I0821898

PIONEERING HISTORY ON TWO CONTINENTS

Pioneering History on Two Continents

An Autobiography

BRUCE F. PAULEY

Potomac Books
An imprint of the University of Nebraska Press

Potomac
Books is an imprint of the
University of Nebraska Press.
Manufactured in the United
States of America.

Library of Congress
Cataloging-in-Publication Data
Pauley, Bruce F.
Pioneering history on two continents:
an autobiography / Bruce F. Pauley.
pages cm
Includes bibliographical references and index.
ISBN 978-1-61234-696-0 (cloth: alk. paper)
ISBN 978-1-61234-698-4 (pdf) 1. Pauley,
Bruce F. 2. Pauley, Bruce F.—Family. 3.
Historians—United States—Biography. 4.
Historiography—United States—History—
20th century. 5. Historiography—Europe,
Central—History—20th century. 6.
Europe, Central—Historiography. 7. Russian Germans—History—18th century.
8. Pioneers—Nebraska—Biography.
9. Russian Germans—Nebraska—
Biography. I. Title.
E175.5.P38A3 2014 973.07202—dc23
[B] 2014003471

Set in Lyon Text by
Renni Johnson.
Designed by N. Putens.

In memory of my courageous ancestors

For my wife

and our descendants

Contents

Illustrations

Following page 174

Preface

When I first started writing this book, my motive was like that of many autobiographers: to provide my children, grandchildren, and later descendants with a record of my life, as well as the lives of my ancestors as far back as I could trace them. As this project progressed, however, I began to realize that my family's evolution reflects in many ways the social and economic history of the United States since the last quarter of the nineteenth century, although the ancestors on my father's side were unusual in being pioneers in both Russia and America.

All my great-great-grandfathers and great-grandfathers were farmers, as were their forebears. My grandfathers left the land to enter the business world at the beginning of the twentieth century. My parents were the first members of their families to go to college, and they belonged to the generation that came to maturity at the beginning of the Great Depression. My father typified his generation in wanting to actively serve his country during World War II, not content to be a passive bystander.

My own story also mirrors the world in which I grew up and the profession I entered. Like most historians, I was born into a stable, middle-class family that valued education and travel more than material possessions. Although mildly nonconformist, I never underwent an emotional rebellion against my parents and indeed always had a high respect for them. Unlike the eighteenth-century British historian and author of the six-volume *Decline and Fall of the Roman Empire*, Edward Gibbon, I did not grow up with "half a dozen chosen servants . . . [while being] the absolute master of my hours and actions."[1] A dignified leisure was never an option for me or for most historians. Consequently, there was never a debate about whether I would attend college. Like other historian-autobiographers, I have had success in publishing scholarly articles and books. Likewise, I closely fit the pattern of having a high regard for the historical profession and a sense of personal satisfaction for having chosen it. Indeed, I have no hesitation in admitting that there was practically no distinction between my work as a practicing historian and teacher and pure enjoyment—correcting piles of examinations being a major exception.

In other respects, however, my career differs from that of most other historian-autobiographers in not being a long series of academic triumphs culminating in an appointment at an elite university. Nor is it a resurrection of historical controversies with other specialists. Rather, it has been one of both devastating setbacks and exhilarating rewards, experiences with which many historians can easily identify. Teaching at a variety of colleges and universities, both public and private, large and small, has given me a broad perspective on the enormous changes in American higher education since the 1950s. I have also included topics not ordinarily described by historian-autobiographers: why I entered the profession, why I chose my particular subspecialty and research topics, and the lengthy and convoluted process of researching, writing, and publishing scholarly books.[2]

This book also differs from most other autobiographies in relying far more heavily on diaries and contemporaneous letters than on one's all-too-fallible memory. I have been fortunate to live when letter writing was still commonplace; expensive, long-distance phone calls, which left no record, were rare. The letters I have written and received since the 1950s do not display the craftsmanship and elegant calligraphy of the Victorian era, but regular written correspondence between friends and close relatives was still the rule, not the exception. Correspondents were often apologetic if their letters were typed instead of handwritten.

Letter writing is just one aspect of my growing up in an age that now, in the twenty-first century, seems archaic. I belong to the last generation to grow up in the shadow of the Great Depression and in the midst of World War II, to be entertained and informed by the radio rather than by television, to not be surrounded by fast-food restaurants, to use trains and steamships for long-distance travel rather than cars and airplanes, and to attend college when *in loco parentis* was still enforced and nearly all professors were men. I also belong to the last generation of historians to take notes by hand and write books and articles with a typewriter rather than with a computer.

Although traveling is part and parcel of most historians' careers, my career has been marked by an unusually large number of trips to foreign countries—over seventy on six continents. Many of these trips influenced the topics I would choose to research and provided me with numerous anecdotes and photographs with which I could add color and insight into both my teaching and my publications. The most influential of these trips, so far as my teaching and writing were concerned, were to countries rarely visited by other historians, let alone American tourists in general. Especially memorable was seeing Prague in the dark Stalinist days of 1957, the Balkans and Hungary under Communist rule in 1964, and East Germany in 1969 and 1987. Even more fascinating were trips to Moscow and Leningrad near the height of the Soviet empire in 1980 and again in 1996 after its fall, and to Yugoslavia and Albania in 1991 when they were in the throes of revolution and disintegration. Other travels to the Caribbean, Europe, the Middle East, Asia, as well as North and South America occurred over such a long period of time—1945 through 2013—that even the nature and means of traveling changed a great deal.

Finally, the dominant theme in this book is the importance of timing, or just plain luck, of which my ancestors and I experienced a great deal, both good and bad. My father's paternal grandfather, Heinrich, brought the family from the steppes of Russia to the Great Plains of Nebraska in 1878 at what turned out to be an ideal time. My grandfathers started their automobile and lumber businesses at the beginning of the twentieth century when the market for their cars and lumber was sky high. My parents, both born in 1908, grew to adulthood under idyllic circumstance until their fortunes were turned upside down by the Great Depression. My birth year of 1937 enabled me to enter the job market in 1963, when the demand for professional historians had never been higher. My being born in 1937 was the gift that kept on giving right down to the present.[3] On the other hand, I am no determinist. Timing and luck were important but *not all-important* in my life or that of my ancestors. Hard work and perseverance were also essential.

No robot delivered the thousands of lectures I gave during my forty-two years of teaching, and no ghostwriter wrote my books. Nevertheless, it would be naive to ignore the role of timing and luck in shaping one's life.

In many ways, writing a family history-autobiography is much like writing any other kind of history. The central questions remain: What do I include and what must I leave out? How do I make sense of the past and create a coherent and interesting narrative without distorting reality? I hope that my readers, and not just historians, will be able to identify with some of my experiences. I also hope that my frequent references to everyday life at home and abroad will awaken long-forgotten memories among a broad range of older readers and serve as a revelation to younger ones about life in the "olden days."

Acknowledgments

Numerous friends and colleagues have been kind enough to read all or portions of this manuscript. I have to recognize above all Dr. Walter Siegl, with whom I shared a room during my junior year of college in Vienna in 1957–58. In addition to his stimulating my early interest in Austrian history, his career as a diplomat enabled me to visit him in Moscow in 1980 and 1996 and Belgrade in 1991, thereby enormously increasing my knowledge of current events. He and his wife, Gundi, gave me the chance to visit sites seldom seen by tourists. Ambassador Siegl also generously read the many chapters in this book that relate to Austrian and Russian history as well as to totalitarianism. Another longtime Austrian friend, whom I met at an international institute in Connecticut in 1961, Dr. Helmut Sohmen, read portions of this manuscript. He and his wife, Anna, made it possible for me to increase my general knowledge of modern history by serving as gracious hosts in London, in Bad Aussee in Austria, and in Hong Kong, where they now live. Still another Austrian friend, Professor Gerhard Botz, generously allowed me to use his Viennese apartment on several occasions while I was conducting research and also facilitated the publication of two of my books.

In this country, the staff at the American Historical Society of Germans from Russia in Lincoln, Nebraska, and especially Pam Wurst, provided me with essential information on the Volga Germans. The Nebraska Historical Society made available microfilmed newspapers essential in tracing the early years of my Nebraska pioneer ancestors. Clarissa Trapp, archivist at the Colorado State University Library, helped me track down important material related to Volga German immigrants. Elaine Sprague of the Harlan,

Iowa, Community Library helped me find articles by and about my mother and maternal grandfather. Interlibrary loan librarians at the University of Central Florida and the Clearview Library in Windsor, Colorado, helped me locate rare books.

A great many friends and former colleagues have read all or portions of this work and offered valuable suggestions. The most detailed and helpful comments were made by fellow Austrian history specialists Laura S. Gellott at the University of Wisconsin–Parkside and Evan Bukey at the University of Arkansas, both of whom read the manuscript in its entirety. Gilbert McArthur, a specialist in Russian history at the College of William and Mary, made especially useful comments about my travels in Russia. Hunt Davis, professor emeritus at the University of Florida, was able to offer helpful observations about our years at Grinnell College. A colleague at the University of Central Florida (UCF), Professor Anthony Cervone, was able to amplify my comments about UCF, as did a former history colleague at UCF, Professor Jonathan Scott Perry, now at the University of South Florida–Sarasota. Daniel Murphree, the assistant editor of the *Florida Historical Quarterly*, graciously volunteered to proofread the entire manuscript. Karen Lane, a professional freelance editor from Merritt Island, Florida, also meticulously proofread the manuscript and helped eliminate extraneous material.

For my chapters on the Volga Germans I profited from the observation of Vladimir Solonari of UCF, who spent his early years in the Soviet Union. The same was true of the comments of Professor Kenneth Rock of Colorado State University. Professor Emeritus Fred Luebke of the University of Nebraska–Lincoln, a specialist on Nebraska history, critiqued the second chapter. A newly discovered relative, James Griess of Lancaster County, Nebraska, a specialist on the Germans from Russia, critiqued the first two chapters. Judge Scott Clugston of Greeley, Colorado, helped me locate my great-great-grandfather's house and farm near Harvard, Nebraska, and uncovered several newspaper articles about my family.

A childhood friend, Gordon Mohrman, helped revive my memories of Lincoln, Nebraska, in the late 1940s and 1950s. A graduate school classmate, Dr. James Bachman, was able to refresh my recollections of our years as PhD candidates at the University of Rochester and our travels to Europe in

1969 and 1974. Friends and fellow UCF faculty members Tom Morgan and Richard Adicks likewise read those chapters dealing with UCF. By far my most indispensable reader has been my wife of fifty years, Marianne. My sister, Patricia Pauley Guy, and my sons, Mark and Glenn, were also able to make helpful observations about our family's history.

Finally, I would like to express my gratitude to the staff of the University of Nebraska Press for the superb job they did in the production of this book. Sabrina Stellrecht, Tish Fobben, Courtney Ochsner, Kyle Simonsen, and especially Derek Krissoff, editor in chief of the University of Nebraska Press, were all a pleasure to work with. Jonathan Lawrence was also highly professional in his work as copyeditor of the book.

Pauley Family Lineage

PHILIPP JACOB PAULŸ (born in 1728 or 1731 in Isenburg, Darmstadt, Hesse [Germany]; died in Norka, Russia, date unknown)

Married to MARIA ELIZABETH (born in 1732, birthplace unknown; died in Norka, date unknown)

JOHANNES PAULŸ (born in 1758 in Isenburg; died in Norka in 1811)

Married to CATHARINA WEITZEL (born in 1768 in Norka; died in Norka, date unknown)

JOHANNES PAULŸ [or Pauli] (born in Norka in 1805; died in Norka in 1869)

Married to CATHARINA HAHN (born in Norka in 1807; died in Norka in 1867)

HEINRICH PAULI (later spelled Pauley) (born in 1834 in Norka; died in Harvard, Nebraska, in 1914)

Married to ELIZABETH ROSS (born in Norka in 1836; died in Harvard in 1896)

CONRAD PAULEY (born in Norka in 1862; died in Lincoln, Nebraska, in 1936)

Married to ALICE YOST (born in Norka in 1866; died in Lincoln in 1936)

LUDWIG HEINRICH PAULEY (born in Harvard in 1886; died in Lincoln in 1946)

Married to LENA ALBERTINA RIGHTER (born in Neligh, Nebraska, in 1888; died in Lincoln in 1984)

CARROLL RIGHTER PAULEY (born in Hebron, Nebraska, in 1908; died in Lincoln in 1987)

Married to BLANCHE MARIE HULSEBUS (born in Defiance, Iowa, in 1908; died in Lincoln in 1992)

BRUCE FREDERICK PAULEY (born in Lincoln in 1937)

Married to MARIANNE BARBARA UTZ (born in Rochester, New York, in 1941)

MARK ALLAN PAULEY (born in Laramie, Wyoming, in 1967)

Married to MARIA CECELIA HART (born in Cali, Columbia, in 1968)

ALENA MARIE PAULEY (born in Lincoln in 1996)

BENJAMIN ISAAC PAULEY (born in Omaha, Nebraska, in 2001)

GLENN HAMILTON PAULEY (born in Laramie, Wyoming, in 1969)

Married to LUCY HANSEN (born in Madrid, Spain, in 1971)

WILLIAM FREDERICK PAULEY (born in Cheyenne, Wyoming, in 2007)

REINA VICTORIA PAULEY (born in Cheyenne, in 2009)

PIONEERING HISTORY ON TWO CONTINENTS

CHAPTER 1

Pioneers on the Russian Frontier

Menschenfänger and *Volgers*

MY VOLGA GERMAN ANCESTORS

This is a story about timing, dates, and luck. Unfortunately, or perhaps fortunately, we often recognize the importance of dates, especially birth years, only in retrospect. As a historian I have found it essential to keep track of dates, especially when they relate to cause and effect. The significance of dates applies as much to family history as it does to history writ large. Before undertaking this study I was only dimly aware of dates in my family history. However, a four-year exploration of my ancestral roots as well as my own life has demonstrated just how crucial they can be.[1]

My family history begins in the 1760s with my great-great-great-great-great-grandfather Jacob Paulÿ, who lived with his wife, Maria Elizabeth, in Isenburg near the city of Frankfurt am Main in west-central Germany.[2] I know nothing about this distant ancestor except that he was a *Handarbeiter* (manual laborer). However, I do know that his home region, the Palatinate, had been especially hard hit by the Seven Years' War (1756–63) when the Austrian empress Maria Theresa tried to regain the province of Silesia, which had been seized by Frederick the Great in the War of the Austrian Succession

(1740–48). The second war had devastated whole villages throughout Germany, and both work and food were in short supply.

The end of the Seven Years' War nearly coincided with the rise to power of Catherine the Great in Russia in 1762. A former German princess, the relatively enlightened new empress was eager to consolidate Russia's control over the region of the southern Volga, which was inhabited by wild Mongolian tribes. Catherine II was not the first ruler to be concerned about the nomadic people living on the southern borders of the Russian Empire. Conflicts with indigenous steppe tribes had been going on since at least 1500. She was, however, the first Russian ruler to practice religious tolerance and not insist that all her subjects belong to the Russian Orthodox Church.[3] On December 22, 1762, she issued a 190-word manifesto in several languages inviting industrious Europeans to colonize the Lower Volga of southern Russia. When the manifesto went largely unnoticed she issued a second and much more detailed 1,350-word manifesto on July 22, 1763, promising colonists the right to settle in any part of Russia and free travel expenses.

Catherine viewed herself as a wise ruler whose goal was the "supreme good" of her subjects.[4] Going far beyond what she was willing to grant the native people of her empire, she also offered would-be settlers freedom of religion, perpetual freedom from military service, freedom from taxation for up to thirty years, interest-free loans to build homes and to purchase farming equipment, and freedom to govern themselves. Finally, if the colonists had a change of heart they were free to return to their country of origin, although in Russia, a country with roads literally no better than cow paths, that proved to be easier said than done. Nevertheless, this "escape clause" was remembered and invoked by the Volga Germans a century later.

Although people from all classes and all parts of Germany, the Low Countries, Sweden, Alsace, and Switzerland responded to this offer, inhabitants of the Rhineland area of Germany were the most numerous. Most of the recruiters were Frenchmen of dubious reputation who were employed by the Russian government as agents in Frankfurt, Ulm, and elsewhere.[5] Paid on the basis of how many colonists they could recruit, not on their honesty, they came be known as *Menschenfänger* (people grabbers) or *Seelenkäfer* (soul sellers) because of their aggressive and misleading recruiting tactics. They claimed that the region along the Volga resembled the Lower Rhine River area of Germany, had fertile soil (an exaggeration), enjoyed an extremely mild climate (a lie), and in general was a veritable paradise. So many Germans responded to these images that after 1766 the rulers of major German cities and principalities in the Rhineland became alarmed and passed decrees forbidding further emigration, although by this time Catherine had exhausted funds for the enterprise.[6] To Jacob and Elizabeth Paulÿ these enticements were apparently irresistible. To go from being a manual laborer to a land-owning farmer represented a huge leap on the social scale.

But first they had to get to Russia. The story of their journey is astonishing and reveals how primitive travel was in the second half of the eighteenth century. Departing Isenburg sometime in June 1766 and traveling by foot, wagon, or raft, they probably needed two months to cover the four hundred miles to Lübeck on the Baltic Sea. There they waited with other colonists, possibly for weeks—but at Russian expense—until their ship, the *Elephant*, was fully loaded before sailing for ten days or more through the Baltic Sea and the Gulf of Finland nine hundred miles to the deep-water port of Kronstadt. Met by bearded Russian teamsters, they and their luggage were hauled to Oranienbaum, a small town twenty-five miles west of St. Petersburg. Their arrival date was August 23, 1766.[7]

A few days later they were transported in small ships to St. Petersburg. There they were eventually assigned a military officer to protect and lead their group to the settlement sites. Many of the colonists were dismayed to learn that with few exceptions, and contrary to earlier promises about being able to settle anywhere in Russia, they would be forced to make their homes in the Volga region south and to a lesser extent northeast of Saratov.

The Paulÿs' journey from St. Petersburg to the Lower Volga was itself monumental, lasting nearly a year. Advertisements had indicated that an overland trip would take only two or three weeks; floating down the Volga would require five to six weeks.[8] Most likely the Paulÿs first rafted up the 45-mile Neva River through the Schlüsselburg Canal to Lake Ladoga.[9] From there they journeyed to the mouth of the Volkhov River, along which they floated for 130 miles to Lake Ilmen. At that point most parties portaged 200 miles or more—the women and children piled into wagons or carts while most of the men walked—until they reached the town of Torzhok on the Tvertsa River, or possibly Kostroma, a city on the confluence of the Kostroma and Volga Rivers, where ice would have forced them to spend the winter. In either case they would have been housed with Russian peasants and their farm animals, all under the same roof. Relief from the stench, smoke, and steam would have come only by stepping outside into the frigid winter air.[10] In the spring of 1767 the Paulÿs were able to resume their journey by floating or sailing another 1,100 miles down the Volga to Saratov.[11] From their enrollment in Germany to their final destination on the Volga, the trip covered around 2,700 miles and lasted at least fifteen months, about average for the German colonists.[12] Of the 7,501 immigrants who arrived safely in Oranienbaum, 16.9 percent died en route to Saratov.[13]

The region was near the fifty-first parallel north latitude, roughly as far north as Saskatoon, Saskatchewan, and had a climate closer to the Canadian plains than to that which their descendants would later encounter in Nebraska. Rainfall, which averaged just twelve to sixteen inches a year, was highly erratic, and the average growing season was only 106 days compared to the 170 days that are generally considered ideal for farming. Late winter storms, which killed thousands of livestock, were an ever-present threat.[14]

Surrounding the colonists were a nearly treeless wilderness, howling winds, and endless thigh-high grass. However, before leaving Saratov each family had been provided with the bare essentials to survive: a couple of ponies, a cow or an ox, an unassembled wooden plow, a simple harness, and parts for a wagon. In addition, they were given pots, pans, kettles, pottery bowls, and other necessary cooking items. They managed to get through the first winter (if at all) only by building *Semlinka* dugouts (sod homes) or riverside caves, both of which often flooded when the snow melted in the spring. The crowded conditions led to epidemics and massive mortality that reduced the Volga German population from 6,433 families in 1769 to 4,858 in 1775.[15] Survivors existed on local wild fruit, such as strawberries, blackberries, cherries, and pears, and on dried fish purchased from Russian serfs. It would take at least three years for the colonists to obtain enough scarce wood to build log cabins. By 1773 there were 104 villages along the Volga with a total population of 25,781.[16] One of those villages was Norka, founded on August 15, 1767. Two of the original 957 settlers, most of whom were from Isenburg, were Philip Jacob and Maria Elizabeth Paulÿ.[17]

This first generation of Volga Germans must have been among those people fittest to survive the colonies' early years. In addition to the miserable and unhealthy conditions described above, the arrival of the colonists coincided with a prolonged drought. Furthermore, in 1774 a would-be usurper of the throne, Yemelvan Ivanovich Pugachev, terrorized the Volga Germans and other people living in the Lower Volga region, destroying much of their property and driving all but the very young and very old into hiding. Still more devastating were the periodic plundering and massacres by so-called Kirghiz raiders. Even after this warfare ended, the colonists still had to fear attacks by ferocious wild animals such as bears and wolves. It took nearly a decade for the warfare and famine to end, by which time the colonies may have lost a third of their original population.[18]

Conditions for the colonists finally started improving in 1775 when the drought ended along the Lower Volga, and they began obtaining seeds from Russian authorities early enough to plant them at the optimum time in the spring. Norka was located in well-drained highlands (*Bergseite*) west of the Volga and was initially blessed with forests of birch, pine, and linden trees; however, unrestricted cutting depleted most of the forests by the 1870s. Although much of the land was rocky, sandy, or alkaline, it was suitable for wheat, barley, oats, hay, and sunflowers, all crops the family could later grow in Nebraska.

After 1785 the lives of the colonists eased considerably, although hardly any of them became wealthy. The virtual absence of trained physicians made early death an ever-present reality. In this respect, however, Norka was comparatively fortunate. In 1784 a Swiss Calvinist pastor, physician, and surgeon named Johann Baptista Cattaneo arrived in the village. He ministered to both the spiritual and medical needs of the settlers on both sides of the river for the next forty years. Perhaps most significantly he vaccinated more than eight thousand people for smallpox—a practice Catherine the Great promoted by risking her own life to be inoculated.[19] Among those inoculated were no doubt some and perhaps all of my Pauley ancestors.[20]

Apart from sheer survival, one of the colonists' first concerns was education. Among the earliest colonists were professional teachers as well as people who had attended German universities. The next two generations of teachers, however, had only elementary educations and spent half the year farming. Teachers faced classrooms having two hundred to four hundred pupils,[21] about the same size as classrooms in American cities between 1823 and the 1850s or even later.[22] The highest qualifications for Norka's teachers were a loud voice and a willingness to work for low wages. Instruction was limited to the four "R's" with religion added to the usual reading (the Bible often being the only available book), 'riting, and 'rithmetic. However, students were severely hampered in practicing the latter two categories by the absence of desks.[23] Moreover, they were in school only three or four hours daily (with double sessions for the teachers) and then only from October to Easter when farming recommenced. Although the Volga German *Volksschulen* (elementary schools) produced literate or semi-literate graduates at a time when the literacy rate in Russia was around 20 percent, the general educational level of the Volga Germans was no higher in the 1870s than it had been in Germany a century earlier and was certainly far behind schools in the recently united German Empire.

There being no theaters, libraries, or taverns in the colonies, entertainment was all "homegrown," as it was on the American frontier. Singing folk songs, ballads, and hymns imported from Germany was quite common, which may explain why my grandfather Pauley and his descendants were so musical. However, visiting one's neighbors and chatting was by far the most common pastime. Women always brought their knitting and needlework along so the time would not be wasted.[24] Children were expected to listen respectfully.

Until they were driven out of the region by Stalin and dispersed throughout Siberia and other parts of the Soviet Union in 1941, Volga Germans clung tenaciously to their language, religious denominations, and customs. Intermarriage with Russians, whom they regarded as less clean and less industrious than themselves, was regarded as a disgrace.[25] To be assimilated into Russian society would have represented an unthinkable cultural retrogression. On the other hand, the Volga Germans made very little progress in industry and agriculture, at least prior to 1860, and may have even regressed. Another thing that did not change significantly was their language. My grandfather Pauley, who grew up speaking German in Nebraska, learned that much of his vocabulary was antiquated when he and my grandmother attended the Berlin Olympics in 1936.

IN SEARCH OF FREEDOM AND OPPORTUNITY

Although the Volga Germans in some respects stagnated culturally, their economic conditions generally improved in the century following their settlement. Promises made by Catherine were renewed by Czar Alexander I in 1804 and 1813. However, their privileged status was changed by a number of laws enacted by the Russian government after 1860. A law of 1871 issued by the reforming czar, Alexander II (reigned 1855–81), eliminated the autonomy promised the colonies by Catherine the Great and gave the Russian government control over the settlements' political and administrative affairs.[26] The subsequent indignation of the colonists is easy to understand. On the other hand, so too is the envy of ethnic Russian peasants who had had no such exemption. One advantage of Alexander's decrees was that they actually made it easier for the Volgers (as the Volga Germans came to be known) to move about the country or even to emigrate.

Three years later, probably in response to Prussia's impressive military victory over France, Alexander II made military training compulsory for every male reaching the age of twenty-one, including those living in the German colonies. Every young man in Russia between sixteen and twenty now had to register for the draft. Military service in nineteenth-century Russia had been a horrendous fate, considered little better than a death penalty for conscripts. Volga Germans had seen crippled Russian veterans begging in their streets because the government had made no provisions for pensioning them after they were no longer fit for service.[27] As recently as 1861, military service had been for twenty-five years. Although the new law reduced service from sixteen to six years (four years for those men who had completed primary school), it was to be followed by nine more years in the reserve. Discipline, though less harsh than earlier, could still be abusive. Such servitude, especially in the first years after the conscript law was enacted, was a terrifying prospect, particularly for Volga Germans who would be commanded by Russian-speaking officers. Conscripts were drafted when most Volga Germans were married and had children or were about to get married. Volga German parents feared that their sons might be Russified or even lured into converting to the Russian Orthodox Church by military service.

The draft law went into effect in 1874, although Alexander II soon modified it to allow Volga Germans ten years to emigrate before the law would be enforced.[28] However, the czar reneged even on this promise, and the first Volga Germans were conscripted in November and December 1874.[29] The new law may have been the final impetus for my great-great-grandfather—who had five sons, two of them of prime draft age—to decide to emigrate, even though over time just one in five draft-eligible Russian men was actually conscripted.[30]

Almost certainly more important than conscription, however, was the land question. The German colonies practiced the same *mir* system of land redistribution as did other peasants in Russia. Farmland belonged to the village, not to individuals. Every five or ten years it was redistributed according to the number of sons in each family. In order to ensure equality, the land was parceled out in strips so that each family would receive some especially fertile land as well as some that was much less fertile. This system resulted in families' cultivating noncontiguous plots, which made farming less efficient; much time was wasted simply going from one plot to another. The *mir* system also gave farmers little incentive to improve the land, since they held it only temporarily.[31]

Norka, on the *Bergseite* of the Volga River, was older and far more densely populated than many villages on the *Wiesenseite* (plains side) of the Volga, much of which had been settled later. No new land could be acquired from the Russian government after 1840, although it was not until 1871, when they attempted to acquire new land, that the Volga Germans became painfully cognizant of this fact. Consequently, available land per adult male in Norka had been reduced to fewer than four acres, small even by European standards of the time. Severe drought caused a series of crop failures starting in 1873, thus making the land shortage all the more acute.[32] No new farming techniques were introduced that might have increased productivity. Meanwhile, the soil, for which no fertilizer was available or ever had been, was becoming ever less productive, especially after 1860. Population pressure alone would have been enough to induce emigration as it did elsewhere in Europe in the second half of the nineteenth century. Alexander II's decrees simply added urgency.

Even before these problems began to crystallize, a preacher named Wilhelm Staerkel came to Norka. After his ordination in the 1860s, Staerkel served as a missionary of some kind in Missouri and Kansas before returning to the Volga in 1869. In 1876 he began a ministry in Norka that was to last until 1908. Following the loss of Volga German privileges in 1871 he began to preach about the opportunities available to his parishioners in the United States, extolling in particular the country's religious, political, and personal freedoms. He also made note of the Federal Homestead Act of 1862, which made free land available to immigrants in what until shortly before had been known as the "Great American Desert." Job opportunities with railroad companies, which were rapidly expanding to the west, were plentiful. Furthermore, railroad companies such as the Union Pacific and the Burlington, desperate for customers, spent $1 million advertising Nebraska alone ($15 million in today's valuation).[33] Agents distributed brochures printed in German, Czech, and the Scandinavian languages, extolling the virtues of the Great Plains. Ethnic Germans were regarded as especially good prospects because they were known for their industry and thrift and their tendency to emigrate in groups.[34] Thus, the very characteristics that were so prized by Catherine the Great in the 1760s appealed to American railroad companies a century later.

Staerkel's exhortations resulted in a meeting in the village of Balzer in 1873, attended by mostly Protestant representatives from both sides of the Volga. The Volga Germans were acutely aware that they had been enticed to immigrate to Russia by grossly exaggerated propaganda. They were determined not to make the same mistake twice. The Balzer meeting resulted in fourteen *Kundshafter* (exploratory emissaries) being commissioned and paid at common expense to explore possible relocation sites in Nebraska, Iowa, Kansas, Arkansas, and Florida.

Two of the scouts selected in the Balzer meeting were Johannes Nolde and Johannes Krieger, both from Norka. They chose to investigate the land near Sutton, Nebraska, and returned with favorable reports concerning the availability of railroad services, farmland, and water.[35] They even brought back samples of soil, prairie grass, and paper money along with railroad advertisements describing the land and opportunities. In no sense, therefore, can one maintain that the Volga Germans were "lured" to Nebraska by duplicitous land agents.[36] Consequently, colonists from Norka began arriving in Sutton in 1876, with a large group arriving in 1877, followed the next year by my ancestors and twenty-seven other families.

By 1878 the stars seemed to be lining up in favor of emigration for my great-great-grandfather Heinrich, his wife, Elizabeth Ross, and their six children, including my fifteen-year-old great-grandfather Conrad. Heinrich's father, Johannes (b. 1805), had died in 1869, two years after his mother, Catharina Hahn (b. 1807), so parental bonds, which might have discouraged emigration, didn't exist.[37] However, Heinrich and Elizabeth undoubtedly had many siblings and cousins who remained in Russia. Apparently, they also had one or more relatives along with some close friends already living in the Sutton area who encourage them to immigrate. In fact, Norka was deluged with letters from America; no fewer than fifty arrived in a single dispatch in 1877.[38]

The earliest American historian of Volga German immigration, Hattie Plum Williams, describes how seven families from Norka, along with two single men, had settled in Ohio in 1875. After digging ditches for two years, they moved to Sutton and wrote enthusiastic letters to their friends and relatives in Norka about their new home.[39] In 1876 Christian Pauli (or possibly Pauly), almost certainly a brother or cousin of Heinrich, arrived in Sutton along with six other families from Norka. Thirty other Volga German families came to Sutton or nearby communities in 1876 and 1877.[40] Among these families was one headed by Heinrich and Catherine Yost. Natives of Norka, they first immigrated to Wisconsin in 1876 and then moved to Harvard, Nebraska, the next year.[41] One of the daughters, Alice, was to marry my great-grandfather Conrad in 1883. Most likely the Yosts also played a role in my ancestors' coming to Nebraska in 1878 and may even have helped them purchase steamship tickets, a frequent practice among the Volga German immigrants already in the United States.[42]

Although there were plenty of incentives to come to the United States, emigration must have been a wrenching experience for the Volga Germans, as it was for most Europeans who left their ancestral homes for the New World. Five generations of Pauleys had lived all or part of their lives in Russia over a span of 111 years. Like other Europeans, with the exception of aristocrats, soldiers, and sailors, they had almost certainly never traveled more than a few miles from their home.[43] They had lived in a compact town, not on an isolated plot of land as was and is the custom in the United States. Leaving Russia meant selling nearly all of their personal possessions to pay for taxes, passports, and the trip to America. Space limitations meant that only the barest of essentials could be taken for the long journey. They must have known a great many of the seven thousand people who lived in Norka in the late 1870s, including friends and relatives they most likely they would never see again.[44]

THE FATE OF THOSE LEFT BEHIND

By coming to the United States when they did, my ancestors spared their descendants a ghastly fate that awaited those family members—and there were no doubt many of them—who chose to remain behind. Russification and "pan-Slavism" increased during the 1880s. In 1881 the colonists were forced to study Russian in school. Much more distasteful for the Volga Germans was being forced to fight other Germans during World War I, and they became scapegoats for the economic shortages and humiliating defeats of the Imperial Russian Army on the German front.[45]

Life for civilian Volga Germans was no better after the Bolsheviks came to power in November 1917, even though the Volgers were not initially hostile to them. But the colonists were triply damned in Bolshevik eyes because they had been loyal to the Romanov imperial dynasty before the war, were devoutly religious, and were firm believers in private property and private enterprise. During the long Russian Civil War (1918–21) the Bolsheviks requisitioned foodstuffs from the Volga Germans. By 1922, war, starvation, and flight had reduced the Volga German population from 600,000 to under 300,000.[46] The fate of the colonists would have been even worse had it not been for the help offered by the Central States Volga Relief Society formed in Lincoln, Nebraska, along with another relief society in Portland, Oregon. Even this aid, however, was a mixed blessing as Josef Stalin, at the time the Soviet commissar for nationalities, thought that anyone who had relatives abroad was a spy and a traitor.

Vladimir Lenin's New Economic Policy, inaugurated in 1921, allowed limited prosperity to return briefly to the Volga region in 1924 and 1925, but it did not reach prewar levels. Confiscatory taxes and Stalin's forced collectivization of farms, beginning in 1929, resulted in the deportation of 65,000 colonists to Siberia. No group suffered more from collectivization than the Volga Germans, and no group resisted more tenaciously. Collectivization also produced a new famine, resulting in the deaths of another 70,000 to 150,000 colonists. The history of the colonies came to an end in September 1941, three months after the start of the German invasion of the Soviet Union. Around 380,000 colonists, mostly old men, women, and children, were falsely accused of collaborating with the Nazis and were given twenty-four hours to leave their homes before being brutally deported in sealed cattle or freight cars to central Asia or Siberia where one quarter of them died.[47] Even though they were eventually cleared of treason, they were not allowed to return to their former homeland after the war. Although the victims of the war are numerous—one should never forget the Russian POWs, the Sinti and Roma (Gypsies), and the Poles—a strong case can be made that of all the ethnic and religious groups in Europe, only the Jews suffered a more horrible fate before, during, and after the war than the Volga Germans.

Even prior to Stalin's expulsion of German Russians to the East, few Volga Germans living in America were tempted to return to their former homeland, and those who did lived to regret it. Those early Nebraskans who came from the German Empire, from Bohemia and Moravia in the Austro-Hungarian Monarchy, from Sweden, or even from the eastern United States always had the option to return to their previous homes if life appeared to be too harsh. Tens of thousands of early migrants to Nebraska in fact exercised that option as a result of the ferocious blizzard of 1888, the crash of 1893, or the drought of the 1890s. In the United States as a whole, an estimated 35 percent of European immigrants eventually returned to the country of their birth.[48] For the Volga Germans, however, there was for all practical purposes no homeland to which they could return, especially after the Bolshevik Revolution. After 1941 there were often not even churches or gravestones to remind them of their past lives. Perhaps that is one reason why they became so rooted in and so loyal to their new country and state. Of all immigrant groups in the United States, only the Russian Jews were less likely to return to their country of origin than the Volga Germans.[49]

Life for those Volga Germans who had immigrated to the United States was not immune from European developments. During World War I anti-German hysteria broke out in the United States, including in Nebraska, which was merely a milder version of what was occurring in Imperial Russia. "Pro-German elements were silenced, jailed, or otherwise suppressed with fervor and thoroughness no era before or since has been able to match," writes historian Robert Sklar.[50] The German language was no longer taught throughout Nebraska, and Volga Germans found themselves disliked and the objects of discrimination either as Germans or as Russians and were sometimes forced to kiss the American flag. German-language newspapers were either shut down or prevented from publishing editorials of any kind. Books in German were sometimes burned, and many ethnic Germans felt obliged to anglicize their names to disguise their background. Indeed, nearly eighteen thousand German Americans were arrested throughout the country merely for speaking German in public.[51]

Although the Pauley family was probably not entirely immune from anti-German prejudices in the United States, without knowing it my great-great-grandfather Heinrich and his wife, Elizabeth, saved the family from the catastrophes that were to beset the Germans in Russia. As they set off for America with their six children in May 1878, the prospect of traveling across two continents and the Atlantic Ocean to a frontier community in central Nebraska must have been both daunting and exhilarating. The family was about to undergo a pioneering adventure for the second time in little more than a century.

CHAPTER 2

A New Life on the Great Plains

"The Door to Success Is Labeled 'Push.'"

SHIPS, TRAINS, AND PLOWS

A new chapter in the history of the Pauley family began on June 5, 1878, when Heinrich, his wife, Elizabeth, and their six children—Johannes, Peter, Catherina, Adam, Heinrich, and my great-grandfather Conrad—arrived in the New World.[1] Another daughter, Elizabeth, was born in Nebraska in 1881.[2] Compared to the family's epic journey from Germany to the Volga, the nearly six-thousand-mile passage from Russia to Nebraska, over twice as long, was a veritable summer excursion. The most arduous part was probably getting to the nearest railroad station in Saratov thirty-five miles north of Norka, a two-day journey along dirt roads (which in some cases are worse today) that could be traversed only after the snow melted and spring rains ended. Thereafter, the trip was relatively easy. Saratov had been linked to the Russian railway network in 1871, the same year the Burlington and Missouri Railroad reached Sutton, Nebraska, Heinrich's ultimate destination. It was probably only a three- or four-day train ride via Moscow, Warsaw, and Berlin to the German port of Hamburg, where they boarded the Hamburg America Line's SS *Wieland* on May 22. On board, the Paulis were not among strangers. Of the *Wieland*'s one thousand passengers, four hundred were fellow Volga Germans.[3]

The 375-foot by 40-foot iron-hulled *Wieland*, built in 1874, was a hybrid ship that included both a steam-driven screw propeller and two masts, the latter to save fuel when winds were favorable. Unlike the ship that took my ancestors from Lübeck to Oranienbaum, the *Wieland* had regular sailing schedules, not waiting to be filled before departing. Heinrich and his family traveled "between decks," which was the German equivalent of "steerage" or third class. If there was a difference it was that between decks was an area just below the top deck. In the 1860s and 1870s this generally meant that there were no separate cabins for families, only separate compartments with bunks for families and other compartments for single men and single women. Ventilation was by hatches that opened to the deck above in good weather but that were closed during storms, thereby creating a dark and musty atmosphere. Meals were served on long tables in the compartments, not in separate dining rooms.[4] These were hardly luxurious accommodations. The best thing about the *Wieland* was probably its speed: the voyage from Hamburg, with a stop in Le Havre, France, took just two weeks.

On June 5, 1878, Heinrich and his family reached Castle Garden, New York, the predecessor of the Ellis Island immigration center. The scariest part about Castle Garden was passing the health inspection. Although only 2 percent of immigrants failed the test, those who did were sent back to their homeland. Gathering their belongings, undergoing brief questioning, exchanging money, proving they had a sponsor (the Burlington and Missouri Railroad), obtaining train tickets directly from a Burlington agent, and being transported to a railroad station probably consumed another day or two for Heinrich's family.[5] The 1,550 miles from New York City to Nebraska were covered in just four or five days. The cost of a third-class ticket was $23.50. This was actually no great bargain; in constant dollars it would be around $345 today. Money for the tickets may have come from relatives already in Nebraska or from the Burlington Railroad in exchange for a commitment to purchase land from the company within thirty days.[6] They allegedly traveled to their final destination on a freight train,[7] although it is more likely that they were in a very rustic "immigrant car" attached to a freight train.[8]

If they weren't on an actual freight train, the immigrants were certainly treated like freight: stuffed into old cars, ninety to a coach equipped with hard wooden seats, heated with a potbellied stove, and having only a hole in the floor to serve as a toilet.[9] What is known for sure is that on June 11, at exactly 11:00 in the evening, Heinrich and his family, along with twenty-six other Volga German families, all of them from Norka, arrived in Sutton.[10]

Heinrich's timing was fortunate both for his family and, ultimately, for his descendants. If he had tried to immigrate thirty years earlier the trip would not have been much easier than Philipp Jacob's epic migration from Germany to the Volga. Long-distance trains were nonexistent in the 1840s both in Europe and America; nearly all oceangoing ships were still powered exclusively by wind and took six or seven weeks to cross the Atlantic. Nebraska was not open for settlement until 1854, and the Homestead Act was enacted only in 1862. If Heinrich and his family had arrived in 1873 they would have been confronted by the Panic of 1873, which threw the whole country into the worst depression in its history up to that time.[11] Assistance from government authorities at the national, state, or local level was minimal.[12] In 1874 Nebraska experienced the beginning of a severe drought, prairie fires, and a terrible plague of grasshoppers, which could wipe out a crop in a single day.[13] Remarkably, these disasters ended in 1877, just one year before Heinrich and his family arrived in Nebraska.[14]

On the other hand, if Heinrich had left Russia in the 1890s he and his family would have arrived in time for the Panic of 1893 and a severe drought lasting from 1893 through 1895, a combination of disasters that was to be a dress rehearsal for the Dust Bowl and Great Depression of the 1930s.[15] Economic conditions were so severe that the state's population, which had grown from 452,402 in 1880 to 1,062,656 a decade later, managed to add fewer than 4,000 people during the 1890s.[16] Nearly all of the arable land in the eastern half of Nebraska had been purchased by 1885. If the Pauleys had come to Nebraska in the late 1880s the nearest available land would have been in the southwestern part of the state or in northeastern Colorado, a semi-arid area that was particularly hard hit by the drought of the 1890s.[17] If they had come around the turn of the century they would have become tenant farmers doing backbreaking work picking sugar beets in the

Nebraska panhandle, eastern Colorado, western Kansas, or the panhandles of Oklahoma or Texas, all areas that were in the heart of the Dust Bowl of the 1930s.[18] If they had arrived in Lincoln around 1900 they probably would have joined other Volga Germans in becoming street sweepers, house and office cleaners, or railroad laborers.

Clay County, where Heinrich and his family settled in 1878, was apparently the site of the first German settlements in Nebraska.[19] Sutton had such a large German population coming from both the Volga and Black Sea regions of Russia that it came to be known as "Russian Town."[20] The area's wide-open and windswept plains must have reminded Russian Germans of the steppes of southern Russia. Almost certainly more important than the familiarity of the landscape, however, were the soil and climate conditions, which were ideal for growing wheat, a crop Volga Germans had learned to cultivate in Russia. So Heinrich's family (and their descendants) was lucky to be part of the first wave of German-Russian immigrants to obtain inexpensive and highly productive land.

Not everything, however, went smoothly for Heinrich and his family after their arrival in Nebraska. They spent their first night in Sutton sleeping in the same train that had brought them to Nebraska. After that they probably remained in an "Emigrant House" in Sutton until the fall of 1878, or they may have moved in with Christian Pauli's family or with other friends they had known in Norka, such as the Yosts. Although the Burlington's Emigrant House provided free housing, food, clothing, laundry facilities, bedding, and furniture, several families had to share the shed-like one-room facility, which was twenty-four feet wide and eighty feet long.[21] When they moved to a farm two miles north of the town of Harvard and thirteen miles west of Sutton, their first home was a fourteen-by-twenty-foot barn. The following June the home caught fire and was completely destroyed, leaving the entire family without food, clothing, or even cash. Neighbors came to their rescue by donating clothing and provisions and helped them build a sod house, much like what their ancestors had lived in more than a century earlier.[22]

Meanwhile, my great-great-grandfather was fortunate in having three sons, including my great-grandfather Conrad; they were old enough to work for the Burlington and give their earnings to their father, as had been the custom in the old country. With these savings Heinrich was able to purchase a 160-acre farm one mile east of Harvard—the price of land per acre having fallen from $8.19 in 1871 to $4.25 in 1882.[23] For a Volga German or for that matter many other nineteenth-century Americans, being a landowner or a homeowner was not just a means to economic security but also a sign of prestige and self-respect, things new immigrants sorely needed.[24]

In keeping with the Volga tradition, Conrad and his two older brothers, Johannes and Peter, were all "assistant farmers" on their father's farm in 1880.[25] It is hard to imagine how a family of nine was able to squeeze into their modest five- or six-room house. However, at a time when many pioneer starter houses, whether sod or frame, often consisted of one twelve-by-fourteen-foot room, the Pauley house was actually substantial.[26] All four of Heinrich's sons grew to manhood in the community, married, and ultimately became prosperous farmers who eventually retired in Harvard.[27] As a sign of the family's rapid Americanization, Heinrich, the name of both the father and one of his sons, was changed to "Henry," Johannes became "John," Catherina was better known as "Kate," and the America-born daughter, Elizabeth, was called "Lizzie."[28]

While growing up I frequently heard in school about the hard lives of the early Nebraskans; compared to my life and the lives of my parents and grandparents, they were indeed grueling. I doubt, however, that my great-great-grandfather and his family felt sorry for themselves. The south-central part of Nebraska to which they moved was, to be sure, barren in its appearance—only 3 percent of Nebraska was naturally forested—and the climate was (and is) harsh.[29] For good reason the University of Nebraska's fight song says that "we'll all stick together in all kinds of weather." On the other hand, the climate was considerably milder and less extreme than the Volga area, where the average January temperature was ten degrees Fahrenheit compared to twenty-six degrees in south-central Nebraska.[30] And unlike the Pilgrims in New England or for that matter early settlers almost anywhere east of the Mississippi River, clearing the land of trees and digging up tree stumps, an extremely hard and time-consuming task, was not an issue in the Nebraska of the 1870s. Nor was it necessary to remove rocks. Trees and rocks were not needed to build fences, because barbed wire had been on the market since 1874. A variety of new and improved plows had just become available, such as seed drills for planting wheat and listers for planting corn where rainfall was scarce, as it was in central Nebraska. It wasn't essential to have a stream on a farmer's land. New well-drilling machines and windmills, which had become a common feature on the prairies by the late 1870s, could extract water from the huge Ogallala aquifer and obviated the drudgery of drawing water from a well with a pail.

Crucial to the settlement of Nebraska, especially west of Lincoln, were railroad companies such as the Burlington and the Union Pacific.[31] From Lincoln to the East Coast, railroads connected already-established towns. West of Lincoln, the railroad came first, then the settlers. To encourage immigration and thereby increase their revenues, the Burlington sold land it had acquired from the government at low prices and low interest rates and with minimal down payments. The Burlington even offered reduced fares in addition to the free temporary "Emigrant" housing to those who bought land.

Within Nebraska, rails increased from 1,868 miles in 1880 to 5,148 ten years later, making the settlement of the frontier and the development of towns far more rapid than it had been further east in the pre-train era.[32] Indeed, the railroads literally founded towns west of Lincoln, establishing a station about every ten miles around which a town usually soon grew. Curiously, towns founded by the Burlington were named alphabetically starting with Asylum, named for a mental institution just west of Lincoln. Harvard was located midway between Grafton and Inland.[33] Trains not only carried the early Pauleys to towns such as Sutton, Hastings, and Lincoln, but more importantly they hauled their crops to markets around the country and, with the aid of steamships, around the world.

My Pauley ancestors had the rare distinction of being pioneers on two continents in two different centuries. But the second round of pioneering in Nebraska was certainly far easier than the initial experience in Russia. Whereas my "Russian" ancestors endured eight years of drought and famine before they could enjoy their first good crop in 1775, Nebraska was blessed with bountiful rainfall and big harvests from the late 1870s to the early 1990s. Clay County's average annual rainfall of twenty-seven inches was well above the twelve to sixteen inches that fell on the Lower Volga. My ancestors were far more accustomed to the kind of dry and erratic climate of central Nebraska than settlers from humid regions further east or those from western or central Europe, all areas that had relatively dependable rainfall. Even grasshopper plagues would not have intimidated them, since they had encountered them in Russia. Heinrich's family would not have been lonely either, because like so many other nineteenth-century immigrants, they were preceded or followed by other families from their village in the old country. Families with whom my ancestors had intermarried, such as the Yosts, Rosses, and Brehms, had also come to Clay County from Norka at about the same time. In fact, all or at least nearly all the Volga Germans who settled in or near Harvard came from Norka.

It was probably just as well that Heinrich settled down as a farmer, because if he had moved to a city such as Lincoln or Omaha he and his family would have found a veritable deathtrap with unpaved streets filled with excrement, garbage, rubbish, and rats. It wasn't until 1878, the very year that the Pauleys arrived in Nebraska, that Omaha even *began* building a sewage system, one that wasn't completed until 1895.[34] A city of 30,500 inhabitants in 1880, only a quarter mile of its 118 miles of streets was paved. Animals would lie in the streets wherever they happened to die.[35] Their stench, along with that from the stockyards, would have been unhealthy and unappealing, to say the least.[36]

If the Pauleys had moved to Lincoln in 1878 they would have encountered a town of less than 13,000 and, like Omaha, lacking in sewers, paved streets, and streetlights. By the end of the 1880s Lincoln's population had mushroomed and the city boasted a new state capitol building, three universities, thirty-five miles of tram tracks, and twenty miles of sewage pipes.[37] However, the 1890s saw Lincoln's population stagnate if not decline, owing to the "Great Depression" (as it was called in the 1890s). Meanwhile, Clay County provided a healthier environment. Its population of 54 in 1870 exploded to 11,294 in 1880.[38] Ten years later it reached its all-time high of 16,310 before beginning a long decline to 6,542 in 2010.[39]

The census of 1900 revealed a good deal about Heinrich. For example, it spelled his name "Paulie" and recorded that he could speak and read English but not write. Being only semi-literate, it is highly unlikely that he had been a tradesman before leaving Russia.[40] Sometime between 1880 and 1886 he purchased his farm near Harvard. There he prospered, as shown by the census of 1900, which stated that he owned the property mortgage-free—typical for a Volga German immigrant—along with 117 farm animals, a very substantial number.[41]

Heinrich's first wife, Elizabeth Ross, died in 1896. The census of 1900 showed that Heinrich—better known by this time as "Henry"—married that same year a fifty-nine-year-old widow named Margaret Kearn (or Maggie), who had immigrated to this country in 1892. Margaret, who had had thirteen children by her first husband (only six of whom were still living in 1910), lived until 1925 and could not speak English. Like Heinrich, she could read but not write.[42] Thanks to the help of his sons and abundant rainfall in the 1880s and again after 1900, Heinrich was able to leave an estate worth $12,000 (close to $300,000 in today's currency) when he died in 1914.[43]

When the Pauleys arrived in Harvard, the town was just beginning to take on the trappings of modern civilization. Its first building was the railroad station. By the time the town was incorporated in 1873 it had already acquired postal service, a dry goods and grocery store, two weekly newspapers, and a $5,000 schoolhouse (worth about $125,000 today).[44] Six years later its population had grown to 650 inhabitants.[45] Several days each summer were devoted to lectures and concerts provided by Chautauqua, a religious, educational, and recreational program founded in upstate New York in 1874.[46]

The real boom years, however, occurred throughout Nebraska during the 1880s. Sod houses were rapidly replaced with frame homes. Social life was picking up with balls and lavish parties and with the founding of literary and dramatic societies. Every lodge, social society, and church had its singers and musical groups.[47] A new local newspaper, the *Harvard Courier*, kept the town's citizens abreast of all these developments. The Gay Nineties, however, were anything but gay in Clay County, because the average annual rainfall dropped from twenty-seven inches to just seventeen. Taxes were high and the price of farm products was low; banks were failing and money was tight. Perhaps the one bright spot was a new two-story schoolhouse, probably the most impressive building in the town, constructed in 1894, just in time for my grandfather Ludwig Pauley to attend.

Economic conditions began improving at the end of the 1890s when a number of large new homes were built along with brick and cement sidewalks, although the streets were not paved until the 1920s.[48] Just after the turn of the century the Stokes' Opera House—used for everything from graduation exercises to the display of agricultural products—was opened with a grand ball. In 1904 three automobiles appeared in the town's streets; by 1911 there were nineteen. In 1907 an electric power plant was opened and four streetlights and a few homes were lit by electricity, although the town was not fully electrified until 1920. In 1913 the town became downright citified when chickens were no longer allowed to roam free. Two years later a handsome neoclassical Carnegie Library, with its solid oak woodwork and door casings, was opened and it is still in use today. Two of my grandfather's younger brothers, Harold and Ray, sang at its dedication.[49]

Today, much of Harvard, like so many small rural communities in Nebraska, is struggling to stay alive, as can be seen in the many empty buildings in its business district. Its 2010 population of 1,013 is not much larger than it was in 1880 and is well below its peak population of 1,261, reached in 1960.

My great-grandfather Conrad Pauley began his adult life with one significant advantage: he had learned to write as well as read, probably reflecting a modest improvement in Norka's school system between the 1840s, when his father was of school age, and the 1870s, when Conrad was in school. He also attended public school in Harvard, although for how long I have no idea. In any event, Conrad's education was probably better than that of most of his age cohorts in Nebraska. Only 39 percent of school-age children attended schools in Nebraska at the beginning of the 1870s. Nine years later the figure was still only 63 percent.[50] A system of secondary schools was not even established in Nebraska until 1881.[51] School attendance was not mandatory until 1887, and then only for children between the ages of eight and fourteen. Even this law was unenforced and frequently flouted, as were similar laws throughout the United States.[52] Nor were early Nebraska schools any better equipped than those of the Volga Germans. Not until 1891 did school districts provide students with textbooks free of charge.[53] Only the small number of students per school might have been an advantage in Nebraska.[54]

In 1883 Conrad married Alice Yost, whose family, as mentioned earlier, had come from Norka in 1876 and whose farm was literally next door. However, Conrad was not the eldest son and thus did not inherit his father's farm or any of his money, most of which was set aside for Heinrich's invalid son, Adam.[55] By 1900 Conrad had only nine farm animals on his mortgaged farm near Sutton.[56] After that, however, he seems to have done well, because he was able to retire from full-time farming in 1908 at the ripe old age of forty-six, a fairly typical age of retirement for Volga Germans in Russia. My father opined in his memoirs that Conrad was probably tired of walking behind a plow drawn by one or two horses.

Conrad's daughter Selma, born in 1895, recalled that "Pa always said if he could get $100 an acre he would sell, which he did."[57] Once again, timing was crucial. Annual rainfall in Nebraska was above normal during the first decade of the twentieth century and helped increase the value of land from $18.95 an acre in 1890 to $49.95 in 1910.[58] In constant dollars this was equivalent of going from $464 an acre to $1,170 today. My father also gained the impression that his grandfather had sold his farm for around $25,000, which would probably be close to $600,000 today.

With his newly acquired wealth Conrad was able to buy seven and a half acres on the north side of Harvard and in my father's words "settled down to a new life of quiet retirement."[59] The new home boasted a bathroom—still unusual in the early twentieth century and lacking in his parents' house—a washing machine, and a furnace strong enough to heat the downstairs but not the three upstairs bedrooms. Conrad did not give up agriculture altogether, however. He and my great-grandmother maintained a large garden, in the Volga German tradition, and together with their eight children still enjoyed eating fresh chickens from their large chicken house, fresh milk from their Jersey cow "Bess," and plenty of apples and cherries, fresh and canned, from their extensive orchard, all stored in a cool cave that was dug below the cellar. My father recounted that when Conrad and Alice moved to Lincoln they made sure that Bess came with them. It became my father's duty to keep the cow well fed, a chore he didn't mind much because he loved Bess's rich cream.

Although my great-grandfather retired from farming, my great-grandmother did not retire from being a housewife. Their house in Harvard had a washing machine, but like my mother, Alice needed to scrub soiled clothes on a zinc scrub board. She also made soap out of lard and lye. Her life was made easier by the recent invention of kitchen ranges, sewing machines, kerosene lamps, and wringers on washing machines.[60] However, as late as the 1920s a typical rural wife spent nine hours a day cleaning, laundering, canning, and preparing meals. Just cleaning out her cast-iron stove, disposing of ashes, and starting a fire consumed an hour a day. Almost certainly, all eight of her children were born at home.[61] If someone in the family got sick the mother typically doubled as a nurse.[62] Although men now purchased ready-made clothes, it is likely that my great-grandmother, like most other women of her generation, still made her own.[63] On the other hand, it is likely that she made good use of catalogs from Sears and Roebuck or Montgomery Ward, which brought urban products to rural households.[64]

When my wife, Marianne, and I visited Harvard in 1983 and again in 2009, we discovered that Conrad's house looked exactly as it had in a picture taken in 1910, with an inviting porch that extended across the front of the house. A tour of the house in 2009 revealed that it retained all of its original woodwork. Guests had been welcomed into a formal parlor that opened to the living room and kitchen but could be separated from them by handsome wooden pocket doors, an innovation of the late nineteenth century. My father wrote in his memoirs about how much he enjoyed riding around in his grandfather's horse-drawn buggy or surrey, "complete with fringe around the top just as in the musical *Oklahoma*."[65] But he also told me that it was much less fun going to his grandfather's outhouse in the middle of a winter night, even though it was a relatively luxurious "three-holer."

Residents of Norka had been forced to engage in cottage industries to make ends meet, particularly as land per family shrank. Perhaps this tradition made it easier for Conrad to go briefly into the harness and sewing-machine business in downtown Harvard; later he bought a meat market, although the latter business lasted only a few months. After that he became a Buick dealer, which enabled my grandfather to buy Buicks at cost into the 1920s. However, undoubtedly the most important thing that he did was to help my Grandfather Pauley establish the first Pauley Lumber Company in Milford, Nebraska, in 1909 and then another and much bigger lumberyard in Lincoln in 1915. The next year, the year that Conrad's son Harold graduated from Harvard High and a year after Heinrich Pauley's death, Conrad and his wife moved to Lincoln, where he remained until his death in April 1936, followed three months later by the death of my great-grandmother, Alice.

EDUCATION, ASSIMILATION, AND URBANIZATION

The eldest of Conrad's eight children was my grandfather Ludwig Heinrich Pauley, who was born in 1886. As a boy he was called Louie or Louis; as an adult he was known by his friends either as Lu or L. H. (never Ludwig). Using the father's first name for the eldest son's middle name was typical of Volga German families. When I was growing up I never thought of him as being in any sense a pioneer. But in his own way he was very much a pioneer when he became the first "Russian" boy to graduate from high school in Harvard in 1902 at the age of sixteen. Most likely he was the first German from Russia anywhere in Nebraska to graduate from high school. In neighboring Sutton, with its heavy concentration of Volga and Black Sea Germans, no "Russian" graduated from high school until 1912, and the two who did were both girls.[66] In nearby Hastings, few Volga Germans even started high school before 1917.[67]

Harvard was typically American in having more girls graduate from high school than boys, whose labor was needed on the farm. Of the ninety graduates of Harvard High School between 1871 and 1901, only twenty-nine were boys.[68] Nationally, 59 percent of all high school students in the United States in 1900 were girls; in the biggest cities they made up no fewer than 75 percent of the high school enrollments.[69] In general, attendance was highest in small towns in the West and Midwest.[70] Harvard also exemplified national and state trends by having eight female faculty members in 1904—all but one of them young—compared to just three male teachers.[71] For smart, ambitious girls, teaching was one of the few professions—besides nursing and secretarial work—that was now open to women. However, it was common for females to teach only one or two years before getting married; only a few districts allowed married women to teach. Male teachers also quickly moved on to higher-paying jobs.[72]

At the turn of the twentieth century the United States was unique in having six thousand free public high schools, which offered modern foreign languages, mathematics, and science every year.[73] Enrollment at American high schools doubled between 1890 and 1900.[74] Nevertheless, only 6 percent of Americans teenagers graduated from high school in 1900. My grandfather may have been inspired to continue his education because his father had enough interest in education to be a member of Harvard's school board from 1902 to 1910, itself a highly unusual post for a Volga German.[75] A more mundane reason may have been the location of the family farmhouse little more than a mile away from the school, an easy walk for my grandfather, compared to other rural Nebraska schoolchildren who were often four or five miles away from the nearest school.[76] In any event, four of my grandfather's siblings—William, Selma, Harold, and Ray—followed his example and graduated from Harvard High School.[77]

My grandfather distinguished himself in debating and dramatic societies and was president and valedictorian of his seventeen-member senior class, the largest class in the school's history and a class size that would not be surpassed until 1917.[78] The graduation ceremony or "closing exercises," which were held at the opera house, included the graduates' all giving brief speeches. In turn-of-the-century America fine public speaking was one of the surest ways of gaining prominence, three-time presidential candidate William Jennings Bryan probably being the best example.[79] My grandfather's "recitation," which the town's newspaper said was "well delivered and called forth hearty applause," was titled "The Door to Success Is Labeled 'Push.'"[80]

This interest in education, showed by both my great-grandfather and his children, was in fact a radical departure from the attitude of most Volga German immigrants, who viewed public schools with a mixture of fear and suspicion. Advocates of public education in the United States saw Americanization through the teaching of English and common values as one of its primary virtues.[81] One of the reasons that Volga Germans left Russia, however, had been the fear of Russification. Their isolation from the rest of the Russian population and even from other colonies had created both solidarity and a "siege mentality." This feeling was reinforced by the near contempt in which they were held by well-assimilated Americans, even by

German Americans. Americanization threatened to alienate children from their parents and grandparents as well as from their German heritage.[82] American-born children of immigrant parents were caught in a dilemma: they were apt to be chastised if they spoke English at home or German at school.[83] The older generation thought that too much education was a threat to the maintenance of the ethnic group, their work ethic, and their religious traditions. Because of these parental attitudes, and more importantly because of their limited knowledge of English, Volga German children were viewed by their teachers and classmates as "dumb" or "slow."[84] Any Volga German who managed to graduate from high school was viewed by his friends with considerable awe.[85]

Shortly before commencement, my grandfather was offered a teaching job in the Harvard School District. By Nebraska standards of the time he was highly qualified, as there was no minimum age for teachers; many were fourteen or fifteen and had only an eighth-grade education.[86] My grandfather's teaching career must have been one of the shortest in Nebraska history. On August 4, 1902, he resigned the position, "finding the lumber industry a more promising field."[87] He was evidently not impressed by his prospective salary, which in Nebraska in 1904 averaged $55.24 per month for men (about $1,200 in today's values); women were paid $41.40 for the same work.[88] My grandfather went to work for the J. H. Yost Lumber Company in Hastings, Yost being a brother of his mother, Alice Yost Pauley. The very next year, when he was still only seventeen, he became the manager of the Inland, Nebraska, branch of the Yost lumberyard. During the next twelve years he managed other branches in Hebron, Sutton, and in 1909 the Yost lumberyard in Hastings, to which he and my grandmother and father moved. In 1915 my grandfather—again with the help of his father—established his biggest and most successful lumberyard in Lincoln at Twenty-Seventh and E Streets, which continued in operation until 1999.

Once again fortuitous timing benefited the Pauley family. Lincoln's population was growing—in contrast to Clay County. The population having at best stagnated between 1890 and 1910 when it was 44,000, Lincoln grew to 55,000 in 1920 and to nearly 76,000 by 1930.[89] Even during the Great Depression, when the state's population fell from 1,378,000 in 1930 to 1,316,000 a decade later, Lincoln bucked the trend by growing to nearly 82,000 in 1940.[90] When the lumberyard burned to the ground in 1925—a front-page event witnessed by thousands of Lincolnites—my grandfather used the insurance money to rebuild and take advantage of Lincoln's growth.[91] His luck ran out during the Depression, however, when his lumberyard barely survived. Residential construction throughout the United States declined from a high of $5.16 billion in 1925, when the country was enjoying the longest housing boom in its history, to just $435 million in 1935.[92]

My grandfather's linguistic ability, his graduation from high school, and his prowess in business enabled him to enter the mainstream of American society much earlier than most other Volga Germans. Although Clay County had been an early gathering point for Volga Germans, ethnic Germans made up only 5 percent of the population of the county as a whole in 1880, considerably less than the state's average of 6.9 percent.[93] And unlike in Lincoln, there were no urban Volga German enclaves in Clay County. The Homestead Act of 1862 had required pioneers to live on and improve the land for at least five years before acquiring a title, thus precluding farm villages of the German type.[94] Moreover, anyone hoping to engage in business with the general population, as my grandfather did soon after the turn of the century, almost inevitably was forced to loosen ethnic ties and become part of the dominant population. Overly strong ethnic ties could have actually been a hindrance to his success.[95]

Almost certainly contributing to my grandfather's early assimilation into mainstream American society was his marriage to my grandmother Lena (a name she disliked and never used) Albertina Righter, on March 4, 1908, in Stockham, Nebraska. Winter was the time when nearly all Volga German marriages took place, farm work being at a minimum.[96] Their marriage was unusual in two respects. In the first place, they were very young: my grandfather had just turned twenty-two, and my grandmother was barely twenty.[97] The average marrying age in 1900 was 25.9 for men and 21.9 for women. Even more unusual was a Volga German marrying an "outsider," something that was almost unthinkable before 1900.[98] Even though my grandmother had a German heritage—her ancestors had come directly from Germany in the late seventeenth century and settled in Pennsylvania—they had long since ceased to speak German.[99] Consequently, although my grandfather did not forget his German, it was not spoken in the household as my father was growing up, this practice being typical of the third generation of immigrants.[100]

My grandparents' wedding was evidently a major local "event," because the *Courier* described it as "impressive." My grandmother was described as "a very attractive young lady, fully qualified to practice the art of domestic science and to make the home blessed."[101] The article also noted that she was a "professional stenographer and proficient at the typewriter keys" and had been an assistant instructor in shorthand at nearby York College.

Although my grandmother later did some bookkeeping (at home) for her husband, her daytime hours were soon had to be devoted to "domestic science." In so doing she was not alone. Only 5 to 9 percent of married American women worked for wages in 1900.[102] Nine and a half months after my grandparents married, my father, Carroll Righter Pauley, was born in Hebron, one of the towns with a lumberyard managed by my grandfather. The marriage and early birth of my father put a premature end to my grandmother's education at York College after her freshman year, a termination she deeply regretted the rest of her life. She may not have been aware that at most only 4 percent of the American population attended college at all at the beginning of the twentieth century.[103] Of the graduates only 17 percent were women.[104]

It is hard to say how happy their marriage was; people with German backgrounds back then generally did not display much affection, especially around others. However, my grandparents traveled a great deal, and trips, especially long ones, can be nerve and marital testers. So they must have gotten along at least tolerably well. Grandfather Pauley seemed austere to me and never showed the kind of affection displayed by my mother's father. He firmly believed that children were to be seen and not heard, especially at the dinner table. I do, however, have happy memories of fall picnics in Nebraska City with my parents and grandparents.

Grandmother Pauley was less austere than either my grandfather or her mother, and did a much better job of enjoying life. She turned out to be by far the longest lived of my grandparents, dying in 1984 at the ripe old age of ninety-six. She and my grandfather were avid travelers, a habit she continued until she was eighty. In 1935 my grandparents traveled *by car* to Mexico. A year later they attended the Berlin Olympics. After my grandfather's death, in 1946, my grandmother continued her travels, going around the world at least once, with India being her favorite destination. She also kept busy during her long widowhood by being president of her Philanthropic Educational Organization chapter and was active on the Bryan Hospital Board of Trustees in Lincoln.

AUTOMOBILES AND HIGHWAYS

The early history of my mother's family is shrouded in even more mystery than my father's. I do know, however, that they were poor German peasants who suffered from farming infertile soil, feared being conscripted into an army—in their case Prussia's—and sought a better life in the American Midwest.

The name "Hülsebus" goes back only to 1812, three years before Ostfriesland, a poor, flat, and low-lying area in northwestern Germany, became part of the Kingdom of Prussia. In addition to every house being assigned a number, every family had to adopt a permanent surname, apparently as a means of facilitating taxation and the conscription of soldiers. No longer could one simply follow the confusing practice of using a father's or mother's first name as a surname, a patronymic custom still practiced in Iceland. No one knows the origins of the name, but according to my mother and a family historian, the name was a shortening of Hülsenbusch, which could mean a bean plant or holly bush.[105]

What is certain is that the first known person to bear the name was Berend Albers Hülsebus (1787–1831). Berend's son Albert Behnen Hülsebus (1812–92) sired no fewer than twenty-four children by three wives. One of these was my great-grandfather Harmon (1842–1922), better known as Harm. Fearing the Prussian draft and longing for more land to farm, Harm emigrated in 1867. Emigration itself was no simple matter. Emigrants had to receive official permission by proving that they had no outstanding debts and were not evading the draft. They also had to give up their German citizenship.

The cost of the passage was daunting: in 1873 it cost between $24 and $32 for a steamship ticket (about $500 in today's currency), which was no bargain for an unskilled laborer who earned only about $7.20 a month in the 1860s or a craftsman who earned only $11.50. Unlike the Volga Germans, whose families emigrated as a group, those from other parts of Europe often emigrated separately. In the case of the Hülsebus clan, the father, Albert, didn't leave Germany until 1874, by which time all eighteen of his surviving children were in the United States, most of them settling in Illinois, Iowa, or South Dakota.

Great-grandfather Harm settled first in Freeport, Illinois, and then Warrensburg, where he worked as a "section hand" for a railroad. Later he became a section boss for the construction of new lines. Such railroad jobs were commonplace for immigrants in the second half of the nineteenth century. In January 1878 Harm married Johanna Keppler, nearly seventeen years his junior. Fourteen months later, my grandfather Fred Albert Hulsebus was born, the umlaut in his family name having disappeared soon after his father arrived in the United States. In 1880 Harm moved the family to Defiance, Iowa, where land could be purchased for little more than $7.00 an acre.

It was on this farm that my grandfather Hulsebus was born and raised. He was not content with farming, however, instead studying mechanical and electrical engineering in Des Moines for two years. In 1902 he married my grandmother Dora Kruger and began working in the hardware and telephone business in Defiance. In 1910 he moved his family to nearby Harlan, a town of around twenty-five hundred, where he established the Hulsebus Motor Company. By 1915 it had ten employees and sixteen thousand square feet of floor space located just a block away from Harlan's main square. His dealership sold Cadillacs, Buicks, and Hupmobiles and included gasoline pumps and a large repair garage.[106]

My grandfather entered the automobile business at a propitious time. Farmers were especially eager to buy cars in order to escape isolation. My grandfather remembered how it had taken him two and a half hours by horse-drawn wagon to travel the fourteen miles between Defiance and Harlan when he was married in 1902. In an advertisement he published in the

Harlan Republican in 1929 he noted proudly that thanks to the automobile a *round trip* from Defiance to Harlan could then be easily and comfortably made in just forty minutes.

There had been fewer than 14,000 cars in the entire country at the turn of the twentieth century when the population was 76 million; the number of cars increased from 7 million in 1919 to more than 23 million a decade later.[107] Of the 123 million Americans in 1930, nearly one in five owned an automobile.[108] No fewer than five out of every six cars in the entire world were owned by Americans on the eve of the Great Depression.[109] In Iowa alone the number of registered vehicles rose from 147,000 in 1915 to over 437,000 in 1920.[110] Thanks to Henry Ford's assembly-line production in 1913 and the rapid increase of installment buying in the 1920s automobiles went from being a plaything of the rich to a near necessity for most Americans, especially farmers.[111] They changed lifestyles more drastically than anything else in the twentieth century with the possible exception of computers and television.[112] The automobile industry was the principal driving force in the prosperity of the Roaring Twenties, and businessmen reached a level of popularity throughout the country never reached before or since.

Speed was not the automobile's only advantage. It is hard to believe in our age of congested highways and auto-produced air pollution that at least for a time the automobile actually *improved* health. When horse-drawn buggies disappeared, so too did the twenty-two pounds of manure deposited on city streets by every horse each day. The dust in the air created by dried horse manure, which caused respiratory illnesses, likewise gradually vanished. Until the invention of air-conditioning, cars also provided some relief for summer heat by enabling owners to find cooling breezes in the countryside.[113]

Automobiles, of course, were useless without good roads, so it is significant that my grandfather also became the president of the U.S. Highway 59 Association, a road that stretched from the Canadian border to Kansas City, Missouri. In 1908 only around 6 percent of American roads had a hard or gravel surface, and almost all of them were in the East.[114] In that year, the fastest car in a famous race from New York to Paris took thirteen twelve-hour days just to reach Chicago, a trip that a train could do in eighteen hours.[115] In Iowa the roads were so bad that after rainstorms travelers were often forced to wait for days for them to dry out before they became passable. Not until 1916 was there a Federal Aid Road Act, which offered federal funds to states to help them organize highway departments with matching federal grants.[116] My grandfather apparently had only limited success, because at the time of his death in 1943, U.S. 59 had not yet been fully paved through Iowa.

My grandfather was not short on self-esteem or shy about dispensing advice. For example, he wrote a four-page single-spaced letter to President Roosevelt in May 1941 recommending that the president appoint former president Hoover to represent the United States to negotiate for world peace and goodwill. He added that "if we must fight in all parts of the world we may lose and Stalin may win" (a prediction that turned out to be at least half right). (Whether Roosevelt actually read the letter is more than doubtful as he received over 15 million letters during his twelve years in office, or about 4,000 a day.) My grandfather conveyed the same idea to Hoover himself and the Republican presidential nominee for 1936, Alf Landon, both of whom wrote brief, noncommittal responses. Alas, my grandfather's single-minded effort to end the war ended in failure.

The last fourteen years of Grandfather Hulsebus's life could not have been happy. His brother Charles died in 1929, followed by his mother a year later, the same year that both the Great Depression and a terrible, decade-long drought began in the Midwest. Of the ten hottest summers in Iowa's history, four occurred during the 1930s. The double whammy of the Depression and the drought dropped the average value of Iowa farms from $35,000 in 1920 to $11,000 in 1935.[117] In a state in which agriculture was by far the most important industry, farmers could not even think of buying a new car.

My grandfather noted the downturn in the business cycle and his sense of personal failure—a very common occurrence in a country that attributed success or failure to individual effort—in letters he wrote to my mother while she was working in France. In a letter dated November 21, 1930, my mother wrote: "I received a letter from you this morning, Papa. I'm worried about business, especially since we have read in the American papers about all the banks which have closed. I hope that nothing happens at home." My grandfather's self-esteem must have been at least somewhat restored a few months later by an editorial in his hometown newspaper praising him for being a "community builder" and "giving freely of his time."[118]

My grandfather managed to survive the Depression financially only through gasoline sales, his repair shop, converting his auto showrooms into offices and apartments, and selling refrigerators and washing machines. Faced with a shrinking income, a family would obviously sacrifice buying a new car before they would cut back on purchasing food or clothing. Many people even regarded it as bad taste to flaunt their wealth by driving a new car.[119] Nationally, car sales dropped from 5.3 million in 1929 to 1.8 million three years later.[120] In some years my grandfather did not sell a single car, and after February 1942, because of the war, no new cars were manufactured. Wartime gas rationing obviously not only reduced his gasoline sales but also the frequency with which cars needed repairs. I remember my mother saying how sad it was that my grandfather did not live long enough to profit from the revival of the auto industry in the early postwar years.

Grandfather Hulsebus's premature death from heart disease in November 1943, four months shy of his sixty-fifth birthday, was one of the great tragedies of my life. I remember that every time we visited him in Harlan he would immediately take me and my sister to a nearby corner drugstore where he would buy us ice cream cones followed by a game of catch. I am sure that I would have learned many practical things from him had he survived even a few more years. He was by far my favorite grandparent, even though I was barely six when he died.

CHAPTER 3

Education, Travel, and the Great Depression

"A long feast of beauty"

MUSIC, DRAMA, AND SCHOLARSHIP

Timing was just as critical in the lives of my parents as it had been for my grandparents. Each was born in 1908, so their youths coincided with the most prosperous period in American history up to that time. Prosperity enabled them to be the first in their families to go to college and travel abroad. Their socially active, carefree, and privileged lives, however, were suddenly turned upside down by the Great Depression.

My mother, Blanche Marie Hulsebus, was born in Defiance, Iowa, on July 19, 1908. Her birth date was later to become something of an embarrassment, because my father never let her forget that she was his elder by five months. He liked to say that he had married an older woman. In 1910 she and her parents moved fourteen miles south to Harlan, where my mother spent the rest of her childhood until she went away to Grinnell College in 1926. Her only sibling, Fern, was born in 1912.

All of my mother's stories about growing up in Harlan indicate that her childhood was a happy one. As noted in the last chapter, her father was a prominent citizen and successful businessman, at least until the onset of the Great Depression. My mother's house was located across the street from the town library; she read so much that her grandmother frequently complained that she was ruining her eyesight. Of course, her grandmother had not had the benefit of electric lights in her youth. My mother was also ahead of her time in learning how to drive when she was a teenager.

The ability to drive was just one advantage enjoyed by both of my parents during the Roaring Twenties. The years between 1922 and 1929 soon came to be known as the "Coolidge Prosperity," the greatest economic boom up to then in American history. The biggest reason for this economic expansion was the increase in car sales. Other inventions, which had been rare or even unknown at the beginning of the decade, such as telephones, refrigerators, vacuum cleaners, electric irons, toasters, washing machines, and radios, had become commonplace by its end. America was now richer than all of Europe including Russia combined.[1] Unfortunately, the decade also witnessed the decline of old habits of thrift and sacrifice that dated back to the Pilgrims. Modern advertisements succeeded in convincing millions of Americans by the end of the 1920s that what had been considered luxuries at the beginning of the decade were actually "necessities" purchased with borrowed money. Consumer credit rose from $2.6 million in 1920 to $7.1 million in 1929.[2] The consequences of this change in philosophy are now all too familiar.

My mother loved school and did well, in part because she had excellent teachers and in part because her father insisted on it and was proud when she succeeded. She showed an early interest in music, especially in singing and playing the piano. She performed numerous solos in her church choir and also in school musicals. When she was in high school she played the piano to accompany silent films in a local theater. Music was to play a huge role the rest of her life. She went to France in 1930–31 in order both to teach music and English and to study piano and voice. For years she directed a thirty-member children's choir at Trinity Methodist Church in Lincoln. Around 1960 she was the president of the Symphony Guild in Lincoln.

My mother excelled both academically and in extracurricular activities during her high school years. Her curriculum included four years of

Latin in addition to physics, general science, music, mathematics, four years of English, and ancient, American, and European history. Except for gym she had no easy classes. Thanks to her straight-A average she was the valedictorian of her senior class of forty-seven students in 1926. She was also the editor in chief of her yearbook (*The Harpoon*), the pianist for the nineteen-member school orchestra for all four years, and the president of the "Irving Society" (a drama club) her senior year. My mother also gained recognition in the Harlan community for both her dramatic and musical performances, especially the latter.

When my mother went off to Grinnell in the fall of 1926 it had fewer than eight hundred students. Like so many other colleges founded before the Civil War, it was located in a small town of the same name, about fifty miles from the temptations of the big city of Des Moines.[3] It was supported by the Congregational Church but was unusual in being entirely free of sectarian control.[4] By the end of the nineteenth century it had established a reputation for academic excellence. Its claim to be the "Harvard of the West," however, was based on its athletic prowess in football, baseball, and track, not academics.[5] For example, during the 1890s its football team defeated the University of Nebraska in two of their three contests.

Grinnell was also a national leader in women's higher education, being only the second liberal arts college in the country (after Oberlin in Ohio) to open its doors to coeds. By the late 1920s female college students were no longer the rarity they had been in Grandmother Pauley's time. In the 1920s women made up 40 percent of all college students and almost a third of all college professors and presidents, figures that would not be surpassed until at least the 1990s.[6] In my mother's graduating class of 1930, women outnumbered men seventy-seven to fifty-five.[7]

My mother majored in music, minored in English, and once again excelled in both academic and extracurricular activities. By the time she graduated she had earned forty-two A's and eleven B's and was elected to Phi Beta Kappa. She retained a passionate love of Grinnell the rest of her life, so much so that my father used to joke that Grinnell for her was not just a college but a religion. My sister and I felt much the same way when we attended, if perhaps slightly less passionately.

Since its founding in 1846 Grinnell had always tried to instill in its students an idealistic ambition to serve the larger community, whether it be locally, nationally, or even internationally. Most likely it was in part owing to this idealism and the influence of a professor, the father of a boy my mother was dating, that she applied for a teaching job at a school in Château-Thierry, a town of eight thousand inhabitants fifty-five miles northeast of Paris.

Her year in Europe was a life-altering experience for my mother and indirectly for me as well. In addition to my hearing about her experiences for years and then visiting the places where she had taught, she left behind two diaries and a set of letters—totaling nearly five hundred pages—that she wrote that year to her parents. Other long letters were published in her two hometown newspapers. These letters, which I inherited after her death, were carefully preserved. They show not only that she wrote clearly and vividly but also that she also had insights into the lifestyle, customs, and politics of the day, especially for France, of course, but to a considerable degree for Italy and Germany as well, which she visited toward the end of her year abroad.

My mother's year in Europe began with her joining a tour organized by the Kiwanis Club of Shenandoah, Iowa. The cost for those people who went to Europe as part of the month-long, all-inclusive round trip from Shenandoah, including Pullman berths on trains, all meals on the ship, and hotels and meals in Paris for the first five nights, was $261 (about $3,400 today), which my mother regarded as "an impossibly low rate." The Canadian *Duchess of Atholl* was part of a new kind of tourism during the period between the two world wars. Prior to 1914, transatlantic ships had been used either by the ultra rich, who sailed first class, or by immigrants, who traveled in "steerage." World War I and postwar American immigration laws drastically reduced immigration to the States. To compensate, new or refurbished ships provided a whole new "tourist third class" of cabins for professional people, families, and students seeking adventure in Europe. This was the beginning of mass tourism, though still far from the scale we have reached in the twenty-first century. My mother described her cabin, which held four passengers, as small but "comfortable," and it included the luxury of a sink. Among the voyagers were a good many "new women" traveling alone for business, education, or pleasure. On many sailings, women outnumbered men two to one.[8] For example, of the 157 members of the Kiwanis group, no fewer than 118 were women, 52 of whom were single.

Launched in 1928, the *Duchess of Atholl* briefly held the record for an eastbound transatlantic crossing of six days and thirteen hours. Older, less luxurious ships soon fell victim to the Depression. For example, my father, who also sailed to Europe on the *Duchess of Atholl,* was one of the last passengers on the ss *Metagama* when he returned to the States in August 1930. Built on the eve of World War I, it was scrapped in 1934 because of declining patronage. Nearly all the passengers on my father's voyage were Polish immigrants heading for Canada. "They sat at long tables and must have eaten some sort of stew three times a day," he noted in his memoirs. "Several big bowls would be placed on long tables and all the diners would stand up and help themselves. . . . The food was terrible and I soon found myself existing on crackers, cheese, and tea."[9]

Mom remained with the Kiwanis group only while it was in Paris. Thereafter she was on her own, except for the $20 per month ($260 today) that her father sent her for piano and voice lessons, concerts, and train fares. She received no income in Château-Thierry beyond her room and board. When in Paris she sometimes walked for miles to save bus fare. Her financial situation improved later in the year when she taught in Grenoble; there her income eventually rose to the princely sum of $30 a month on top of free living expenses, a salary well above the $20 a month paid to French schoolteachers but far below the annual income of $1,000 earned by professors at the University of Grenoble.[10] A twenty-five-day trip at the end of the year from Grenoble to Avignon, Nice, Florence, Bologna, Munich, Nuremberg, Stuttgart, the Rhine River, Cologne, and back to Paris including train fare but not meals cost $68 ($900 today).

Soon after the ship's departure my mother wrote her family that "the three young men in the party seem rather bashful, although one of them did come up to me yesterday morning and exchanged a few remarks." He was "traveling alone and [was] both seasick and home sick. . . . He's a nice, good looking, tall fellow, and men are scarce." That young man was to be my father, and the conversation marked the beginning of a romance that did not end until my father's death in 1987. My mother told me that someone in the Kiwanis group from Lincoln had told her that she should ignore my father because he was engaged, which was, in fact, the case. Once the ice was broken my father wrote that "within twenty-four hours . . . I had ascertained that [she] was a Methodist and a Republican and that she liked tomato soup and peanut butter. I was enthralled!"[11]

It is not surprising that many young men pursued my mother, all of them nice looking and intelligent. Mom never considered herself a great beauty. She was, however, poised, attractive, and vivacious. She also had great taste in clothing and interior decoration. My mother was obviously smart, as indicated by her grades in high school and college. She was also adventuresome and later traveled with Dad literally all over the world. Most of all she was devoted to her family.

During the fall semester of 1930 my mother taught music and English at the Methodist War Memorial School, otherwise known as "A Community House of Friendliness," in Château-Thierry. Located appropriately enough on the Place des Etats-Unis (square of the United States), the school was established in 1919 by the Methodist Church in a 150-year-old former hotel that had been ravaged by the "Great War," as World War I was known at the time. The school's initial purpose was to aid refugees returning to their ruined homes in one of the most devastated parts of France. It soon evolved into a home for infants and young children from destitute families. It also included a well-heated library for adults, with good lighting and comfortable chairs along with fifteen hundred books, newspapers, and magazines in both English and French. The children's library was the second of its kind in the country.

The town was located near the site of the Battle of Belleau Wood, where the American Third Infantry Division played a key role in thwarting a German attack in June 1918. Travel agencies such as Thomas Cook and American Express brought more than seventeen thousand tourists a year, most of them Americans, to Château-Thierry to see the battlefield, the American military cemetery with its twenty-two hundred graves, and a war memorial in the town's main square. They also toured the Memorial School and, without being asked, left donations that funded it.

My mother's pupils were girls of various nationalities who came from poor or broken homes. They were eager to learn English and other practical skills, because doing so would get them good jobs in Paris in shops filled with American tourists.[12] Even though my mother was supposed to teach entirely in English, she quickly discovered that she needed to speak at least some French; she was poorly prepared to do so, however, despite having studied the language during her freshman and sophomore years at Grinnell. In the middle of the academic year the school closed because its director retired. "How I hate to leave Paris" she lamented in early January just before leaving for Grenoble in the French Alps.[13]

In most respects my mother was enchanted by France and by Europe in general. When she returned home she described the Continent as a "paradise" for music lovers. She particularly loved attending the opera and concerts in Paris, where she saw Maurice Ravel conduct one of his compositions and Richard Strauss do the same for his opera *Der Rosenkavalier*. She attended a concert by Sergey Rachmaninoff, who, she said, "played like an angel and a devil, with tender sweetness and fiery vigor. Such crystal and liquid and deep tones! The two hours passed like fifteen minutes; we were nearly the last to leave the hall, clapping until the stage lights were off."[14] She was also enthusiastic about visits to the world-renowned Louvre art gallery. Culture didn't occupy all of her time, however. Once she moved to Grenoble she went skiing and played tennis nearly every day. She admired French families for their love of "promenading" and conversing. "Conversation is to them a game and a fine art!"[15] She was impressed with France's paved highways, which were uncluttered by billboards and lined with old trees.

However, Mom was by no means uncritical of Europeans and complained about extreme French nationalism. She wrote her parents that "French girls don't know anything but cooking and sewing and don't think of anything but finding a husband."[16] French business practices were overly traditional, unimaginative, and uncompetitive. Her students of high school age studied as hard as the better college students in the United States, but she disliked the emphasis on memorization and the lack of opportunities for self-expression.[17] After seeing many people in third-class train carriages with "red noses, purplish red cheeks, and glassy eyes," she thought that "the French need a little of our emphasis on health, exercise, sports, and hygienic living quarters."[18]

My mother also made some interesting political and cultural observations in a diary she kept of her trip to southern France, northern Italy, and Germany after her teaching ended in Grenoble. She noted that France no longer seemed like a foreign country. She even identified herself with the French so much that American tourists she encountered looked "glaringly" like they "didn't belong." She was impressed with the cleanliness and efficiency of Italian trains compared to those in France—perhaps it was really true that Mussolini made the trains run on time. She found Italian men "the most handsome creatures [she had] ever met, but [didn't] trust them an inch." She thought there was so much art and historical treasures to see in Florence that she was "fairly dizzy with the responsibility of seeing everything in just a few days!" When she arrived in Germany she felt that "it is my country. I have such a feeling of peace and deep quiet thrill—as though I were coming *home* as I enter Germany. I like the look of the people—they are solid and honest and good." Later she remarked that it was an "awful thing . . . not to be able to speak the language and I feel so German." However, she also noted that she liked the sound of French better than she did German.

Mom was also aware of the political mood among Germans in 1931. While in Grenoble, a university city of eighty-six thousand people among whom were included many foreign students, she noticed that "the young generation [of Germans] is not so pacifistic as the older people who have suffered in the last war. There is somewhat of a spirit of revenge among the young."[19] "Hatred for the Germans seems to be born into the French and hatred for the French is born into the Germans," she wrote.[20] One German woman told her that she believed in the "survival of the fittest," a very Hitlerian idea. Germany seemed "sad and quiet. The people are poor and do not find life easy or happy." Germany, she wrote in her diary on July 5, "has known twelve years of horror, poverty, and sorrow. They have no future. They cannot have families—are too poor—there is not room enough for more people. They have no hope in the future. Many are out of work."

On July 16, 1931, Mom remarked in her diary: "My last day in Europe! I wonder if I shall ever have another so varied and interesting. I am coming back and I am not going to forget what I have learned this trip!" How right she was. The powerful impressions Europe had made on her were also reflected in the last of several articles she wrote for the *Harlan Republican* in which she said that the year had

> meant more than I can now appreciate. . . . [It] has been a long feast of beauty. The sky was a deeper blue in France; the air had a light golden green and the flowers, especially the roses which grew in great quantities everywhere, were nothing less than gorgeous. . . . The architecture of France, of all Europe, is beautiful. . . . Here [in the States] a house that is ten years old is torn down for something up-to-date. There, a house, a church, is built for centuries. . . . The Europeans have beauty of art, painting and music that we here with our advertisement posters and our jazz cannot realize. Europeans do not have our physical comforts . . . but because of this lack, life is simpler, more leisurely, deeper and more beautiful.

My mother's year in Europe was transformative. Already in September 1930, just two months after her arrival in France, she recorded in her diary that "Today, doing my laundry, I seemed to arrive at a new state of mind, of realization of myself as an independent individual, and a joy in it. I must begin to arrange my life with that idea, my environment has changed from that of the small family circle and the sheltered ordered schools, to the broad world in which I must find my own way, think out the right plans, make decisions." Consequently, she had no desire to accept a job offer at Harlan High School, which she turned down in part because "on the whole [she] did not like [the town]."[21] (A popular World War I song was "How you gonna keep them down on the Farm after they've seen Paree?") Instead she spent two years teaching at a private girls' school called Sea Pines on Cape Cod, where she was able to earn the magnificent sum of $1,850 ($29,000 today) a year. Most of this money she returned to her parents, much of it being used to pay for her sister Fern's freshman and sophomore years at Grinnell. She was particularly attracted to Sea Pines because it was close to Boston, which she regarded as "the most European city in the United States."

My father was also impressed by his trip to Europe, which greatly increased his already substantial interest in history. After Paris he visited Geneva, Lucerne, Heidelberg, Frankfurt, Cologne, Mainz, Koblenz, Berlin, Potsdam, Amsterdam, The Hague, Brussels, Bruges, and finally London and the nearby Shakespeare country. Although he managed to see an extraordinary number of interesting and important sites (for example, the Kaiser's Palace in Berlin, which was gutted during World War II), his tour was evidently not quite the mind-bending experience that Europe was for my mother. In his autobiography he barely mentions anything about the trip besides meeting my mother and the relative quality of the two ships on which he sailed. Compared to my mother's full year in Europe, Dad spent barely three weeks in Europe, from July 25 to August 14; sixteen days were at sea. Six other days were spent in Montreal and Quebec and traveling by train to and from the Canadian ports. This breakdown makes it is easy to understand why American trips to Europe were still relatively rare in the 1930s and up to the beginning of extensive Atlantic air travel in the late 1950s. How many people today can take off six weeks for a European vacation?

Whatever letters my father may have written to his parents during his trip have not survived. A few years ago I did discover a fairly detailed diary he kept while on the trip. It lacks the thought-provoking observations about the European way of life or Europe's beauty found in my mother's letters. His interest in historical sites, however, was indicative of his lifelong avocation. He also showed an acute awareness of the difference in modernity between Paris and Berlin, noting in particular the electric lights of the German capital compared to the old-fashioned and dimmer gas lights of Paris, notwithstanding the latter's renown as the "city of light."

THE "ACTIVITIES MAJOR"

My father was an avid traveler and had a much earlier start touring than my mother. Europe was merely more exciting and educational than the many trips he had already taken in the United States with his parents. Three earlier trips had been to Yellowstone National Park, the East Coast, and a long, eventful journey to the West Coast by way of New Mexico and Arizona. The trip east was the easiest, because highways east of the Mississippi were paved; on the other hand, campgrounds were harder to find. The trip west in 1925 was undertaken in a "touring car," with its canvas folding top but no sides. He and his parents camped out wherever they could—there being few campgrounds as such—occasionally in someone's backyard. His mother cooked over an open fire. Paved roads were nonexistent, with only a few exceptions in California. Most mountain roads were one lane wide. A descending car had the right-of-way because brakes were often unreliable. The ascending car was supposed to back down to the first by-pass at a time when there were few guardrails. My father described this maneuver as "an extremely stimulating experience, even for a confidence-filled 16-year-old boy."[22] Driving two hundred miles a day was considered quite an accomplishment. He noted toward the end of his European diary that he stopped in St. Louis on his return trip from Europe and that St. Louis was the only major city in the United States that he had not yet seen. However, none of these boyhood trips was to the Deep South, which many northerners still regarded as somewhat foreign in the 1920s. Together, these trips created my father's lifelong love of travel, and, by inheritance, my own as well.

Dad went to the very same elementary school (Prescott) that I did thirty years later. In high school he was, if anything, even more involved in extracurricular activities than my mother, although without the same high grade-point average. He called himself "somewhat of an 'activities major.'" He took minor parts in several plays, became a member of two prestigious clubs, including the Mummers (for actors). He was also a homeroom representative and a member of the Boys Glee Club, orchestra, debate team, student council (secretary), and band (captain). He was also the treasurer of his graduating class. He admitted in his memoirs that "as a result [he] entered the University of Nebraska less than fully prepared for college."[23] However, just graduating from high school in the 1920s was still a considerable achievement. As late as 1922 fewer than 20 percent of Americans had that distinction.[24]

A photocopy of his grades reveals that indeed many of his courses were in band, orchestra, and chorus and relatively few in the natural sciences.

However, he did take two and a half years of Latin and four years of English. He was able to study German only in his senior year, 1925–26. Not until the U.S. Supreme Court in 1923 declared unconstitutional a Nebraska law restricting the use of foreign languages, and wartime Germanophobia finally dissipated, was the language offered again at Lincoln High.[25] (Only a decade earlier no fewer than 24.4 percent of all American high school students had studied the language; in 1922 the percentage had fallen to 0.6.)[26] In the 1920s grades were measured in percentages rather than by the letters A to F. My father's best grades, ranging from 85 to 95, were in history, including ancient Greece and Rome, as well as in American and modern European history. What is remarkable about his transcript is its revelation of the enduring importance of classical subjects such as Latin and ancient history in American high schools during the 1920s. The other notable fact is how closely his interests resembled my own three decades later.

Although graduating from high school in 1926 was no longer the rare occurrence it had been in Grandfather Pauley's time, a descendant of a Volga German going on to college was altogether another story.[27] Emma Schwabenland-Haynes, writing in 1927, said that "it is practically impossible to point to any [German-Russian] that has attended an institution of higher learning," although she cites Colorado as a partial exception.[28] Like intermarriage, it was not until the middle of the twentieth century that it became commonplace for descendants of Volga Germans to attend a university.[29]

Even though the "golden age" of the University of Nebraska had occurred before World War I, one distinguished historian who taught there in the late 1920s, when my father was a student, said that the school "carried the brightest torch for learning to be found anywhere between the Missouri River and the Pacific Coast."[30] The school, with over ten thousand students, was also the tenth largest in the country.

My father's admission about his lack of preparedness for university is borne out by the transcript of his grades, although comparisons are difficult to make because of grade inflation that has been going on in academia since the late 1960s.[31] Dad's grades were mostly in the 70s and 80s, though he did score a 90 both semesters in English composition. His writing ability was demonstrated in his autobiography, which is astonishingly clear and engaging for someone who had had no experience in composing such a long work. In his only history course, a two-semester survey of England, he received an 80 the first term and an 83 the second.

Dad's less-than-spectacular grades probably again reflected the number of extracurricular activities he engaged in during his college years. He was president of his Delta Upsilon fraternity, a member of the Business Administration's Executive Council, and president of his senior class. He regarded his three-plus years in the Reserve Officers Training Corps Band, now known as the University of Nebraska Marching Band, as his most enjoyable activity. In his senior year he was both its captain and drum major. It must have been quite a sight to see him, six feet, two inches tall and wearing a tall drum major's Busby, strutting onto the field of Memorial Stadium before thirty-five thousand spectators.

My father's interest in extracurricular activities was far from unique in the 1920s, a time when only one in seven Americans attended college.[32] Robert Knoll, for forty years a professor of English at the University of Nebraska, pointed out in his history of the university that its third quarter century, from 1920 to 1945, was marked by a "culture of aspiration." Universities, not only in Nebraska but elsewhere in the United States as well, were institutions where one could become "accredited socially as well as professionally." The 1920s were also a time when self-made men such as Grandfather Pauley, who had not gone to college, wanted their sons to have the campus experience they had never had themselves and to associate with young men from well-established, educated families.[33] A high school diploma, which had smoothed the way into the white-collar class for my grandfathers at the beginning of the century, no longer sufficed for business executives in the 1920s.[34] Moreover, contacts could be made that would be useful in various ways after graduation.[35] This was undoubtedly true of my father, who retained many of the friendships he developed at the university, especially with his fraternity brothers, for the rest of his life.

My parents corresponded for three years before they finally tied the knot on a hot summer's day in Harlan on June 20, 1933. During the interval my father was trying to establish his career with his father at the Pauley Lumber and Coal Company during the worst years of the Great Depression.

Meanwhile, my mother probably had an easier time teaching music at Sea Pines. They were able to see each other only during some of my mother's summer and Christmas vacations when she returned to Harlan. For my father the trip was made more difficult because the highway from Lincoln as far as Omaha was still gravel (it would not be paved until the end of 1935). The highway went through the middle of every town in Nebraska and Iowa, including Omaha and Council Bluffs. Cars had to share two-lane roads with farm equipment traveling no more than ten miles an hour.

The old cliché that opposites attract certainly did not apply in the case of my parents. Actually, most people fall in love with people very much like themselves.[36] Besides my parents' common love of peanut butter and tomato soup, they both came from conservative, Republican, Methodist families. Their fathers were successful businessmen, at least prior to the onslaught of the Great Depression. Both were very active socially and musically during high school and college, although my mother was far more successful academically. Both had traveled widely before marriage, my father more in the United States than my mother, but my mother had spent far more time in Europe. Although my mother had begun her year in France as a prohibitionist, she admitted in her diary—but not to her parents—that she had developed a taste for both wine and beer by the end of the year. My father headed for a tavern as soon as he reached Montreal before the sailing of his ship for Europe. Despite their political conservatism, neither was an American nationalist; they continued to express a strong interest in and respect for foreign cultures, which they passed on to me.

SURVIVING THE GREAT DEPRESSION

It was no doubt these common values and common interests that enabled my parents to endure the terrible years of the Great Depression and World War II, years my father vividly described in his memoirs. He constantly worried about keeping a roof over our heads and food on the table. He once told me that he was so worried about how he was going to support a wife in 1933, the worst year of the Depression, that his weight dropped ten pounds in the last days preceding his wedding. In fact, huge weight losses, brought on by worry alone, were common during the Depression. The marriage rate also fell by 22 percent between 1929 and 1933, and the birthrate declined by 15 percent during the same period.[37]

My father had good reason to be anxious. The Depression turned out to be second only to the Civil War as a social trauma, causing not only a loss of jobs but also a loss of savings, businesses, and status.[38] When he and my mother got married the unemployment rate had reached 24.9 percent, the highest level of the whole Depression. In the meantime the GNP had fallen to half of its 1929 value, and the stock market had lost nearly 85 percent of its pre-crash value.[39] Only a third as many automobiles were manufactured in 1933 as in 1929. The situation was even worse for farmers, whose income dropped nationally from $6 billion to $2 billion.[40]

Nebraska was one of the states hardest hit. Terrible heat waves and a prolonged drought were interrupted only by floods in 1935 and a blizzard in 1936.[41] The price of corn in 1932 was one-fifth what it had been in 1929, while the price for hogs and beef dropped to one-fourth of their previous levels.[42] This was especially devastating in states such as Nebraska and Iowa, where the incomes of people living in towns and cities depended to a large extent on the prosperity of farmers in the region. Although eastern Nebraska was only on the fringe of the notorious Dust Bowl, the prolonged drought produced dust storms so severe that day was turned into night and many people suffered from "dust pneumonia." To keep out the dust my mother hung wet sheets or towels over the windows. In Harvard, just eighty-five miles west of Lincoln, dust banks piled up as high as six feet during the terrible summer of 1934.[43]

Evidence of the Great Depression and the drought of the 1930s lasted into the early postwar years. I can remember seeing throughout the city, but particularly near the state capitol, numerous basements with nothing but a ceiling overhead. My parents told me that these were buildings whose construction abruptly ended when money ran out because of the crash. In a suburb of Lincoln called Bethany there stood an empty shell of a building that had been Cotner College until, like hundreds of private schools around the country, it had been forced to close its doors in 1933. A north-south boulevard of the same name had lost at least half the majestic elm trees that once lined the street because of the drought. Still another reminder of the Depression was the large number of cars on the streets in the early postwar years that dated back to the 1920s because Lincolnites had not been able to replace them in the 1930s.

The Great Depression, which lasted from 1929 to 1941, was not the first economic crisis in American history, but it was the worst. Even among the three-quarters of the population that remained employed, a third worked only part time.[44] These figures do not include women who were passed over for work in favor of a man. Businesses and the federal government discouraged the hiring of married women and mandated that they be the first to be fired in cutbacks. Twenty-six states actually enacted laws prohibiting the hiring of married women.[45] Fifty percent of school districts fired women who got married.[46] As in Victorian times, women were supposed to return to their "natural" sphere as a wife and a mother.[47] Construction, which was obviously vital to the success of the Pauley Lumber Company, fell nationally by 26 percent in 1930, 29 percent in 1931, and 47 percent in 1932.[48]

The rise of unemployment and the decline in construction and the stock market were not steady but fluctuated up and down, sometimes wildly. By April 1930 the stock market had recovered 20 percent of its losses of the previous autumn and was at the same level it had been at the beginning of 1929.[49] Consequently, President Herbert Hoover was prompted to say on May 1 that that he was "convinced we have passed the worst and with continued effort we shall rapidly recover."[50] The next month he told a delegation seeking a public-works program that the "depression [was] over."[51] Grandfather Pauley evidently believed these reassuring words. Dad noted in his memoirs that his parents funded his trip to Europe in 1930 as a college graduation present because they thought that the economic downturn was only a "Wall Street phenomenon and not apt to have much effect in the farm areas of the Midwest."[52] Indeed, the country's economic situation in the spring of 1930 did not seem nearly as dire as it had been as recently as 1921, when there had been a 24 percent decline in the GNP—double the downturn for the whole of 1930. And the unemployment rate of 11.9 percent in 1921 was worse than the 8.9 percent in 1930.[53]

However, it was precisely during the six weeks of my father's graduation trip, from mid-July to late August 1930, that the economic crisis reached the Midwest with a vengeance. Upon his return my father was informed that sales at the lumberyard were declining rapidly. As it turned out, the "Depression," originally a euphemism coined by President Hoover because it sounded less dire than "crash" or "panic," was anything but temporary. Although the unemployment rate declined to 14 percent by the beginning of 1937, it rose again to 19 percent later that year and still stood at 14.6 percent in 1940 and 9.9 percent the following year. Not until 1943, at the height of World War II and rearmament, did unemployment return to pre-Depression levels.[54]

Fortunately, my father was never unemployed during the Depression, although the Pauley Lumber Company just barely survived, unlike the 110,000 businesses that failed throughout the country between 1929 and 1932 alone.[55] He managed to draw a salary of just $100 a month when he first started working for his father, a salary that was reduced to $75 a month in 1931 as the Depression worsened, although it was restored to $100 ($1,660 today) in 1933 once my father became a married man.[56] He worked in an office with no air-conditioning from seven in the morning until six at night, six days a week except for Saturday afternoons in July and August, a schedule that was only slightly shortened when I was growing up in the 1950s. He told me that some nights during the 1930s Lincoln's overnight low would be ninety-two degrees. My father supplemented his income by joining the National Guard soon after his marriage, which paid for the family's medical bills. He bought a house on South Sixteenth Street at an auction for next to nothing and miraculously managed to rent out its second-story apartment. Consequently, his total income may have been slightly higher than the national annual average of $1,500 and was certainly higher than the $12 a month paid to truck drivers at the Pauley Lumber Company and the $15 earned by the yard foreman.[57] Only in the late 1930s would his salary at the lumberyard "skyrocket" to $125 per month. The U.S. census of 1940 revealed that he worked fifty-four hours a week and had a total income of $1,800 the previous year, half that of his father.[58]

The Pauley Lumber Company was in an especially precarious situation because it had built a number of speculative houses, which, like other houses in Lincoln, could not be sold at almost any price. Finding a renter was not much easier, as extended families often doubled up. Precarious finances at the lumberyard meant that paying the company's phone bill was a touch-and-go proposition. The lumberyard had so little cash on hand that my father would sometimes have to make change for a five- or ten-dollar bill at a nearby mom-and-pop grocery store. Conditions remained so poor at the lumberyard in 1940 that my father took a job in real estate in Wichita, Kansas, but soon quit because his handsome $200 paycheck invariably bounced. Toward the end of 1941 he moved our family to Lansing, Michigan, after taking a job with Nash Kelvinator (later known as American Motors). He arrived in Lansing on December 7, 1941, Pearl Harbor Day; my mother, sister, and I joined him a few weeks later.

The Depression was a traumatic experience for my father, as it was for most Americans who lived through it. It is no accident that he devoted a third of his memoirs to describing it. My mother told me that once, when he was in the midst of writing them in 1976, he returned home from his office looking so utterly bedraggled that she became alarmed and asked him what was wrong. "Oh, I was writing about the Depression today and it all came back to me," he replied. My uncle Gordon told me in 2002 that my father was so convinced that the country's profligate ways would eventually lead to another depression that he had a contingency plan all worked out for the Pauley Lumber Company when that day arrived.

The Depression was just as hard, if not harder, on my mother. She was no longer living with adoring parents. When she married my father she epitomized trends that had started around the middle of the nineteenth century. During this period more and more unmarried American middle-class women could hope to acquire a good education and enjoy some economic independence as teachers, nurses, or secretaries. However, this independence was expected to come to a screeching halt once they married or at least when they began having children.[59] In my mother's time most women still usually accepted this dependence as part of the natural order of things, however jarring the contrast with their premarital life may have been. My mother's only long-term job outside the home was directing a children's choir—by far the largest of the four choirs at Trinity Methodist Church—which sang sacred classics once every six weeks or so (for which she received many accolades). Thirty years later, educated women in particular were no longer so willing to make this sacrifice.[60]

For my mother, cooking and cleaning without a dishwasher and automatic washing machine or dryer in a house without air-conditioning, and always under the critical eye of her mother-in-law, must have required a huge adjustment for someone used to winning public acclaim for her musical and acting performances. The one luxury that my father provided her soon after their marriage was a refrigerator to replace their icebox.

My mother's sister, Fern, was perhaps more seriously affected by the Depression than anyone else in our extended family. She exemplified the consequences of being born in what later proved to be a bad year: 1912. Whereas my mother graduated from Grinnell in the spring of 1930, before the full effects of the Depression had become apparent, Fern started at Grinnell that fall, when it was all too apparent that the crisis was severe. Even with the money my mother sent home from Sea Pines, my grandfather could no longer afford to keep Fern in school after the spring semester of 1932. She spent the remainder of the Depression doing secretarial work for her father and the local public school. The census of 1940 revealed that her annual salary was $720.[61] Harlan's small size severely limited her chances of marriage. Only after her father's death in 1943 was she able to leave Harlan for a job in New York City. She never married.

My parents were fortunate in being born near the beginning of perhaps the biggest boom in American history, 1900–1930, a period that was far more prosperous than that experienced by their parents and grandparents and was perhaps the most optimistic in American history.[62] Their youths were almost idyllic. However, when they embarked on marriage and their adult lives they encountered horrible circumstances that their children and grandchildren could later hardly imagine. Somehow they managed to endure, for which they have my profound admiration. The memories of the Great Depression remained with them for the rest of their lives, and in a sense they passed them on to me. My father often said in his later years: "What this country needs is another depression." What he meant was that too many Americans were living far beyond their means and that only a depression would cure their extravagance. If my father had lived to see the "Great Recession" of 2008, he would have said "I told you so."

CHAPTER 4

War, Peace, and Prosperity

"Peace—how pleasant thou art!"

BLIND LUCK: MY EARLY CHILDHOOD

I was born in Lincoln on November 4, 1937. Few people could have known at the time that 1937 was to be an ideal birth year. It was the eighth year of the Great Depression, and unemployment had declined only modestly since its worst level in the winter of 1932–33. The U.S. population had grown by 16 percent in the 1920s and was to grow by 15 percent in the 1940s. However, during the 1930s birthrates were so low that the population grew by only 7 percent, from 123 million to 132 million, figures that are now dwarfed in the second decade of the twenty-first century.[1] In Nebraska, economic conditions were so bad that the state's population actually *declined* by 62,000 during the 1930s.

About the only upside for the state during the decade was the University of Nebraska football team. The Cornhuskers already played a unique role in the state at that time. With no other major college or professional football teams to divide loyalties, people from Fall City to Chadron supported the team, which during the 1930s won 65 games, lost 21, and tied 8. In 1937 the team started out with a 14–9 victory over mighty Minnesota, a team that had lost only one game since 1932 while winning three national championships. The victory set off a huge celebration in downtown Lincoln and was followed by Nebraska's shutting out five of its nine opponents that year—an unthinkable achievement for any college team today. However, the team scored only 99 points itself during the whole season, a far cry from today's high-scoring games.

Internationally, 1937 was a peaceful year with no great diplomatic crises. Little did anyone know that the day after my birth Adolf Hitler would hold a meeting with his top military and diplomatic leaders—known later by the name of the transcriber as the Hossbach Conference—in which the führer would outline the possibilities for territorial expansion into Czechoslovakia and Austria, steps that would lead (in reverse order) to World War II in 1939.

Unlike my sister, Patricia (or "Patty" as she was called then), who was born barely ten months after our parents' marriage, I was planned. It may be that my parents were encouraged to expand their family by the decline of the unemployment rate, which had dropped from 24.9 percent when President Franklin Delano Roosevelt took office in March 1933 to "only" 14 percent in early 1937.[2] Demographers have noted that birthrates bear a remarkable relationship to economic conditions nine or ten months earlier.[3] The number of unemployed people in the country had dropped from 13 million in 1933 to 7 million in early 1937, and the GNP for the whole of 1937 actually exceeded that of 1929, having grown 12 percent a year since 1933. The Dow Jones Industrial Average, which had fallen from a high of 381 in September 1929 to a low of 41 at the beginning of 1933, was back up to around 179 in January 1937.[4] Personal income had risen from $50.2 billion in 1932 to $74.1 billion five years later.[5] Lincoln's *Evening State Journal* noted on New Year's Day that "the stock market swung farther up the recovery trail with business in 1936 reaching the highest levels in five years."[6] A week later, Roosevelt informed Congress that he expected to balance the budget and begin reducing the national debt in fiscal year 1939.[7] A sign of recovery in Lincoln itself was a story carried by the *Evening State Journal* on January 5 announcing plans to construct a new student union at the University of Nebraska.[8]

Little did my parents know when I was conceived in February that Roosevelt's attempt to balance the budget by cutting government spending in 1937, together with the start of Social Security taxes (benefit payments did not begin until 1940), would by August contribute to the economy's downhill slide.[9] By October the market would drop by more than a third; by the following March it had lost half its value. Four million more workers would lose their jobs during the winter of 1937–38; corporate profits nose-dived by 78 percent, and industrial production was down by 40 percent.[10] The unemployment rate would rise to 19 percent.[11] Nineteen thirty-seven came to be known as the "depression within the Depression." The Depression was beginning to look like a permanent way of life.[12]

My mother told me that she and my father wanted a daughter first and then a son, so in that respect they got exactly what they wanted. It is interesting that my father's grandfather Conrad had eight offspring, and my mother's grandfather Harm sired seven. Just one generation later my grandparents on both sides of my family had only two children, as did my parents. In the country as a whole it had taken well over a century for the birthrate to fall from eight to two per family.[13] That decline took place in the Pauley and Hulsebus families in a single generation. My wife and I have continued the two-child tradition, as have our sons. No doubt the evolution from farming to business to the professions has had a great deal to do with this change, although the Depression also played a role.

My birth and my mother's two-week stay in the hospital—usual for that time—cost my father all of $75 ($1,100 in constant dollars) compared to a U.S. average of $32,000 today. Being born in a hospital, however, was still fairly uncommon in 1937. Two years earlier only 37 percent of American women had chosen this type of delivery.[14] However, since the 1920s middle-class urban women were opting ever more frequently to give birth in a hospital.[15] I was brought home to a duplex at 1600 Dakota Street. The walls separating the two units were so thin and I was so noisy that my "nursery" was the bathroom, as far removed from the neighbors as possible. My sister, who evidently was hoping for a sister, suggested to my mother that she "throw the baby in the garbage can." I may have been noisier than my own children and grandchildren, because in the 1930s a highly popular book by John B. Watson, *Psychological Care of Infant and Child*, insisted that babies be fed according to a rigid schedule and not necessarily when they were hungry. A popular book, *Behaviorism*, also counseled parents "Never hug and kiss them, never let them sit in your lap," although I doubt very much whether my parents followed this advice.[16]

My mother noticed that as a boy I behaved quite differently from my sister. I loved to get into things and liked to smash my toys. When I was a little older but still too young to walk, I threw myself from one piece of furniture to another, not caring much if I fell or not. Because of the noise problem and relatively high cost of the rent, we soon moved to a very ordinary house on the corner of Sixteenth and "C" Streets not far from Trinity Methodist Church. The new quarters were far from satisfactory, however, because they had a terrible floor plan and the bedroom where Patty and I slept was impossible to heat. I eventually caught a cold that developed into bronchial pneumonia, resulting in my spending several days in the hospital. Summers, on the other hand, were so hot that I would don a straw hat—and nothing else—to stay cool, until my mother spotted me and clothed me again.

Our next move was to a neo-Tudor house at 1861 Dakota Street, which I was to consider home until my third year of college in 1957. (In those benighted days streets were still called streets instead of lanes, coves, courts, terraces, drives, avenues, circles, ways, places, and parkways as they are today.) Unbeknownst to me, it was located just two blocks away from what had been the airfield where Charles Lindbergh had learned to fly in the 1920s. The house had been built by the Pauley Lumber Company late in 1929—just in time to remain unsellable.

Compared to the often monstrous houses of the late twentieth and early twenty-first centuries, our house was pretty modest, having just fifteen hundred square feet.[17] However, even that was considerably larger than the national average of just under a thousand square feet in 1950.[18] Post–World War I houses were much smaller than those of the Victorian era, which were built for larger families and often for servants as well. Despite the smaller size, prices were higher than before the Great War because of the far more technologically advanced kitchens and bathrooms of the newer homes.[19] Our house did have a living room large enough to accommodate my mother's grand piano. My parents' bedroom was also sizable. Patty's bedroom was medium size; the dining room was just large enough for a table and chairs. My room was by far the smallest of the three bedrooms, although I liked having two windows that looked out onto the backyard. The kitchen, with its linoleum floor, was small and compact, a drastic change from earlier centuries when kitchens were one of the largest rooms in the house and the site of children's games, visiting neighbors, Saturday-night baths, and even childbirth. Our bathroom was tiny, also the norm from the 1920s to the 1950s. It was about the size of a walk-in closet today, with a bathtub but no shower. We felt fortunate in having a second toilet in the basement. Not surprisingly, we had to take turns using the bathroom. Being the youngest member of the family, I was the first to use it in the evening and the last in the morning. There was no such thing as a "family room" in the house; in fact, the term had not yet even been invented. Nor was there a master's suite, guest room, theater room, music room, study, exercise room, bonus room, or any other such room that has now become commonplace.

The house was unusual for its time in having a two-car garage attached to the back of the house, but that meant the driveway consumed most of the backyard, leaving little space for grass. Having two cars also meant that, unlike most teenagers, I had ready access to a car once I turned sixteen and had no desire to have a car of my own. About a third of the basement was taken up by a coal bin. I was fascinated by my father taking out the "clinkers" (unburned pieces) every night when he came home from work. The largest room in the basement was for laundry. My mother had a washing machine with a wringer for getting out excess water from the clothes and a scrub board for getting out stains. There were also clotheslines in the basement for drying laundry in the winter when it was too cold to hang clothes outside. There was a good reason why Monday was still called "washday." Needless to say, our house was not air-conditioned, although a window air-conditioner was installed in the kitchen when I was in high school. I can remember many nights when the temperature never dropped below eighty-two degrees and I would lie in a pool of sweat trying to fall asleep.

MY "WAR YEARS"

World War II dominated the early years of my life as our family joined the 30 million Americans—one in four—that migrated around the country.[20]

The attack on Pearl Harbor occurred five weeks after my fourth birthday. I was a little too young to remember that historic event, but its consequences determined where and how we lived for nearly the next four years. My father, fearing the draft—actually very unlikely for a married man with two children—decided to join the navy in 1942. His more compelling reason, however, was revealed in his memoirs. "History was being made and I was a part of it, in a sense, but only in a peripheral manner. I talked to Blanche about my problem (she later claimed that she didn't understand the full implications of our talks) and tried to make her understand that I felt impelled to play a military part in World War II."[21] My mother apparently thought Dad was only talking in broad, philosophical terms. However, when he actually received his training orders in December 1942 or early the next month, "the full implications [of his decision] were now being driven home to [my mother] with a vengeance and to say that she was none too happy about the entire matter, would be putting it mildly."[22] In fact, she complained off and on about the decision for the rest of her life. On the other hand, she admitted to me December 1989 that she was proud of him for serving his country. I was equally proud when he visited my kindergarten class at Prescott Elementary School in the spring of 1943, apparently when he was between training assignments. It must have been a special day for parents; I vividly remember my father standing out and above the others and wearing his handsome naval officer's uniform.[23]

My father's memoirs give an excellent account of his thirty-two weeks of training. He began at Dartmouth College in New Hampshire in March 1943. My mother, my sister, and I joined him at his next training site early that summer in Princeton, New Jersey. We next moved to Columbus, Ohio, where we lived from July to September. I have no meaningful memories of any of these sojourns except for the beauty of the Princeton campus and that we were living above a grocery store near a slum in the Ohio capital. I remember more clearly our next move, to Miami, where my father attended a Submarine Chasing School in the late fall of 1943. By that time I was in the first grade; I remember attending Biscayne School, a multi-story building that was only one classroom wide. It had no glass windows, just large openings in the walls to allow breezes to pass through. I was fascinated by the tall coconut palms and was always begging my father to open a nut, which, of course, was no easy task. I also enjoyed strutting next to the sailors when they marched in formation to or from their classes.

Our stay in Florida turned out to be short-lived, as my mother, my sister, and I returned to Harlan because Grandpa Hulsebus became seriously ill and died that November. I spent the spring semester in the Harlan elementary school while Mom took care of her father's estate. The Harlan school I attended must have still been as good as in my mother's time. Whereas I had received reasonably good grades in all subjects at Prescott, my grades in Harlan ranged from "satisfactory-plus" in music to "unsatisfactory-minus" in arithmetic (a harbinger of things to come in that subject). When I returned to Lincoln for the second grade in 1944–45, I again received "satisfactory" in all subjects.

My father's naval training finally ended in the spring of 1944, and he was assigned to a destroyer escort called the USS *Holder*, one of over 450 such ships built during the war. Lightly armed, they were used to escort convoys of merchant marine ships. Designed primarily for anti-submarine warfare, they also provided some protection against planes and smaller attack vessels. Starting on March 24, the *Holder* led a convoy of ships hauling supplies to Allied forces in the Mediterranean. According to my father, this convoy was the first to have an American escort screen protecting it until it reached its final destination; all earlier convoys had been met by British ships at Gibraltar. Fortunately, the convoy's crossing of the Atlantic was uneventful because the Battle of the Atlantic against Hitler's submarines had been won by the Allies a year earlier. However, Dad's journey into the Mediterranean was anything but placid. His memoirs describe in gripping detail how his ship was nearly sunk on April 11 when it was struck by a German torpedo plane, causing two large explosions. Ten percent of its crew of 175 men were either killed or wounded, but alert damage control kept the ship afloat. My father was knocked out by the explosions (for which he received a Purple Heart) and was nearly swept overboard. Things could have been even worse, however. With all its power lost the *Holder* was "dead in the water" and thus a sitting duck for another torpedo, which fortunately never arrived.

The navy, not knowing what to do with the ship, ordered it towed back, along with a skeleton crew, to the Brooklyn Navy Yard. It must have been about this time that I asked my father how many Germans he had killed. I was taken aback when he said: "None and I hope I never have to kill any." On the other hand, he told me when I was an adult that "when someone is shooting at you with intent to kill, you get vindictive in a hurry."

My mother, my sister, and I spent the summer of 1944 in Brooklyn, where I devoted much of my time trying to understand the "Brooklynese" of my playmates, who thought I was equally exotic. However, my stay in Brooklyn turned out to be brief, because my sister and I returned to Lincoln to live with our grandparents while Mom stayed behind with Dad and worked in the gift shop of the Metropolitan Museum of Natural History.

Although I was aware of the presidential campaign of 1944, my earliest memory of a specific historical event dates to April 12, 1945, when we were briefly home between my father's assignments. I was listening to one of my favorite children's programs when it was suddenly interrupted by an announcement that President Roosevelt, the only president I had ever known, had just died. I ran into the living room to tell my mother, who was taking her usual afternoon nap. She woke up just long enough to say that I must have misunderstood the announcement. A few minutes later my program was interrupted again, this time for good. Once more I hurried into the living room with the news. This time she believed me and said: "Oh no! That means Truman is president!"

Another vivid recollection I have is the dropping of the atomic bombs on Hiroshima and Nagasaki in August 1945. I doubt if I was as elated to hear the news as those marines who soon learned that it would not be necessary to invade the Japanese home islands. However, I did absorb the common feeling that we were now living in a new age. I recall being frightened that someday an atomic bomb would be dropped on our country.

The exploding of the two bombs occurred during my father's last assignment in Curaçao in the Dutch West Indies in the fall of 1945. When he arrived in Curaçao the war in Europe was over, but the Pacific War against Japan was still very much in progress. After some time my mother, my sister, and I were allowed to join him, even though the Pacific War had ended in the meantime. Far from being a hardship, our two months in Curaçao turned out to be more like a tropical vacation. The flight to Curaçao was my first ever. No one outside Nazi Germany had as yet produced jet planes, and commercial air service was still in its infancy. Our flight was leisurely and included numerous stops on islands along the way. What stands out to me in retrospect is how much time the stewardesses (as they were then called; there were no male flight attendants until the late 1960s) had for casual conversations with the passengers. I was also fascinated to be able to fly above rainbows, something that my friends believed to be impossible.

Dad's job was to help keep oil flowing through the Panama Canal to the Far East. All ship captains had to report to his office to pick up sailing instructions. My father was able to rent a nice house on the edge of Curaçao's capital, Willemstad, and wrote that "we readily adjusted to the relaxed life of a tropical island. Blanche was able to endure the strain of getting up from the breakfast table and walking to the porch glider while our big, black maid did the dishes and scrubbed the tile floors. Nor did the picking of mangoes and limes from the trees in our ample orchard seem to burden her unduly. I had no more night watches—only 8 to 5 banker's hours. We shopped for groceries at the army PX or for fruit and vegetables at the waterfront native market. Peace—how pleasant thou art!"[24]

Like my school in Miami Beach, our house had no glass windows, just large openings to let in sea breezes. Every night I slept under a mosquito net. My sister and I loved riding in a jeep the navy had provided for our father and watching thousands of huge lizards scurry out of our way. The only unpleasant memory my sister and I have was our maid, Ida, standing behind us to make sure we finished our awful-tasting powdered milk.

Curaçao was the first foreign country (or colony to be exact) I had lived in, and it made a lasting impression on me. I can still remember its stereotypical Dutch architecture, a floating bridge (which still exists but is now used only for pedestrians), and boats filled with flowers, fruits, and vegetables. Rural areas were a sharp contrast to the relatively modern capital. My twelve-year-old sister described native huts as being "so dirty and ragged that they look as though a good strong breeze would blow them over." Outside the huts were naked infants playing in the dirt. When were drove around the island we were "amazed at the ease and grace with which [the native women carried] their heavy loads in baskets on their heads."[25]

There was no English-language school for me to attend, so my mother tutored my sister and me instead. In my case she had little success, though; I was far more interested in climbing trees, swinging from a backyard trapeze, and swimming than in studying. The "vacation" ended early, however, when Dad received word that his father had had a serious heart attack and he was needed back in Lincoln. Our arrival home on November 11 marked the end of my "war years."

For me the war meant more than simply moving from place to place. It stimulated a lifelong interest in travel and current events. I followed the news and was very much aware that the war was "total" every time I picked up a magazine, watched a "newsreel" at the movies, or listened to the radio. As one can still see on television, a great many movies were intended to inspire support for the war. Posters and even advertisements were filled with references to the war. Prescott School played its part. Periodically we had air-raid drills in which we had to leave our classrooms and move to the interior of the building. In retrospect, I think the chances of the Germans or Japanese bombing Lincoln were pretty slim to say the least. As young students we also participated in the numerous scrap drives that took place throughout the country. I frequently took old newspapers, "tin" cans, and even empty toothpaste tubes to school. Saving and making do became almost a part of my generation's DNA. The later idea of "planned obsolescence," and using the equity in one's house as a piggy bank, still strikes us "children of the Depression and World War II" (as I call my generation) as downright immoral. The war was so omnipresent in our lives that I vividly remember asking my mother what news was like in peacetime. I recall her mentioning reports of auto accidents and petty crimes and thinking that peacetime sounded pretty boring. As it turned out, my interest in war and its causes became a lifetime fascination.

Ironic and even callous as it may sound, for my family, as for a great many Americans, the war marked the end of the Great Depression and the beginning of an exciting adventure filled with travel, no doubt mixed for my mother with periods of loneliness and anxiety about my father's safety. The country was united to an extent never seen before or since.[26] For my father and many other Americans, the war was the most interesting and exciting time in his life.[27] He was able to see history in the making as he had hoped and had survived without serious injury. Not surprisingly, he devoted a full third of his memoirs to his war years. For me the war was one memorable experience after another.

BACK TO SCHOOL

My return to "civilian" life was not without difficulty, as I am sure was the case for many other children whose parents had been in the military services. Since kindergarten I had moved around from Lincoln to Harlan, Princeton, Columbus, Miami, Brooklyn, and Curaçao. In each school I found that I was either behind or ahead of my classmates. My parents seriously considered putting me back a grade, and I managed to stay with my third-grade class only with the help of a tutor. I might have been better off if I had been held back, or "red-shirted," as so many youngsters are nowadays. I had started school two months shy of my fifth birthday; like many boys, I was neither precocious nor diligent in my studies. Such remained the case until I reached college.

The grades I received not only from kindergarten through high school but also during my first two years of college gave no indication of a scholar in the making (although in this respect I was by no means unique among future historians).[28] The only subjects in which I received consistently good grades were music—where grades were almost meaningless—and social studies. Even in the latter subject my grades were rarely top notch. In math my grades ranged from mediocre to poor, which doesn't surprise me because I always found abstract subjects boring.

Comments from my teachers were mixed. My early travels did produce some positive reactions. My kindergarten teacher in Harlan wrote that I had "entered into our conversations with his experiences, and I liked that." This observation was echoed by my kindergarten teacher at Prescott, who said that I "liked to give reports on [my] activities." My third-grade teacher also noted that "he contributes to our Social Studies [discussions]." Given my passion for reading as an adult, I am surprised that I occasionally struggled a bit with that subject. Nevertheless, my favorite day of the week was Friday when our class spent time in the school library. I always headed for books about geography or history. My mother also encouraged my interest in books by reading to me every night while I was in bed.

The biggest accomplishment in grade school was a report I gave on Alaska in the sixth grade. My teacher, Edna Thompson, was so impressed that she sent a letter home to my mother that read: "I wish you could have heard the very scholarly report that Bruce gave in Social Studies last week. He had been very careful in its preparation. The children were attentive and were anxious to hear it all through to the end. I think that is a real test of a good report. He does so well in the things he has much interest in; he really should be more careful in all his written work. I was glad I could put him into one of our hardest readers."

My work at Irving Junior High School, grades seven through nine, did not greatly improve except in social studies and sometimes in English and physical education. Irving had been built in 1927 when junior high schools were expected to ease the transition from elementary school to high school. They were also supposed to prevent social class divisions by extending the curriculum to include vocational classes and extracurricular activities as well as "assemblies" where students of all abilities could witness concerts, talks, and patriotic exercises.[29] As I recall, my vocational training was limited to classes in drafting and woodworking, but my only accomplishment in the latter was building a shoe-shining box. My report cards at Irving were a real hodgepodge. I did very well in social studies in both the seventh and eighth grades.[30] My science accomplishments were another story, with my teachers mentioning that greater effort on my part would have yielded better results.

At Lincoln High School my grades were, if anything, even more mediocre than in junior high. The low point was a dismal grade in tenth-grade algebra, which I improved somewhat in geometry the next year. However, my distaste for math was so strong by then that I was determined to avoid other math courses as much as possible. My work in Spanish—rumored to be the easiest foreign language the school offered—was only slightly better.

I later regretted that I had not gotten started in German, which would have proven far more useful to me professionally.

My one truly bright spot in high school was music. My musical career, however, had not gotten off to a promising start. I had been in my mother's children's choir at Trinity Methodist Church, not that I had any choice in the matter. As was true in many middle-class families, my parents, or at least my mother, insisted that I take piano lessons in grade school. Each morning she sat down next to me on the piano bench and tried to get me to practice. It was the most tortured fifteen minutes of the day. Each spring, my piano teacher, Mrs. Steckelberg, held a recital in her house in order to show off the accomplishments of her twenty or twenty-five pupils to their proud parents. The worst students played first, and the best, among whom was my sister, came last. By my third year of lessons I had risen all the way up to second from the bottom in the pecking order. I recall the drive to the recital that year as resembling a trip to the guillotine. When my turn came, I got completely confused and Mrs. Steckelberg had to help me through the remainder of the piece. A few days later my mortified parents gave me the wonderful and unexpected news that I wouldn't have to take lessons any longer. Sometimes it pays to be bad at what you don't enjoy doing. However, I still have recurrent dreams about not being prepared for some kind of presentation, although it is usually a role in a play or a lecture.

My musical career improved in the ninth grade when I was given a lead role as Mr. Fix-It in an operetta called *Up in the Air*. My best grade as a sophomore was in Boys Choir. It was probably for that reason, plus a tryout, that I was selected by a tall, distinguished man named Hugh Ranger to sing in the eighty-three-member Lincoln Boys Choir. With the exception of my mother's choir, this all-city choir, which included boys with both changed and unchanged voices ranging from soprano to bass, was my first exposure to the classics of choral literature by such composers as Bach, Mozart, and Schubert. I suspect that the choir made quite a positive impression on me, even though I was not enthusiastic about having to attend two-hour rehearsals on Saturday mornings. I can't remember where and how often we performed, except that I do recall that we traveled all the way to Cleveland, Ohio, for a major concert.

Much more prestigious than the Lincoln Boys Choir, or even the lead role I had as the elderly burgomaster, Jan van Borken, in Victor Hugo's *The Red Mill* in my senior year, was singing in the Boys Octet during my junior and senior years. My voice had apparently made a good impression on an older classmate who was later to gain national fame as a television talk-show host and columnist for the *New York Times*. Dick Cavett wrote in my sophomore yearbook, *The Links, 1953*: "Bruce, one of the best singers I have ever sat by—I know you'll be the star of the 8-octet next year—Good luck and all that stuff." Interestingly enough, Cavett was perhaps best known at the time as a magician; next to his signature in my yearbook he drew a hat with a rabbit popping out. However, he was already gaining local recognition as the master of ceremonies of the school's talent show, "Joy Night," and was the president of the Student Council his senior year among a host of other activities, including the National Honor Society.

Another Lincoln High School "Link" who gained national fame was Sandy Dennis, who was in my own class of 1955. Although her passion for acting was well known in the school because of her roles in the junior and senior plays, no one who I knew imagined she would become a Hollywood movie star in the 1970s, winning an Academy Award for her role in *Who's Afraid of Virginia Woolf* and also playing leading roles in *Up the Down Staircase*, a drama set in a high school, and in a comedy with Jack Lemmon called *The Out-of-Towners*, about a midwestern couple that encountered endless travails during a job interview in New York City. Tragically, her career and life were cut short by cancer in 1992.

The Boys Octet sang (for free) all over the city for various women's clubs and civic organizations. I counted forty-four such performances my junior year and twenty-four during my senior year. Unlike the Lincoln Boys Choir, we sang popular songs like "You'll Never Walk Alone" (which had old ladies in tears), "Mood Indigo," and "Mr. Sandman, Bring Me a Dream." I didn't appreciate it at the time, but the popular songs of the 1950s were actually quite good, with their pleasant melodies and intelligible lyrics. Somehow I was chosen to be our spokesman, so I became accustomed to public speaking, sometimes before large audiences such as school assemblies, where there might be over fifteen hundred students and teachers in attendance. That experience probably eased my road to classroom teaching a decade later.

The Boys Octet turned out to be a real esteem booster for me, because unlike my parents, I did not engage in a great many extracurricular activities, let alone hold any prestigious offices. There were three obvious reasons for this underachievement. First, most of my courses were required and in subjects of little interest to me. As mentioned above, I did quite well in social studies, which was basically history. I am sure that I would have done well in geography, but, as in most other American school systems then and since, it was never offered as a stand-alone subject after sixth grade, much to the detriment of Americans' knowledge of the outside world. The second reason for my poor performance was my unwillingness to study hard. I thought that if I did an hour or so of homework each night I was going above and beyond the call of duty. Finally, although I had some good teachers in high school, particularly in English, none of them inspired me to pursue a career in academe. It may be that I was unlucky or simply avoided the best (and hardest) teachers. It wasn't until I got to college that I was really exposed to great teachers, and then studying hard was something I wanted to do and was not simply a means of academic survival.

Contributing to a low esteem and lack of self-confidence, at least prior to my being selected for the Boys Octet, was my being terribly skinny throughout junior and senior high school. By the tenth grade I had reached my adult height of just under of six feet, two inches, but I weighed a puny 135 pounds. I had improved to around 150 pounds by the time I graduated from high school, but it wasn't until the end of my sophomore year of college that I reached a respectable 170 pounds. Consequently, even though I was the quarterback of a neighborhood football team in grade school, I had no chance of being a member of the football team in high school. Nor did I have the ability to be on the high school basketball team; the competition for that honor was fierce because of the huge size of the school—fifteen hundred students for just three grades. I did, however, play basketball in a church league, but I was no star.

Golf was the one sport in which I did fairly well in junior and senior high. We lived just a block away from the Lincoln Country Club, which I passed on the way to and from Prescott School and later Irving Junior High. The game looked like fun. One day when I was twelve, I discovered some old hickory-shafted golf clubs that had been used by my mother, probably for a college course in physical education. Armed with these clubs and accompanied by a couple of neighborhood kids, I sneaked onto the course through a gate in the wire fence on Twentieth Street. However, after hacking our way through a couple of holes we were chased out by the club's pro.

After a few such incidents my parents decided it was preferable, and more legal, for me to play at Pioneers Golf Course, at the time the only eighteen-hole public course in Lincoln. Lacking any sprinkling system for the fairways, it wasn't much of a course, especially from 1952 to 1954 when Lincoln was suffering from a terrible drought—only the greens and tee boxes were watered, leaving the fairways parched and hard as concrete. However, the price was right. As I recall, a junior membership for unlimited play cost $25 ($200 adjusted for inflation) for an entire season. Naturally, I carried my clubs; pull carts had not yet been invented. A few years later, when motorized carts began to appear, I thought they were the most decadent device imaginable. How lazy could one get? Nowadays I couldn't get along without one, at least not for eighteen holes.

Before I leave the subject of school altogether I should mention two practical courses that I took in junior and senior high. The first was typing, which I took in the eighth grade. Little did I know at the time that I would have so much use for that skill throughout my life. The other was photography, which I took before our trip to Europe in 1954; it taught me the basic principles of composition. It also proved useful in my professional life, especially for taking slides of historical sites I could show my students.

LINCOLN IN THE LATE 1940S AND 1950S

By 1950, Lincoln's population had grown from 75,000 when I was born to nearly 99,000. Despite this growth, Lincoln was extremely homogeneous; nearly all of its citizens could (like the Pauleys) trace their heritage to central or northern Europe. Only about 1 percent of the population was what we then called Negroes (the term "African American" had not yet been coined), and even these were all biracial. At Lincoln High School they were well represented in athletics, but they ate by themselves in the school's lunchroom, and interracial dating was unheard of. The city's main sources of income were largely the same then as now: state and city-county government, higher education, and insurance. Consequently, the city was very middle class with few rich people but also virtually no poverty.

The capital city's homogeneity had one big downside: a lack of foreign-food restaurants. Asian and Mexican restaurants were completely nonexistent. Anyone hankering for Italian food had to go to Omaha. I seriously doubt if there was a single Chinese restaurant in the state. Making the culinary scene even worse was the inability of restaurants to serve liquor by the drink. Liquor sales had been banned in Lincoln since 1909, depriving restaurants of a major source of revenue.[31]

My parents loved to eat out, so the lack of good restaurants necessitated desperate measures. Better-than-average food could be obtained at the YWCA cafeteria downtown. The cafeteria on the "Ag Campus" of the University of Nebraska was also rumored to have decent food. I believe that when I was a graduate student we ate at a rooming house near Wahoo—thirty miles north of Lincoln—which served family-style dinners to the public on Sundays. For ninety-nine cents one could get a pretty good steak dinner twenty miles away in Seward, albeit at a very ordinary grill. When my wife and I lived in Lincoln in 1964–65 we drove to Nebraska City—fifty miles to the east—where there was a truck stop that was known for its good vegetables, although my wife was not impressed.

Lincoln was also homogeneous in its automobiles, 99 percent of which were American. Only rarely did one see even a British sports car. When my father bought a Volkswagen Beetle in 1958 it drew stares because of its small size and unusual shape. The car was very basic, lacking both turn signals and a gas gauge. If it started to run out of gas there was a lever on the floor which, if turned by one's foot, would open a one-gallon reserve tank. Detroit was indifferent to the Beetle. It was about this time that I read an article in my father's *Wall Street Journal* quoting a top executive of General Motors who said that his company had no intention of "lowering its automotive standards" to meet what he thought would be a minimal demand for the diminutive new import. Car advertisements always emphasized style and increased size, never gas mileage. Forty years earlier railroad officials had been equally slow to recognize the threat posed by automobiles.[32]

Detroit automakers' attitude toward international competition was all too typical of the complacency that Americans felt toward the outside world during the 1950s. I recall my eleventh- and twelfth-grade social studies teacher saying that the proper attitude to hold toward foreigners was to "feel sorry for them because they hadn't been born in the United States." This attitude, even though insufferably arrogant when viewed from abroad, was under the circumstances at least understandable. In 1945 the United States produced half the world's manufactured goods and services. Unfortunately, it was all too easy for Americans in the late 1940s and 1950s to assume that a status that had resulted in large part from the strictly temporary destruction of the German and Japanese economies and the weakening of the British and French economies would last indefinitely. Nor could we even imagine that by the end of the century the United States would be faced with stiff competition from China, India, Brazil, and South Korea. We are now paying dearly for that complacency.

Another way in which Lincoln in the 1950s differed from today's city was its downtown area, which was a lively retail and commercial center. The downtown was so busy in part because it was adjacent to the University of Nebraska, and the long-standing debate as to whether the latter should be moved to what is now known as the East Campus had finally been resolved in favor of leaving the main campus in its original location.[33] The commercial center had four department stores as well numerous smaller clothing stores, banks, and hotels. The Burlington depot was still fairly busy, although not nearly as jam packed as it had been during the war, when travel by train reached its historic peak in the United States and tickets for civilians were next to impossible to come by. The last of Lincoln's streetcars ceased operation as soon as allowed by the federal government at the end of the war. It is fortunate that the United States still had a halfway decent mass-transit system during the war, or else gas rationing would have had far more drastic consequences.

Buses were well patronized much of the time in the 1950s and had standing-room only during rush hours. Because Lincoln was still fairly small and compact, you could reach most parts of the city from the downtown area within fifteen minutes. Our house on Dakota Street was only about three blocks from the extreme southern end of town. Today, the location seems almost "close in" and is only about a ten-minute drive to the downtown area and the university. Many of the lots on our street were still vacant when I was in grade school, providing space for a baseball diamond and a football field. By the time I was in junior high those lots had pretty much filled in.

Prescott, my elementary school, was just over a mile from our house, so like 60 percent of American schoolchildren, I walked to and from school every day. Unlike today, when around 90 percent of children either ride to school on a bus or are driven by their parents, the only time I took a bus was for a field trip, usually to hear the Lincoln Symphony Orchestra. Only when I was at Lincoln High School, a good two miles from our house, did I take the school bus home. (In the morning I would ride to the Pauley Lumber Company with my father and walk the three additional blocks from there.) All this walking was probably one reason why my schoolmates and I almost never got fat.

Actually, children in those days were almost never obese—I knew of only one such boy throughout all my school years in Lincoln. To some degree this may have been a legacy of World War II, when food was rationed and Americans of all income levels became accustomed to eating healthful foods.[34] There was no television to watch or computer games to play. Instead of staring for hours at a screen, I would play football or baseball in the warmer months and sled down our steep street in the winter. Moreover, fast-food restaurants such as McDonald's were completely unknown in Lincoln. By the time I was in high school there was a Dairy Queen three or four blocks from our house, but we burned off the calories walking there and back. Not until I moved to Florida in 1971 did I live anywhere near a fast-food restaurant, and by that time my eating habits were well ingrained. In addition, there was not much chance of getting fat at regular restaurants in the 1950s because portions were only about two-thirds the size they are today. Consuming high-calorie drinks was also literally more difficult in the 1950s than it is today. Cup holders for automobiles, grocery carts, and movie-theater seats had not been invented. Golf carts and cart girls, with their drinks and snacks, were also nonexistent.

By no means, however, were all health-related habits superior in the 1950s. Not having even heard of cholesterol, our family put heavy cream on our cereal and desserts. The cream, which was thick enough to whip, could be scooped from milk that had not been homogenized and was delivered to our house in reusable glass bottles. Cigarettes were also omnipresent in the 1950s, as can be seen in virtually any movie produced during that era. They were advertised so frequently on TV that many people doubted whether "free" TV could exist without their catchy tunes and slogans. Cigarette vending machines were omnipresent. When my father, who was chairman of the board of trustees at Bryan Memorial Hospital, suggested that a hospital was not an appropriate site for such a dispensary, he was scoffed at and outvoted.

In general, the 1940s and 1950s were something of a golden age as far as the American diet was concerned. Fruits, orange juice, and vegetables were available the year round. Beef consumption had dropped significantly from pre–World War I levels.[35] Good eating habits were actually reinforced by food rationing during World War II. Like other children of the war and early postwar years I was frequently reminded to think of the 400 million starving Chinese—although I never quite understood how cleaning my plate would help feed them.[36]

Television was slow to reach Nebraska, and our family did not acquire a set until I was a senior in high school. Until then we were perfectly satisfied with the radio for the latest news and entertainment. I was a faithful listener of *The Lone Ranger* and other children's programs, such as *Sergeant Preston of the Yukon* and *Big John and Sparky*. In the evening the whole family enjoyed comedy shows such as *George Burns and Gracie Allen*, *Edgar Bergen and Charlie McCarthy*, *You Bet Your Life* (with Groucho Marx); and especially *Jack Benny*. Their comedy was timeless, free of profanity, and still available on DVD or online.

When television belatedly came to Lincoln in the mid-1950s, its broadcasting hours were brief and the pictures were black and white and "snowy." There were, however, some good programs, such as *I Love Lucy*, *Milton Berle*, *Twenty Questions*, Sid Caesar's *Show of Shows*, and the *Ed Sullivan Show*. The year after we acquired a TV I went off to college. Even though the dormitory where I lived had one set (for the entire building), I rarely had time to watch it. That was even truer of graduate school. Consequently, to this very day, I have never been a television addict, limiting my viewing mostly to news, travel programs, and an occasional historical documentary or classic movie. Outside the home, miniature golf and outdoor movies (better known as "passion pits"), both located on Forty-Eighth Street, were popular in the 1950s, especially on hot summer evenings. Both of them, but especially the latter, fell victim in the 1960s to air-conditioning and daylight saving time.

In 1945 fewer than half of all Americans had telephones, and those who did rarely had more than one.[37] Cell phones, of course, could not have even been imagined, but public payphones were plentiful and cost only five cents a call, a price that hadn't changed since the 1930s.[38] The telephones of my childhood had two big advantages. For one thing, when you made a phone call even to a big business, you could expect to hear a live human being at the other end of the line. The second advantage was that there were no advertisements, live or recorded, commercial or political, that interrupted our meals. Answering machines, which admittedly do have definite advantages, didn't become commonplace until the 1980s. Long-distance phone calls were expensive and could be made only with the help of an operator. Therefore, letters were still the typical means of long-distance communication, which had fortunate consequences for historians and autobiographers.

Weather was of major importance in Lincoln in the late 1940s and 1950s, as it has nearly always been throughout Nebraska's history. In January 1949 Nebraska was hit by a blizzard that rivaled the legendary storm of 1888. I can remember that trains—still by far the most important means of long-distance transportation for both people and freight—were brought to a standstill for up to a week by huge snowdrifts. Thousands of stranded cattle froze to death. Of course, for me it was a great opportunity to miss school and to build a tunnel in a deep drift in our front yard.

The very next year, a nearly seven-inch downpour caused Salt Creek and other areas of town such as the Russian Bottoms to flood. Nine people drowned and there was $53 million ($270 million today) in property damage, some of which involved the Pauley Lumber Company. I remember going to the lumberyard with my father late in the evening and observing how the flood had filled the basement of the office, the new hardware store, and the lumber sheds with thick, gooey mud. Fortunately, the flood was bad enough that Salt Creek was soon deepened and straightened, thereby reducing the likelihood of severe flooding. Compared to a disaster like Hurricane Katrina, which hit New Orleans in 2005, the Salt Creek flood of 1950 was small potatoes. Still, it gave me some idea of what a mess a flood can leave in its wake.

As if blizzards and floods were not enough, Nebraska was hit by several summers of severe heat and drought in the early 1950s. I particularly recall one day in the spring of 1953 when a dust storm that blew in from the west was so bad that it turned day into night, and lights had to be turned on in our classroom in the middle of the afternoon. The storm was reminiscent of the ones that had been commonplace in Nebraska and the southern plains during the Dust Bowl years of the 1930s, although, unlike then, it was a solitary event.

Saturdays were exciting, especially during the school year. Starting when I was around eight or nine, I would walk two blocks to the nearest bus stop and for a nickel take a bus downtown. For nine cents I could go to a movie at the Husker Theater, which showed reruns of Roy Rogers and Gene Autry cowboy movies. Theaters showing first-run movies charged 25 cents (about $2.25 in constant dollars) for children in the evening and 50 cents for adults. For 10 cents I could get a box of popcorn. When buttered popcorn was introduced in movie theaters in the early 1950s it cost an outrageous 25 cents. All movies were what would later be called "G-rated," so my parents and I would often go to two movies a week in the summer, although in large part it was because the theaters were the only places in town that were air-conditioned.

Other common prices in the 1950s now seem almost incredibly low, although in large part it was because the dollar was worth about eight times as much then as it is today (2014). "Penny postcards" literally cost one cent for both the card and the stamp. Regular mail, delivered to our front door twice each weekday and once on Saturday until the early 1950s, cost three cents (unchanged since 1932), six cents for air mail. Coffee cost just five cents a cup (albeit with no free refills), although I wasn't allowed to have any because caffeine was widely viewed as being harmful to children.[39] At some point in the early or mid-1950s restaurants began charging ten cents for coffee. That increase created a nationwide outcry, forcing many restaurants to compromise at seven cents. When haircuts reached a dollar, many older people wondered what the world was coming to. Coca-Cola, however, remained five cents a bottle, as did other soft drinks, also unchanged since the 1930s. Cigarettes—which (thankfully) I was forbidden to smoke—were 25 cents a pack. Hot dogs cost 15 cents throughout the 1950s, and hamburgers were always 25 cents (up from six for a quarter in the 1930s) until McDonald's introduced their 15-cent hamburgers. Gasoline cost about 25 cents a gallon, and the tank was filled by attendants at "service stations" (the term still meant something) who would cheerfully clean your windshield and ask if you wanted your oil and tire pressure checked. Inflation remained low throughout the 1950s, so these prices seemed permanent to my generation. Current prices for the above items seem utterly fantastic. As I type these lines I notice that my keyboard does not have a readily accessible symbol for cents, which itself is telling.

The best Saturdays were in the fall, especially when the Cornhuskers had home games, even though the team was in the middle of the worst era in the program's history, later known as the "dark ages" (1941–61). Between 1890, when Nebraska fielded its first team, and 1940, the year the team went to the Rose Bowl, it had suffered only three losing seasons. However, during the remainder of the 1940s it never won more than four games a season. The team's glorious past seemed like a fairy tale to me, but not to my parents' generation.

Starting in about the sixth grade and lasting through high school, I was able to attend every home game, thanks to 50-cent "knothole" tickets. They were poor bleacher seats at the south end of the stadium, but I was still able to soak up the atmosphere and become an avid fan. (The knothole section disappeared after Bob Devaney's first year as coach when a string a sellout games began which has lasted to the present day.) The annual Band Day, begun in 1933, was another way the university could put warm bodies in the normally far-from-sold-out stadium.[40] High school bands with their colorful uniforms came from all over the state and literally covered the entire playing field during their halftime performances. Further increasing attendance, or at least making the whole Saturday-afternoon experience more enjoyable, was the special energy-efficient football train that deposited fans from Omaha at the Lincoln station just two blocks from the stadium. Like knothole tickets and Band Day, since the mid-1970s the football train is also a thing of the past, although there has been some talk recently of restoring it.

A few differences in the game itself are notable. Nebraska fans could count on home games beginning at two o'clock, and because there were no long TV timeouts, the games would be over well before dark. There were no night games until the early 1980s. Kickoffs were from the 40-yard line, and face masks had not yet been invented. A 240-pound lineman was considered huge. A football player weighing 300 pounds was unimaginable.

Every November my mother would let me use her ticket and sit with my father as a special birthday present. I don't think it was much of a sacrifice for her, because she was not an ardent fan and by November the weather was usually chilly. My parents had incredibly good tickets in the first row of the west stadium on the 35-yard line. Football was the only sport that interested my father, so going to a game was a special treat for both of us. As in so many other Nebraska families, the football team bonded the generations and the whole state together. In later life I discovered that it is a major common denominator for "exiled" Nebraskans living outside the state.

Admittedly, we "old-timers" tend to idealize the time of our youth. Nevertheless, while I was growing up Lincoln was a safe and wholesome city. Until there was a murder spree in 1957 by a young man named Charlie Starkweather, the crime rate was so low that Lincolnites left their back doors unlocked so milkmen could make deliveries directly to their refrigerators. The schools were decent, though not great. Illicit drugs were unheard of and girls rarely got pregnant out of wedlock, and if they did they disappeared before their pregnancy became obvious. The divorce rate was low, and doctors still made house calls. (Trips to a dentist, however, were dreaded because drills in those days seemed like jackhammers.) The University of Nebraska provided plenty of inexpensive entertainment, and Lincoln had an excellent symphony orchestra. All in all, it was a good time and place in which to be born and raised.

CHAPTER 5

The Audacity of Youth

"One glorious experience after another"

SUMMER JOBS

By now it should be abundantly clear that I showed few scholarly attributes from the beginning of my formal education right through high school. My mediocre classroom performance and poor study habits did not, however, prevent me from making an audacious decision when I was just seventeen and barely three weeks out of high school: I wanted to be a history professor. Although I made the decision very suddenly one day in June 1955, many events, both positive and negative, led to this choice.

First the negative influences: My first job was taking care of our yard. Household chores in the postwar years were still very gender specific.[1] My father was the breadwinner, and my mother ran the household: cooking, cleaning, paying the bills, and shopping for clothes, even for my father. My sister helped around the kitchen, a place my father and I rarely entered except to eat breakfast. Around the age of ten I began to take care of our lawn. By the time I was twelve I also mowed my grandmother's much larger yard, and by the time I was fourteen or fifteen my father had me mowing and weeding the tiny lawn and washing the windows of his hardware store, part of the Pauley Lumber Company.

When I was old enough to drive, my father put me to work delivering sand for children's sandboxes and unloading boxcars of lumber. To say the least, I wasn't thrilled about these jobs and asked if I could work instead in the hardware store, which had the enormous advantage of being air-conditioned. My father vetoed the idea, saying (correctly) that I didn't have the expertise for the job. However, I suspect that he feared being accused of favoritism by his employees if I didn't start at the bottom of the pecking order. Unloading boxcars of lumber was miserable work. The lumber had to be brought out piece by piece and slid down a long, wheeled ramp. Even with heavy work gloves I managed to get numerous splinters in my hands.

A much worse job was in the summer of 1955 just after my graduation from high school. Although I didn't realize it at the time, my father was grooming me for a position in the lumberyard. One day in the spring he came home from his office and served notice that I would be working that summer at the Hawkeye Building and Supply Warehouse located near First and J Streets. I suspect that "Hawkeye" had reluctantly agreed to give me the job because my father was one of its better customers.

It was not only the worst job I ever had, it was about the worst job I could even imagine having in Lincoln. Hawkeye was a huge warehouse filled with all sorts of basic building supplies such as hundred-pound bags of cement, insulation, drywall, corrugated steel, boxes of nails, and various other items I can no longer recall. That summer turned out to be one of the hottest on record. There were something like sixty consecutive days in which the temperature topped 100 degrees, with 104 being common. The cavernous interior of the warehouse was not air-conditioned, but after I emerged from a boxcar I had been unloading—a boxcar that had been sealed and standing in the sun for several days—the interior of the warehouse actually seemed cool for a few minutes. For my troubles I was compensated with the princely wage of $1.10 an hour. Adjusted for inflation, the $9.00 hourly wage was at least substantially better than today's minimum wage of $7.25. By the end of my eight-hour day, when I caught a bus home, I was a sweaty, dirty, stinking mess. When I complained about the sweat, my father said that it was my "badge of honor." I'm not sure that my fellow passengers on crowded buses thought it was such an honor to be standing next to me.

My wretched experience at Hawkeye quickly convinced me of one thing. I didn't want to do that kind of work for a living, not that it had ever been a serious consideration. More importantly, I didn't want to have anything more to do with building supplies. In attempting to prepare me for a career at the Pauley Lumber Company, my father had inadvertently closed that door.

My next work experience had nothing to do with determining my profession, but it did have a great deal to do with where I wanted to live, at least in the summer and fall. I think my father must have had somewhat of a guilty conscience about consigning me to the hellhole that was Hawkeye, because he consented to my working at a resort in the Colorado Rockies in the summer of 1956. I wouldn't go so far as the popular folk singer John Denver, who in his song "Rocky Mountain High" claimed that he was "born in the summer of his twenty-seventh year," but I was thrilled to work just outside the western border of Rocky Mountain National Park. I had a menial job as a dishwasher and busboy, working from early in the morning to late in the evening six days a week with only a brief break in the morning and perhaps another two-hour break in the afternoon. However, the fifteen or so college kids who worked there had a great time together even on workdays. Late in the evening we would sometimes go to a tavern and drink 3.2 beer (legal at that time for eighteen-year-olds in Colorado) and dance until midnight or later. Amazingly, both boys and girls would get dressed up for such occasions; I would be sure to wear a sportcoat and tie, as I did for all my dates through college and graduate school. On my day off I would literally head for the hills and hike in the national park, taking lots of pictures along the way. By the end of the summer I had fallen in love with the mountains, the low humidity, and the brilliant blue skies.

NEIGHBORHOOD RELICS AND SUMMER VACATIONS

Fortunately, there were positive influences, starting early in my childhood, that eventually pointed toward a career as a historian. As noted in the preceding chapter, World War II was a vital part of my early life, certainly contributing to my interest in current events. I also have vague memories of visiting the Gettysburg Battlefield with its impressive monuments sometime during the war, perhaps while our family was in Princeton in 1943. Several times during and after the war my sister and I lived with our grandparents on Twenty-Sixth and "B" Streets while I was attending Prescott School. The walk from the school to my grandparents' house took me through some of the oldest parts of Lincoln, which were filled with mansions dating back to the turn of the twentieth century. I would often vary my route just to study different houses. I was particularly interested in those few that still had hitching posts and sometimes even steps next to the curb from which people riding in horse-drawn buggies could easily descend. It seemed to me that these remnants of the past were ancient relics, whereas in reality it had been at most only about thirty years since they had been functional.

Prescott School was also just a block away from South Street, where Lincoln's last tram ceased operation in September 1945. Built in 1908, it had been one of the city's longest streetcar lines, carrying passengers from the downtown along Sheridan Boulevard to College View, a suburb in the southeastern part of the city.[2] I recall watching the removal of the tracks on my walk home from school. Streetcars survived in Omaha until at least 1955, and I often regretted not having the chance to ride on one. It is ironic that a half century later streetcars, now often given the more updated name of "light rail," have made a comeback in Denver, Portland, Calgary, and around thirty other cities, and there has been some discussion about bringing them back to downtown Omaha.

Another neighborhood relic that intrigued me in the late 1940s was old cars on the streets of Lincoln, many of them dating back to the 1920s. As noted earlier, my grandfather Hulsebus's automobile dealership was drastically affected by declining sales after 1929, long before the war brought the manufacturing of new cars to a screeching halt in 1942. Nor could the demand for new cars be filled overnight once the war ended. Consequently, Lincoln's streets were filled with antique cars, some of which still had cranks in front for ignition. Ice and milk wagons pulled by horses were also a common sight in Lincoln, although they quickly disappeared after the war, probably because gas was no longer rationed and trucks for civilian purposes were being manufactured again.

This early fascination with old cars and houses, bygone streetcars, and indeed almost anything else that was old has led me to speculate that my interest in history was somehow inherited from my parents, especially my father, and not merely an outcome of trips to historic sites, important as they would turn out to be. Much the same could be said of my love of classical music. My familiarity with classical music was limited to the choral masterpieces sung by the Lincoln Boys Choir. Unfortunately, I had had little exposure to symphonic music, let alone opera. The one exception was the annual field trip to hear the Lincoln Symphony Orchestra, which usually performed nothing more sophisticated than Sergey Prokofiev's *Peter and the Wolf.*

Adding to my love of history were the many postwar trips we took as a family to historic sites and faraway places. The earliest postwar trip of which I have a fairly vivid memory took place in 1947 when we followed the Oregon Trail across Nebraska into eastern Wyoming and the Black Hills of South Dakota. I recall seeing Ash Hollow, where the pioneers made a difficult crossing from the South Platte to the North Platte; Chimney Rock, with its iconic spire; Scotts Bluff, a huge bluff near the western Nebraska town of the same name; Register Cliffs in eastern Wyoming, where we could still see names, dates, and messages left by the pioneers; and finally, Fort Laramie, which was the highlight of the trip even though it had not yet been restored. The summer of 1948 was less historical but more scenic as we saw Yellowstone National Park and the Grand Tetons in Wyoming. The summer of 1949 was even more ambitious as our family went to Tacoma, Washington, where my father underwent two weeks of naval reserve training. On the way back to Nebraska we saw the redwood trees of California and the ghost town of Virginia City, Nevada, whose population had declined from twenty-three thousand in its gold- and silver-mining heyday in the 1870s to a few hundred. Whenever we encountered a roadside historic marker on these trips, my father would stop so we could find out what had taken place at that site.

The most exciting trip our family took while I was still very young was to Mexico in 1950. Nowadays, I'm sure that 99 percent of the people making that trip all the way to Mexico City from Nebraska or nearly anywhere else north of a border state would fly. We, on the other hand, drove the entire distance. The trip was almost certainly inspired by a similar one taken by my paternal grandparents and my uncle Gordon in 1935 (while my father stayed in Lincoln minding the Pauley Lumber Company). The drive through Kansas, Oklahoma, and Texas was routine, and the only thing I remember is oil wells in front of the state capitol in Oklahoma City and the Alamo in San Antonio. Motoring through Mexico, however, was anything but ordinary. We frequently drove on unpaved roads and even more frequently crossed rivers by ferryboats or simply drove through them. I remember seeing people living in huts and small children running around shoeless if not completely naked. Mexico City, on the other hand, was quite modern. I was struck by the enormous difference between the extremely wealthy people, who lived hidden behind very high walls with broken glass embedded in the top, and poor people, who lived in squalor. I didn't realize at the time that such enormous differences in wealth were and still are what characterizes most third-world countries.

Less exciting but still interesting was our trip to Manitoba in the summer of 1951. I remember picking wild blueberries along the roads and then taking them to a restaurant to have them for breakfast in Winnipeg. After leaving the provincial capital we boarded a little tourist boat and cruised up and down huge Lake Winnipeg, delivering mail to isolated villages along the way.

All of these trips were made by car, sans air-conditioning and, of course, on two-lane roads that invariably went through the center of every town, large or small. My sister and I tried to keep ourselves entertained by spotting non-Nebraskan license plates and reading Burma-Shave brushless shaving cream signs with their hilarious punch lines. Finding a hotel or motel (the latter term, combining the words *motor* and *hotel*, was coined in 1925 but not commonly used until after World War II) was something of an adventure, because there were no chains until the Holiday Inns were franchised in 1957. There were still plenty of motor courts boasting that they had "modern cabins" with running water. We relied on the recommendations of the American Automobile Association for lodging and a gourmet named Duncan Hines for restaurants. Carrying luggage was more difficult than today, because suitcases had no wheels or pull-out handles. On the other hand, the distance from the trunk of a car to a motel room was a good deal less than the long concourses of today's airports. All in all, auto trips were slower and much less luxurious than today, but travel was probably more interesting and varied compared to driving on interstate highways with their nearly identical motels and fast-food restaurants at every exit.

During the summers of 1950 and 1951, I also attended a Methodist youth camp called Camp Comeca near Cozad, Nebraska. It wasn't much of a camp, situated as it was on top of a nearly barren plateau. The few trees that had recently been planted were tiny, and there was no swimming pool, although there was a nearby lake. The camp was run in part by fundamentalist Methodist ministers, who tried mightily to get us to follow in their footsteps while indoctrinating us in Methodist beliefs. One preacher told us that faith could *literally* move mountains. I had a hard time believing I could move Pike's Peak a single inch no matter how hard I might try.

Another one of our pastoral leaders, obviously still not reconciled to the end of Prohibition less than two decades earlier, warned us about the horrors of alcohol. I later found out that Nebraska, and especially its native son and three-time presidential nominee, William Jennings Bryan, had been one of the driest of the dry states. Our camp leaders had come of age just when Prohibition became the law of the land in 1920, and Methodists had been among the movement's strongest advocates.[3] I angered one of the preachers by disputing his argument that it would be better to commit suicide than to become a bartender. Oddly enough, the Methodist Church at that time was much less adamant about smoking than it was, for example, about drinking wine. I had a more positive religious experience at Trinity Methodist Church in Lincoln when the dignified and scholarly minister, Dr. Theodor Leonard, was in charge. I also enjoyed hearing my father sing the bass part of hymns. Otherwise, church services seemed like the longest hour in the week.

EUROPE IN 1954

Far surpassing our earlier summer vacations was our three-month trip to Europe in the summer of 1954. During the preceding academic year I had developed a close friendship with an American Field Service (AFS) student from Switzerland named Werner Brandenberger, who lived down the street from us.[4] "Brandy," as he was popularly known, turned out to be an enormous influence on my life. Almost two years older than I, he spoke fluent English in addition to French, Italian, and his native German. He had also studied Greek and Latin in his Swiss high school near Zofingen, a school attended many years earlier by Albert Einstein. What impressed me most about Brandy was his eagerness to make the most of his American experience. Every weekend he would take out a new girlfriend and attend a different church service. During school vacations he traveled to remote parts of the country. Making the most of opportunities became an objective I tried to follow later in my own life.

While Brandy and I were developing our friendship, my father became convinced that the only way he could cure his stomach pains (aside from eating baby food), which had no apparent physical cause, was to take a long, relaxing vacation.[5] Brandy, with the help of his parents, managed to find us a rental apartment on the second story of a chalet in Vitznau, a village of less than a thousand people on the northern shore of the Lake of Lucerne, fifteen miles east of the town of Lucerne. Thus, on May 30 we embarked by train on what turned out to be an exciting and life-changing adventure.

Our thirty-six-hour trip from Lincoln to New York was something of an ordeal because we had no sleeping compartments. On the other hand, I was thrilled by the Burlington's "vista dome" cars, which were enjoying their brief heyday during the 1950s. Our two days in New York included visiting numerous sights, including the United Nations, before we set sail on the RMS *Georgic*, a five-hundred-foot-long British Cunard–White Star Line vessel built in 1932. Of the ship's 1,650 passengers about half were Irish returning to the old country for the first time in decades. Many of them celebrated the momentous occasion by getting drunk by midafternoon.

My father was almost notoriously frugal as a result of his experiences in the Depression; as a chief petty officer in the navy he was known as "pinchpenny Pauley." Consequently, he asked a friend at an Omaha travel agency to find the cheapest way of getting to and from Europe. I think the agent found it. Dad described the voyage in his memoirs as "ten miserable days in conditions remarkably similar to those I had experienced years before on the SS *Metagama*," the ship on which he had returned from Europe in 1930. The *Metagama*, in turn, was not nearly up to the standards of the *Duchess of Atholl*, the ship on which he had met my mother. My father noted that "on the *Metagama* I had but one roommate, while on the *Georgic* I had eight or ten. Men and women were berthed separately and Bruce and I were in the extreme bow of the ship at about the waterline with nothing between us and the ocean except the steel plates of the hull."[6]

The *Georgic* had been used to transport British troops during World War II before being sunk in the Red Sea by German aircraft in 1941; later it was raised and refitted. The effects of the explosion that sank it could still be seen in its concave and convex bulkheads. Our accommodations were probably not a whole lot better than steerage in the nineteenth and early twentieth centuries and were similar to those for immigrant passengers on the *Titanic*, which was built only twenty years earlier than the *Georgic*. Indeed, most likely they were not terribly different from what my great-great-grandfather Pauley's family experienced on the *Wieland* in 1878.

A typical day aboard the *Georgic* involved sitting on deck wrapped in a winter overcoat. Activities were limited to shuffleboard, playing cards, and dancing, which were no doubt entertaining for some passengers but not for me. Unlike today's cruise ships, the *Georgic* had no casinos, Las Vegas–style performances, magic show, pools, fitness center, or shopping, let alone excursions. Only bingo has bridged the decades. The lone break from the boring routine was a huge storm that produced swells as high as the third deck. Walking down corridors littered with puddles of vomit while the ship violently tossed about required considerable agility. However, I suspect that if I had found someone of the female persuasion with whom I could pass the time the whole voyage would have seemed a good deal less boring. My sister, who attracted the attention of two recent graduates from Yale, has entirely different memories of the *Georgic* than do I.

I didn't realize it at the time, of course, but I was witnessing not only the *Georgic*'s last year of service but also the last chapter of a nearly century-long period when steamships were the most common mode of transatlantic travel. In the mid-1950s airplanes surpassed ships as the most popular way of reaching Europe, a trend that was accelerated by the introduction of jet service in 1958. At almost the same time, rail transportation in the United States was giving way to the automobile and airplane for long-distance travel on land. I bitterly regret the virtual disappearance of trains in the United States, but my experience on the *Georgic* cured me of nostalgia for lengthy North Atlantic voyages.

Despite my boredom, I'm glad I made the crossing to Europe by ship. In so doing I was not only able to get a good idea of travel in the era before jet planes but was also able to grasp how much of the world consists of oceans. To go day after day seeing nothing except water and an occasional freighter in the distance made a huge impression. Jets virtually make the oceans disappear.

Fortunately, the rest of our trip was vastly better than its prelude. My father was quite right when he wrote in his memoirs that "our transit to Europe was like darkness before the dawn because from the time we arrived on the Continent until we left, we had one glorious experience after another."[7] We spent our first week in Paris and vicinity, where we saw the usual sights: Notre Dame Cathedral, the Louvre (several times), the Place de la Concorde with its statues representing the French provinces, the Champs-Élysées, the Place Pigalle, Sacré Cœur church, the opera house, the Arc de Triomphe, and the Eiffel Tower, among other famous monuments, churches, and museums. What impressed me most was the enormous size of the Palace of Versailles and its gardens, and Des Invalides museum, the site of Napoleon's Tomb. One of the courtyards of Des Invalides, a former military hospital built by Louis XIV in the late seventeenth century, was the site of numerous cannons that had been dragged back and forth across the Rhine by the French and German armies as trophies of war. Even at my tender age of sixteen this sight struck me as symbolic of the futility of war.

After a brief visit to Château-Thierry to see the school where my mother had taught in the fall of 1930, we headed to Germany, first to Heidelberg and then to Karlsruhe. Along the way we went through the Saar district, at that time still controlled by France and still a tangled mass of ruins left over from World War II bombing. The most interesting part of the trip was a conversation we had with a former Wehrmacht officer who told us that he and his comrades realized already in 1941 and 1942 that the war was lost. However, he said with some pride that West Germany no longer had rationing, whereas Britain still did.

Heidelberg had not been bombed in the war, although its castle had been badly damaged by Louis XIV during the War of the League of Augsburg (1688–97) and had never been reconstructed. Karlsruhe presented a sharp contrast to Heidelberg. A once beautiful, rationally planned princely capital, it had been devastated by the war, and its rebuilding was far from complete. The purpose of our visit, however, was to see a German family that was extremely grateful for the help my mother's Philanthropic Educational Organization chapter had given them after the war. The family had literally walked across Germany from Poznán (Posen), a partly German-speaking town that was annexed by Poland in 1919. The only possessions they managed to take with them were the clothes on their backs and the father's violin. The latter was put to use when the family entertained us with music and food.

From Karlsruhe we passed through Switzerland to Italy, stopping for three days in Florence to tour the palaces, churches, and art galleries that had so impressed my mother in 1931. Then it was on to the Bay of Naples in southern Italy to satiate my father's passion for Roman history. The six days we spent in this area were in many ways the highlight of the whole trip. In Naples we spent several hours exploring the National Museum with its huge collection of ancient Roman artifacts, including many items related to everyday life such as dishes, food, and medical instruments. We saw Pompeii on two different days, the second time at a leisurely pace. I especially liked Herculaneum, which was much better preserved than Pompeii. Whereas the latter had been slowly covered in volcanic ash, Herculaneum had been also instantly buried in lava from Mount Vesuvius, which meant the lack of oxygen prevented the wood from being more than charred.

After spending two days relaxing on the Isle of Capri with its emerald waters and driving by bus along the spectacular Amalfi drive, we headed back north to Rome, where we devoted five days to exploring the Forum, the Coliseum, numerous churches including St. Peter's Basilica, and the ancient Roman seaport of Ostia. The latter, with its broad, arcaded streets, mosaic sidewalks, and balconies, had once been a very livable city. I was later able to use slides I took in these cities to illustrate life in classical antiquity to students in my History of Western Civilization classes. It was only many years later that I learned that Benito Mussolini had ardently supported the excavation and partial restoration of ancient Roman ruins as a way of instilling national pride.

After three days in Nice we spent a day in Grenoble, where my mother had taught in 1931. On July 10 we arrived in Vitznau, where we remained for nearly six weeks. An hour away by ancient paddle-wheel steamboats from Lucerne, Vitznau was famous for its spectacular mountain scenery and its rack-and-pinion rail line built in 1871, the first of its kind in the world. One early passenger, Mark Twain, gave a vivid account of the terrifying descent he made by train in 1878 from the top of Mount Rigi.[8] He obviously loved the Lake of Lucerne as much as we did.[9]

Our apartment had an ideal location: two blocks from the center of the village and three blocks from the dock for ferryboats, which was adjacent to the rail terminal. The chalet had a long balcony with a spectacular view of the lake. I would learn only later in Austria that our seven-room Swiss home was considered spacious by European standards. More typical of Europe of 1954 was its lack of a refrigerator, which meant that we had to go marketing twice a day. On the other hand, we were impressed that we could make phone calls anywhere in Switzerland without the assistance of a telephone operator, long before direct, long-distance dialing became the norm in the United States.

Our location in the very center of Switzerland enabled us to explore nearly every corner of the country without having to overnight elsewhere. The longest excursion was a six-hour round-trip train ride to Geneva. On the way we met a former Red Cross prisoner of war inspector who had scrutinized camps in Nebraska several times during the war. It had taken the German POWs three days to reach their destination in Nebraska. Because of covered windows, some of them became convinced that their train was going in circles to make them think that the country was larger than it actually was, an anecdote I related many years later to students in my course on World War II.

The only downside to our stay in Switzerland was that it turned out to be the wettest summer in fifty years. However, on nicer days we would hear concerts at the nearby Park Hotel, go swimming in the frigid waters of the lake, hike, or ride the Rigi-Kulm train to the top of Mount Rigi, or in my case, rent a bicycle and ride fifty miles around the mountain, stopping to take pictures in villages along the way. We also made fairly frequent trips into Lucerne to sightsee, shop, or have lunch. Altogether it was a glorious stay, and it even seemed to alleviate my father's stomach problems.

On August 17 we left Switzerland and arrived in Bregenz, just across the Rhine River and the Swiss border with Austria. It has a beautiful location on the Lake of Constance. Although it struck me at the time as a charming town, what I remember most were two French soldiers eating quietly in a restaurant, the only indications I would ever see of the Allied occupation soldiers in Austria; a year later the occupation ended. My only other mention of the occupation in my diary, made during a brief excursion to Salzburg, was that the roads in the province of Salzburg, which was part of the American zone of occupation, were newer than those in Tyrol and Vorarlberg. The latter two provinces were occupied by the French, who were almost as poverty stricken as the Austrians in the early 1950s.

From Bregenz we traveled further east to Innsbruck and saw the Renaissance emperor Maximilian's tomb with its bronze statues of twenty-eight of his relatives. We also saw a huge panorama of the war between Tyrolean peasants and Napoleon's army. We stayed in a private home with a man and his family who entertained us with zither music. His long complaint about the loss of South Tyrol to Italy at the end of World War I was my first exposure to the South Tyrol issue.[10]

On our way back to Paris and ultimately to our ship we stopped for two days in Zürich, which impressed me (as did all of Switzerland) not only by its cleanliness, but also by its relative modernity. After Zürich we proceeded to Zofingen to see Brandy (who, like many exchange students, was having a terrible time readjusting to life back at home). There we visited a cheese factory and two castles, one of them having a moat. After having seen so much of Swiss tidiness, Paris struck me on the return visit as being "junky." I also wrote in disgust that it was so expensive after Switzerland that it was "impossible to get a meal for less than a dollar [$8 today] and then it would be no good." On the other hand, we noticed that Paris had changed in one very positive way. The sound of honking horns, which can be heard so clearly in George Gershwin's *American in Paris*, had been miraculously silenced by an ordinance prohibiting their use.

The return voyage on the *Georgic* differed little from the trip over, and other than mealtime conversations with a professor from Princeton University and an Indian engineering student, the trip was even more boring than the voyage to Europe.

MY EPIPHANY

By the time I got back to Lincoln I felt like a changed person. Like many travelers who have spent considerable time abroad, I saw the United States with fresh eyes, having learned nearly as much about my home country as I had about Europe. Traveling to Europe in those days was still unusual, although only a few people showed much interest in my adventures. I recall with a shudder inviting fellow members of the Boys Octet to show them nearly all 327 slides that I had taken. I've learned the hard way that one is lucky to have an audience sit through more than about a quarter of that many of pictures.

Probably the highlight of my senior year of high school was our family's hosting an AFS exchange student from Milan, Antonietta Di Pietro, better known as "Toni." Her presence led to frequent serious conversations around the dinner table comparing European and American culture and served to increase my interest in European history still further.

Hence it was on that June day in 1955, just a couple of weeks after my graduation from high school and Toni's departure, that I sat eating my sack lunch at the Hawkeye Building Supply Warehouse thinking about what I wanted to do with my life. I knew that I had done reasonably well in my history courses but poorly in abstract subjects like algebra. I knew that I was passionate about traveling, especially to Europe. I also took into account my newfound love of photography. How could I combine those interests? I quickly dismissed the idea of becoming a high school history teacher, because I knew that neither the pay nor the respect they received was very good and I had had no inspiring models in high school to emulate.

Almost by a process of elimination I decided that I should become a history professor. This choice would fit all three of my passions.

That evening I told my parents about my decision. Looking back nearly six decades later, I am struck my audacity. I had almost never even stepped onto a college campus. I don't recall ever having even spoken to a professor, let alone heard one lecture. Given my academic performance in high school and earlier, my parents must have thought I was being wildly unrealistic. I think it was my mother who pointed out that I would have to do a lot of research, but I replied that that didn't bother me. Surprisingly, my father never tried to change my mind, either then or later. Perhaps he remembered that working for his father at the Pauley Lumber Company had been no picnic. He may have been pleased that I shared his interest in history. In later years he took pride in knowing that I had at least pursued his avocation. The parental support I received as well as our family travel is typical of people who have entered the historical profession.[11]

Many years later, in 2002 to be exact, while I was a guest professor at the University of Nebraska–Lincoln, my wife and I were having dinner with Aunt Phyllis and Uncle Gordon, my father's brother and his wife. I don't remember the context, but I happened to mention my surprise that my father had written relatively little in his memoirs about his life following our trip to Europe in 1954. When I asked my father about this he said that nothing terribly important had happened to him after that date. Life was mostly a matter of going to work in the morning and returning at the end of the day. At that point my uncle interjected rather adamantly: "Yes," he said, "working at the Pauley Lumber Company was forty years of dullsville." My forty-plus years as a history professor were to be anything but dull. Indeed, at times I would wish for a little less excitement.

CHAPTER 6

From Grinnell to Vienna and Back

"It's a great profession if you're independently wealthy."

"I dread the day when I'll have to leave."

GRINNELL COLLEGE

By the time I decided on a career in June 1955, I had long since made up my mind about where I wanted to go to school: Grinnell College in Grinnell, Iowa, the same college that both my mother and my aunt Fern had attended and which was perhaps best known for two of its alumni—the movie star Gary Cooper and the New Dealer and President Roosevelt's right-hand man Harry Hopkins.

Choosing a college was easy. Being the mild nonconformist that I was, remaining in Lincoln and enrolling at the University of Nebraska, as most other Lincoln High School graduates did, was not a very exciting or adventuresome prospect. Besides, I had found Lincoln High much too large for my comfort level. A small school like Grinnell, with around nine hundred students and small class sizes, was much more appealing. My mother had tried to persuade my sister to go to Grinnell two years earlier, but Patty had opted for Nebraska. During our summer in Europe, however, Patty decided that she could not bear to return to the Lincoln campus because she had become bored both with sorority life and her home economics major. Somehow my mother was able to get her admitted to Grinnell at the last minute. So off she went to Grinnell that autumn and immediately loved the school; I followed her a year later.

My matriculation at Grinnell was another example of my good fortune of having been born in 1937. People born just a few years earlier would have encountered a campus with several flimsy and temporary buildings built for the massive influx of World War II veterans taking advantage of the GI bill. Older professors said it was a golden age of teaching, with classes filled with mature and motivated students. However, stiff competition and crowded classrooms and dormitories were probably not so wonderful from the student's point of view, especially if you were not a veteran yourself. If I had been born five years later I would have competed for admittance with people born when the birthrate was far higher than in my birth year. As it was, in 1955 Grinnell was eager for suitable applicants, not only because of the low birthrate in 1937 but also because fewer than 40 percent of all high school graduates entered college at that time.[1] My mother, in fact, was paid $50 ($400 today) by the college for each student she could recruit and was successful in a half dozen cases.

Because of the Depression, World War II, and low birthrates, Grinnell had changed little from my mother's time. In 1928, during her sophomore year, it had 783 students, only about a hundred fewer than when I attended.[2] The Depression created budget deficits and low enrollments. Some faculty had to be cut, and those who remained saw their salaries slashed by 20 percent. Two men's dormitories were built during World War II, as was Darby Gymnasium; the college's first gymnasium, built in 1899, was still used by women. A new science building had been constructed sometime after the war. However, all four buildings that constituted the entire college, after a tornado had completely destroyed the campus in 1882, were still around, as was Carnegie Hall, which housed the library. A strictly temporary building constructed during World War II made do as a student union. Otherwise, the layout of the campus had changed little from my mother's time, including the fact that the men's and women's dorms were on opposite sides of the campus, clearly separated by a railroad track.

The biggest difference between Grinnell in the late 1920s and three decades later was the change in the gender ratio of students and faculty. My mother's graduating class of 1930 had seventy-seven women and fifty-five men. Excluding physical education instructors, there were forty-one male professors and sixteen female. By contrast, my graduating class of 1959 included ninety-three men and eighty-five women. The change in the professoriat was even more dramatic. Again excluding physical education instructors, the number of female professors *declined* by 50 percent, to eight, two fewer than in my freshman year. Meanwhile, the number of male instructors *grew* by over 50 percent, to sixty-seven.[3]

The ethnicity of the faculty and administration remained virtually unchanged. All professors and administrators were white in 1930, whereas only my sophomore biology professor, Guillermo Mendoza, was not a Caucasian. All but three students were of European descent in 1930, whereas twenty-nine years later there were three female black students and six black males. An odd similarity was that neither men nor women smiled for their yearbook picture in 1930. Men and women again moved in lockstep in 1959, but at this time smiles and grins were almost universal for both students and faculty—again, changes that occurred throughout the country.[4]

The physical separation of men and women was a major aspect of the doctrine of *in loco parentis*—"in the place of a parent." Curfew for women was 10 p.m. on weeknights, midnight on weekends. No such restrictions existed for men, because it was assumed that if coeds were literally locked up the chances of men getting into trouble would be negligible. Nor did men have elderly "house mothers," a position that had been eliminated just prior to my freshman year. To further maintain respectability, men still wore jackets and ties for dinner, which was served by student-waiters. Little did we know that we were witnessing the end of an era. *In loco parentis* was eliminated nationally by the landmark *Dixon v. Alabama* decision in 1961. Soon after my graduation from Grinnell in 1959 the dormitories were made coed, jackets for men at dinner were no longer required, and Sunday chapel services were eliminated.

Intellectually, however, changes were brewing that would raise the college's profile to national status. Howard Bowen took over as president during my freshman year. In his nine years at the helm Grinnell advanced on many fronts: new buildings were constructed (after I left), academic standards rose, highly competent faculty were attracted, the size of the endowment was increased, and old ideals were restored. Bowen, a specialist in economics, also set an example to the faculty by teaching a course every year.

Traversing the 220 miles from Lincoln to Grinnell was a breeze during my freshman and sophomore years. I simply boarded a train at the Rock Island depot on O Street in Lincoln and five hours later I was in Grinnell. From the depot it was a six-block walk to my dorm room in Smith Hall. By the time I was a senior, "progress" had eliminated this cheap, convenient, and energy-saving form of travel.

Almost literally from the day I set foot on Grinnell's campus in September 1955, my attitude toward studying underwent a metamorphosis. Whereas I had felt as if I was going above and beyond the call of duty to put in an hour a day on homework in high school, I now almost raced back to my room after class to start reading my textbooks. Fortunately, almost everything about Grinnell facilitated study. Not only was its enrollment little more than half that of Lincoln High School, but the compactness of the campus also meant that little time was wasted getting from class to class. In fact, nearly all of my classes were held in just one building, the Alumni Recitation Hall, better known by its initials. ARH was only a block away from my room in Smith Hall, which I could readily use for studying if I had as little as an hour between classes. With few exceptions the college did not allow students to bring cars to the campus, and the town of Grinnell—population seven thousand—offered next to nothing in the way of distractions. All socializing and entertainment occurred on the campus itself and was included along with tuition, room, and board. The comprehensive fees in 1955–56, by the way, were about $1,500, rising to $1,750 ($13,000 in constant dollars) in my senior year. In 2013–14 the fee was over $53,000. It is easy to understand why the percentage of students at private colleges and universities has declined so much since the 1950s when such schools enrolled roughly half of all students.[5]

Best of all, my classes were usually small, the professors knew most of their students by name, and they were excellent teachers. Teaching was taken very seriously at Grinnell. Class participation was lively and often continued after class, either one-on-one in the professor's office or sometimes when the professor would accompany a group of students to the nearby student union. I made sure my professors knew who I was so that when it came to ask for recommendations for graduate school they would not have to resort to writing a generic letter. On Fridays outstanding visiting speakers would talk on topics of general interest at Herrick Chapel; the subject would be discussed that afternoon in the large lounge of one of the dorms (Yonkers). Grinnell students were generally bright, and I soon learned that I was one of the few who had not graduated from high school in the top 10 percent of his or her class.

My experience at Grinnell seems all the more impressive when viewed from a distance of nearly sixty years. Unlike the experience of 50 percent of first-year students at today's major research universities, not one of my classes at Grinnell was taught by a graduate student or part-time "adjunct" professor.[6] We had huge reading assignments in every class, and nearly all exams involved writing essays. In only two or three classes were there tests involving multiple-choice or true-false questions.

I loved Grinnell virtually from day one. My only problem was that I quickly became painfully aware that, like my father, I was poorly prepared for some of my classes, particularly in science and German. I was grateful to eke out a C in biology. Consequently, my GPA during my freshman year was a less-than-impressive 2.6 on a 4.0 scale, and dropped to 2.4 my sophomore year when I had to take even more required courses. However, there were far more such courses in those days than most universities have today, even Grinnell. I can recall only one class that could be described as easy. Grade inflation at Grinnell was unknown in the 1950s when nationally the average GPA was 2.52 (in 2006 the national average was 3.11).[7]

My choice of major was quickly confirmed. I gave some thought to being a professor of political science or even German, but soon dismissed those ideas in part because the political science department was not one of Grinnell's strongest. When I discovered that learning German was a struggle and that I would probably spend most of my time teaching beginning courses in grammar, that idea also quickly evaporated. Moreover, political science and German did not offer nearly the breadth of subject matter that history did. The Foreign Service remained my "plan B" as late as graduate school in case a career as a history professor proved impossible. I reasoned that history would be an excellent background for either career.

Many students considered Grinnell's history department the best in the college, which helps account for its having the largest number of majors. In the late 1950s, World War II was still fresh in the minds of my generation, and best-selling books such as Alan Bullock's classic, *Hitler: A Study in Tyranny*, had only recently been published. The Nuremberg trials, the Berlin blockade, the Korean War, the death of Stalin and de-Stalinization, the Hungarian Revolution of 1956, and the launching of *Sputnik* by the Soviet Union were all riveting events that stirred the interest of my generation.

Having made an early decision about a career proved advantageous. I knew from the get-go which courses I needed, so I never complained that my courses were "irrelevant" (an oft-used term in the 1960s), even if the thought did occur to me. For example, I knew that I would have to study German and French if I wanted to get a PhD, so I would have to take those subjects whether I liked them or not.

I was also lucky in having an especially inspiring history professor my very first semester at Grinnell: Frederick L. Baumann. Professor Baumann, or simply "Baumann," or even "Freddy," as we called him behind his back, had just begun phased retirement. A member of the faculty since 1929, he amazed us by saying that he had been born in 1888 and could recall the Panic of 1893, when unemployment reached 18.4 percent, the highest ever prior to the Great Depression.[8] He also entertained us with stories about his experiences in an ambulance corps in northern Italy during and just after World War I.

Baumann was definitely a member of the old school of teaching. He firmly believed that scaring the wits out of students was the best way to make them study and learn. Girls found him so intimidating that some of them would burst into tears when he barked at them while they gave an oral report. Nowadays his demeanor might be described as bullying, but it was gender neutral and certainly produced results. As for myself, I didn't need any scaring; my parents had already warned me that I would surely flunk out if I didn't study harder than I had in high school.

Before long I had Baumann figured out. Beneath his gruff and almost tyrannical exterior was a man with a soft heart and a love of history that he was eager to pass on to his students. Only a few weeks into that first fall semester I walked into his office and announced that I had decided to be a history professor. His response was: "Well, I was afraid of that. It's a great profession if you're independently wealthy." There was much truth in this observation. As late as 1940, Ivy League schools such as Yale had "dollar a year" faculty who were so wealthy that they were willing to work for literally nothing.[9] When Baumann began his career, the average pay of professors nationally often did not even meet basic living expenses.[10] Salaries dropped even lower during the Great Depression at a time when enrollments were increasing nationally by 20 percent. By the mid-1950s the national average annual salary for assistant professors was around $5,000.[11] For senior professors in all fields it was about $7,000 (around $58,000 today), and I seriously doubt whether Grinnell's salaries were even that high, especially for historians. In terms of purchasing power, salaries had actually declined nationally by 2 percent since 1904. By contrast, elementary school teachers had seen their incomes rise by over 100 percent during the same period, and auto workers by 140 percent.[12]

Another teacher who influenced me was Joseph Frazier Wall, a professor of American history who had graduated from Grinnell in 1940, served in the war, and joined the Grinnell faculty in 1947. He later wrote a Pulitzer Prize–winning biography of Andrew Carnegie. Professor Wall seemed to develop a liking for me, and he gave me some excellent advice about graduate schools (about which more later). He became such a respected and beloved figure long before his retirement in 1985 that it was almost impossible for his former students to imagine the college without him.

Unlike many other historians, I can't say that that my exposure to an inspiring college professor was decisive in my decision to become a history professor. As noted earlier, I had made that decision even before setting foot on Grinnell's campus. Nevertheless, the history professors at Grinnell did *confirm* me in my professional choice. It wasn't just their lecturing that persuaded me to follow the path of a historian. It was their whole style of life, and indeed the whole intellectual and cultural milieu of the campus.

Intellectual stimulation was not limited to the classroom at Grinnell or even to out-of-class discussions with professors. Particularly during my sophomore and senior years, "bull sessions" with roommates and other friends in my dormitory proved to be thought-provoking and informative. I was especially lucky to have as a roommate a young man named John Price. I had met him during the spring of my freshman year when he was visiting the campus; we immediately hit it off and agreed to be roommates in the fall. John was from Manhasset, an upscale suburb of New York on the North Shore of Long Island surrounded by historical sites and cultural outlets. His mother, who was from Iowa, thought it would be broadening for him to get a taste of the Midwest. After graduation John won a Rhodes Scholarship and graduated from Harvard Law School. Later, he was special assistant to President Nixon for urban affairs, succeeding Senator Daniel Patrick Moynihan of New York in that position. Part of his job was working on the president's health insurance proposal, which (interestingly enough) included universal coverage.[13] Still later he became an international banker. He has been a trustee of Grinnell itself for the past forty years.

John and I and the other member of our three-person suite, Dave DeLong, spent long hours talking about life, politics, careers, our professors, and, of course, the relative merits of numerous members of the opposite sex. In looking back on our conversations and friendship, I feel sorry for students who never had a college roommate and haven't fully participated in campus life. Classes were only part, albeit an important one, of my undergraduate experience.

Meanwhile, Grinnell offered me numerous musical outlets. I quickly joined the college chapel choir, which sang the great hymns of the Christian musical repertoire every Sunday morning. I was also a member of the Men's Glee Club, which sang both serious and lighter fare and performed for high schools throughout Iowa and also at the Art Institute of Chicago. In my sophomore year I played the role of Prologue in the short comic opera *Pyramus and Thisbe*, although I have absolutely no memory of the story. I think it was also in my sophomore year that I joined the chorus, which sang Handel's *Messiah*. Likewise, I was in a chorus of the Brahms *Requiem* during my senior year. In that same year I was chosen (probably with the help of

John Price) to be in the Scarlateers, a male octet similar to the Boys Octet I had sung with at Lincoln High. All this singing and exposure to choral masterpieces had two consequences. On the one hand, it increased my appreciation of serious music; on the other hand, it utterly spoiled me. In later years I was never tempted to join a church choir or any kind of chorus that didn't perform the classics.

EXPLORING THE OLD WORLD

Our family's trip to Europe in 1954, my decision to become a history professor, Grinnell and its eloquent history professors, and even my exposure to great music at Grinnell and earlier in Lincoln all led to the next major turning point in my life: my junior year abroad. In the fall of my sophomore year I met a senior who had just returned from a semester in Vienna, thanks to an American organization called the Institute of European Studies (IES). He was enthusiastic about the program and pointed out that it was amazingly inexpensive and that he had received full credit from Grinnell for the courses he took in Vienna.

IES was founded in1950 by a young Austrian, Paul Koutny, and two equally young Americans, Clarence and Alberta Giese. Koutny, who had spent a year and a half in prison for anti-Nazi activities, studied for a year in the United States in 1949–50. These two experiences convinced him of the need for international understanding. His idealism led to the founding of IES and the first group of American students to study in Vienna in the fall of 1950. Since then IES has served more than eighty thousand students, and it now has programs in twenty-one countries. Probably its best-known alumnus is the novelist John Irving.[14]

I wasted little time in telling my parents about IES. Although I don't remember all of my arguments, I'm sure I pointed out that such an experience would aid my admission to a graduate program in history, greatly facilitate my learning of German, and improve my teaching ability, all of which proved true. My parents were receptive to the idea, perhaps in part because the program would not be much more expensive than Grinnell. They did, however, try to persuade me to spend just the spring semester in Vienna rather than entire academic year. I stuck to my guns, however, and they eventually relented. I have no way of knowing for sure, but I can well imagine that it was my mother who persuaded my father to allow me to spend the whole year abroad. After all, she had been in Europe for a full year compared to my father's three weeks, and she knew the relative merits of a longer stay, especially with regard to learning a foreign language.

Even before leaving for Europe I was determined not to become part of an American "bubble," a real danger when studying at a sizable American institute abroad.[15] Consequently, instead of joining the other fifty-two IES students on the luxurious *Queen Mary* and visiting London and Paris before going on to Vienna, I traveled alone on a Holland America Line ship, the *Zuiderkruis*. The idea of staying out of a bubble was sensible; I had already seen Paris and would later see London thoroughly. However, not traveling on the *Queen Mary* was perhaps a mistake, given the fun I probably missed, although my choice may have been logistically unavoidable given my other plans. Oddly enough, unlike the *Georgic*, I remember little about the *Zuiderkruis* except for the brief reference in my diary that there were only three hundred passengers and the food was excellent.

I set sail on September 12 after traveling with my parents to Norfolk, Virginia, to see my sister and her first child, John Carroll Holmes, the middle name, of course, being the same as our father's first name. After my parents and I visited colonial Williamsburg, the Yorktown battle site, and Civil War battlefields near Richmond and Petersburg, I headed off on my own to visit John Price in idyllic Manhasset, somewhat apprehensive about being truly on my own for the first time in my life.

I didn't have long to be concerned. After the nine-day voyage on the *Zuiderkruis*, there were my parents, smiling and waving at me as the ship docked in Rotterdam. They had made plans for their own auto tour of northern Europe but had been delayed in their own itinerary. So instead of wandering around the Netherlands on my own, I traveled with my parents through several Dutch and German cities in a little English Ford they had purchased, stopping to see Hans Christian Andersen's home in Odense, Denmark, before spending several days in Copenhagen and vicinity. Although we were impressed by that city's beauty and royal palaces, what interested us most was Denmark's welfare system. We discovered that Danish child-care centers are open from 5:45 a.m. to 5:30 p.m. for children between two and a half and six whose mothers worked outside the home. The Danish centers provided children with a free hot lunch, as did the public schools. For women over sixty and men over sixty-five there were five hundred institutions around the country where for $1.25 a week ($10 in today's currency) they could get a room of their own, meals, physical therapy, and lots of interesting entertainment. Both institutions were decades ahead of our own child-care centers and assisted-living facilities.[16]

After my unexpected nine-day excursion with my parents I headed for Trier in extreme western Germany by way of Brussels and Luxembourg City. In Trier, with its ancient Roman ruins, I teamed up with a former AFS exchange student, Dieter Freese, whom I had befriended during my senior year at Lincoln High. He helped me buy a used bicycle for $20 (about $150 today), and off we went down the Mosel River as far as Koblenz, visiting along the way a number of quaint villages filled with half-timbered medieval houses and, of course, the valley's famous vineyards.

Our itinerary included Bad Ems, the Rhine and Main Rivers as far as Frankfurt, Heidelberg, and the Neckar Valley, which included Eberbach and Schwäbisch Hall. Next came the Kocher River and the little towns of Aalen and Nördlingen, the latter a medieval walled city similar to Rothenburg ob der Tauber, although less famous. Eventually we reached the Danube River and Regensburg, the largest unbombed city we had encountered. Here, Dieter and I parted company. I continued cycling to Passau, where Hitler had spent part of his childhood, and Linz in Upper Austria, which the führer considered his hometown.[17] Having by now cycled nearly five hundred miles across Germany and part of Austria, I got lazy and completed my journey to Vienna by rail, arriving on October 14.

Cycling was not always easy. Dieter was in much better shape than I (and let me know it), having just completed a tour of Ireland. I hadn't ridden a bicycle for years and had never done any long-distance cycling. The trip was a revelation about how cheaply young Europeans could travel. By sleeping in 15-cents-a-night youth hostels (three of which were located in mountaintop castles) and by purchasing food in dairy stores and delicatessens, we managed to live on two dollars a day for two weeks without starving. I proudly informed my parents that the trip had cost $70 less (about $600 in today's valuation) than if I had traveled with the IES group. I had explored charming medieval villages and castles, city halls, museums, and baroque and rococo churches everywhere I went. The youth hostels themselves were interesting places, albeit very basic in their amenities. The youth hostel movement had actually begun in Germany around 1900 before spreading to other European countries and the United States. Regrettably, whereas there are around 530 youth hostels in Germany and over 4,000 worldwide, there are little more than 50 in the United States, probably because our country does not easily lend itself to either cycling or train travel, the two favorite modes of transportation for European youth hostellers.[18] The unfortunate result is that young Americans rarely have the chance to visit foreign countries unless they (or their parents) can afford what have become expensive study-abroad programs.

VIENNA IN THE LATE 1950S

After arriving in Vienna and searching for three days to find my luggage and bicycle (which I had checked through to Vienna when I boarded the train in Linz), I finally got settled in a room at 41 Billrothstrasse, in Vienna's Nineteenth District. My room was in a rather dreary late-nineteenth-century structure located near Vienna's famous Grinzing neighborhood, one of the many areas where Beethoven once lived. It was (and is) also renowned for its wine gardens, where both the Viennese and tourists still go to socialize, sip new wine, and listen to zither music.

My room had never been modernized, and its only source of *potential* heat was a ceramic coal-burning stove in a corner of the room. Since it took around an hour to heat the room, it was rarely worth the trouble. I would be off to class well before the stove could make a significant difference. (I managed to stay halfway warm by wearing long underwear from the end of October to the beginning of May.) Consequently, I spent as little time in the room as possible, seldom doing more than sleeping there and eating my breakfast while dressed in a heavy overcoat, or *Loden*. The bathroom wasn't much better. One had to build a fire in a little oven there to have a hot bath.

Fortunately, there was a tiny gas water heater for the washbasin. Needless to say, I didn't take a whole lot of baths that year. During the day, when I was not in class or eating my lunch and dinner in the IES headquarters on the Neuer Markt, I stayed warm by studying at the British Council Library and caught up on the news at the Amerika Haus, both products of the Cold War and popular with the Viennese because they were warm and free.[19]

Fortunately, my humble room did have one enormous advantage which I described in a letter to my parents as a "miracle": an Austrian roommate named Walter Siegl. The nephew by marriage of Paul Koutny, Walter had asked his uncle if he could have an American roommate. I soon was amazed to find out that I was the only IESer to ask for an Austrian roommate, so the match was easily made. We got along famously from the beginning. Walter was good about talking to me in German as much as I could possibly understand, at which point we would switch to English. Thanks in part to him, in part to my meeting other Austrian students at two international clubs, and in part to a radio I purchased for three dollars, I probably acquired more fluency in German that year than I had in the two years I had formally studied the language at Grinnell—not an uncommon experience. Walter was just as interested in history as I was, and he passed on to me his extensive knowledge of his country's history. He went on to have a distinguished career in the Austrian Foreign Service.

For the first time in my life I discovered that I was better prepared for my classes than many of my classmates. Because I had already studied German, I was excused from that requirement and could concentrate on courses of my own choosing, especially history, music history, the history of philosophy, and the history of European art. Most of my professors, who also taught at the University of Vienna, were good lecturers. Their reading assignments were light to nonexistent (I averaged about three hours of homework per weekday and more on Sundays), and the academic year was frequently interrupted by religious and secular holidays, especially in the spring. Consequently, I had plenty of time to explore the city and its art galleries and gorge myself on classical music, the outlets and affordability of which were probably unmatched in the world. Indeed, the number of musical and dramatic performances each week was (and remains) staggering.

One young person I met in the IES dining room was not even an IES student. He was a Hungarian in his mid- to late twenties who had fled his native country during the revolution the previous year. As a refugee he had little or no income, and IES officials allowed him to eat at the institute on Neuer Markt plaza for free. We had many fascinating conversations about the revolution, communism, and how he escaped Hungary. I recall him telling me about his sense of exhilaration when he reached Austrian soil.

In 1957, signs of World War II and postwar Allied occupation were still obvious. The ongoing impact of war, during which Austria was a part of Hitler's Third Reich, was readily apparent in the fact that my landlady, Frau Rimböck, who was probably in her fifties, had lost her husband in the war. Her mother, who lived with her, had been widowed in the Great War. The impact of World War II could also be easily seen in buildings. The most badly damaged buildings had been repaired or replaced, but many others were pockmarked with bullet holes and shrapnel. Throughout the city I also noticed the mysterious letters LSIH written over the entrance to apartment complexes, an acronym for "Luftschutzkeller im Hof" ("air raid shelter in the courtyard"). Much more obvious were the enormous antiaircraft towers built by the Nazis. They remain to this day too big and solidly built to destroy without wrecking entire neighborhoods.

The Allied occupation of Vienna by the United States, France, Great Britain, and the Soviet Union was of even more recent vintage, having ended only in May 1955 and leaving Austria as a neutral state. The Russian occupation was readily apparent in street signs painted with Cyrillic letters on corner buildings and in the decrepit conditions of many buildings in the districts that the Russians had occupied. Most obvious of all was the monument to the Russian soldiers who, while suffering huge casualties, had liberated (or conquered) the city in the fierce fighting of April 1945. To the Viennese it was affectionately known variously as the monument to the unknown looter, father, or rapist.[20] Austria had been forced to keep the monument by the terms of the State Treaty that ended the occupation in 1955, but the Viennese were at least able to hide it at night by placing an illuminated and high-spouting fountain in front of it.

I was surprised to find out from various Viennese that the occupation had had one significant advantage: each of the four occupying powers had tried to impress the Viennese with their culture. As a consequence, Vienna had an ongoing spectacle of Russian, French, British, and American music and military parades.

A little less obvious to the untrained eye was the fact that Vienna had by no means recovered from World War I. In many respects the city had been frozen in time, too poor since 1914 either to grow or to modernize itself with new buildings. However, these facts merely increased the city's appeal and induced me to write my parents, shortly after my arrival, that "Vienna looks like the most interesting city in Europe, and it will certainly take me all year to see it and get to know it."[21] As the most important city of the Austro-Hungarian Empire, it had served as a magnet for the monarchy's population, which reached 52 million in 1910. Vienna's population was 2.1 million, which put it in a virtual tie with Chicago as the fifth-largest city in the world (the first four were London, New York, Paris, and Berlin). Less than half a century later that population had shrunk to 1.62 million, due in part to a cessation of in-migration and a very low birthrate. Equally important, however, was the expulsion of the country's nearly 200,000 Jews, most of them Viennese, by the Nazis. Around 65,000 Austrian Jews were slaughtered in the Holocaust, a subject that Walter and I discussed at length because his family had lost many Jewish friends.[22] Another factor in Vienna's declining population was the departure of a good many Czechs who had once migrated to the city from Bohemia and Moravia and moved back Czechoslovakia after it gained independence in 1918.

In 1957 a large proportion of Vienna's population consisted of elderly people who could still recall the glory days when Vienna was the *Kaiserstadt* (imperial city) of the Austro-Hungarian Monarchy, one of the five or six great powers of Europe on the eve of World War I. Many of Vienna's streetcars in 1957–58 had been in service in imperial times. The painting and exhibits of Vienna's great museums had obviously not been changed since before World War I. The nostalgia for the monarchy was (and still is) apparent in the number of postcards for sale of the emperor-king, Franz Joseph (reigned 1848–1916), and his wife, Elisabeth, whose tomb was always decorated with fresh flowers.

Austrian traditions dating back to the monarchy were also apparent in

1957–58, albeit probably in weakened form. It was common for a man, even from the working class, to kiss a woman's hand when greeting her and saying "Küsti Hand gnädige Frau" (literally, "I kiss your hand, gracious lady"). Colorful local costumes for women called dirndls, though not as common in cosmopolitan Vienna as in the countryside, were still a frequent sight on the streets of the Austrian capital and elsewhere.

A stroll through the central district of Vienna was a history lesson in itself. Every building in which some historic event had occurred or where some important person had once lived (with the notable exception of Hitler) was marked with a Viennese flag and a plaque describing the building's importance. The emperors' two palaces (the Hofburg in the old city and Schönbrunn in the outskirts), the Belvedere (home to the ill-fated archduke and heir apparent, Franz Ferdinand, whose assassination in Sarajevo in 1914 helped touch off World War I); the Rathaus (city hall), the Burgtheater, the Parliament building, the Staatsoper (state opera), and St. Stephen's Cathedral were merely the more famous buildings of Vienna. Lesser-known monuments could be found on virtually every street and in every park, particularly in the old city center.

Making the whole year more enjoyable—and more affordable for my parents, who were paying for it—was the strength of the U.S. dollar in 1957–58, which, more than a half century later, one can only view with a mixture of nostalgia and disbelief even when multiplied by a factor of 7.5 to account for inflation. A ride on a streetcar cost the equivalent of 8 cents. A haircut was 25 cents, as was a standing-room ticket with an excellent view at the Staatsoper (less-desirable standing-room tickets cost 15 cents). A student-discounted seat at a concert hall would be about 33 cents; a decent meal in one of the non- touristy parts of the city could easily be had for under a dollar. Movies (in which I frequently indulged to improve my German and to stay warm) cost about 20 cents depending on the location of the seat. A huge exception to these incredibly low prices was the cost of a phone call to the United States: $3 a minute for a minimum of three minutes (nearly $70 in constant dollars). (Today the cost is 3 *cents* a minute.) Needless to say, I was never tempted to call my folks. The other big exception was the cost of flying. My one-way ticket back to the States from Glasgow on Icelandic Airlines cost $224 (at least $1,600 in constant dollars).

Although the low prices I encountered in Vienna can be ascribed in part to the strength of the dollar, that is not the whole story. Streetcars, trains, health care, parks, hiking trails in the Vienna Woods, and even the opera were paid for or heavily subsidized by the local or federal government. Relatively large areas were set aside for standees at all the concert halls and theaters. Consequently, poor people, and students like me, could enjoy the charms of the Danubian capital nearly as much as the wealthy. My mother made the same comment about France in 1931: "It isn't a hardship to be poor in France; rather it's interesting to see how cheaply yet pleasurably one can live."[23]

A WEEKEND IN STALINIST PRAGUE

An added attraction to Vienna in the late 1950s, at least as far as I was concerned (although not to the average American tourist), was the proximity of the city to three Communist countries: Czechoslovakia, Hungary, and Yugoslavia. A three-day excursion to Czechoslovakia in November 1957 proved to be the first of many trips I would take behind the Iron Curtain and in some respects the most memorable. Stalin had been dead since March 1953, and the general secretary of the Soviet Communist Party, Nikita Khrushchev, had launched his "de-Stalinization" campaign in 1956 with a not-so-secret speech denouncing Stalin's crimes. However, the Czechoslovak government remained defiantly Stalinist. Since 1955 it had been the site of the world's most massive statue of Stalin, measuring over 185 feet in height and weighing some seventeen thousand tons. Not until 1962 would the monument, which conspicuously overlooked the Moldau River, be destroyed, and even then only on the orders of Khrushchev. Once the statue was blown up, the Czechoslovak regime proceeded to root out all photographs of the monument in the fashion of George Orwell's *1984*.

The grim impact Soviet communism had had on the Czechoslovak economy and society was apparent as soon as our group of eight IESers crossed the Austro-Czech border. Owing to France's desire at the Paris Peace Conference of 1919 to turn Czechoslovakia into an anti-German ally, and because of the relative passivity of the British and American delegations in the face of French demands, the Czechs had inherited the richest provinces of the Austrian half of the Austro-Hungarian Monarchy. During the interwar period Czechoslovakia far surpassed Austria economically, but it had become an economic basket case by the late 1950s. The hardworking "Sudeten" German minority of 3.25 million had been "ethnically cleansed" after the war, as was apparent in the many deserted villages and farmhouses we saw on our way to Prague. The elimination of all private enterprise and a pay scale that placed laborers above former capitalists and university professors helped devastate the Czechoslovak economy.

Since the fall of the Iron Curtain in 1989, Prague has regained its early-twentieth-century glitter and has become a mecca for foreign tourists. Such was hardly the case in 1957. Foreign tourists and vehicles were such rarities that we twice attracted crowds of curious children, adults, and soldiers, who literally pressed their noses against the windows of our Volkswagen autobus as if looking at creatures from another planet. Fortunately, the Czechs were always friendly. Prague was grayer than the sky and so devoid of vehicles that we could have camped out in the middle of the most important intersections. So as not to "contaminate" the local population, our group was housed in the only hotel where Westerners were allowed to stay, although it was quite comfortable and the food was good. Some members of our group also reported being followed as they explored the city.

Prague, and in fact the whole country, was in official mourning for the death of the Czechoslovak president Antonín Zápotocký. Every shop window had his picture and bust, next to which were flowers and the Czechoslovak and Soviet flags. I noted in my diary that shops seemed to be vying to outdo each other in the lavishness of their displays. Russian flags were also apparent at a special exhibit of Russian photographs of smiling, sweating young workers standing in front of blast furnaces and young girls joyfully working in wheat fields. Books by Russian poets and novelists filled bookstore windows, but most of the books were related to science, industry, farming, and the history of communism. The Russian influence was even obvious in the performance I attended of Tchaikovsky's opera *Eugene Onegin*. The audience at the opera house in Prague was very drably dressed, in sharp contrast to the elegantly attired audiences at Vienna's Staatsoper.

Our group learned during a guided tour of the city that a Czechoslovak citizen who was "patriotic and a good worker would not be bothered if he went to church on Sunday." (No one asked our guide who evaluated "patriotism" and "hard work.") When I later did some window shopping along the city's main boulevard, Wenceslas "Square," I discovered music shops that were selling 78 rpm records and phonographs that had become obsolete in the United States twenty years earlier. Another store window on the same street displayed Russian prize photographs of sweating young workers in front of blast furnaces; others showed young girls working in a wheat field. A department store was selling very unstylish dresses and suits at prices that consumed a quarter of a worker's monthly wages.

CHRISTMAS IN AUSTRIA

After an "exhausting" autumn filled with concerts, operas, movies, and visits to museums and wine cellars, I was ready for a vacation. While the other IES students went on a skiing trip in the Alps, I traveled on my own by train through northern Italy, Switzerland, and Germany, spending Christmas with Walter Siegl and his family along the way and later visiting my old Swiss and German friends, Brandy and Dieter.

The trip started out in spectacular fashion when I got my first good look at the Austrian Alps. As I approached the Semmering Pass separating the provinces of Lower Austria and Styria, the ground was covered with a fresh blanket of snow. When the sun came out the scene turned into a dazzling spectacle. My first night was spent in Villach in the province of Carinthia, where I stayed in an unheated youth hostel next to the train station for five Austrian schillings or twenty American cents. By the next night I was in Bozen, or Bolzano as the Italians call it, in the South Tyrol. This was my first visit to this region, which was given to Italy at the Paris Peace Conference as a reward for fighting on the Allied side, even though the annexation clearly violated the ninth of President Woodrow Wilson's famous Fourteen Points. It didn't take me long to understand why the Austrians in general and the South Tyrolese in particular so adamantly objected to this blatant violation of national self-determination. The South Tyrol's population had been 98 percent German-speaking in 1918. By the 1950s, thanks to Mussolini's policy of Italianization, the region had become one-third Italian-speaking. Bozen in particular had been swamped with workers from all over Italy, lowering the proportion of its German-speaking population to 25–30 percent. The central part of the city still looked very Austrian, but the newer buildings were in a modern fascist style. The most obvious sign of fascism was a large monument to the Italian "victory" over the by-then disintegrating Austro-Hungarian army in November 1918.

After a brief look around Bozen I took a *Personenzug* (milk train) to Brixen (Bresseone in Italian). The ride was eye-opening because every passenger was dressed in traditional Tyrolean costumes, the men wearing tight green jackets, knee-length lederhosen, long green stockings, and feathered hats; all the women wore dirndls with blue aprons. The lonely-looking conductor was the only real Italian on the train. In Brixen I hiked up a mountain and passed numerous religious shrines along the way. It was easy to imagine Beethoven being inspired to write his *Pastoral* Symphony in such a setting. I half expected to see colorful peasants dancing around a Maypole while a thunderstorm approached in the distance.

After spending a few hours in Innsbruck the next day I visited Walter and his family in Dornbirn, in Austria's westernmost province of Vorarlberg. That was a memorable experience in itself because I was able to witness a three-day Christmas celebration almost completely devoid of the commercialization that had overtaken the holiday in the United States. The Siegl family—three boys, of whom Walter was the oldest, and one girl—had been forced out of the Sudetenland and had resettled in Vorarlberg. Although the father's income was probably well above the Austrian average, the family was poor by American standards. The kitchen and bathrooms in particular were what one would have found in the States twenty or thirty years earlier. They didn't seem able to afford much heat either, as the three Siegl brothers and I slept in a large, unheated dormitory-type room. Nevertheless, the daughter came into the already frigid room and threw open a window in the morning to allow in sub-freezing air. Seemingly to thaw out, the children drank warm milk. They all thought it was disgusting that I would drink milk any other way.

The family's Christmas tree didn't make its appearance until Christmas Eve. While the Siegl children and I waited in the bedroom, the parents decorated the tree with real burning candles, cookies, and paper chains. Once the tree was decorated, the children were allowed to see it and the father read the Christmas story from the Bible. At midnight we all went to a mass, admiring the town's Christmas lights on our way to and from the church.

While I was in Vorarlberg, Walter and I made a quick trip to the Lilliputian country of Liechtenstein. He thought it a bit odd that I should be interested in a country of just sixty-two square miles. In part I wanted to confirm my theory that the smaller the country, the more likely its citizens are to make maximum use of every square yard of land, with the opposite often being the case as well. We climbed up to the prince's castle, which dates from the tenth century and from which we could see the two-thirds of the country lying on the eastern side of the Upper Rhine River across from Switzerland.

After that, the Siegls and I explored a nearby skiing village and enjoyed a thirty-five-minute ski lift up to the tree line, from which we could almost see the whole of Vorarlberg. Soon afterward I headed off to Switzerland to see my old friend Werner Brandenberger in his hometown of Zofingen. He also showed me his small apartment in Basel, where he was attending a university. I couldn't help noticing how much wealthier Switzerland was than Austria, the result of avoiding both world wars.

From Basel I headed north to Strasbourg. Its history as a trophy of war for Germany and France was apparent in its architecture: its medieval and late-nineteenth-century sections were thoroughly German, whereas its twentieth-century architecture was French. Unfortunately, the styles didn't mesh well. I cared only for the half-timbered houses in the medieval part of the city along with the city's famous Gothic cathedral. Strasbourg also made me realize what a disadvantage it was to be in a city where I didn't know the local language, although I did find a few German signs and some people could speak either German or English. After Strasbourg I went to Düsseldorf to meet up with my friend Dieter Freese and two German girls I had known as exchange students at Lincoln High. I discovered Düsseldorf to be a completely rebuilt city with wide avenues and modern buildings.

After an all-night train ride, I arrived back in Vienna in the early afternoon. Compared to the boring modernity of the rebuilt German cities, Vienna's charming architecture never looked better. It was now January and the middle of the ball season. At one ball I discovered the delightful Viennese practice of girls asking boys to dance before midnight. I noted in my diary that "they were . . . real beauties. It was quite something just to be able to pick out a beautiful girl and then walk over to a place near her and look eligible! . . . It was a magnificent scene to see the room filled with couples whirling around to the strains of a Viennese waltz. Unfortunately, the results weren't so good when I tried to whirl. In the first place, I didn't know the step, and then I kept getting dizzy and breaking into a sweat." The dancing lessons (which were and are commonplace for young Austrians) that I took a few days later were of only marginal value. Regrettably, aside from the balls, I couldn't meet Viennese girls without a formal introduction as per the Austrian custom.

SPRING SEMESTER TRAVELS: FROM SOUTHERN EUROPE TO THE BRITISH ISLES

My travels during the spring semester continued unabated. In February I devised my own itinerary for travel through Yugoslavia to Greece at the cost of $12 for a special student ticket (worth $90 today), over to Turkey, back to Greece, and then up the Italian peninsula to Austria. Yugoslavia grew poorer and less developed the further south I ventured. At my first stop, in Zagreb, the capital of the Yugoslav Republic of Croatia, I immediately noticed a big difference from Czechoslovakia. Although the people were practically dressed in rags, they could watch American movies and buy products from capitalist countries. They also enjoyed freedom of religion and could own their own homes.

By the time I reached Skopje, the capital of the province of Macedonia, I felt like I was in the Ottoman Empire. Indeed, the city had belonged to the Turks for centuries up to 1912. On one side of the Vardar River lay the old Turkish city with numerous minarets piercing the sky, although the mosques themselves were often closed. Ethnic Turkish men were wearing traditional fezzes, and women wore baggy red pantaloons, both of which had been banned in Turkey in the 1920s by its reforming president, Kemal Pasha Atatürk.

After spending a few days in Istanbul I ventured southwest to see the ruins of Ephesus near the Aegean Sea. Nowadays it is overrun by tourists, but when I was there the place was deserted and I spent eight hours exploring every nook and cranny of what had once been a splendid Hellenistic and Roman town. It was fascinating to return to the site in 1998 and again in 2007 to see the progress archaeologists had made in restoring the city to its former glory as one of the four largest cities of the Roman Empire.

I headed back to Vienna by way of Athens, Delphi, the Island of Corfu, and Italy. Athens was a disappointment. To my surprise, except for the Acropolis, the recently excavated Agora, and a very small Byzantine church, it was a modern and noisy city. On the other hand, I was impressed by Delphi's spectacular mountainside location. Nearly as interesting, however, was the Greek island of Corfu with its Venetian-style architecture. It was also the site of the summer residence of the traveling Austro-Hungarian empress-queen Elisabeth; the palace was deserted at the time but has since become a tourist attraction. She must have been enamored with ancient Roman civilization, because many of the interior walls were painted with a special red color often found in the ancient villas of Pompeii. Some parts of the palace were completely deserted. The kitchen, for example, still had the stoves that had been used in imperial times. The bathrooms once had hot and cold running fresh water and sea water.

During our three-week spring break I traveled with the IES group to Italy as far south as Sorrento, where I broke away for six days in Sicily. My favorite sites were the Norman cathedral in Palermo, the baroque architecture and well-preserved Roman amphitheater in Syracuse, and the Greco-Roman theater in Taormina with its gorgeous view of the sea. I rejoined the IES group in Rome in time for an audience with Pope Pius XII. (I was astonished that his entry into St. Peter's Basilica atop a throne was greeted by what seemed like undignified cheers from the faithful.) Stops in Ravenna, Florence, Siena, and Verona completed our Italian tour.

Also memorable was a weekend excursion I took in May by train and bicycle into Austria's easternmost province of the Burgenland, which had belonged to Hungary as late as 1923. To reach my destination in the central part of the province the train stopped in Sopron, a town that Hungary retained after a disputed election in 1920 in which thousands of dead people allegedly voted for Hungary. My excursion took place just eighteen months after the Hungarian Revolution of November 1956. It was apparent that the Hungarian government was taking no chances of any more people trying to escape the country: the train was lined with soldiers.

On the same excursion I encountered an elderly lady—she was probably younger than I am now—and asked her what she could remember about the days when Burgenland was still part of Hungary. She replied that people didn't have any basis of comparison then, but she did admit that she loved the uniforms of Hungarian soldiers. I later learned that handsome uniforms were a major means of recruiting for European armies prior to World War I. When I asked her what she could remember about Franz Joseph, the Austro-Hungarian emperor-king, she replied: "Er war vergöttet" ("He was deified").

When the school year closed at the end of June I traveled for three weeks with the IES group again, our ultimate destination being the Iberian Peninsula. En route we stopped long enough in Lucerne for me to take a ferry to Vitznau. I was still impressed by Switzerland's natural beauty, but I was already missing the baroque architecture of Austria. In the south of France we saw the Papal Palace in Avignon and the Roman and Romanesque architecture of Arles and Nîmes, including the imposing Roman aqueduct called the Pont du Garde. In Spain we saw the usual tourist sites in Barcelona, Toledo, Seville, and Granada. I was especially impressed with the Moorish architecture of the Alhambra in Granada and the cathedral in Córdoba that had been built in the middle of an enormous mosque. Much less impressive were the rural areas of Spain, which I found "primitive and poor." The most memorable thing about Madrid was eating supper at 10 p.m. and seeing throngs of people still walking the streets at 2 a.m. Portugal we found refreshingly cool after the torrid temperatures of southern Spain.

When the group headed back to Vienna I broke away in southwestern France in order to see the pilgrimage town of Lourdes before heading north to the British Isles. On my way from the famous cathedral town of Canterbury to London I had a brief taste of early train travel. My third-class coach had obviously been built well before World War I. Each compartment was entered from the outside rather from an interior corridor. By the time I reached London I was covered with soot from the steam engine. From London I teamed up with one of my IES friends, Pat Witte, and began a two-week hitchhiking tour of western England, Wales, Ireland, Northern Ireland, and Scotland (where we were thoroughly drenched by almost continuous rain). We met lots of interesting people along the way before flying back to the States from Glasgow.

My parents once asked me how I could learn anything when I had such long vacations. I responded, and I think even in retrospect quite correctly, that "it will be my non-academic experiences of this year that I am really going to remember and profit from, not the academic ones, although I have learned very much in this area too. . . . What good is it just to study a foreign language if you never use it, or to study opera if you never see one? The sensual experiences always last longer."[24] In early May I wrote in my diary, "I feel vitally alive. Every day is like a new adventure. I'm never bored. I am constantly finding new interests. I dread the day when I'll have to leave."

Like my mother's year in France, and like the experiences of so many other future historians, my year in Europe was life-altering.[25] I summarized the year in the last entry of my diary this way: "It's terribly hard to pack up and end this year, for there will never again be a year quite like this one. . . . It's terrifying to think of leaving Vienna. I didn't know it was possible to love a city so much!" I had traveled by steamship, automobile, bicycle, train, ferry, hitchhiking, bus, and finally airplane to every part of Europe south of Norway and Finland and west of Poland. I had seen ancient Greek and Roman ruins; medieval castles; Romanesque, Gothic, baroque, and rococo churches; and countless art galleries and historical museums. I must have seen at least twenty-five operas and operettas and too many concerts to count. My German had improved to the point where I could carry on a reasonably intelligent conversation and easily read newspapers—even old ones written in the neo-Gothic script—without resorting to a dictionary more than occasionally. I had learned about nationality conflicts, border disputes, and the direct effects of Communist rule, not to mention a great deal about European history, politics, music, art, and architecture. My interest in history had been not only confirmed but enormously intensified. Moreover, I had come to realize the usefulness of history in appreciating art, architecture, and music. Like my mother, I ended the year determined to return to Europe again and again. I had also decided that Austrian history would be my specialty.

Prior to my return to Lincoln I wrote my parents one last letter from Manhasset, where I was again visiting my friend John Price. "Well, this wonderful year is just about over. It sort of staggers my mind to think of all the wonderful experiences I've had. . . . I think I gained a lot of permanent impressions that will always stick with me, and that will always be an inspiration to me the rest of my life. . . . I am anxious to pursue all the new interests that I gained this year. I just hope that someday I'll be able to give my son the same opportunity that I had this year. Certainly, there are not many 20-year-olds luckier than I!"[26]

AN AGE OF OPTIMISM

Like most people who have spent a year abroad, whether it is an American in Europe or a European in America, returning to my home country and in my case to a small town was not without difficulty. I had fallen in love with Vienna just as my AFS friends had fallen in love with Lincoln. I still loved Grinnell, but it was not Vienna, and the Iowa cornfields were not the Alps. Nevertheless, during my junior year I had matured as a student; my grades during my senior year were vastly better than those of my freshman and sophomore years, in part because I was studying eight to nine hours a day, six days a week, about double the national average at the time and nearly quadruple the current average for undergraduates.[27] I was confident enough in my senior year to regularly sit in the first row of a history classroom and pepper the professor with questions—probably to the dismay of my professors and other students in the class. The history faculty, impressed by my work ethic and grades, asked me to tutor a freshman. By the second semester of my senior year I did the best of my three years at Grinnell. I even got an A in my independent German reading class and was ranked second among all senior history majors on the Graduate Record Examination.

My senior year at Grinnell ended in June 1959 and I went through the graduation exercises with my classmates even though I had not yet fulfilled the mathematics requirement. Consequently, I took a course in college algebra during summer school at the University of Nebraska, the first math class I had taken in six years. The class got off to an ominous start when I overheard a student say that this was the third time he was taking the course. The first time he had dropped it; the second time he flunked. Nevertheless, the first day of class seemed a repeat of what I learned in high school algebra, and I could manage to understand what the instructor was saying the second day as well. By the third day, however, I realized that I was already over my head. The instructor, a graduate student, had the disconcerting habit of putting long problems on the board without explaining what she was doing. When finished she spun around and asked if there were any questions. Since no one had the faintest idea what she was saying, she would proceed to the next problem, which was even more difficult than the first.

My father, who had also been weak in math, felt personally and biologically responsible for my predicament and suggested that I hire a tutor at his expense. My tutor, a math major, could hardly put a subject and a predicate together in the same sentence. Nevertheless, he not only knew his math but also knew how to painstakingly explain it so that even a knucklehead like me could understand it. Thanks to him I managed to scratch out the equivalent of a C, just barely good enough to transfer the credit to Grinnell and allow me to officially graduate. That experience taught me that people can be smart in some ways and dumb in others. I continue to remain in awe of people who are good at mathematics, the natural sciences, and technology, all of which have remained mysteries to me. On the other hand, I have also met people in these fields who are equally intimidated by history.

So ended my undergraduate days. In many ways they were the happiest and most carefree of my life. I had established friendships that would last to the present. During my junior year I had been free to travel anywhere in Europe I pleased. The world was at peace. Grinnell, like other campuses around the United States in the late 1950s, remained a quiet place of learning.[28] Later, people of my vintage would be called the "Silent Generation."[29] The years from the end of World War II to the end of the Eisenhower administration, the very years I was growing to adulthood, seem like an especially fortuitous period in retrospect, perhaps resembling the three decades preceding the Depression. The 1940s and 1950s were, relatively speaking, an era of national consensus. The war had reduced economic inequality, discredited fascism, and confirmed American values, which were then reaffirmed by postwar fear of the Soviet Union. Unlike earlier (and later) American wars, World War II engendered no "buyer's remorse." With 6 percent of the world's population, the United States in 1945 produced half the world's manufactured goods.[30] Nearly everyone "liked Ike." He had ended the Korean War in 1953, and Stalin's death in March of the same year eased the Cold War substantially. The Hungarian Revolution of 1956 and the subsequent massive Russian military intervention heightened war fears only temporarily.

The Depression and World War II had created enforced savings and a pent-up demand for consumer goods and housing, which in turn spurred high employment and unprecedented prosperity. Between 1945 and 1960 the GNP grew by nearly 250 percent and per capita income by 35 percent.[31] Inflation throughout the 1950s was 1 percent annually, and unemployment averaged 3 percent. The dollar was strong, and the federal budget was nearly balanced. One in four Americans was still poor in the mid-1950s (compared to 15 percent in 2012), but real wages were increasing faster than at any time in the previous half century, and economic inequality was much less than in the 1920s or today.[32] No one worried about terrorism, mass shootings, or global warming. The threat of nuclear war still existed, but it was not as strong at the end of the decade as it had been at the beginning. Certainly there were issues such as civil rights for racial minorities and inequalities for women that at best were only beginning to be addressed. But such controversies had not yet resulted in riots or racially motivated murders. Probably only the three decades preceding the Great Depression witnessed so much optimism in the United States. Life was good, especially if you were a white male who had recently graduated from college. My carefree life, I was convinced, would continue in graduate school, especially because I would no longer have to take all those disagreeable non-history courses.

CHAPTER 7

The Ordeal of Graduate School

"Think of what you have and what you have accomplished—not what you have yet failed to do."

A QUICK END TO ILLUSIONS

My belief that graduate school would be easy did not survive my first semester. Graduate school for me, and I suspect for most other graduate students in history of my generation, was a grind, a hurdle to survive, and not a time to be fondly remembered like our undergraduate days.[1]

My second illusion—that my Grinnell degree, my year in Europe, my fluency in German, and the good grades I had received in my junior and senior years would suffice to get me admitted to an elite graduate school—had dissolved even before I left Grinnell. Evidently they were not impressed by my 2.91 grade point average; unfortunately, my mostly A grades from Vienna were not included in the GPA. I can't remember which graduate schools I applied to, but Yale and Princeton were among them. Apparently, I didn't have enough sense to apply to somewhat less prestigious schools, although I was admitted to Fordham.

Not getting into a graduate school of my choice was a real blow to my self-esteem. The prospect of returning to my hometown after being more or less on my own for four years seemed downright humiliating. I even wondered if it would even be worthwhile going to Nebraska at all. On that score I was reassured by Professor Wall, who offered me the following advice:

> I fully understand your desire to do your graduate work at a larger university with better library facilities than the University of Nebraska has to offer. . . . My own feeling is that an M.A. degree [from Nebraska] would be respected anywhere in the country. . . . Then too I am opposed to the idea of your having to work 15–20 hours a week in order to go to Columbia. I know that many graduate students do this, but I think it is to be avoided if at all possible because the demands of graduate school are such that to do a first-rate job it demands most of your time and energy. I have seen graduate students working for the Ph.D. and also working for a living extend their schooling over years and it is a deadening process.

Fortunately, I took Professor Wall's advice, thus avoiding the fate of 40 percent of PhD candidates who never finish their degrees.[2]

My other concern was about what it would be like living at home. Would my parents treat me like an adult, or would I feel as if I were still in high school? As I mentioned in the last chapter, I had had a major disagreement with my parents about how much time I should spend in Europe. My father had also wanted me to take some courses during the spring semester that I thought would impede my career plans. Fears about my parents trying to control my life turned out to be completely unfounded. Although my father's legal problems resulting from his father's tangled business dealings dragged on until 1967, I think the worst of them were resolved by 1959. Increasing his sense of financial security was the thought of no longer having to pay college tuition for my sister and me. Dad may have also simply thought that I was now an adult and his role as a parent had been completed, at least to a substantial degree.

My parents had moved into a new house at 3535 Calvert Street during my senior year at Grinnell. I was given the guest room on the main floor. It was a fine place to sleep, but it had no space for a desk or bookshelves and was too close to the den, where the television set was located. To solve the issue of where I would work, we created a study in the unfinished basement by nailing a huge under-carpet to a two-by-six-inch exposed wooden beam in the ceiling. To improve the atmosphere I pinned a huge *National Geographic* map of Europe onto the makeshift room divider. My father found a big secondhand desk for me, and we moved the single bed I had used on Dakota Street into this "room." I also had a comfortable chair for reading, my old dresser, some familiar photographs, my Grinnell diploma, and a simple bookshelf. The room could be made virtually soundproof by simply closing the door at the top of the stairs. It turned out to be a perfect arrangement for studying. In fact, I was able to study so long and hard that my father would occasionally come to the head of the stairs and ask if I'd like to take a break and watch *Gunsmoke*, *Perry Mason*, or *The Twilight Zone* with him and my mother. After my performance in high school, I think they were amazed that I could study for so many hours without interruption.

Unlike the other history graduate students, I had no distractions to get in the way of my studying. I didn't even apply for a teaching assistantship, which was becoming a common means for graduate programs across the country to accommodate rapidly increasing undergraduate enrollments. I didn't think I was ready for one—although I may have been unnecessarily cautious in that regard. I also kept in mind the advice Joe Wall had given me about avoiding time-consuming work. Moreover, I didn't need the money. The ridiculously inexpensive tuition—something like $100 a semester—was paid by my parents. I didn't have to shop for food let alone prepare it, wash dishes, or even take care of the lawn. My parents' new house, unlike our old one, was fully air-conditioned and had a beautiful enclosed backyard with a patio, where I occasionally read or enjoyed an outdoor meal. Altogether, it was an ideal arrangement, so ideal that my classmates expressed some good-natured envy when I once had them over for a backyard barbeque.

I had some excellent professors during my two years at Nebraska. The only problem as far as the history department was concerned was that some of its best professors moved on to other universities during the time I was there, or soon thereafter, a consequence of the great and all-too-brief period of academic mobility during the 1960s. I had an excellent two-semester course in American foreign policy from David Cronin, who left the next year for the University of Wisconsin, arguably the best public university in the country at that time; he later became the head of its history department.[3] My first mentor, Robert Koehl, also eventually accepted a job at Wisconsin. My French history professor was Robert Forster, who was lured away by Johns Hopkins University. My medieval history professor, William Bowsky, accepted a position at a state university in California. But at least I had the services of these outstanding professors while I was at Nebraska. I may have also received more individual attention from my professors than I would have at a much larger university with a more prestigious reputation. I found out later that graduate students at some of the largest schools could find their major professors only if they happened to run into them in an elevator on their way to give a presentation or about to leave for an overseas research trip.[4] There was nothing mediocre about Nebraska's workload for students either. One of my classmates, Jessie Stoddard, a pleasant and ambitious young woman who went on to get her PhD at the University of California at Berkeley, wrote to a mutual friend that the standards were "a good deal lower there than at the University of Nebraska."[5]

Undoubtedly, relatively low salaries, which had been a problem since the agricultural depression of the early 1920s, caused the university to lose some of its best professors.[6] The appearance of the campus in those days was also nothing that would have inspired loyalty. Between the history offices and classrooms in Burnett Hall and Love Library were two large, unpaved parking lots, the site of surplus army barracks in the late 1940s when GIs sent enrollment skyrocketing from 6,500 in 1940 to 14,000 in 1948. Student enrollment had been nearly 10,400 in 1928 when my father was a student.[7] The Depression, however, had led to a decline in the birthrate that was especially severe in Nebraska, one of the states worst hit by the economic disaster. Enrollment, around 7,000 in 1955, was between 8,500 and 9,000 while I was at the university. Declining enrollment and, of course, the Depression and World War II had delayed the construction of new buildings. Notable exceptions were the student union, which opened in 1938, and Love Library, built in 1940. Depression and war had also stood in the way of the beautification of the campus. Moreover, Lincoln still lacked many of the cultural outlets that it would later acquire.

My other illusion—that graduate school would be easy because I would be taking only history courses and no math or science—was quickly dispelled. I soon learned that graduate school was a whole new ballgame. The emphasis was as much on original research as it was on examinations and accumulating credit hours. Like many other American universities, the University of Nebraska considered research a distinguishing characteristic.[8] I had acquired a broad factual knowledge of history while I was at Grinnell and in Austria and had written a good many term papers. Nearly all of them, however, were under ten pages and had involved little research into primary sources. My weak background in research was exposed as soon as I took a course in historiography, the history of historical writing. Although I worked hard, I could manage only the equivalent of a C, an unacceptable grade in graduate school. I immediately found myself on academic probation.

The historiography class was the low point of my two years at Nebraska. Thereafter, my writing rapidly improved and I was able to get top grades on such things as critical book reviews. I still struggled my first year on classroom examinations, in part because I was so well prepared that I would go into too much detail on some parts of the test and not have sufficient time to answer other questions. However, by my second year I was getting B-pluses in all my courses, and I finished with two solid A's during my final summer term.

When I was at the University of Nebraska, all master's candidates had to write a thesis. Many graduate programs in history no longer have this requirement for students who do not plan to obtain a doctorate. However, even today a master's thesis is regarded by most graduate programs in history as a good preparation for writing a doctoral dissertation, and in fact, some dissertations are extensions of master's theses. A thesis can vary considerably in length, although most history theses are around one hundred to two hundred typewritten, double-spaced pages. More important than length, however, is that the thesis be based on original research and that the finished product not simply be a summary or condensation of what is already known.

I had four important concerns when I chose a thesis topic. First, I wanted it to have something to do with Austria. Second, because I still considered the Foreign Service a possible career choice, I thought a subject related to the twentieth century would be more useful than one limited to an earlier century. Third, by limiting myself to the twentieth century I would reduce the likelihood of having to read handwritten letters in archaic German script (I found out many years later that learning to read antiquated German script is not quite as difficult as I had assumed). Finally, since National Socialism was such a hot topic at the time (and has remained one), I wanted to research something that involved the Austrian Nazi Party.

Fortunately, Professor Koehl was an excellent historian of National Socialism. He had recently published a book on the Nazis' forced resettlement policies during the World War II and was working on a book about the infamous SS, published several years later as *The Black Corps: The Structure and Power Struggles of the Nazi SS*.[9] He was agreeable to my interests and suggested that I work on something I eventually called "The German Policy of Peaceful Penetration in Austria, 1933–1936." Of the work's eight chapters, only the first was exclusively on Austrian domestic affairs: the others were primarily on German foreign policy. Nevertheless, my research into Austrian history at the graduate level had begun.

As is customary with master's theses, my original research was confined to printed and microfilmed documentary sources, not unpublished ones. I also used memoirs (some of them in German), scholarly monographs, general histories, and a few newspaper articles. My central argument was that Hitler's decentralized and almost laissez-faire policy toward Austria and the Austrian Nazi Party after his takeover in Germany in January 1933 had resulted in a failed Nazi putsch in Austria in July 1934. The putsch created an international outcry and a united anti-German international front, and it became the lowest point in Hitler's prewar diplomatic career. The new German ambassador to Austria, Franz von Papen, instituted a new policy toward Austria by persuading Hitler to exercise much tighter control over the Austrian Nazi Party. This policy of "peaceful penetration" resulted in a false sense of security both within Austria and internationally, thus helping to lead to Austria's eventual annexation by Hitler's Third Reich in 1938.

Several things about this project stand out half a century after its completion. My first draft, which did not include a preface or bibliography, was 265 pages long. One chapter had no fewer than 80 pages. Professor Koehl, who read the first draft while on a research leave in Berlin, praised my "abundance of excellent research" but pointed out that my style was "clumsy" and that I needed to get rid of parenthetical statements and shorten my sentences. Just after I finished the draft, he turned my project over to a colleague, Professor Albin Anderson. Without even bothering to read it, Anderson said: "Cut it in half." I was horrified. I had gone to an enormous amount of work to write those 265 pages; how could I possibly eliminate half of them without destroying the integrity of the project? As it turned out, I didn't quite cut it in half—the final product was still 158 pages long—but I came close to fulfilling Professor Anderson's demand. I have to admit that the final version was vastly better than the first. The process of editing proved enormously useful in later research projects by training me to be as succinct as possible with short chapters, short paragraphs, and short, uncomplicated sentences. When Professor Koehl saw my finished work, for which I had received an A-minus, he was so impressed that he asked me if I had actually written it myself. I took his question more as a compliment than an accusation.

Another interesting feature of my thesis is how it was reproduced. Somehow I managed to find an excellent typist who typed my whole manuscript for twenty-five cents a page, footnotes and all. (Footnotes were a nightmare to type because it was almost impossible to guess how much space to allow for them at the bottom of the page.) Although the first Xerox image had been created in 1938, photocopy machines were not yet available at the university.[10] Consequently, my typist had to make carbon copies. My own copy must have been about the third or fourth sheet down, making it barely legible.

It had taken me two academic years and two summer school sessions to get my master's degree. But get it I finally did in July 1961. Although working conditions at home had been ideal, and although my grades improved substantially my second year, my experience at the University of Nebraska had been grueling, and at times I had wondered if it was worth it. Many years later, however, when given a distinguished alumnus award from the University of Nebraska Alumni Association, I gave a brief acceptance speech in which I said that it was at Nebraska that I "had learned what it took to be a scholar."

The graduation ceremony was in the new eighty-thousand-seat Municipal

Auditorium on Fifteenth and N Streets with Governor Frank Morrison as the main speaker. I remember nothing about the governor's speech, but I do vividly recall that afterward my father hugged me and, with his sense of family history, proudly pointed out that I was the first Pauley to receive an advanced degree.

ON TO SNOWBOUND ROCHESTER

By early 1961, I faced the issue of where to continue my graduate work. Professor Koehl was leaving, and in any event he was not a specialist in Austrian history. I knew there was a prominent specialist in Austrian history at the University of Texas in Austin by the name of R. John Rath. He edited the *Austrian History Newsletter*, which would soon become the *Austrian History Yearbook*. I applied to Texas and was not only admitted but was also offered a full scholarship. The catch was that I would have total responsibility for teaching a section of their History of Western Civilization course; this meant I would have to prepare nearly ninety lectures from scratch and grade countless exams. Teaching such a wide-ranging course was a daunting prospect which I estimated—I think realistically—would take most of my time, especially the first year, if I were to do a respectable job. Eventually, I turned the offer down, although in some respects I later regretted that decision. Once I met Professor Rath, I discovered him to be a charming and courtly gentleman who almost certainly would have given me more assistance than I had from the mentor I had at Rochester. Teaching "Western Civ" (as historians still like to call it) would have indeed been time consuming, but it would have enabled me to get a fast start once I found a tenure-earning position. Professor Koehl, however, warned me that Texas was not a particularly prestigious school to be "from" at that time.

Meanwhile, I had run across a book called *The Hapsburg Monarchy, 1867–1914*, by a University of Rochester historian named Arthur J. May, whom Professor Koehl described as a "first-rate scholar." I was somewhat concerned about his age—he was sixty-three at the time—but Koehl assured me that "his age is of no significance," an opinion that later proved disastrously faulty. May's book was much broader in scope than anything Rath had written, was quite readable, and displayed a sympathetic but not uncritical attitude toward the monarchy, which I shared. I wrote him a letter mentioning his book and telling him about my year in Vienna, my knowledge of German, my master's thesis, and my desire to specialize in Austrian history. That did the trick. I soon received a full-tuition scholarship plus a fellowship of $1,500 a year (worth over $10,000 today). In exchange for being financially independent for the first time in my life, I would merely have to preside over a small discussion section one hour a week for a Western Civ course, along with grading the class's exams and book reviews. The course lectures would be given by one of the members of the history department. A friend of my parents had seen the University of Rochester (which I soon found out was usually referred to as the "U of R") and described the campus as handsome with harmonious architecture. Ever since I had visited John Price on Long Island I'd had an idealized vision of what it would be like to go to an eastern university. I knew that the University of Rochester was not an Ivy League school, but it did have a good reputation, especially in the Northeast. The fit seemed perfect, so I accepted the offer sight unseen.

During the summer of 1961, after my acceptance at Rochester, a Nebraska classmate, Harl Dalstrom, who lived in Omaha, introduced me to a friend of his who had started graduate studies at the U of R two years before. His name was James Bachman, and he was to become a lifelong friend and faithful correspondent. Jim was friendly and had a great sense of humor. After we discussed the U of R at length we decided to room together that fall in a house a few blocks from the campus.

My first semester at Rochester did not get off to a promising start. Jim decided that he could better prepare for his comprehensive examinations if he remained in Omaha during the fall. I discovered that Elmdorf Avenue, where the rooming house was located, was in a depressed and depressing part of town. To make matters worse, the first week or ten days I was in Rochester were about the hottest and most humid I had experienced anywhere. Even though it was September, I found myself dripping with sweat. Furthermore, I had passed up an opportunity to be a dorm adviser, which would have given me free room and board.

Next, I learned that the U of R history department had been decimated by research and sickness leaves. The latter included the professor—John Christopher, the author of a well-known textbook in Western Civ—who was supposed to teach the course for which I and other graduate students were scheduled to assist. His last-minute replacement was a retired professor from the City College of New York who came highly recommended by one of its distinguished professors. As it turned out, the replacement was an elderly gentleman who was well past his prime, if indeed he'd had ever had one. His lectures did little more than regurgitate what was in the textbook to the utter wrist-slashing boredom of both the undergraduates and the graduate assistants who sat through them twice a week. Students would literally bring their textbook to class and underline passages as he read them aloud nearly verbatim.

One bright spot was my experience as a teaching assistant. Such assistantships had been introduced at the beginning of the twentieth century by none other than Woodrow Wilson, at the time the president of Princeton University. Known as the "preceptorial system," the program was designed to stimulate critical thinking and create a close relationship between students and faculty. By the 1960s, however, at Princeton and elsewhere, graduate students had replaced faculty as discussion leaders.[11]

I can vividly recall the first day I walked into class and how terribly unnatural it seemed to sit down behind a desk at the front of the class rather than with the students, as I had been doing for the previous nineteen years. Despite my apprehension, my discussion section went rather well, because Rochester's students were bright and willing to answer questions. The second year of my assisting was far more enjoyable than the first, because the lectures were delivered by Professor Hayden White, an engaging speaker and a rapidly rising star in the profession.

Practice teaching was another positive experience I had at the U of R, and something that is badly neglected in many doctoral programs.[12] All too often, new PhDs in history are better prepared to teach a graduate seminar on a topic related to their doctoral dissertation than they are to teach an undergraduate survey course.[13] Typically, brand-new professors are tossed into deep teaching waters and left to sink or swim.[14] Faculty frequently assume that "teaching is an art that is either too simple to require formal preparation, too personal to be taught to others, or too innate to be conveyed to anyone lacking the necessary gift."[15] At the U of R, however, Dexter Perkins, the renowned scholar of American diplomatic history and later president of the American Historical Association, initiated a program in 1947 in which all PhD candidates gave about six lectures, each one as a guest speaker in a different class and under the close supervision of the course's instructor.[16] All my lectures, including two of the large survey course in Western Civ, seemed to go quite well, and the professors in whose class I had lectured were always very complimentary and made only minor suggestions for improvement. I felt completely comfortable in front of the students, probably in part because of the public speaking I had done while in the Boys Octet. The only thing that bothered me was that I spent about a week reading everything I could get my hands on for each lecture. How, I wondered, could I possibly prepare nine lectures or so in one week if it took one week for just one lecture? The thought was scary.

Another encouraging development was the improvement in the weather. Once the initial heat wave had passed, Rochester enjoyed five or six weeks of mostly glorious weather. Because of abundant year-round precipitation, Rochester, in western New York State on the south shore of Lake Ontario, is blessed with lush vegetation that turns to beautiful shades of red and yellow in the fall. Unfortunately, autumn in upstate New York is far too short and is followed by interminable winter. I soon began to call Rochester "the land of eternal ice and snow." By late October the days were shorter and cloudier, and by early November the overcast skies were almost uninterrupted by sunshine. Then it started to snow, about three weeks earlier than was usual in Nebraska. By December it was snowing at least a little nearly every day, and the temperature rarely rose much above freezing. Once a week there might be a really sunny day and the snow would sparkle, but the following day it would be dark and snowy once again, a pattern that continued until late March or early April.

My housing situation improved my second year when I became a dorm adviser. I received no money for this job, but I did get a nice little apartment and free meals, with practically no responsibilities beyond handing out keys at the beginning of the semester and collecting them at the end. Fortunately, students had to work so hard at Rochester that they had little time for mischief beyond occasionally opening their windows and cursing the school. In addition to my bedroom, I had a comfortable living room and a private bath. The meals were the best part of the deal, because all the dorm advisers plus some other history grad students habitually ate together. They say that misery loves company, and since there was plenty of misery to go around I developed some close friendships with other doctoral candidates. We had a great opportunity to have serious conversations about our courses, our politics, and our career aspirations.

THE INSTITUTE OF WORLD AFFAIRS

Relief from the almost ceaseless three-year grind of graduate school came during the summer of 1962 when I attended a seven-week seminar at the Institute of World Affairs (IWA) near the idyllic village of Salisbury in the beautiful hills of northwestern Connecticut. My Austrian friend Walter Siegl, who had been studying at McGill University in Montreal, had attended IWA the previous summer and highly recommended it. Tuition, room, and board were free to the select few who were accepted. Applicants had to have already graduated from a university. With nothing to lose, I decided to apply—and was accepted.

Once I reached the campus I discovered that IWA was supported by three extremely elderly, philanthropic, conservative, and idealistic women, the most important of whom was an eighty-one-year-old lady named Maude Miner Hadden. Although the institute was founded in Geneva in 1924, World War II forced its transfer to the United States. Peter Gay, a German Jew who had a distinguished career as a historian after immigrating to the United States in 1941, was one of its more illustrious students in 1945.[17]

The institute was attended by around forty-five students. Fifteen or so were from the United States; the remainder came from some twenty different countries, including many commonly referred to in those days as belonging to the third world. The international students were generally older than the Americans, who were mostly fresh out of college. (I was one of the older Americans.) Most of the lectures were delivered by political scientists with a specialty in international relations, plus at least one former general. The lectures, discussions, sleeping quarters, and eating facilities were centralized in a fairly new building overlooking a small but charming lake. The dorm rooms were like cells, having little more than a bed and a single, bare forty-watt bulb for illumination. The institute's library was ridiculously inadequate for the research projects we were supposed to pursue, containing at most a few hundred books, few of them scholarly. Most of the speakers were as elderly and ultraconservative as the three ladies who ran the program. I recall one speaker, a retired general, who insisted that Marx was a Russian, not a German.

Making up for these deficiencies, however, were the stimulating and informative discussions we had every day. Most of the students were bright and sociable. Because of my fondness for Switzerland and Austria I immediately gravitated toward three central Europeans: Seraina Kind, a tall girl from Switzerland; Peter Gerlich, from Austria; and most of all, Helmut Sohmen from Linz, Austria. Helmut, who had early ambitions to be a professor of law, eventually became the CEO of a major shipping company based in Hong Kong. He turned out to be the only student with whom I retained a lifelong friendship. Coincidentally, I later put him in contact with Walter Siegl, and they, too, became great friends.

One incident during the summer not directly related to the institute sticks out in my mind. A small group of us went into town to get much-needed haircuts. One of us, while sitting in the barber's chair, saw a sign on a wall stating the prices for various services. He noticed that a regular haircut cost something like $1.50 (about $10.50 in today's valuation) but that "difficult-to-cut hair" was three times as much. When he asked about the discrepancy, the barber casually replied that "that price is for niggers. If they want a haircut I'll give it to them, but that's what they'll have to pay." Having been isolated from such blatant racism while growing up in Nebraska, I had thought that such attitudes were confined to the Deep South.

DROPPING INTO AN ABYSS

The fall semester of my second year at Rochester proved to be one of the worst periods in my entire life. I was beginning to study for my comprehensive

PhD written and oral examinations. The history department's rule was that a doctoral candidate had to be prepared to discuss no fewer than one hundred books in each of five subfields. My subfields were central Europe in the nineteenth and twentieth century, Russia since Peter the Great, the Renaissance and Reformation, early modern Europe to 1789, and Japan after 1868. It never seemed to cross the minds of whoever came up with this idea that it would be nearly impossible for anyone with an IQ lower than an Albert Einstein or a Thomas Edison to even memorize the authors and titles of that many books, let alone discuss their contents. I'm no psychologist, but my guess is that when people are confronted with what they regard as an impossible task, they are more likely to despair than to work more diligently. I recently read with great envy that when the distinguished diplomatic historian Norman Graebner took his comprehensive examinations at the University of Chicago in 1937, he was given access "to the files of all previous questions asked on written examinations in [his] *three* [my emphasis] fields."[18]

In any event, despair overtook me for several weeks and I descended into a deep depression. The workload was only part of my problem, albeit probably the biggest. A year-long correspondence with a member of the opposite sex had ended with a thud while I was at the IWA (more about that in the next chapter). By early November the doom and gloom of another Rochester winter was setting in, leaving my mood about as dark as the leaden skies. My ability to concentrate disappeared so completely that after reading a page I hadn't the slightest recollection of its contents. Like most depressed people, I also had trouble sleeping. My mood improved when I attended class or ate with my colleagues, but as soon as I was alone my depression returned with a vengeance. A few trips to a university psychiatrist did no good. He would listen politely to what I had to say but suggested no remedies. I read many years later that I would have had just as much chance of emerging from my depression if I had bought a cat (which, in any case, wouldn't have been allowed at the U of R). Fortunately, my depression didn't last long enough for me to consider jumping off a bridge into the icy waters of the nearby Genesee River, but I could understand how people who have endured years of deep depression, and perhaps are also in constant pain, could easily entertain such thoughts. The one good thing to emerge from the episode is that I gained a much greater understanding of clinical depression and sympathy for those who experience it.

By the middle of December I admitted to my parents that I was feeling in the dumps. My father responded with some excellent advice:

> I want to pass on to you a few of my thoughts with regard to your life in general and your present problem and state of mind in particular.
>
> I am positive that a successful assault at a PhD degree requires more than wishful thinking and more even than remarkable talent. Lack of willpower to make oneself "pay the price" of a semi-monastic life; inability to overcome periods of despondency induced by endless years of intense concentration and study or just plain lack of self-discipline to stick it out have certainly caused many otherwise well-equipped candidates to fall by the wayside and wind up as an elementary school teacher with a nagging wife and a household of kids. You have set a goal for yourself—how come you are now feeling inadequate to meet it? Dark winter days have a strong tendency to make all of us despondent—including me. Many, many times I review my life and regret my sins of commission and omission. Don't feel that you are pioneering a new field of human experience when these periods come to you. On the other hand, you must not and cannot allow yourself the luxury of dwelling on your own inadequacies. Think of what you have and what you have accomplished—not what you may have yet failed to do. You have done a marvelous job so far and you are almost over the "hump"—please Don't let down now. Remember, I love you and have faith in you.[19]

Fortunately, my depression eased considerably when I returned to Lincoln for Christmas vacation. Although it resumed to some extent when I got back to Rochester, it wasn't as bad as it had been in November and December. The depression disappeared altogether when I started dating the most beautiful and charming girl I had ever met. But that story will have to wait for the next chapter.

CHAPTER 8

Romance and Marriage

"Everywhere you look there is beauty and history."

EARLY MISADVENTURES

The sudden success I enjoyed during my last semester at the University of Rochester had no precedent. My success with girls in high school about matched my unimpressive academic performance. My skinny physique prior to my senior year at Grinnell did nothing to enhance my confidence so far as girls were concerned, although it evidently had never been a problem for my father, who had been a real beanpole as a teenager and well into his adult years. My lack of athleticism (except for golf) and all-too-serious nature also undermined my confidence around members of the opposite sex.

I did have one *almost* spectacular success in my junior year of high school. I asked the school's homecoming queen, Judy Hartman, for a date, and lo and behold, she actually accepted. I was thrilled. However, a few hours before our date she called me from Omaha to say that she was visiting her father and couldn't make it back in time. In retrospect, I think she was genuinely sorry to break our date, but at the time, rather than brushing the matter off and suggesting an alternative time, I allowed my feelings to be hurt and never asked her out again.

Grinnell women on the whole were better known for their brains than for their beauty. I dated a few during my freshman and sophomore years, but only one of them stands out in my mind today. I succeeded in getting a date with a girl who had recently been named "Miss Iowa," no less, and was a genuine beauty. It turned out to be one of the most boring dates I ever had. I couldn't get her to converse about anything, no matter how many questions I asked. She was an elementary education major, a major that Grinnell soon abolished as being unworthy of an elite liberal arts college. After that miserable experience I silently vowed that I would never date an education major again.

During my junior year abroad I'd had the good fortune to dance with some beautiful Viennese girls, but I never established a real relationship. There were some serious and reasonably attractive girls in the Institute of European Studies, at least one of whom was interested in me, but I was much too busy exploring the city and traveling independently throughout Europe to develop a romantic relationship.

I did discover an attractive and smart girl named Gretchen my senior year at Grinnell. There was one big problem, however. My former roommate, John Price, had dated her in the spring, and their relationship, as he wrote me, "was just starting to blossom" before the school year ended, and he was hoping for better things when he returned from a semester of study in Washington DC in the fall of 1958. He told me about Gretchen but at first wouldn't even tell me her name, for fear, as he said, that I "would sweep her off her feet." When he finally divulged her name I took her out a few times, and we had a good time. However, as the time for John's return to Grinnell grew closer I felt more and more like a cad. If I continued the relationship with Gretchen, a sophomore, it would probably end later that year when I graduated. In the meantime I might permanently alienate one of my best friends. With considerable regret, I decided to end the relationship, probably hurting her feelings in the process, because I didn't have the gumption to explain my reasoning.

There were almost no female graduate students in history at the University of Nebraska or for that matter in most graduate programs in history in the United States at that time. Only 2 percent of the PhDs handed out in 1962 were given to women, and women earned only 10 percent of all PhDs between 1930 and 1970.[1] The lack of female doctoral students was also reflective of, or perhaps even in part caused by, the absence of female professors in history departments at Grinnell, Nebraska, and Rochester.

In any case, I was far too busy for dating. I did help to organize and was the president of a university-wide Graduate and Professional Students Association at Nebraska, one member of which was a nice-looking girl from Panama who was obviously interested in me. The feeling, however, was not mutual.

My parents were probably getting somewhat concerned about my marital prospects while I was living at home. Nowadays, when the average marrying age for men is 28.7 and 26.5 for women, they probably would not have been concerned. However, in the early 1960s the average marrying age was at a historic low of just 22.8 for men and 20.3 for women.[2] Toward the end of my second year at Nebraska, which was Gretchen's senior year at Grinnell, I decided to reestablish contact with her. She and John had not gotten back together, and John had gone off to Oxford on a Rhodes Scholarship. Gretchen wrote a friendly letter in response to mine, and I decided to go to Grinnell and attend her graduation. She had evidently not forgotten me, because we hit it off that long week far more than when we had been dating two years earlier. A few days later her mother even telephoned me in Lincoln and asked if I would come up to Minneapolis to celebrate Gretchen's graduation. I was tempted but was frantically trying to finish my thesis, which was due before the end of July, so I regretfully declined. Gretchen spent the next year teaching in Thailand, and we corresponded regularly. However, whatever interest she had in me waned just before her return to the States. She did come up to Connecticut to visit me when I was at the Institute of World Affairs, but the visit was anything but productive.

SUCCESS AT LAST

In the spring semester of my second year at Rochester (1963), I registered for a course in totalitarianism that was being offered for the first time. I don't remember much about the course itself except that we read a very difficult book called *The Origins of Totalitarianism*, by Hannah Arendt. Soon after the course began I became much more interested in a beautiful young woman who sat two or three rows in front of me than I did in the course itself. I had noticed her earlier, because she punched meal tickets at the Women's Center cafeteria where male students were allowed to eat lunch. I soon asked a grad student friend of mine, Gilbert McArthur, who seemed to know the names of all the good-looking girls on campus, the name of that gorgeous ticket-punching blonde. Without a moment's hesitation he said: "Oh that's Marianne Utz, but she wouldn't be interested in you because she comes from a very wealthy family." I wasn't about to be deterred by Gil's assessment. Besides, it seemed unlikely that a girl from a rich family would need to work her way through college. In any event, I recalled that my uncle Gordon had once told me that "rich girls are just as easy to marry as poor ones," although he had not followed his own advice. As I soon learned, Marianne came from a family of modest means.

So, having learned the her name, I called Marianne and told her my name. Her response was: "Who?" I obviously hadn't caught her attention nearly as much as she had caught mine. After explaining that I was a classmate in the totalitarianism class, I asked her for a date. The most she would promise was to sit in the first row of class the next day and allow me to introduce myself. Even then she agreed only to meet me later for coffee at the student union. We met that afternoon and quickly struck up a conversation. I haven't the slightest clue, after all these years, of what we discussed, except it must have included what year in school we were (she was a senior) and our majors. I no doubt told her where I was from and that I intended to be a college professor. Beyond these pleasantries, what immediately impressed me about Marianne was how effortlessly she could converse. Whereas it had been like pulling teeth with most of the girls I had dated earlier, Gretchen being an exception, talking to Marianne was effortless. Only recently have I learned that words are actually "the fuel of courtship."[3]

There were many things that impressed me about Marianne from the very beginning. Like most men, I was immediately attracted to her most obvious feature: her beauty. Standing just under five feet, six inches tall, she had thick, wavy blonde hair and green eyes. In high school she had been a fashion model at a department store and had also been a model for a Kodak photographer. Adding to her attractiveness was her taste in clothing. She dressed well even for classes and looked especially sensational when we were on a date. Her manners were also impeccable. Last, but certainly not least, she was an excellent student, disproving the stereotype of the dumb blonde. Born and raised in Rochester, she had graduated third in her high school class and was voted the girl most likely to succeed as well as the girl with the friendliest smile. At the U of R she had won many honors, including being on the Dean's List nearly every semester, Junior Prom Queen, Sweetheart of Sigma Chi, and May Queen, the last being for superior grades and service to the university. Part of her service was on the prestigious Judicial Board, which handled cases involving social life at the Women's Center. Only after we were married did I realize that she was actually very much like my mother, although even more attractive. The only downside about Marianne that I soon discovered was that she was an elementary education major. So much for my earlier vow never to date one! As it turned out, her major and career were very compatible with my own.

Once I started dating Marianne, it was amazing how quickly my depression disappeared. Greatly facilitating our romance was my ability to borrow a car from a fellow grad student. It was an old wreck of a Nash, if I remember correctly. It was in such bad shape that second gear didn't work; I had to shift directly from first to third. I didn't care, and thankfully neither did Marianne, whose other boyfriends hadn't had access to *any* cars. The borrowed car enabled us to spend a leisurely afternoon at a local park called Mendon Pond and join other history grad students for a picnic at beautiful Letchworth Park in the hills south of Rochester. On another occasion we drove over to Niagara Falls and enjoyed the sight from the Canadian side. I soon discovered that Marianne loved classical music as much as I, so we went to see an excellent performance of Mozart's *Don Giovanni* by students at the Eastman School of Music. We also frequently went out to eat and danced at the Genesee Park Inn. Somehow my comprehensive exams no longer seemed quite so daunting or important.

The more I found out about this gorgeous young woman, the more I was impressed. She had been a cheerleader and a member of a sorority in high school but had given up those pursuits at the U of R in favor of academic and service-related activities. In high school she had worked with handicapped children at a nearby summer camp. Her parents had emigrated from Germany in 1930, and even though they had not spoken German to their children, Marianne had picked up a good deal of the language by listening to her relatives and by taking three years of German in high school.

Once, when I asked Marianne for a date, she said that I would have to pick her up at her home just off Winton Road in Rochester where she was spending the weekend. After a long drive in the dark I finally managed to find the Utz house. Marianne's mother, an attractive fifty-one-year-old woman, was sitting next to the television set. Without a moment's hesitation I walked up to her and said: "Es freut mich Ihre Bekanntschaft zu machen" ("I'm pleased to make your acquaintance"). Mrs. Utz seemed flustered and only managed to stammer a response in English. Marianne had never before brought home a boyfriend who could speak German. Despite her surprise, I think Mrs. Utz was favorably impressed. As the spring went on she would ask Marianne what she was doing that weekend; Marianne would reply that she was going out with Bruce Pauley. Marianne's mother probably sensed what was going on, but rather than acting overly inquisitive she merely said: "Oh, you seem to be seeing quite a lot of him lately."

A few weeks later I had a chance to meet Marianne's father. He was a rather shy and somewhat short man with an even stronger German accent than Marianne's mother. When I later happened to mention her parents' accents to Marianne she said: "Really, I never noticed." Mr. Utz proved to be an observant man. He later mentioned that when he saw how easily Marianne and I interacted, he sensed that this was nothing like Marianne's earlier relationships.

I had a chance to meet Marianne's other relatives—like her parents, all Germans who had immigrated to the United States in the 1920s and 1930s—at her graduation party. They were all nice-looking, friendly people with whom I immediately felt comfortable. Marianne's aunt Rose was especially gracious, and I sensed that she was hoping that Marianne and I would get married. I later learned that she was also one of Marianne's favorite relatives.

Before the end of the school year, in late May or early June, when Marianne and I had dated for barely three months, I decided that she was the one and asked her to marry me. She said yes, although she later claimed that, lacking an engagement ring, she had not yet considered our engagement official. As soon as I got back to Lincoln we began exchanging letters at least every other day. Once a week we would splurge and talk on the phone for ten minutes or so. We agreed that she would fly out to Lincoln for a long weekend in July to meet my parents.

When July 11 finally arrived I drove to pick up Marianne at the Omaha airport. As was appropriate in those days for any occasion more formal than a picnic or a swimming party, I was dressed in a brown, plaid sport coat and tie; she was wearing a new green-and-white suit. When I first saw her I felt like a starving man who hadn't eaten for weeks. I could hardly wait to get her out to my parents' car and give her a long, passionate kiss. Just then a little boy passed by and remarked to his parents in a loud voice: "I saw some real romance!" Marianne and I laughed about that incident for years.

If there was ever any doubt concerning our marriage plans, that weekend in Lincoln put them to rest. My parents were nearly as enthusiastic about Marianne as I. After the visit my mother wrote Marianne that "although your visit with us was a short one, it was long enough for us to feel that you are already a member of our family—a *well loved* member!" She went on to say that Marianne had "charmed everyone who met you. They are all unanimous in their approval—which makes Bruce glow with pride and makes us happy, too." My father told me that he didn't "see how I could have a more perfect person for a lifetime mate." A loving and respectful relationship was quickly established which lasted as long as my parents were alive. My aunt Phyllis told me in 2002 that my mother went so far as to brag about Marianne to her friends. Helping matters considerably was the fact that Marianne and my mother had much the same conservative taste in clothing and interior decoration, so Marianne did not hesitate to ask my mother for advice on these and other matters and my mother was happy to give it. My mother even passed on some of her elegant clothes to Marianne, who was delighted to have them. I soon established an equally warm relationship with Marianne's parents, so we never had any in-law problems. Quite the opposite: our parents proved to be enormously helpful, especially when our sons were born.

Even before we were "officially" engaged, the issue of a wedding date arose. During her spring break and before our dating became serious, Marianne had landed a teaching position in the Boston area. With the help of Professor May I had been awarded a Fulbright-Hays Fellowship that would take me to Graz, Austria, for a full academic year. What to do? We both recognized that three or four months of dating was not an ideal length of time for getting to know each other prior to getting married. On the other hand, I didn't want to take a chance of losing this jewel of a young woman and had no desire to undertake another year-long correspondence. I also thought it was nearly as important for her as it was for me to spend some time in Europe.

There was no easy solution. Ultimately, Marianne convinced me that having a real wedding would require lots of preparation time; trying to squeeze final comprehensive exams and a wedding into the same week would not do justice to either event. Following our formal engagement we agreed that Marianne would continue working at Kodak for the remainder of the summer and would substitute-teach in the fall. She would live with her parents and save as much money as possible for a Volkswagen Beetle, which we would purchase in Germany. Meanwhile, after taking my exams I would get started on my research project in Austria and would return to Rochester shortly before Christmas for our wedding. It seemed like a sensible thing to do but meant that following our weekend in Lincoln I would see her for only about a week in early September when I was taking my PhD examinations. All in all, between early June and late December we would see each other for a grand total of twelve days.

In retrospect, I can see that a major reason for our successful romance was perfect timing, just as timing was critical in so many other aspects of my life. When I met Marianne she had recently ended a relationship and was completely unattached. She had no intention of going to graduate school, although she did have that teaching job in the Boston area. I was nearing the end of my residency at Rochester and obtained the Fulbright soon after we met. We were both at a stage in our lives when we were ready for a commitment. We hadn't dated nearly as long as would have been ideal, but we had seen a great deal of each other in the short time we had been together at the U of R.

By contrast, the timing of my relationship with Gretchen had been terrible to the point of making a future together virtually impossible. I had forfeited any chance of really getting to know her at Grinnell, and in any event we were both too young and had too many academic plans to think about forging a serious relationship. Our brief reunion at her graduation weekend was far too short for us to develop really strong ties. It proved equally impossible to develop a close relationship from a distance of ten thousand miles during a year when she was teaching in Thailand (although her letters describing Thailand and her travels throughout Asia and Europe provided a welcome relief during a lonely period in my life). When she returned she was anxious to go to graduate school at Georgetown just when I was eager to return to Europe.

SIX MONTHS OF TORTURE

The six-plus months from the time I left the U of R for home on June 10 to my convoluted forty-eight-hour return trip to Rochester from Graz on December 15 were interrupted only by that all-too-short July weekend and the week in early September when I took my written and oral comprehensive exams. I wondered if I could ever survive such a long wait. The summer was probably the worst period because, except for Marianne's letters and weekly phone calls, I was studying ten to twelve hours a day. Auditing a class in Russian history and a seminar on Nazi Germany from Professor Koehl were my only diversions.

To read the required five hundred books alluded to in the previous chapter was an obvious impossibility. I decided I would skim only the most important ones and read reviews of those that were less important. The University of Nebraska library, where I found the necessary books, still had no photocopying machine, so I had to spend innumerable hours transcribing the most important portions of reviews by typewriter, whereas nowadays, of course, reviews can often be read online and printed with the click of a mouse. By the end of the summer I had amassed a huge folder of notes. My only physical recreation was a one-mile neighborhood jog around midnight. During one of these nocturnal runs a perplexed policeman stopped to ask if anything was wrong.

It is customary for mentors of PhD candidates to ask most of the questions in comprehensive examinations and to lead the discussion during the oral portion of the test. Consequently, I devoted more attention to Austrian history than to my other four fields. That strategy proved to be a complete waste of time. Professor May, who always spent his summer in a vacation home in Maine—"the first of June sees the last of May," he used to announce to his class—decided that he couldn't be bothered to return to Rochester a few days early for my exam. As a result, not a single question about Austrian history came up on the test.

I have no recollection of the written portion of the examination except that I am sure that I did not do particularly well. On the night preceding the oral test I was determined to get a good night's sleep, so I took a sleeping pill and went to bed early. Two restless hours later I took a second pill, and later a third. I got a grand total of one hour of sleep that night and began the exam feeling like a zombie. When I was dismissed from the room so my inquisitors could discuss my fate, I fully expected to be flunked, which frequently happened to history grad students at Rochester. But to my astonishment, the committee gave me a "conditional pass" but said I could expect to receive an especially tough grilling on my doctoral dissertation. I was not only enormously relieved but genuinely surprised. My only explanation was that I had done well in my course work and the committee did not want me to lose my Fulbright grant, which, I suppose, gave the department a certain amount of recognition.

A few days remained before I was to leave for Austria. The Austrian Cultural Institute in New York was going to host a get-together for the fifteen or twenty Fulbrighters who were about to embark on their year abroad. I thought Marianne should at least have this opportunity to meet other Fulbrighters and learn about the program. She managed to persuade her parents to let her accompany me to New York, where we spent five delightful days seeing the sights in addition to meeting the Fulbright students and professors. It was the first time I realized that Marianne enjoyed sightseeing as much as I did.

All good things have to end, however, and the day of my departure arrived all too soon. I can still vividly recall seeing Marianne crying on the dock as my ship, the SS *Constitution*, pulled away. Despite our carefully reasoned decision to wait until December for our wedding, I wondered if I had done the right thing leaving her again for over three months. Fortunately, my friend John Price was with her on the dock and helped her catch her flight back to Rochester.

The *Constitution* was a vast improvement over the archaic *Georgic* that I had taken to Europe with my parents in 1954. Built in 1951, it had both outdoor and indoor swimming pools, game rooms, and a movie theater. It had been used for several episodes of the sitcom *I Love Lucy* and had been featured in the 1957 film *An Affair to Remember* with Cary Grant and Deborah Kerr. I was totally unaware of the ship's history at the time. For me, the best part about the voyage was that it took a southerly route to Europe through the Straits of Gibraltar and ultimately dropped off our Fulbright group in Genoa. The result was that we entered the Gulf Stream with its pleasant, warm, sunny weather after just one day of cold weather, in contrast to the ten cold, miserable days I had experienced on the *Georgic*.

The voyage was more like a vacation cruise than a simple transport of passengers across the ocean. We made several interesting sightseeing stops along the way at the Madeira Islands (where I was surprised to discover the tomb of the last Austro-Hungarian monarch, Karl I), Casablanca, Gibraltar, Barcelona, Cannes, and finally Genoa. After seeing Christopher Columbus's birthplace we headed for Vienna in a first-class sleeper, arriving on the morning of September 16, twelve days after our departure from New York.

Although I was a faithful writer during the whole trip, the correspondence got off to a shaky start. I wrote Marianne a few lines every day while the ship was at sea and then mailed my mushy, eight-page letter from our first stop at Madeira. Two days later I sent her a postcard from Casablanca with a belly dancer on one side and a matter-of-fact message on the other. As luck would have it, Marianne, who had gone ten days or so without a word from me, got the postcard first. She wasn't too thrilled. Fortunately, her spirits rose the next day when my long letter arrived. (Marianne later told me that her mother noticed tears rolling down her face as she read my letter and asked if anything was wrong. Marianne merely shook her head.)

I had written Marianne no fewer than thirty-eight letters during the summer and was to send her another thirty-seven letters and eleven postcards in the fall for a total of eight-six. By an amazing coincidence, Marianne posted me exactly the same number. All of these exchanges have been carefully preserved and provide a priceless account of a crucial period in our lives, something that would be unheard of in our current era of phone calls, e-mails, and text messages.

Arriving in Vienna was like a homecoming. At the station to greet me was my former roommate, Walter Siegl. A few days later I was able to get together with Helmut Sohmen, who had just finished guiding a group of inattentive IES students through Western Europe before returning to his law studies. In my first letter to Marianne from Vienna I wrote that "I was a little afraid that I might not be as thrilled by Vienna as I was before, but my fears were certainly unnecessary. For the last five years I have been just starved for beauty and culture and now I can really gorge myself! All day long I have felt like skipping or shouting for joy."

The Fulbright Commission organized a wonderful twelve-day orientation for all the award winners. Its thirteen-page booklet, which I still have, meticulously listed all the lectures we would hear, where we would eat, what was playing each night at the theaters, excursions we would take, and places of interest in Vienna. During the orientation I became pleasantly surprised by how well prepared I was to begin my Fulbright year, thanks to my experience abroad during my junior year abroad and the term papers and seminar papers I had written on Austrian history while at Grinnell and the University of Nebraska. Most obviously, I was thoroughly versed in how to navigate my way around Vienna. I also soon discovered that my German was better than I realized. During the orientation we were asked to join one of three German-language classes: beginning, intermediate, or advanced. At first I chose intermediate, but I quickly learned that it was too easy. A lecture on the history of Austria given by a professor at the University of Vienna I found too general to be of much use, and I knew enough about the

Austro-Hungarian Monarchy to challenge his contention that it had been held together solely by the Habsburg dynasty. The orientation included a tour of Vienna, an excursion to the Burgenland as far as the Iron Curtain border with Hungary, and a trip through the romantic and mountainous "Wachau" region of the Danube as far as the famous baroque monastery at Melk. On September 29, I boarded a train for Graz, where I remained for most of the academic year.

GETTING SETTLED IN GRAZ

My good fortune continued once I got to Graz, the capital of the province of Styria and, with 250,000 inhabitants, Austria's second-largest city. I soon came to love Graz at least as much as Vienna. Its compactness and relatively small size made it easier to explore. It had proportionately less industry than Vienna and relatively more space devoted to parks. The foothills and peaks of the Austrian Alps were also closer. The operas and concerts of Graz, not surprisingly, were fewer in number and slightly lower in quality than those of the Austrian capital, but they were plenty good enough to be supremely enjoyable. A concert by the internationally acclaimed tenor Fritz Wunderlich was especially memorable.

Greatly adding to my pleasure was the family with whom I lived during the fall. Walter Siegl and I had had only a very formal relationship with our landlady in Vienna. I can remember just one occasion when we were invited into her living room for a glass of wine. By contrast, I was treated almost like a family member by my hosts, the Moosbrugger family. They lived on the outskirts of Graz in a lovely, residential suburb called Mariagrün. They were accurately described by a Fulbrighter who had lived with them the year before as "extremely intelligent and refined . . . and always available for companionship when one wants it. The whole family went out their way to make me comfortable and feel at home and was wonderful in correcting my German. I found it an ideal situation."[4] I came to share those sentiments entirely. Adding to my pleasure was the proximity of hiking trails in the nearby woods and mountains, which I used on numerous occasions that fall, accompanied by members of the Moosbrugger family. Soon after my arrival I wrote Marianne: "You have no idea how nice it is just to go for a walk here. Everywhere you look there is beauty and history."

Frau Dr. Hedwig Moosbrugger was the de facto head of the family and also my official landlady. She taught two courses in the theory of physical education at the University of Graz; her husband, Dr. Herbert Moosbrugger, who was in rather frail health because of a war injury, was a civil engineer. The children were Reingard, five years younger than I, who spoke excellent English; her nineteen-year-old brother, Helfried, who I thought was unusually mature for his age; and their twenty-six-year-old nephew, Peter, whose father had been killed in the war. Also living with them was a fifteen-year-old servant girl, Ilse.

Compared to the room I shared with Walter in Vienna in 1957–58, I was living in the lap of luxury in the fall of 1963. I had a large, centrally heated room, complete with a desk and a sink with hot running water. The walls were painted a cheerful yellow, and I had plenty of closet space and a comfortable extra-long bed. From my window I had a beautiful view of the woods and hills surrounding Graz to the east. I was free to eat breakfast anytime between 7:30 and 9:30. Dinner, which I ate with the family, was announced with a loud gong around 6:00. The food, which was quite similar for breakfast and supper, consisted of made-to-order eggs, ham, wurst, two or three kinds of cheese, homemade marmalade, fruit, coffee (tea for supper), and always plenty of delicious hard-crusted Austrian bread. I was on my own for lunch, when the Moosbruggers had their main meal. However, that was fine with me, because it gave me an opportunity to investigate some of Graz's restaurants.

When my birthday arrived on November 4, Frau Moosbrugger arranged a special dinner for me complete with a fancy torte for dessert. Before dinner, each member of the family lined up, shook my hand, and gave a brief congratulatory speech. Incidentally, the birthday handshake was nothing exceptional. I shook hands with the Moosbruggers when I first saw them in the morning and again before I went to bed at night. Such formality extended to small shops, including barbershops, where everyone would say "auf Wiedersehen" when I left.

Conversations around the Moosbrugger dinner table were exclusively in German, and consequently my German soon improved by leaps and bounds. In time I learned that although many Grazers had studied English, few spoke it fluently, not even teachers of English who were self-conscious about speaking it around native English speakers. Moreover, there were only a few Fulbrighters in Graz, and these I saw infrequently; I often went for days without speaking a word of English.

One exception to this concentration on speaking German came in November when I was invited to participate in a conference of teachers of English held at the Seggan Castle near Leibnitz, several miles south of Graz. Situated on a hilltop overlooking the Mur River valley, it was surrounded by high mountains. All I had to do was lead informal discussions, for which I was paid a modest but welcome sum. One of the teachers there wanted me to explain segregation; someone else wanted to know the differences between the Republican and Democratic Parties. Neither question was easy to answer in the early 1960s.

Another opportunity for speaking English and also meeting Austrians was at the Austro-American Society, which consisted mostly of Austrians who had studied in the United States under a Fulbright grant or in the American Field Service program. In late November the society had a memorable banquet with excellent food. The mood was dampened, however, by the recent assassination of President Kennedy, which seemed to be mourned almost as much in Austria as it was in the United States. The day after his death, Graz was bedecked with black flags.

The Moosbruggers included me not only in long walks but also occasionally for auto excursions. One time Frau Moosbrugger and Helfried invited me for an afternoon outing that took us to the Yugoslav border. On another occasion, Herr Moosbrugger took me with him on a business trip into the heart of the Alps as far as Bad Ischl, the favorite hunting reserve of Kaiser Franz Joseph, a region where wearing colorful traditional costumes and kissing ladies' hands were still commonplace.

All the Austrians I met that fall were friendly. In part their friendliness resulted from my being able to speak their language tolerably well, which of course is true in most countries one visits as a foreigner. One incident that exemplified a distinct pro-Americanism sticks out in my mind. One day on my way back to the Moosbrugger home, I decided to get off the streetcar one stop early and explore the Hilmteich Park with its charming little pond surrounded by bushes and flowers. After I had been sitting on a bench for a few minutes, an elderly woman began speaking to me in a heavy dialect, which I was pleased to be able to understand. After expressing amazement that I was an American—most international students in Graz were from Greece, Iran, or Norway—she gratefully mentioned the fact that the United States had saved her from starvation after both world wars.

The one thing that did not favorably impress me about Graz was the quality of the lectures at the university. I wrote Marianne that "the lectures I've heard here, on the whole, are much inferior to the ones I've heard in the States (though I've heard some bad ones there, too). The worst thing here is that the professors read their lectures, often straight from a book. I find this both boring and childish. It would be far easier to mimeograph and distribute the lectures to the students. . . . I also find it quite irritating that students here consider the professors such gods that they never ask any questions." When I repeated these observations to Helmut Sohmen, he wrote back that "your suggestion concerning the mimeographing of lectures has been realized to a large extent at the Law School and many of my colleagues see their professors only at exam time. But the whole system is rotten . . . and can't be compared at all with the American way of teaching."[5]

Austrian universities at the time were still suffering from the economic consequences of two lost world wars, and some of its best professors had emigrated.

AVERTING DISASTER

I kept busy during the fall of 1963, but as I wrote Marianne, "every day without you is real torture." About a week before I was to fly back to the States for our wedding, a potential disaster struck: I came down with the flu. At first I wasn't too alarmed, assuming I would recover before my scheduled departure. However, as the time approached I didn't seem to be getting any better. The Moosbruggers could not have been more solicitous and tried their best to nurse me back to health.

By the day before my scheduled departure my fever was finally gone, but like most people who have just had the flu I still felt terribly weak and wondered how I was ever going to make it back to the States. If I could have flown from Graz to Rochester or even from Vienna to New York it would have been far less daunting. However, I was scheduled to fly on good old Icelandic Airlines, the airline of poor students, whose nearest airport was in Luxembourg City. To get there I had to overnight in Vienna, fly the next day to Zürich, and change planes before flying on to Luxembourg. In Luxembourg City I had another long wait before embarking on a twenty-four-hour flight to New York, where I changed planes once again before completing the last leg to Rochester. Altogether, the trip took forty-eight hours. Fortunately, Marianne was unaware that my return to Rochester was ever in doubt.

I would like to say that the wedding came off without a hitch, but that was hardly the case either. My parents and my grandmother drove all the way to Rochester from Lincoln, picking up my sister and brother-in-law in Farmington, Illinois, along the way—three days in each direction. When they reached the border of New York State they were halted by a blizzard, which closed the New York State Thruway. When it reopened in the middle of the night, they immediately set off again for Rochester.

Fortunately, the wedding and the reception went smoothly. John Price was my best man, and Jim Bachman and Marianne's brother, Dick, were ushers. A Grinnell friend, Ted McConnell, officiated. Marianne's maid of honor was a close U of R friend, Maret Ralph, and my sister was the matron of honor. The reception was held in the suburb of Pittsford at the Spring House, which was built in the 1820s as an inn for travelers on the Erie Canal. Its rear windows, near where we ate, looked onto a beautiful snow-filled backyard.

Marianne and I left the reception before it was over, following the rather silly custom of the time, thereby missing out on a party that all our friends had at the Utzes' house. Our wedding was followed by a second near disaster. On our drive to "romantic" Buffalo, where we spent our first night, we were nearly stranded by a blizzard. Because it was our wedding night, I decided to be wildly extravagant and spent the enormous sum of $10 ($70 adjusted for inflation) for a room at a Holiday Inn. The next day we drove to Toronto, where we did a little sightseeing before attending the American Historical Association convention in Philadelphia, where I looked for a job, about which more later. After a brief stopover in Manhasset to see John Price, we flew to Europe to start our new life.

CHAPTER 9

Seven Months of Bliss

"Five hours a day in libraries, perhaps six. Then Vienna is ours."

MEETING MY GERMAN IN-LAWS

The timing of my Fulbright year was ideal. The United States was at peace—our involvement in Vietnam was still minimal—and the dollar was still strong. Consequently, my Fulbright and the half scholarship I received from the University of Rochester went a long way. I had the opportunity to complete research on my doctoral dissertation, improve my German, and increase my knowledge of European history, culture, and geography. At the same time, however, it was a fantastic way to begin a marriage. I had no lectures to prepare, and Marianne had no lesson plans to write. The limited hours of the archives and libraries where I worked gave us plenty of time to explore our first hometown of Graz, Austria.

Following three exhausting days of job interviews at the American Historical Association, Marianne and I left New York on January 2, 1964, and flew to Luxembourg City on Icelandic Airlines. Because Icelandic was the last major airline to use propeller planes, our flight took around twenty-four-hours (which we didn't mind because we had two seats to ourselves at the back of the plane), interrupted by a breakfast in Reykjavík. From

Luxembourg City we proceeded by bus and rail to Crailsheim in the German state of Baden-Württemberg, where Marianne had the chance to see some of her German relatives for the first time. It was quite a sight when her nearly toothless eighty-five-year-old grandmother finally got to meet her twenty-two-year-old granddaughter. Both were immediately in tears. Grandmother Utz was a sweet old lady who spoke German with a thick Swabian accent. Marianne had gotten used to hearing a watered-downed version of that dialect when she was growing up, so she had a pretty good idea of what her grandmother was saying. But even though my German was on the whole much better than Marianne's, I could barely understand one word in ten. Marianne noted in her diary that it was "even more fun hearing and speaking German than I imagined! I'm going to love Europe."

We also met Marianne's aunt Frieda, her uncle Georg and his family, and her uncle Fritz. Their World War II experiences had been in sharp contrast to those of my family. An uncle's toes were frostbitten and amputated while he was on the Russian front. Another relative returned to Nuremberg at the end of the war to a burned-out house he had built himself. Aunt Frieda lost her husband and seventeen-year old son near the end of the war and never remarried. Uncle Otto, who had immigrated to the States in 1929, fought in the Philippines. It is no wonder that while Americans look back on the war with a certain amount of nostalgia or at least pride, Germans and most other Europeans see the war—and war in general—as an unmitigated disaster.

From all of Marianne's German relatives we received the same heartfelt gratitude that my family and I had experienced in Karlsruhe nine years earlier. I, of course, was completely undeserving of such plaudits, and Marianne, as a little girl, had done little more than accompany her mother to a post office when she mailed CARE packages to Germany after the war.[1] Those boxes, with their priceless contents of coffee, lard (for making soap), fruit preserves, honey, raisins, chocolate, sugar, spam, and other basics, often saved Germans fortunate enough to have American relatives from malnutrition, disease, or even death. Nevertheless, we were both treated as though we were personally responsible for what had been desperately needed help. Uncle Georg, who looked like her father's twin, also plied us with *alten Geschichten*, entertaining stories about his youth and that of Marianne's father. Crailsheim itself was typically German, with narrow streets and a few half-timbered houses being among the 15 percent of the town that had not been destroyed during the war.

Uncle Georg enabled us to buy a Volkswagen Beetle by cosigning our check for $1,350, about $500 less than we would have paid in the States. With our bluish-green Bug complete with a sunroof (which proved to be ideal for viewing the Alps), we set off to see my friend Dieter in the university town of Tübingen, my Swiss friend Brandy in Basel, and Walter Siegl's parents in Dornbirn. After Dornbirn we made a slight detour into Liechtenstein to see a small portion of the prince's fabulous collection of Dutch and Flemish paintings, as well as a stamp museum, stamps being one of Liechtenstein's major industries. While we were heading east toward Graz, Marianne marveled at the snowcapped mountains of Vorarlberg and North and South Tyrol.

Before moving into our rental home we visited the Moosbruggers. Marianne was impressed by their warmth and cordiality. "My first thought is that Bruce had been well taken care of during the fall," she wrote in her diary. After an hour's conversation I carried Marianne over the threshold of our new home, which was just a block away. Shortly before my return to the States, the Moosbruggers had discovered that the cottage was owned by an Australian who turned out to be more than happy to rent it to us. It was a charming little story-and-a-half yellow, plaster-covered house, albeit with only about eight hundred square feet of floor space. Its large backyard was filled with fruit trees. Only six years old, the cottage boasted an electric stove, a small refrigerator, a twelve-by-fifteen-foot living room, a large master bedroom, and a modern bathroom with a huge tub.

The only serious problem was the absence of central heating. Marianne wrote in her diary that it was "a bit stark, but a perfect size for us. . . . Unfortunately, the house had not yet been heated." Two days later she wrote:

> [We] have been busy as bees and it feels as though we have been camping. By this I mean that it is so cold and wet in the house and the hot water is not running so that we have the "conveniences" of tent living.

Every room is also dirty and grimy from the soot of the oven. The walls in the halls, bath, and kitchen are actually covered with ice. An electric heater warmed the kitchen gradually and, of course, the ice on the walls became water—what a mess! Since the living room was the warmest room in the house we slept there for two nights, waking up every few hours to rebuild the fire.

Love conquers all, however, and four days after our arrival Marianne could write that "at last kitchen, bathroom, halls, living room and bedrooms [are] emptied of suitcases and cleaned. Until tonight it felt as though we were living in a barn, not a house." With the house in shape she was able to go shopping in an open market in downtown Graz on the *Hauptplatz* (main square). She wrote that "it's rather fun being a foreigner who is able to communicate, though brokenly, with the Grazers. Everyone was helpful and believe me so was my dictionary." Once a week Marianne treated herself to the luxury of a *Damen und Herren Friseur* (hair salon) where for one dollar, including a tip (about $7 in today's valuation), she could have her hair washed and set. Marianne was one of the few Fulbright wives who could speak decent German. For those who couldn't, life could be lonely or even miserable.

THE EVOLUTION OF MY DOCTORAL DISSERTATION

Dr. May had given me some excellent advice when I applied for a Fulbright-Hays Fellowship. In a letter from Vienna he wrote that "while you should try for a Fulbright Scholarship, there is a strong feeling in the [Fulbright] office here that awards are, by preference, granted to young scholars who have not yet had experience in Europe."[2] On another occasion he said that I could improve my chances by asking to work in Graz, instead of Vienna, the choice of most applicants. He suggested that I say that I wanted to research the history of Graz during the period of the Dual Monarchy, 1867–1918. I was not excited about doing a strictly local history, but I had no objection at all to living in Graz.

Researching a dissertation or book is sheer drudgery for a scholar with little interest in the subject; the results will likely be at best pedantic.[3] Doctoral dissertations in history must be on original topics that require the use of documentary sources. Almost always these requirements result in topics of very limited scope, which can be especially off-putting for anyone who enjoys history on a large format. On the other hand, one prominent scholar has noted that such original research gives a "responsible historian . . . a saving sense of how far removed he or she is from firm fact, and one becomes more aware of the level of invention inherent in the concept being used [in a class]."[4]

My former mentor at Nebraska, Robert Koehl, had encouraged me to do something on right-wing extremism in Styria between the wars, for which my master's thesis had already provided a good background. He also said I should not make any decision until I had familiarized myself with the historical controversies in Styria and had seen the relevant archives. Soon after I arrived in the Styrian capital I discovered that a long and detailed history of Graz covering the years 1867 to 1928 had already been written, so that let me off the municipal-history hook. Fortunately, I had no difficulty persuading the Fulbright Commission to accept a proposed new research topic with the deliberately bland title "A History of the Private Political Armies of Styria, 1918–1938."[5]

Professor Koehl also thought "the topic [the history of Graz] rather big and vague." "See whether you can do something with the attitude toward the role of the South Slavs in the province," he wrote. "I think you will find the roots of some of the later Nazi movements."[6] Andrew G. Whiteside, a professor at Queen's College in New York, had an even more specific idea. He suggested in March 1963, shortly after I had been awarded the fellowship, that I investigate the "Styrian origins of Nazism (or at least Austrian Nazism) and the peculiar strength and virulence of Nazism in Styria in the thirties."[7] By July I had modified my research still more to include the Styrian Heimatschutz.[8] As it evolved, I was able to include both the Heimatschutz and the Austrian Nazis into one project because the Heimatschutz, a right-wing paramilitary formation, was ultimately absorbed into the Austrian Nazi Party. In retrospect I wonder if I would have received a Fulbright if the commission in Vienna had suspected that

I intended to work on anything so politically incorrect and controversial as Austrian Nazism and right-wing extremism.

The political incorrectness of my topic was dramatically brought home to me early in my research. I had learned that there were trial documents at the Provincial Court of Justice involving two major figures in my research. One evening I went to the home of the man who controlled access to these documents, which had never before been made available to any historian, foreign or Austrian. After making some small talk, the man asked me my opinion of the Nazis. I was now on the spot. I could forfeit access to these crucial documents no matter what I said. The Nazis had called Graz the "Stadt der Volkserhebung" ("city of the people's uprising") because so many Grazers had demonstrated in favor of annexation by the Third Reich in the days preceding the infamous Anschluss in March 1938. If this man had been one of those sympathizers, I might offend him if I denounced the Nazis too unequivocally. On the other hand, if he had been a pronounced anti-Nazi he might have been equally indignant if I said anything that soft-pedaled Nazi outrages. After trying desperately for a few seconds to think of a diplomatic answer, I came up with a truly Delphic response: "Well," I said in German, "they weren't *all* bad." "That's right," the man blurted out. "But you can't say that!" How exactly to grapple with Austrian Nazism, and later Austrian anti-Semitism, in a way that would be seen by Austrians as fair and convincing was an issue I would have to resolve for much of my career.

In time I discovered that Austrians maintained political correctness by simply not mentioning the Nazi era. It was a "curtain of silence" drawn between the present and the past. I later wrote in *Hitler and the Forgotten Nazis* that "former party members are not eager to tell their children or grandchildren about their past activities or motivations for joining [the Austrian Nazi Party]. The younger generation, they fear, growing up in completely different and happier times, would never understand the anxieties, frustrations, and hopes that governed their actions four decades earlier."[9]

During my year in Graz I came to realize that Nazism could not be explained by pure individual wickedness, although I had not been inclined to accept so simplistic an explanation anyway. The issue was not why bad people do bad things, but why otherwise good people sometimes did things that turned out to be dumb, reckless, or even wicked. My experiences in Graz did reinforce, however, my determination to find the causes of the Nazi phenomenon beyond goodness and evil, black and white.

Nazism had been so widespread in Styria because it was a border province; in imperial times its southern regions had been predominantly Slovene before the province was partitioned at the Paris Peace Conference after World War I. Border provinces in both Austria and Germany had usually been the site of fierce struggles between competing nationalities and aroused ethnic consciousness on both sides.

Another reason for the "curtain of silence" that was still so prevalent in Austria in the 1960s was that the country was weary of political quarrels. During the interwar period it had been divided into three camps, or *Lager*. The largest party, the Social Democrats, ideologically and rhetorically clung to the Marxist idea of atheism, class warfare, and the inevitability of a proletarian revolution, even though in practice the party could act quite moderately. Nevertheless, the Socialists scared the wits out of non-Socialists. The Roman Catholics in the Christian Social Party were horrified by the secularism of the Socialists. The pan-Germans, who were scattered in a variety of parties but were nearly all eventually absorbed into the Austrian Nazi Party, rejected the Socialists' anticapitalism. Each group regarded their rivals not as honest-if-misguided opponents with whom they could reason but as mortal enemies who had to be eliminated by one means or another. The newspapers of the time, which were all organs of political parties, attacked their enemies with brutal vitriol and vicious sarcasm. (The same kind of extremism existed in the Jewish community, especially during the 1930s, when Zionists, anti-Zionists, and ultra-orthodox Jews all denounced each other.)[10] Although the verbal acrimony among Austrians had died down by the 1960s, they still remained divided into three camps. Anyone who changed camps was regarded as a traitor not only by his former political allies but even by his new party affiliates. By contrast, my books were credible with Austrian readers precisely because I was viewed as a neutral observer.

After a couple of weeks in Graz, our lives settled into a routine. Most of my research involved reading newspapers at the provincial library. Since its hours were very limited, 8:30–1:00 and 3:30–6:00, I would try arriving as early as possible, but household chores and a long tram ride usually prevented me from getting there before 9:45. It is indicative of the primitive research technology at the time that I had no means of photocopying and microfilming the hundreds if not thousands of newspaper pages I read. Fortunately, Marianne's German was good enough that she would come with me in the morning and literally hand-copy passages I marked in pencil. By so doing she saved me weeks, if not months, of tedious labor that enabled us to make exciting trips which otherwise would have been impossible.

I would usually get home around 6:30. Following dinner, about three times a week we would go to a movie, an opera, or a lecture at the Urania, a community activity center in central Graz. We loved the ornate opera house. Built in 1899 during Imperial Austria's final boom years, it was lavishly decorated and recently refurbished. Its white walls contrasted sharply with red carpeting and drapery.

The provincial library was open only in the morning on Saturday, so in the afternoon we often hiked up the Schlossberg—a big hill or a small mountain, depending on one's definition—in the center of town. The only thing left of the Schloss, a fort destroyed by Napoleon in 1809, was the city's iconic clock tower. The mountain had been used for bomb shelters during World War II, but when we were there it was honeycombed with tree- and flower-lined walkways that led to a restaurant at the top with magnificent vistas of the city and surrounding countryside. The only downside to our walks was the sight of victims of the war or years of strenuous manual labor: one-legged men, deformed children, and unusually large numbers of very short adults. Many old women were bent over from years of hard work.

On Sundays we would often hike in our own neighborhood with its many orchards and gardens, a favorite site for the Grazers themselves. Soon after our arrival we drove to the Burgenland to see the castles (*Burgen*) for which it was named. Its Hungarian heritage was readily apparent in the layout of the villages, where farmhouses were side by side facing the street. Geese were still used, as they had been since the Middle Ages, to keep the streets clean by scavenging. On another Sunday we drove as far south as the Yugoslav border, which we noted was not nearly as strongly fortified and guarded as the Hungarian border, an important indication of Yugoslavia's relative openness compared to the Soviet satellites.

Winter was also enlivened by the city's ball season (*Fasching*), which occurred during the weeks preceding Lent. My dancing had not improved since my Vienna days, but we enjoyed balls sponsored by the Technische Hochschule (Institute of Technology) and the Bauern (Peasants') Ball. The Technology Ball began with the entrance of the school's dignitaries and the dancing of a polonaise by selected couples: girls in white dresses and men in tuxedos and white gloves. We found the Bauern Ball more to our liking, however, because of the colorful native costumes, especially the dirndls worn by young women, including Marianne herself. (She still owns and occasionally wears that dirndl today.)

In mid-February Marianne got her first look at Vienna. She recorded in her diary that she could "never forget a moment of that glorious trip. Vienna is like no other European city that I've seen so far—huge, glamorous, exclusive shops, and opera, theater, and concerts at their best. . . . Bruce and I only drove around the city before picking up his Austrian friend, Helmut Sohmen. With him we walked to St. Stephen's Cathedral and St. Peter's church and then drove to Schönbrunn, the mid-eighteenth-century summer palace of the Habsburgs. Schönbrunn is the essence of beauty and splendor, and one is awed by the handwork and ornateness."

In the evening we saw a superb performance of Verdi's *La Traviata* at the Staatsoper, where we had to pay all of 32 cents (about $2.25 today) for excellent standing-room tickets. The following night we saw a play with Helmut and Walter Siegl. Afterward we all went to one of Vienna's wine cellars, where we sat on wooden benches while being serenaded by a small group of musicians. We could not resist the conclusion, confirmed by many later trips to Austria, that Austrians and other Europeans led more relaxed, more enjoyable, and even more healthful lives than do most Americans. Mark Twain reached the same conclusion during his first trip to Europe in 1867.[11]

One reason for our quick trip to Vienna was to make arrangements for our forthcoming three-week tour of southeastern Europe and Turkey. Although we were having a marvelous time in Graz, I was working much harder than I had at the Institute of European Studies in 1957–58, and Marianne was doubtless getting tired of housework and note taking. Neither of us had seen much sun since October. Winters in eastern Austria are not terribly cold and are relieved by a glittering and affordable night life. Nevertheless, the days are short at a latitude equal to Duluth, Minnesota; nightfall comes around 4:30 in January. By mid-March we were ready for sunshine, green vegetation, and new adventures.

Communist Yugoslavia, the first country we entered, provided little relief from winter, but it was interesting from a political and economic perspective. The first city we passed through was Maribor (Marburg in German) in what is now the independent state of Slovenia. Until 1918 it had been an almost purely German-speaking town and the second largest in Styria. Thanks to the Treaty of St. Germain, which the Allies imposed on Austria in 1919, it had been handed over to Yugoslavia much like the South Tyrol had been awarded to Italy. When we saw it in 1964, city blocks lined with old buildings were being torn down and replaced with modern roads at the expense of the city's former charm. People and shops displayed little of the prosperity that was so evident in Austria. As we headed further south, the Alps and the snow faded away behind us to be replaced by a landscape that could be described only as dreary.

To save time we bypassed Belgrade, which had contained little of historical interest even before it had been almost entirely destroyed by German bombers in 1941. Not stopping in the Yugoslav capital, however, almost had disastrous consequences. Our fuel gauge kept dropping alarmingly as we sped along the new *autoput*, a two-lane highway described as "super" because it was paved. We soon discovered that the government had not bothered to provide filling stations. Finally, in desperation, I saw a little Serbian farming village in the hills a mile or so off the highway. Assuming that the inhabitants had tractors, I reasoned that they must also have gas. I drove into the community and pointed to my fuel gauge to the first people we encountered. Fortunately, my sign language worked and we were soon on our way again.

Our first overnight stop was in Skopje in Yugoslavia's southernmost republic of Macedonia. The city had endured a terrible earthquake since I had last been there in 1958. Sunday strollers, many of them dressed in colorful native costumes, seemed oblivious to the destruction and poorly constructed one-room houses. The oldest part of town still displayed a very Turkish atmosphere, with both women and girls wearing traditional baggy pants.

By noon of our third day we were greeted by blue skies, snowcapped mountains, and green fields covered with fruit trees loaded with pink and white blossoms—a sight for sore and winter-weary eyes indeed. We noticed immediately that the small towns of Greece were far more prosperous than those of Yugoslavia. Houses were usually painted white, but some were pink, blue, yellow, or green. By that evening we were surrounded by the turbulence of Athens, a city of 2 million (now about 3 million). However, Athens had declined to virtual insignificance during the Middle Ages, so we limited our sightseeing mostly to the Acropolis—five blocks away from our two-dollar-a-night hotel (the equivalent of $12 today)—the adjoining Agora or marketplace, and the National (archaeological) Museum.

Although Athens was interesting, we were not sorry to leave for the serenity and beauty of the Peloponnesus Peninsula, where we explored the ancient ruins of Corinth; Mycenae, the center of Minoan civilization and site of its 3,500-year-old Lion's Gate; and Epidaurus. At the latter site, with its magnificent theater where ancient Greek plays were still performed in the summer, we were treated to an acoustics exhibition by a local photographer who proved that we could hear him whisper, rub his hands together, or strike a match from two hundred feet away on the top row of the twenty-thousand-seat edifice. Adding to the beauty of the architecture were daisies, bluebells, and buttercups. The drive through central and northeastern Greece was much less exciting than the Peloponnesus; we regretted every time we left the main highway because the side roads of Greece were still primitive. However, we did encounter a couple of Gypsy caravans along the way and noticed that people were staring at our clothes and even our car because they were not accustomed to seeing Western tourists.

Our first stop in Turkey was Bursa. Lying on the Asian side of the Sea of Marmara, this city of two hundred thousand had been the capital of the Ottoman Empire before Constantinople was conquered by the Turks in 1453. It had some interesting mausoleums, mosques, and fountains, but perhaps its most interesting aspect was Turkey's attempt to modernize and catch up with the West. However, the modernization was confined mostly to one wide street. Along the cobblestoned side streets life continued much as it had for centuries. I enjoyed getting a straight-edge shave for ten cents and a shoe shine for five cents.

Bursa's main square featured a statue of Turkey's equivalent of George Washington, Kemal Pasha Atatürk. Actually, he was far more revolutionary than Washington. In addition to overthrowing the Ottoman Empire and establishing a republic, Atatürk replaced Arabic script with the Latin alphabet, secularized the state, and gave women legal equality in voting, divorce, custody, inheritance, and education. Women's equality seemed more on paper than in reality in 1964, because rarely did we see them on the streets. Women did much of their shopping by dropping a basket from upper-story windows down to passing vendors on the street.

In Istanbul we saw the usual sights, starting with the old sultan's palace built between the fifteenth and nineteenth centuries. Later we saw the Hagia Sophia, the sixth-century Byzantine church and architectural masterpiece that influenced not only all later Byzantine churches but Moslem mosques as well, including the nearby Blue Mosque, the most beautiful of the five hundred mosques in the city at that time. Marianne probably enjoyed the covered market the most, because she could put her excellent bargaining skills to work to buy several decorative copper pots we still display today. Much less impressive were the dilapidated apartment houses and the torn and dirty clothes worn by its inhabitants, probably in part due to the country's population explosion and the rapid migration of peasants into the big cities. Children seemed to be everywhere.

Whereas capitalist Greece appeared to be much more prosperous than Communist Yugoslavia, the opposite was true when we crossed the border from Turkey into Bulgaria. The collectivized farms at least appeared to be neat and well organized (in contrast to the dysfunctional farms of the Soviet Union), a fact that probably had more to do with Bulgarians' long having had the reputation of being the "Prussians of the Balkans" than it did with the organization of the farms. Bulgarian shops were well stocked, but the quality and style of the goods were poor. We discovered that Sofia, the capital, had grown from 200,000 to 800,000 since 1945. Its spacious streets were almost devoid of cars, a pleasant but revealing contrast to the nightmarish traffic of both Athens and Istanbul. We enjoyed attending a performance of an operetta that included women wearing peasant costumes. However, in contrast to both Graz and Vienna, the very ordinary looking auditorium was only about one-third full.

Bucharest, our next stop, was a relatively modern city and far better looking than those we had seen in Yugoslavia. Like Sofia, it lacked the slums of Istanbul. The newer parts of the Romanian capital were completely planned with twelve-story apartment houses surrounded by their own shops, elementary schools, and parks. They weren't ugly, but they were depressingly uniform. All families in these buildings, regardless of their size or incomes, had to live in three-room apartments. Our private guide bragged about the advantages of the new housing but also confessed that he personally would prefer a house of his own. Housing consumed only 5 percent of a Romanian's income, but food accounted for no less than 50 percent. We were fortunate to be able to travel in Romania at all, because it had only recently been opened to Western tourists. However, Romanians could not travel abroad because of the non-convertibility of their currency, or so we were told. We also noticed that there were no non-Communist Western newspapers and magazines available in bookstores or in our hotel.

Crossing the old border of Romania into Transylvania—annexed from Hungary after World War I—was like entering not just a different country but a whole new region of Europe. As the boundary between Romania and Austria-Hungary, it was also the border between central and eastern Europe. We were now back in what had been, until 1918, the multi-ethnic Habsburg Monarchy. One village might be Romanian-speaking; the next six would be Hungarian speaking and looked exactly like the villages of Burgenland. When we reached Braşov (Kronstadt in German), the medieval Gothic architecture of the city hall and cathedral was purely German, and German could still be heard on the streets and seen in one newspaper. Those buildings constructed during the Dual Monarchy looked exactly like those of Graz.

Budapest, our last major stop, seemed almost dead. The site of fierce fighting between the Germans and Russians in the winter of 1944–45, Budapest still revealed many of its buildings to be little more than bombed-out shells; others were pockmarked with shrapnel and bullet holes. Except for some medieval buildings on the Buda side of the Danube, the city appeared to have been born in the nineteenth century when Buda and Pest were united as one great metropolis and the city became the capital of the Hungarian half of the Austro-Hungarian Dual Monarchy. It then suffered a near death when the Habsburg Monarchy collapsed at the end of World War I in 1918 and again at the end of World War II.

We were lucky to be in the Hungarian capital at the very time when the Soviet leader, Nikita Khrushchev, was in town to meet with his Hungarian counterpart and other Communist leaders. The city was bedecked for the occasion with Russian and Hungarian flags and thousands of red tulips. Because attendance at the parade was by written invitation only, we caught only a glimpse of Khrushchev as he sped by us in a car going at least forty miles an hour. His reception was infinitely less enthusiastic than the one the ill-fated Archduke Franz Ferdinand received in Sarajevo in 1914. I couldn't help wondering whether if Franz Ferdinand's car had traveled equally fast, instead of coming to a full stop a few feet away from the archduke's assassin, the whole history of the twentieth century would have been different.

On the positive side, we found the Hungarians to be friendly, the restaurants to have long and varied menus, and the food to be excellent. A four-course meal cost a dollar. A performance of Puccini's *Madame Butterfly* at the opera house was outstanding; every seat was filled and the audience was tastefully dressed, reflecting the traditions of the Habsburg Monarchy. Another welcome sight was the *New York Times* for sale in our hotel, the first time we had seen a Western newspaper in a satellite country.

By April 5 we were back in Austria. Marianne noted in her diary that we were "happy to be home! Graz never looked better! One certainly appreciates its setting, its wonderful green mountainsides after being away. How prosperous Austria looks after [our] having traveled in Eastern Europe!" The trip had wonderful benefits for us both personally and professionally. While we were in Greece, Marianne wrote in her diary that "this has truly been another honeymoon. Bruce and I are having the best time of our lives and grow closer and more in love each day. It's marvelous to share so many memorable experiences and sights." For my part, I was able to store away a kaleidoscope of impressions and memories related to Austria-Hungary and its neighbors that I was later able to put to good use in *The Habsburg Legacy, 1867–1939*.

FAMILY VISITS AND RESEARCH TRIPS

In early May my parents visited us for a week filled with exploring Graz and its environs, Vienna, the romantic Wachau region of the Danube River, and Salzburg. Soon after their departure I received permission to use two important federal archives in Germany: the Political Archive of the German Foreign Office in Bonn, the capital of West Germany, and the Federal Archives in Koblenz, further down the Rhine River. Both proved very useful. During our three days in the West German capital we noticed how much more prosperous it was than Vienna or Graz, in part because it was not bombed during the war. The city was filled with flower beds and fountains, the latter being illuminated at night. Visiting Beethoven's birthplace was, of course, a must.

During my last few weeks in Styria I devoted considerable time to interviewing some survivors of the political wars of the 1930s, including Karl Maria Stepan, the governor of Styria prior to the Anschluss and the leader of the Fatherland Front, the only legal party in Austria between 1934 and 1938. The person I was most eager to meet, however, was Dr. Walter Pfrimer, the former leader of the Styrian Heimatschutz and for a brief time also the federal leader of the Austrian Heimwehr. Pfrimer gained notoriety for the infamous Pfrimer Putsch of 1931 in which he attempted to overthrow the Austrian government in much the same manner as Hitler's ill-fated "Beer Hall Putsch" in Munich in 1923. Given the strong anti-Semitic ideology of the Heimatschutz, it is ironic that he lived in Judenburg, which in English means "Jews' town."

The circumstances of the interview turned out to be more interesting than the information I obtained, most of which I already knew. He introduced himself quite accurately as "one of the last monuments of this [interwar] age." His home resembled a huge hunting lodge and was filled with scores of antlers mounted on the walls. He seemed eager to make a good impression during our interview, which must have lasted close to two hours. At the end he invited Marianne and me to see his flower garden and gallantly cut several roses for Marianne. I was probably the last person to interview him, as he died just a year later.

Marianne's mother came for a visit in June, shortly before we left Graz for good. Once again the Moosbruggers proved to be gracious hosts, and we had a very pleasant evening of conversation, laughter, and food. My mother-in-law had quite a time keeping her languages straight. She tried her best to speak the cultivated Hochdeutsch she had learned many years earlier in school. However, she couldn't help mixing in both English and her Swabian dialect. By the end of the evening she was exhausted.

Our last few days in Austria were spent in Vienna. Marianne noted in her diary that the visit was

> more pleasure than business. We spend about five hours a day in libraries, perhaps six. Then Vienna is ours—Frau Merlingen [the owner of our bed-and-breakfast] serves a nice breakfast, continental of course, in our room. We break at the library for a long lunch and then read the paper. Evenings, after eating at the *Stadt Brunn*, we take walks, go to the opera or a concert. Dinner is with American and/or Austrian friends [when we engage] in two hours of wonderful conversation and laughter. We are still defending Graz. . . . Married almost six months. Bruce and I are happier than ever!

During our last few weeks in Europe we traveled north into Czechoslovakia, stopping to see the Nazi concentration camp at Mauthausen near Linz along the way. Czechoslovakia still looked decrepit, but was a little more attractive with its early summer vegetation than it had been in the fall of

1957 when I last saw it. However, Marianne described the historic city and formerly prosperous and tidy Sudeten German town of Cesky Krumlov (Krumau in German) as "depressing." The town, now a UNESCO World Heritage Site, boasted handsome architecture "but was run down to say the least. [It] consisted of rows of houses whose sides were black with soot and pealing from age. Neglect characterized every corner. The streets were full of debris and rubble and reeked like a latrine. Gypsy boys . . . begged for chewing gum and chocolate." On the other hand, we did enjoy Prague with all of its wonderful spires and romantic fourteenth-century Charles Bridge. With our strong dollar we were able to eat like kings: a lobster meal with wine cost a dollar.

Our glorious seven-month honeymoon concluded with ten days of sightseeing in France, including Alsace, the romantic châteaux district of the Loire Valley, and Paris. The latter was my concession to Marianne, because, having already seen Paris twice, I would have preferred Normandy. Marianne was enchanted by all the beautiful churches and palaces and by the many art museums. Like most tourists, however, we were worn out by the enormous amount of walking we had to do.

We left France on July 23 on the SS *United States*, a luxury liner built in 1952 to capture the transatlantic speed record. It was Marianne's first and only crossing of the Atlantic by ship and my sixth and last. Marianne spoke for both of us when she summarized our five-day voyage in her diary by saying that "the excitement is rapidly decreasing [and] I have the realization that our wonderful year in Europe is over. Europe has meant so much—first the beginning of a wonderful marriage; second a new world of knowledge and experience. This ship is already America—the people, food etc., and I miss Europe. Now to a 'normal' life with work and much less play. However, we have wonderful memories and the good possibility of returning and I shall always be grateful that I had the chance to spend seven months abroad."

Our seven months of bliss were over. For me it was now time to apply my new knowledge of European history to preparing lectures and writing my dissertation. For Marianne it was time to begin full-time teaching.

CHAPTER 10

Three Jobs in Three Years

"Well, you're hired."

ENTERING THE JOB MARKET

When Marianne and I returned to the United States in July 1964 we both had jobs waiting for us. I had been hired as an instructor at the College of Wooster, in Wooster, Ohio, and Marianne had landed a job teaching third graders at Melrose Elementary. We were both entering our professions at an ideal time. Most college freshmen had been born in 1946 at the start of the postwar baby boom. Third graders had been born in 1956 when the boom was at its height. Meanwhile, universities were struggling to produce enough PhDs and education majors to keep up with the demand. Whereas only 7,695 PhDs were granted in history in the United States between 1873 and 1960, 5,884 were issued during the 1960s alone.[1] College enrollments increased from 3.2 million in 1959 to nearly 8.5 million a decade later; the percentage of eighteen-to-twenty-one-year-olds enrolled in a college rose from 33.2 to 48.[2] With the possible exception of the early 1920s, when specialists in European history were in great demand, the job market for PhDs in history had never been as favorable as it was in the 1960s.[3]

After our brief honeymoon in Toronto, and before departing for Europe, Marianne and I headed to Philadelphia for the annual meeting of the

American Historical Association (AHA). Commonly known as the "slave market," these meetings were where most job interviews, especially for specialists in European history, took place. In those days the AHA and the Organization of American Historians—the two largest organizations for historians in the country—had not yet developed procedures and standards for conducting searches, and the federal government had not established any mandatory nondiscrimination rules.[4] In short, no formal regulations regarding hiring or even public notification of available positions yet existed. In some cases family influence could be decisive in landing a job at a prestigious university.[5] More common, however, was the "old boy" system. A department having an opening contacted a "big name" in the field to ask if *he* (emphasis intentional) had a top student looking for a job. Applicants were interviewed primarily at the AHA convention, if they were interviewed at all.[6] Indeed, some offers were made and accepted in the course of a single telephone conversation.[7] Nowadays it is more common for history departments to use the AHA meeting merely to screen their more promising candidates. The best prospects (usually three) are then invited for a more thorough on-campus interview, where each candidate makes a presentation and is interviewed by the entire department and often by the dean of the college.

The job market was so good for historians in December 1963 that I had one interview after another, each lasting about an hour, for three full days, at least fifteen in all. Today a candidate would be lucky to get three or four interviews at a convention. I brought Marianne with me to all my interviews to take notes. She was just as interested in our move as I and had her own questions about school systems. Even so, by the end of each day I was exhausted.

One of my interviews graphically illustrates the differences between interviewing then and now. The interview was with two members of the history department of the University of Western Ontario in London. Nowadays, Canadian universities are not even permitted by federal law to interview foreigners unless there are no Canadians with suitable credentials. But in 1963, after telling us about the cultural advantages of London and the excellence of its public schools, one of the interviewers asked if I was a Mormon.

He seemed genuinely surprised and disappointed by my negative reply, saying that he "thought he could always tell one." American (and Canadian) laws now make such personal questions strictly illegal.

Another interesting aspect of that first AHA meeting I attended that year was the smoke. Every other chair, in each room where a session was being held, was supplied with an ashtray. By the end of the presentations the rooms were so filled with smoke that the speakers were shrouded in haze. It was still an age when smoking was the norm, and nonsmokers were seen as rather prudish, if not downright antisocial. How times have changed. It has been decades since I have seen an ashtray at a history conference.

It was a reflection of the times and not my job-interviewing skills or academic credentials that my interviews in Philadelphia produced three firm job offers. Here I was, just twenty-six years old, having barely begun my doctoral research, having never taught a course, and having no publications, yet getting job offers from three schools. Today few if any doctoral candidates with such a modest résumé would even bother beginning a job search at a four-year college or university. Indeed, they are lucky to land a tenure-earning job before turning thirty.

Another drastic change in the interviewing procedure is the venue. In 1963, departmental representatives, almost always men, conducted interviews in their hotel room, or occasionally in a suite. Some women felt intimidated by being interviewed by two or three men in what amounted to a bedroom. When in succeeding years their complaints grew louder, the AHA decided to hold interviews in massive halls or ballrooms where each group of interviewers had their own little cubicle surrounded by black curtains. The new venue, though perhaps more gender neutral and less intimidating, had all the charm and comfort of a cattle auction.

I should add that the hiring process for academics has become steadily more elaborate over the last four decades in the United States. For example, at the University of Central Florida, where I was to spend the majority of my career, the history department's hiring procedures since 2004 are in a four-and-a-half page, single-spaced document outlining not only such things as the composition of the search committee but also the types of questions that may and may not be asked of candidates. The system, in large part

1. Four generations of Pauley men in 1909. *Left to right*: Great-grandfather Conrad, born in 1862; Grandfather Ludwig Heinrich, born in 1886; Great-great-grandfather Heinrich, born in 1834; and my father, Carroll Righter.

2. My father's female ancestors with my father on his first birthday in 1909: *Left to right*: Great-great-grandmother Lena Willa, born about 1829; Grandmother Lena Albertina Righter Pauley, born in 1888; and Great-grandmother Lena Righter, born in 1864.

3. My mother's parents about the time of their wedding in 1902: Fred Hulsebus, born in 1879, and Dora Kruger Hermina Hulsebus, born in 1882.

4. My father and Grandfather Pauley on a fishing trip to Yellowstone in 1920. Note my grandfather's suit, tie, and hat and the car's two spare tires. This trip probably marked the beginning of my father's lifelong *Wanderlust*.

5. My father, a lieutenant in the U.S. Navy, my sister, Patricia, and I next to our tropical orchard in Curaçao in the Dutch West Indies in the fall of 1945.

6. Werner ("Brandy") Brandenberger, my American Field Service Swiss friend during my junior year at Lincoln High School. On the back side of the picture he wrote: "To my best and most loyal friend, Bruce Pauley."

7. My parents on top of Mount Rigi near Vitznau, Switzerland, in 1954. Note my father's sport coat and tie.

8. Some of my junior-year-abroad friends at the Institute of European Studies at the University of Vienna, 1957–58. *Left to right*: Bill Maroney, Fran Wanat, Bill Storch, Patrick "Pat" Witte (with whom I hitchhiked through the British Isles in July 1958), and myself.

9. (*Above*) Grinnell College friends in 1959. *Left to right*: David DeLong, Bill Wycoff, myself, and John Price. Our dormitory, Smith Hall, is in the background. John Price later served as special assistant to President Richard Nixon, and still later was the president and CEO of a bank in Pittsburgh.

10. (*Above right*) Two graduate school friends at the University of Rochester, James ("Jim") Bachman (*left*) and Gilbert ("Gil") McArthur (*middle*). Jim became a professor of American history at Tarleton State College in Texas, and Gil became a professor of Russian history at the College of William and Mary in Williamsburg, Virginia. I am on the right.

11. (*Bottom right*) Climbing Mount Schökl with my Austrian "family" near Graz, Austria, fall of 1963. To my right is Peter Moosbrugger, whose father was killed in the war. An engineering student, he later played a leading role in the building of the Rhine-Main-Danube Canal connecting the North Sea to the Black Sea. Next to him is Reingard Moosbrugger (now Vollnhals), who studied and languages and law and worked for the Langenscheidt publishing company. Next to her is the *Dienstmädchen*, Ilse. Standing are the father, Dr. Herbert Moosbrugger, an engineer, and his son, Helfried, who later became a professor of psychology and a dean at the Goethe University in Frankfurt am Mein.

12. My bride, Marianne, and my junior-year-abroad Viennese roommate, Walter Siegl, at the Prater amusement park in Vienna, late spring of 1964. The famous *Riesenrad* in the background, at the time of its construction in 1897, was the largest in the world. Walter later became the Austrian ambassador to Kenya, Yugoslavia, and Russia. At the end of his career he was the political director general in the Austrian Ministry of Foreign Affairs, giving him the greatest influence in policy making. In 1964 he was serving a mandatory year in the Austrian Army.

13. Our cottage and Volkswagen Beetle in Graz, 1964. Both the house and bushes had doubled in size when we saw them in 2013.

14. Our sons Glenn, three, and Mark, five, on the Island of Elba, 1972.

15. My parents, my sister, and I at my parents' fortieth wedding anniversary, Lincoln, 1973.

16. I am addressing a crowd as chairman of the Faculty Senate at Florida Technological University (soon to be renamed the University of Central Florida) during the inauguration of President H. Trevor Colbourn, 1978.

17. My longtime friend Helmut Sohmen and I enjoying a relaxing conversation in London, 1980. Helmut, educated in both Austria and the United States, joined the World Wide Shipping Group in 1970 and became its chairman in 1986. He has held numerous public offices around the world, including chairman of the Pacific Basin Economic Council. He has also served for many years as an economic adviser to the chancellor of Austria.

18. Our family in 1986. Mark (*left*), nineteen, was a sophomore at the University of Florida in Gainesville. Glenn, seventeen, was a senior at Oviedo High School. Marianne was in her second year of teaching homebound and hospitalized students in Seminole County, Florida.

19. Exploring the world. Marianne and I at the Taj Mahal, Agra, India, December 2009.

20. Dr. Christian Prosl, Austrian ambassador to the United States, and myself just prior to the awarding of Austria's highest prize for scholarship, the Ehrenkreuz erste Klasse für Wissenschaft und Kunst. Orlando, 2010.

21. The youngest Pauleys, Cheyenne, Wyoming, 2011. *First row*: William ("Will") Frederick and his sister, Reina Victoria, both children of Glenn, who is behind his daughter. *Second row*: Benjamin ("Ben") Isaac, Mark's son; Maria, Mark's wife; Mark; Glenn; Lucy, Glenn's wife; and Alena Marie, Mark's daughter.

required by federal regulations, is certainly fairer and more inclusive than in the old-boy days, but it does not guarantee positive outcomes.

Anyway, by February 1964, when Marianne and I were well settled in Graz, job offers arrived in the mail from four very different schools. One of them, Keuka College in New York, had not even interviewed me but was willing to use the old-boy approach of accepting the opinion of Professor May. The most lucrative proposal of the other three schools was for an assistant professorship paying the enormous (for then) salary of $7,250 (or around $50,000 in constant dollars) for nine months at Lock Haven State College in central Pennsylvania. This was the highest salary, I was assured, they could pay for someone in my position.[8] There were several problems with this offer, however. The position was for teaching early European history, which was far from either my strengths or my interests. The town of Lock Haven had a population of just twelve thousand and was in an extremely rural part of Pennsylvania, five hours from Philadelphia and with no sizable towns nearby. With a heavy teaching load and a tiny library of eighty-five thousand volumes, it would have been difficult if not impossible to publish my way into a better job. At the time and in retrospect the job looked like a dead end.

Considerably more tempting was an offer of an instructorship at Ohio State University. The position offered little or no possibility for earning tenure, and it paid just $5,800 a year. On the other hand, I would be teaching only multiple sections of Western Civ and would have access to an excellent library. On the negative side, the campus was next to a poor and potentially dangerous part of Columbus. The prospect of teaching at a giant university with thirty-eight thousand students was also unappealing. Although Ohio State would have been easier to use as a springboard to another job than Lock Haven, I have not agonized about turning that offer down.

THE COLLEGE OF WOOSTER

Much more attractive was the third firm offer I received, from the College of Wooster, also in Ohio. The job was tenure earning and paid $6,300 per year (or $44,000 today). The town of Wooster had 17,500 residents, considerably larger than Lock Haven and much better located, or so I thought. Being just fifty-five miles south of Cleveland, Marianne and I could frequently commute to soak up the strains of its famous symphony orchestra, or so I imagined. The college had fourteen hundred students, only slightly more than Grinnell, and had a highly selective admission's policy. History majors comprised 20 percent of the students, and the school had a generous sabbatical program. Indeed, Wooster seemed like the fulfillment of my dream of returning to a small liberal arts college similar to Grinnell. So, with Dr. May's approval, I gladly accepted the offer.

Wooster did have its advantages. The campus was attractive, the history department had some outstanding senior members as well as promising junior faculty, and the students were as good as advertised. We found a reasonably priced unfurnished apartment on the second story of a gift shop in a Victorian-era house within walking distance of the campus. Rochester was roughly five hours away by car. We were also delighted to discover that the town was in the middle of Amish country, so we got to see a lot of the Amish wearing their mid-nineteenth-century outfits and riding around in horse-drawn buggies.

Despite the unquestioned advantages of Wooster, I was soon disillusioned. Some of the letdown was inevitable. There was, first of all, the basic problem of moving from a beautiful Alpine city with a flourishing cultural life to a small town with not so much as a good restaurant, let alone a performing arts center. We soon discovered that there was no public transportation of any kind between Wooster and Cleveland, and in any event season tickets for the Cleveland Symphony Orchestra were expensive and sold out long in advance. Cleveland did have a good art museum, but the drive to Cleveland was far from scenic and took us through the middle of a slum. The college had its own golf course, but I had almost no free time to play. The weather turned out to be much like Rochester's: hot and humid in the summer and cold and damp in the winter, although it received a good deal less snow than Marianne's hometown.

Our apartment had its own problems, the most basic of which was its need to be furnished. Most of what we bought had to be secondhand, and the rest we built ourselves. We created bookshelves the old-fashioned way out of bricks and one-by-twelve raw lumber, which we varnished and shellacked. The shelves, minus the bricks, followed us around the country for several years. We bought a little old six-drawer cabinet—the only item from our Wooster days that we still own today—and some used bedroom furniture. Only a couch and chair were new. Marianne did a wonderful job decorating the apartment with mementos we brought back from Europe. None of this could overcome the fact, however, that guests could reach the bathroom only by walking through our only bedroom. Not surprisingly, the apartment house was torn down soon after we moved.

I enjoyed my first attempt at full-time teaching, although I soon discovered that I was nearly overwhelmed by the workload. My first class was at 7:45, well before the sun was up and well before my students were fully awake. I distinctly remember running out of material before the end of the class period the first time or two I delivered lectures in my Western Civ class. I had no choice but to simply dismiss the puzzled students. Only a few years later I had the opposite problem: how to condense all the information I had in my head or in my notes into a fifty-minute lecture.

I ran into a near revolt from my nine junior and senior history majors that were in my required seminar called Independent Studies. They objected to my proposal that each of their papers be critiqued by a class member in addition to me. After some fast talking I managed to convince them that this would not be an exercise in mutual annihilation. I also taught a required course for freshmen called Liberal Studies, which amounted to a "great books" course. I remember only that it required a good deal of grading.

Meanwhile, I was getting absolutely nothing done on my dissertation. Worse, I could barely envision the time when it would be finished. I had passed up an offer of a year-long extension of my Fulbright for financial reasons. With my twelve-hour teaching load at Wooster I would have at best only the summers to write. I estimated that it would take at least three or four frustrating years before I could submit my dissertation to my graduate committee; this would be the very "deadening process" that Professor Wall at Grinnell had warned me about as I was entering graduate school. Having completed my research, I was champing at the bit to start writing. In part my eagerness resulted from a letter I had received from Dr. May while I was still in Graz. "The reports on your investigations make really exciting reading," he wrote, "and I am delighted that you are uncovering so much material, little, if at all, examined by an historical scholar before."[9]

Marianne was also none too pleased with her situation. She found her third-grade teaching job to be even more exhausting than mine and worsened by recurring bouts of asthma, which at least twice landed her in a nearby hospital. We both thought that we would be better off in Colorado, where Grandmother Hulsebus had found some relief from asthma.

What I did next was so audacious that it astonishes me even now. Sometime in early November I informed my department chair, Aileen Dunham, that I was resigning because of Marianne's health, which, of course, was only partly true. My intent was for us to move to Denver—where Marianne again was able to land a job sight unseen—and I would complete my dissertation while she supported us both. Nowadays, if a history professor gave up a tenure-earning position with no other job in hand, his or her sanity would be seriously questioned. But again, it was a sign of the marvelous times in academe that such a move could be reasonably contemplated. The really good jobs went to those people who had a PhD in hand, not to those who were merely working on their degree.

MY RETURN TO THE UNIVERSITY OF NEBRASKA

Our plans to move to Denver suddenly changed on May 6. Out of the blue I received a phone call from James C. Olson, the chairman of the history department at the University of Nebraska, asking if I would be interested in a one-year appointment as an instructor.[10] There was no chance that this would become a tenure-earning position, since the department already had a specialist in central European history, and in any event it had a policy against hiring its own graduates. Nevertheless, the offer had many advantages. My teaching load would decline from twelve hours a week to nine, while my salary would rise from $6,300 to $7,000. I would teach only the History of Western Civilization, and although my classes would be large, around 120 students in each one, I would have a teaching assistant to conduct discussion sections and grade the majority of the examination. Professor Olson also assured me that "with the schedule we propose you should be able to devote considerable time to the completion of your dissertation which we know you are concerned about."[11]

Although I was delighted to get the job offer and eagerly accepted it, I was a bit mystified about how I had been chosen for the position in the first place. My best guess is that pre-registration for the fall semester far exceeded expectations. The university's enrollment, which had been 8,700 when I was a graduate student there in 1960, was up to 13,000 in 1964, and would reach 19,000 in 1968.[12] As a consequence, the history department evidently found itself shorthanded. It is also possible that Professor Olson encountered my parents at some social occasion and discovered that I would be unemployed in the fall.

Physically, the campus hadn't changed much since I received my master's degree four years earlier. Thankfully, the two parking lots between Burnett Hall and Love Library were now paved. But campus beautification didn't begin until 1966, and the merger with the University of Omaha occurred only in 1968.[13] However, the history department had grown, and its membership was beginning to stabilize. I shared an office with Ed Homze, who was to remain with the department until his retirement at the turn of the new century, during which time he wrote several books on Nazi Germany that became standard works. James Rawley, an Abraham Lincoln scholar, was also a newcomer to the department and spent the remainder of his long and distinguished career at the university.

I quickly discovered that being an instructor, even though I was at the very bottom of the faculty totem pole, was infinitely more pleasant than being a graduate student. Unlike some Ivy League schools and state universities, the history faculty at Nebraska was not hierarchical, so Marianne and I felt welcome at social functions.[14] Far from being bothered by the large size of my classes, I seemed to thrive on them, and my strong voice probably helped keep my students' attention. Discussions are difficult when a class has much more than forty or fifty students. Moreover, the history background of most college freshmen at a public university (and no doubt at many private ones as well) is so weak that they don't have enough knowledge to carry on an intelligent dialogue about historical controversies. (This generalization does not apply, of course, to advanced undergraduate history courses, and most definitely not to graduate-level courses.) I was also fortunate in having an excellent graduate assistant, an army veteran who did a first-rate job of grading exams. I did have to spend several weeks preparing new lectures on ancient Greek and Rome, subjects not covered in Wooster's survey of Western civilization. Many of my other lectures also needed to be upgraded, as lectures given for only the second time almost always do. These were not enormous tasks, however, and by the middle of the fall semester I was able to get back to work on my dissertation. Nor did I resent teaching an introductory survey course like Western Civ, which I did for nearly thirty years. I felt that a course with such a broad scope kept me from becoming too narrow in my interests and provided an excellent reason to visit and photograph historical sites all over Europe and the eastern Mediterranean.

If the appearance of the campus had changed only modestly, the same could not be said of the football team. In 1961, a year after I obtained my master's, the school had hired Bob Devaney as its new coach. (At first there was some confusion about how to pronounce his last name until someone came up with the admonition: "Get off your fanny and support Bob Devaney.") Devaney had established an outstanding record at the University of Wyoming before coming to Lincoln. In his first year the Huskers won nine games and lost only two compared to the three games they had won the year before. The year I was there the team went undefeated during the regular season, losing only to Alabama in the Orange Bowl, 39–28. All this gridiron success resulted in Memorial Stadium's being enlarged twice between 1963 and 1965 from 38,000 seats to 54,000.

My year in Lincoln proved pleasant in most other respects as well. Marianne had little difficulty getting a teaching job, this time at Eastridge Elementary School teaching fourth graders. We were able to find a nice bilevel apartment at Twenty-Fifth and A Streets just across the street from my grandmother, who had moved out of her house on B Street in 1959. The apartment was far nicer than the one we had in Wooster. The duplex in which it was located had probably been built in the 1950s and was well maintained. We had a large bedroom for ourselves and a second one I could use as a study. I think my grandmother enjoyed having us nearby, and we certainly enjoyed her cinnamon rolls, which had regularly won prizes at the Nebraska State Fair. My only regret is that I did not quiz her at length about the "olden days," especially with regard to family history. My parents, of course, were overjoyed to have us in town. The only downside to the year was that Marianne's health continued to be problematic, and she wound up in the hospital suffering from asthma attacks on more than one occasion.

SEARCHING FOR A JOB—AGAIN

Because my job was temporary, I couldn't get too comfortable in Lincoln. For the third straight year I went job hunting, this time at the AHA meeting in San Francisco. The location of the convention was itself historical. Since the association's founding in the late nineteenth century, its annual meetings had always held in the East—Boston, New York, Philadelphia, and Washington—except for an occasional foray into the "West," namely, Chicago. This venue was not particularly surprising, as most of the country's best universities were indeed in the East, and traveling for several days by train to attend a convention was simply impractical. Jet planes, of course, changed all that.

The two interviews I remember were with Colorado Women's College in Denver and Texas Western University in El Paso, soon thereafter renamed the University of Texas at El Paso. A few weeks later I was invited to Denver for an interview. The campus, on the east side of Denver, was small but attractive. I thought the interview itself went extremely well and returned to Lincoln convinced that the job was "in the bag." A few days later I was stunned to discover that my confidence had been unjustified. The irony is that my rejection was a blessing in disguise. After several years of declining enrollments, Colorado Women's College went bankrupt and closed its doors in 1982.

The interview with Texas Western produced more positive results. I was made a firm offer by phone without being asked to go to El Paso for an on-campus interview. I was reluctant to move to a school without first seeing its campus, meeting the history faculty, and especially seeing the town. Somehow I learned that although the school's salaries for assistant professors were good but that those for full professors were not. After some soul searching I decided to turn the offer down. Once again, I can't believe my brashness. I had rejected a firm offer for a tenure-earning job without having another offer in my back pocket. Although my gamble to resign from Wooster had paid off, I'm still not sure I did the right thing in declining the El Paso job.

It wasn't long, however, before another job opportunity came along. One day in March my former thesis co-adviser, Albin Anderson, told me that he had just met the chair the history department at the University of Wyoming at the annual meeting of the Missouri Valley History Conference in Omaha and learned that Wyoming was looking for a specialist in German history. He recommended that I look into it.

The next day I met with the history chair, Professor T. A. Larson. A tall, dignified man with a white mustache, Larson, who was born on a farm in eastern Nebraska in 1910, was best known at the time for his *History of Wyoming*. He and I had a nice long chat about my teaching experience, my dissertation, what courses I might teach, the salary range, and various benefits (which were very good). After about an hour he suddenly announced, "Well, you're hired." I was astonished. I had expected, at most, an invitation for an on-campus interview. I was a little disappointed not to have the opportunity to meet the other members of the department, but by now my one-year contract was winding down and I was in no position to argue.

LARAMIE AND THE UNIVERSITY OF WYOMING

Besides, in contrast to the El Paso offer, I had at least seen the Laramie campus. Marianne and I had spent the previous summer in Boulder while I was busy writing the first four chapters of my dissertation. Just as my father had never missed an opportunity to look over a lumberyard or hardware store when he was on a vacation, I was always interested in exploring college campuses. So on our way to Boulder we made a detour to Laramie to look at the university. When we were there in June, Laramie was having one of its spectacular summer days. It was about seventy degrees, and the sky was a luminous blue. The campus was filled with raised flower beds, and the harmonious architecture featured native stone in soft shades of pink and beige. I learned that Wyoming was a land-grant university (like Nebraska) with seven thousand students—a nice medium size in my opinion. I concluded that Laramie, being between two mountain ranges and just a day's drive from Lincoln, would be a great place to teach. In many respects I was right.

Thanks to that brief visit to Laramie I had no hesitation in accepting Dr. Larson's offer, which was accompanied by a handsome salary of $8,700 (about $58,000 in today's currency). However, I learned several years later that the circumstances of my hiring were unfortunate. At least one member of the history department, understandably, resented that he and the rest of the department were not included in the hiring process. What was less understandable was that he would later take out his resentment on me.

My parents, particularly my father, were thrilled with my new job. My father had a strong attachment to the West. As soon as the spring semester ended he suggested that we drive to Laramie and look for an apartment. With his help we found one on Grand Avenue, just a block from the history department offices. Back in Lincoln I enthusiastically told Marianne about our new home and Laramie's location between two mountain ranges. I think I overdid it. Years later, after we had moved from Laramie, she admitted that her "heart sank" when she first got a glimpse of our new hometown. Apparently our visit the previous year had not left much of an impression, because we had been mere sightseers. Now that we were about to become residents, she saw only a small city in the middle of the thirty-mile-wide Laramie Plains, with not a tree in sight for miles around except for the town itself, and not always even there. She was good, however, about keeping her disappointment to herself.

Most people who have lived in Laramie either loved it or hated it. I immediately belonged to the first category. To be sure, the town, which then had a population of twenty-one thousand, lacked some of the amenities of a metropolis. It had no shopping centers with big department stores, so major purchases of furniture or clothing needed to be made in Cheyenne, forty-five miles to the east, Fort Collins, sixty-five miles to the south, or even in Denver, another sixty miles to the south. The older parts of town, where we lived, had no planning, so houses were often jammed too close together and lacked architectural harmony. The south side of town across I-80 featured an ugly, pollution-spewing cement plant and some even uglier houses and signs.

Then there was the wind, which frequently howled in the winter and spring and could be so strong even during the relatively calm summer and fall months that I sometimes had trouble standing still while trying to putt on the golf course. Winter seemed to last forever. The first hard frost could come any time after early September. The first snowfall could be expected in October at the latest. Whereas March had always shown definite signs of spring in Nebraska, and the whole of April was indisputably a spring month, winter seemed to acquire a new lease on life in Laramie during those months. Historically, April was the snowiest month of the year with March close behind. At least some snowfall was a virtual certainty in May, and one year while we were in Laramie it even snowed in early June.

Nevertheless, for me at least, the town's plusses outnumbered its minuses. Even the weather was not as bad as advertised. True, the winters were long, but never dreary and seldom even bitterly cold. Pollution from the cement plant, along with the burning of garbage, ended while we were in Laramie, giving the town some of the cleanest air in the country. Sunshine was the norm the year round, and winter was frequently interrupted by balmy days in the forties and fifties. The sun is so strong at Laramie's elevation (seventy-two hundred feet) that we sometimes went sunbathing in our backyard in February when the temperature was around forty. Our location in the middle of the "treed" part of town gave us some protection from the wind. Consequently, I never came close to suffering from the kind of weather-induced depression I had experienced in Rochester.

Laramie was a relatively compact town. From our apartment we could reach nearly every locale by car in five minutes. No part of the campus was more than six blocks from our home, and the downtown area was less than a mile away. The town's compactness facilitated socializing, in contrast to many of our sprawling cities nowadays where one's friends and colleagues may live a half hour or more away. The University of Wyoming, like other universities its size, provided plenty of inexpensive entertainment: concerts, plays, lectures, and football games. Laramie's golf course had only nine holes during the five years we lived there, but it was inexpensive and well maintained. By the time we returned later for numerous summer vacations, another nine hilly and challenging holes had been added to the course.

The mountains were the most appealing aspect of life in Laramie. The Snowy Range, with its twelve-thousand-foot peaks, was thirty miles to the west. It lived up to its name so much that the highway crossing it remained closed from the first major snowfall, usually in late October or November, until around Memorial Day, by which time snowplows managed to blast their way through drifts as high as fifteen feet. Once the snow started to melt, beautiful wildflowers emerged between lush green pines and rocky outcroppings. Picnic areas were scattered throughout the range, as were hiking trails. Between Laramie and the Snowy Range were the Laramie Plains, which could appear pretty bleak in the middle of the day. On the other hand, when we were traveling east the setting sun cast long shadows across the undulating prairies, creating a spectacular beauty of its own. To the east of the town was the Laramie Range. Its highest point was not much more than nine thousand feet, and it didn't receive nearly the precipitation of the Snowy Range. Nonetheless, it featured some spectacular rock formations, especially in Vedawoo, a picnic area twenty miles east of Laramie.

Marianne had had her fill of teaching in Wooster and Lincoln and expressed no interest in a third consecutive year. Her decision was fortunate, because she soon became pregnant. With that unexpected news we had to start thinking about finding larger living quarters. Our apartment on Grand Avenue had only two bedrooms, one of which I used as a study. It had to double as a nursery as soon as our son, Mark, was born in April 1967. He was a month early and we had not even bought a baby crib, so a plastic tub had to substitute for a few days. We spent several weeks looking for a house, but nothing appealed to us very much. We wanted to avoid the newer parts of town, which lacked trees, were too far from the university to make walking practical, and were generally too costly for our budget.

After several weeks of house hunting we got lucky. The nicest houses in terms of price and location were usually sold without even being advertised. We learned from a member of the history department that a friend of his had just accepted a job at the University of Virginia. His house, a charming New England–style two-story structure, was located at 1406 Custer Street, just three blocks from my office. It cost a grand total of $25,500 (about $165,000 today), considerably less than the new houses on the "Hill" on the southeast side of town but $5,000–$7,000 more than most houses in the older parts of Laramie. With an advance in my inheritance from my grandmother we were able to take over the 5.25 percent mortgage, so our monthly payments including insurance were a very affordable $139 ($900 today) even though Marianne did not teach during the time we were in Wyoming.

We loved our new house, and in many respects it evokes in me the same fond memories that the Dakota Street house in Lincoln did for my father. It had an impressive history. A neighbor, Wilson Clough, who had joined the English department in 1924 and authored the university's first history, told us that our house had been built in the 1920s by Professors Clara Frances McIntyre (1877–1960) and Laura Amanda White (1882–1948), both of whom came to Laramie in 1913 when just 222 students were enrolled at the university.[15] Unlike the University of Rochester, which hired its first female professor only in 1910, sixty years after the school's founding, the University of Wyoming, like other land-grant universities, had been open to both male and female professors and students since its founding in 1886.[16]

Professor White was appointed chair of the history department in 1914, a position she held until her death in 1948. Until a second historian was hired in 1922 she taught *all* the history courses, both American and European, even though her specialty was the antebellum South. She was also instrumental in establishing a Phi Beta Kappa chapter at the university and was a major contributor to Clough's *History of the University of Wyoming*. In 2001 she was named an "Outstanding Former Faculty of the College of Arts and Sciences." The two lifelong friends, White and McIntyre, made their home "the scene of many pleasant gatherings."[17]

Both women remained single, not that they had any choice in the matter; matrimony would have cost them their jobs and possibly their professions. It wasn't until 1971, under pressure by the federal Office of Economic Opportunity, that Wyoming faculty were free to marry other faculty members and still retain their jobs at the university. McIntyre and White had such distinguished careers that two ten-story campus dormitories, the tallest buildings in the state, now bear their names.[18]

The two lady professors were part of a wave of highly educated women who entered academe in the 1910s and 1920s. Only 10 percent of graduate students were women in 1890, but 41 percent held that status in 1918.[19] My chairperson at Wooster, Aileen Dunham, had joined the history department there in 1924, and women were well represented at Grinnell during my mother's college years in the late 1920s. The Great Depression and the prejudice against two-income families decimated the female professoriate, as had been all too apparent to me at Grinnell, Nebraska, and Rochester.

Our new house was just a five-minute walk to the campus and my office, close enough that we could occasionally entertain students in our living room. In five years I think I drove that distance exactly twice and then only to bring home a huge pile of library books. Consequently, I fueled our Volkswagen Bug about once every three weeks. If the tank was nearly bone dry a fill-up would cost around three dollars. One of the hardest aspects about our departure from Laramie was leaving our first house just four years after buying it.

Meanwhile, my profession was keeping me busy. In June and July of our first summer in Laramie I put the finishing touches on my dissertation and sent it off to my dissertation committee. After my dismal performance in my oral comprehensive examinations in 1963, I had been warned that I would face an especially rigorous cross-examination when I defended my dissertation. Making things even more ominous was the refusal of Professor May, once again, to interrupt his vacation in Maine to return to Rochester for the exam. I needn't have worried. The roles were now reversed from what they had been three years earlier. I was now the expert and my examiners were the novices. Consequently, on September 8, 1966, I was able to breeze through the exam without ever facing a question I couldn't easily answer.

Even before returning to Rochester for the defense of my dissertation, I had been frantically preparing to teach my first classes at the University of Wyoming. Fortunately, I was in good shape for my course in Western Civ, which, counting multiple sections, I had already taught five times and had revised at Nebraska. Consequently, my student evaluations were on the whole very good. I was occasionally criticized (probably correctly) for speaking too fast, and a few students complained about having to take so many notes.

However, for the first time in my career I had to teach an upper-division course, a broad two-semester survey of European history in the nineteenth and twentieth centuries. While at the Institute of European Studies I had taken "Europe between Two World Wars" and "Europe since 1945." At Nebraska I took "Modern Germany" and the "Era of the French Revolution," and at Rochester I had a course in the "Age of Revolutions, 1789–1870." Nevertheless, a professor learns how little he knows about a subject as soon as he is faced with teaching it. There is a great deal of truth in the saying: "If you really want to know a subject, teach it" (or write a book about it). I was usually just one lecture ahead of my students during the whole year.

Nonetheless, I received respectable evaluations for the course, with comments ranging from positive (that I was enthusiastic and seemed to enjoy teaching) to negative (that I gave too much detail and spoke too fast). At Wyoming evaluations occurred only for tenure-earning professors and then only in the first and last years of the probationary period, so I have no way of knowing how my teaching compared with that of other professors in my department. Dr. Larson, however, seemed pleased with the evaluations, noting only the number of students who thought I spoke too quickly.

During my second year at Wyoming I taught another two-semester course in "The History of German-Speaking Europe." I had deliberately picked this title to enable me to devote about a third of my time to Austrian history, which I reasoned would be too specialized to be taught as a separate course. Even though central Europe was already my specialty, preparing at least eighty new lectures again made me realize how much I still needed to learn, especially for the first half of the course, which began in the Middle Ages and ended with the dismissal of Chancellor Otto von Bismarck in 1890. Aside from a one-semester course in modern German history that I had taken at Nebraska, my knowledge of central European history was based on the very narrow research topics I had explored as a graduate student. That information was sufficient to fill one or two lectures. The rest had to be prepared from scratch. Altogether, my two advanced courses necessitated reading more than four hundred books during my first four years at Wyoming. When the course on the history of German-speaking Europe was evaluated in the spring of 1970 nearly all my students gave me a 9 or a 10 in every category and called the course "hard but reasonable."

While I was busy preparing lectures, Marianne was busy having babies. She had found teaching exhausting and when we moved to Laramie she was determined to improve her health before having any children. In general Laramie was a good place to raise kids. Traffic was light, crime was nearly nonexistent. (The notorious murder of Matthew Shepherd was an isolated incident that occurred many years later.) We had many friends, such as Wayne and Peggy Calloway and Ron and Joy Surdam, who had children about the same age as ours and with whom we could exchange babysitting duties. Washington Park, which had an excellent playground, was only three blocks away. Marianne found a nice preschool for Mark and his younger brother, Glenn, who had been born in 1969, where they went for a few hours, two or three days a week. The boys loved to be taken to the university's Experimental Farm, where they could watch chicks and other poultry being hatched. If we had remained in Laramie, almost certainly they would have loved learning to ski, hunt, and fish.

By Christmas 1969 we were feeling well settled in Laramie. Our family was complete; we had no intention of having more than two children, not only for our own sake but also because we took seriously the threat of overpopulation to our nation's natural resources. We loved our house, and I loved my job. Marianne sometimes felt overwhelmed with child rearing and domestic chores, which were made more difficult by her somewhat precarious health. However, we could easily imagine spending the rest of our lives in Laramie. But it was not to be.

CHAPTER 11

Publishing and Perishing

"You cannot be expected to know the intricacies (to put it politely) of the game."

THE NEW EMPHASIS ON SCHOLARSHIP

Up to and including my first few years at the University of Wyoming I had been extraordinarily lucky in most aspects of my life, thanks in large measure to my parentage and to the time and place of my birth. I had been able to go to an excellent liberal arts college, had met and married a beautiful and intelligent young woman, had made three extended trips to Europe, and had had no difficulty obtaining three good jobs. By the end of the 1960s I had a comfortable home, two young sons, and work that I loved. Everything seemed to be going my way. The early 1970s would see this luck evaporate.

My five years at Wyoming coincided with rising expectations for tenure at major universities throughout the country. The process had started with a trickle in the late nineteenth century when a few American universities, starting with Johns Hopkins University and the Ivy League schools, began adopting the German model of PhD programs for the advancement of research.[1] By the 1930s scholarship was becoming the hallmark of academic achievement at the larger and more established universities, although it was not essential for an appointment, tenure, or promotion. This relaxed attitude toward research and publication began changing soon after the end of World War II, led by Harvard University. The faculty's task was no longer the mere dissemination of knowledge but its creation. Good teaching was assumed to be the product of distinguished research.[2] During the 1960s the emphasis on research and publication dramatically increased when the production of PhDs in all fields tripled in just ten years. Between 1958 and 1972 the number of doctoral programs doubled.[3] Proponents argued that research led to new ideas and prevented intellectual stagnation. Publishing would also bring national and even international recognition to a university as well as to the researcher to an extent that could not be matched by teaching alone.[4]

The relationship between research and the quality of teaching has remained controversial ever since the 1890s. Professors have been accused of writing in "'stupefying and inscrutable jargon' that served only to mask the vacuous and trivial nature of their content. In their lust to fulfill their own professional careers . . . professors . . . busily engaged filling up whole libraries with 'masses of unread, unreadable and worthless pabulum.'"[5] It is easy, of course, to ridicule esoteric titles of articles and books, the overall importance of which the general public is unlikely to understand. And doubtless some research does more to promote a professor's career than it does to "advance the frontiers of knowledge." However, it is often these same esoteric articles and books that help lead to new, wide-ranging books and scientific breakthroughs that benefit the general public.

My own observations over the course of more than forty years have convinced me that research does not *guarantee* great teaching. I know plenty of good teachers who have done little or no publishing. Extroverts who can display a certain degree of showmanship are more likely than introverts to be successful in teaching large undergraduate classes. On the other hand, showmanship is of little value in conducting a seminar. *Not* conducting research, however, is even less a guarantee of effective teaching, especially over a long period of time. One thing is certain: my best lectures have been based on my research. Publishing the results of their research also exposes scholars to withering examination by peers that can't be duplicated in a classroom, since undergraduates are more likely to be influenced by style than substance. Teaching research methodology to graduate students without having conducted research oneself over a long period of time is especially difficult for me to conceive.

The University of Nebraska was well ahead of Wyoming in placing a new emphasis on research. Although James Olson had published his biography of J. Sterling Morton in 1942, the real push toward publishing did not occur until the 1950s. Albin Anderson, the professor who co-directed my master's thesis, had been hired shortly after World War II and was eventually promoted to full professor without ever publishing a book, although he had published a few articles. But when Professor Koehl came to Nebraska in the early 1950s it was on the strength of his book *RKFDV: A History of the Reich Commission for German Resettlement and Population Policy, 1939–1949*, which was published by Harvard University Press in 1957. He was replaced in 1965 by Edward Homze, who was able to leave Emporia State College in Kansas and come to Nebraska because of his forthcoming book *Foreign Labor in Nazi Germany*, published by Princeton University Press in 1967.

This new emphasis on publishing was just getting started when I came to the University of Wyoming. During his brief tenure in office (1964–65) President John T. Fey had touted the importance of original research. This emphasis increased during the administration of William D. Carlson (1968–78), who quickly made it clear that he wanted to "put Wyoming on the map academically," and that depended on the "national reputation of its faculty for scholarship, performance, and research."[6]

The dean of the College of Arts and Sciences, E. Gerald Meyer, was especially eager to see that this new stress on research was implemented in his college. With Carlson's blessing he hired renowned research scholars to guide graduate programs in physics and chemistry. Dean Meyer was equally determined to upgrade the history department by insisting that it be the first social science department to offer a PhD. There was some plausibility to his rationale. The department benefited enormously from its affiliation with the American Studies Program, which had received a significant endowment from William Robertson Coe of Cody, Wyoming, and New York City. His gift had created the School of American Studies along with the American studies wing of Coe Library, where my office was located. It also provided for faculty additions, library accessions, and undergraduate and graduate fellowships.

Nevertheless, Dean Meyer seemed oblivious to the needs of a truly viable PhD program in history and to the fact that the demand for PhDs in history, although strong in the mid-1960s, was not likely to last indefinitely. (The dean's belief in an ever-expanding need for PhDs turned out to be much like the assumption, so widely held in the early twenty-first century, that housing prices would always go up.) The history department objected to the introduction of the program, arguing quite reasonably that its faculty and budget were inadequate for such an ambitious undertaking.[7] The department's scruples were later borne out when their PhD program was not listed as "acceptable" by the American Historical Association and was dropped.

In the meantime, however, Dean Meyer was determined to see the PhD program implemented by someone who shared his enthusiasm. Apparently he didn't believe that the history department's chairman, T. A. (Al) Larson, was that man. Relations between the two men evidently deteriorated when Meyer refused Larson's request for three new positions at a time when the physics department, with half the students and double the faculty, was rumored to be receiving five.[8] However, Dr. Larson, who had been chair of the department since 1948, probably hadn't endeared himself to the dean in 1967 when he approved the granting of tenure to a member of his department who had never published anything. Consequently, Larson resigned in 1969 and was replaced for a year by an acting chairman before a permanent chair was hired in the fall of 1970.

I came to Wyoming completely unaware of this controversy over the doctoral program and the tension between the department and Dr. Larson on the one hand and the dean of the college on the other. Nevertheless, I was well aware that there was a PhD program in history as well as the "publish or perish" syndrome. My only misconception was in not knowing how long it could take to get published and how politicized and convoluted the tenure process could become.

MY TENURE STRATEGY

I had what I thought was a sensible strategy for publishing and gaining tenure. I would devote most of my first two years to preparing lectures in my two new advanced courses before concentrating on publishing. This timetable was upset when Dr. Larson asked me to offer graduate seminars starting in 1967 and to give the first half of my course on Europe since 1815 to Deborah Hardy, who had been hired to teach Russian history.[9] I was unenthusiastic about the idea, because it meant preparing another thirty or forty lectures for what would become a two-semester course on Europe in the twentieth century. However, refusing was not a realistic option.

While preparing my new courses I sent my dissertation to a number of specialists on Austrian fascism to solicit recommendations for its improvement prior to submitting it to publishers. Neither of my dissertation mentors was knowledgeable in the area. Dr. May was probably the foremost scholar of Austrian history in the United States, but his expertise ended with the fall of the Habsburg Monarchy in 1918. A. William Salomone, who became the co-mentor of my dissertation after my return from Europe, was a distinguished scholar of Italian fascism but knew little or nothing about Austria. The other members of my dissertation committee were even less knowledgeable about my topic.

Getting busy scholars in Austria to read an unpublished dissertation in a foreign language written by a freshly minted PhD was not easy. The person whose opinion I most valued was Ludwig Jedlicka, the director of the Institute for Contemporary History at the University of Vienna, who had given me some guidance while I was researching the topic. Although he promised to read it, the most I could get from him was that I had exhausted available materials.[10]

By the summer of 1968 I decided that I could no longer wait for expert commentaries. I had shortened the text in some places and lengthened it in a few others in order to clarify the narrative. I also added a few pertinent facts and footnotes and made some stylistic changes, although I was aware that still more background information was needed for the general reader. The issue now became where to send it. I feared that the topic, which was limited to fascism in a single Austrian province, might be too narrow for an American publisher, although I may have been overly pessimistic in that regard. I also suspected that the topic would be politically radioactive in Austria, where the ruling dogma was that Austria was "the first victim of Nazi aggression." This concept originated in the so-called Moscow Declaration of November 1943 when the Allied powers attempted to separate Austria from the Third Reich. The second half of the declaration, rarely mentioned in Austria after the war, insisted that Austria contribute to its own liberation. The concept of Austrian victimization persisted until the Waldheim affair (to be discussed in chapter 13) severely undermined it in the late 1980s.

I thought my best bet was to seek a publisher in Germany, a firm that would be happy to reveal that fascism had not been confined to Germany between the world wars. I asked Reingard, the daughter in the Moosbrugger family in Graz where I had lived in 1963, to translate a condensed version of my text. I sent the abstract to several German publishers, together with a covering letter, starting in June 1969. All of the responses were negative except one I received in September from the Europäische Verlagsanstalt in Frankfurt. Even its response was ambiguous, saying that it could not publish my manuscript because it was concentrating on current political themes. However, it was taking the liberty of forwarding my manuscript to its colleagues at the Europa Verlag in Vienna. Given my track record of rejections, I didn't get overly excited about this response.

I heard nothing further for ten months. Finally, in late July 1970, I unexpectedly received a response from Vienna. Incredibly, the letter had been sent by *regular* mail, in other words, by ship, and had taken a full month to reach me. The editor, Gottfried Kammerer, asked me to send the Europa Verlag the entire manuscript and requested a three-month option during which time they would make a decision. I still didn't quite know what to make of this development, but I did inform the acting chairman of this new situation.

Almost certainly helping my case was the critique of Professor Franz Göbhart of Graz. He had been a member of the Ostmärkische Sturmscharen, a conservative (but not right-wing) paramilitary formation during the 1930s and one of the people I had interviewed during my Fulbright year in Graz. Göbhart wrote that my study "had been written with an ability to sympathetically understand Austrian conditions not shown by other Americans. It displays an astonishing knowledge of details, and an impressive ability to find the right sources, which isn't easy with this subject. The author deserves the thanks of Austrians for his objectivity and the admiration of historians for his methodology."[11]

August passed, then September and October, with still no response from Vienna. In the meantime the tenure committee had met and voted three for and three against my receiving tenure, a positive vote being needed. The acting chairman told me that the outcome was caused by my "lack of scholarly productivity." In desperation I wrote to Herr Kammerer on November 16 asking if a decision had been made—still no response. Then on December 18, while I was attending the wedding of my former Grinnell roommate John Price in Riverside, California, Marianne called with news: a telegram from Vienna had just arrived. "Europa Verlag will publish your book 'Styrian Heimatschutz,'" it read. "Contract will be sent soon."

The news was thrilling, but it came too late, as it turned out, to reverse the tenure decision. The newly hired chairman, whom I will call Professor John Doe, even though not formally having a vote, had disapproved of my getting tenure, a decision seconded by Dean Meyer. Had the initial response been sent by air mail, and had the Europa Verlag stuck to its promise to respond within three months, the book would have been accepted by October 1, well before the tenure decision was made. I later learned that the Europa Verlag made negative decisions quickly; positive ones took more time to traverse a bureaucratic maze.

EVALUATING *THE HABSBURG LEGACY*

My dissertation was not the only egg I had placed in my tenure-earning basket. Another possible book originated from a paper I gave on the Styrian Heimatschutz at a meeting of the Missouri Valley History Conference in Omaha in March 1969. It so happened that Professor Keith Eubank, a renowned scholar of European diplomatic history, chairman of the history department at Queens College, and editor of the Berkshire Studies in European History, gave a paper at the same session.

While we were waiting for the session to begin, Professor Eubank asked if I would be interested in submitting a proposal for a book in the Berkshire series. I was dumbfounded. Here I was, an untenured and unpublished assistant professor, being asked to contribute to the oldest and best-known series of historical essays in European history in the country. Established in 1927, the Berkshire series featured a veritable who's who of American and Canadian historical scholarship. Sidney B. Fay, who contributed *The Rise of Brandenburg Prussia*, was a past president of the American Historical Association and the author of the groundbreaking two-volume study *The Origins of the World War*. Wallace K. Ferguson, a Canadian, was the premier North American scholar of the Renaissance. Owen Connelly's *The Epoch of Napoleon* was the third of his ten books. George Mosse's Berkshire contribution, *The Reformation*, was his second of twenty-five books and for thirty years a best-seller.[12] Joachim Remak's *The Origins of World War I, 1871–1914*, was his third of at least seven books and followed his prize-winning study of the assassination of Archduke Franz Ferdinand. My own mentor, Arthur J. May, had published a book in the series on *The Age of Metternich*.

Even though I was not the first relatively young scholar to be invited to contribute to the Berkshire series, I can well imagine that many of my colleagues at Wyoming thought I was hopelessly unqualified to contribute to such an elite collection. I can't say I blame them. An invitation to submit a proposal was hardly the same as being offered a book contract. And a book contract does not equal a completed manuscript accepted for publication. First I had to think of an interesting topic about which I was already reasonably prepared to write, something that was both original and interesting enough to appeal to undergraduates, especially freshmen, who would be my likely audience.

My travels throughout the former territory of the Habsburg Monarchy on both sides of the Iron Curtain had convinced me of the irony of history. The monarchy had been denounced by its opponents before and during World War I as a "prison of the peoples." Its many nationalities had allegedly "suffered under the yoke of Habsburg oppression." Its breakup at the end of the war was followed by the establishment of new nation-states, or at least states like Poland, Czechoslovakia, Romania, and Yugoslavia, in which one nationality dominated numerous ethnic minorities. This metamorphosis had been celebrated in much of Europe and North America as the dawn of a new age of democratic nationalism. Yet everywhere I had traveled in the former territory of the monarchy, with the partial exception of the Republic of Austria itself, I had seen a region that was in most respects vastly worse off than it had been in 1914. I was aware that nearly all books dealing with the area had either ended or begun in 1918, thus making comparisons impossible. As I later noted in the preface to *The Habsburg Legacy, 1867–1939*, the book was "dedicated to the proposition that neither the Monarchy nor its legacy can be properly understood without careful comparisons between the pre–World War I and inter-war years." To do so I had to be free of any bias for or against nationalism. I simply wanted to see which type of state had produced the most security and prosperity for its citizens. In the conclusion I stated that "what to some observers in 1914 looked like an oppressive, corrupt regime, now looks tolerant, honest, and even progressive in comparison to what followed."[13]

A week after the conference in Omaha I sent Professor Eubank a four-page, single-spaced abstract broken down chapter by chapter, along with a two-page covering letter. I pointed out the lack of any competition for the book I proposed and indicated how my previous research and travel experiences qualified me for the task of writing it. "A book of this kind would have a great appeal to undergraduates," I wrote, "since it would deal with so many vital issues: the origins of the two World Wars, the minority question, the collapse of a great empire, the rise of fascist movements, and Nazi foreign policy."[14] With the exception of changing the title of one chapter, the completed manuscript adhered precisely to my abstract. A few days later Professor Eubank responded by saying that my "proposal was well done (would that others did as well). . . . I feel that such a book is needed and ought to have a good sale. I have given Cliff a very favorable recommendation."[15] Clifford Snydor, the history editor at Holt, Rinehart and Winston, indicated his approval to me by letter on April 30, 1969, although I did not receive a contract until October.

FACTIONALISM AND PROFESSIONAL MERIT

I was given a deadline of September 1, 1971, a goal I reached five months early (almost unheard of in the history profession). A grant proposal I made with the support of our acting department head was approved by a faculty committee for the summer of 1969; I used it to hire a part-time secretary to type research notes. In a three-page letter to Eubank, a copy of which I showed to my chairman, I discussed various themes I had decided to pursue.[16] By June 1970, I had read around 150 books and 36 articles and had filled four file boxes with research notes that then required seven weeks to read and summarize. By mid-August I was able to start writing, and by late September the first two chapters were on their way to Eubank.[17]

In his reply of October 14, 1970, Professor Eubank suggested that I "pay more attention to personalities, anecdotes, and all those stories that undergraduates like in lectures. . . . You could also go back and try to tighten [the manuscript] up by making cuts. But do this only after you have finished the manuscript." In a separate letter to the acting chairman, a copy of which he sent to me, he wrote:

> These chapters are well written and quite readable. They are well suited for the college level at which the Berkshire Studies are aimed. The chapters that I have read reveal a mastery of the necessary monographic works and a command of the material. I was happy to see that the chapters were so well planned. . . . I have been highly pleased with these chapters. Except for an act of God, I expect to recommend to Holt, Rinehart and Winston that the complete manuscript be published as soon as I have approved it. . . . These chapters give every indication that the final book will be a significant historical work even though it will lack the elaborate footnotes found in the usual university press book. Because it is in the Berkshire Studies, it will be more widely read.[18]

Meanwhile, the first two chapters had also been read by our incoming chairman, Professor Doe, who was asked to pass on his evaluation to the tenure committee. Without commenting on my chapters, he wrote obliquely about two young colleagues, one of whom found research and writing distasteful, and asked himself whether that young man would have been happier at an institution that would not require him to publish.

In response I referred to Professor Eubank's positive evaluation and added that I "would have a right to complain [about the tenure decision] only if I am denied a year's extension to complete my book [actually, I needed only two or three months] before a final decision on tenure is made." I went on to say that "at a recent conference Dean Meyer seemed to feel that I was not really interested in writing and would abandon it as soon as my current book is completed. . . . Research and writing have been tremendously satisfying for me and I have no intention to give them up."[19]

Professor Doe replied that I had "to place only limited trust in Eubank's reactions. . . . If he has serious doubts, or intends to ask for major revisions, you will likely not know it until the completed manuscript is submitted. . . . You cannot be expected to know the intricacies (to put it politely) of the game. . . . I have wondered . . . what would have transpired if you had not been offered such a tempting opportunity, but had first tackled the more conventional monograph or articles that beginning scholars produce."[20]

The incoming chairman seemed to be completely unaware that my research topic had been approved not only by Professor Eubank and the history editor of Holt, Rinehart and Winston but also by a University of Wyoming faculty research committee that had awarded me a grant that in turn was endorsed by the history department's acting chairman. Moreover, of course, my doctoral dissertation, then being considered for publication by the Europe Verlag, was a conventional monograph, although Professor Doe apparently was unaware of its existence.

When I saw Dean Meyer he assured me that delaying a final tenure decision would break no rules—I was only in the first semester of my fifth year of probationary tenure instead of the sixth year as was customary at most American universities. In 1940 the American Association of University Professors (AAUP) had introduced practical routinization of job security by establishing three-year and six-year evaluation periods. In addition there was to be a one-year notice of termination, for a total of seven years. Most American universities followed these guidelines scrupulously in 1970. Harvard was a major exception.[21] The University of Wyoming was another. A few years later that was to change, but too late to do me any good.[22]

Only six weeks after these developments, Marianne phoned me in California with the news about the Europa Verlag's publishing my dissertation. By this time I had completed all but the concluding chapter of *The*

Habsburg Legacy. As soon as I returned to Laramie I again saw Dean Meyer and informed him of these developments and asked for a reversal of the tenure decision. The dean said he would leave it up to the new chairman. I ran into Professor Doe a few days later at the meeting of the American Historical Association in Boston. By then he had heard about the acceptance of my dissertation by the Europa Verlag. His response to my question of what he intended to do about the tenure decision was to say that "things wouldn't be the same" if I remained at Wyoming. He offered no explanation.

Many years later, in 1984, I resolved to see if I could get a more definitive answer as to why I had been terminated. In his response, Professor Doe, who was by then no longer the chairman, blamed the decision on the department's factionalism. I evidently had belonged to the "wrong" faction, which enjoyed living in Laramie, whereas members of the opposing faction "resented the misfortune that had brought them to Wyoming. . . . A great many more factors than simple professional merit have always entered into such decisions."[23] In a second letter, written six months later, he related how he had learned only recently that the acting chairman had been "very hard on, and destructive of, junior faculty. That is something, of course, I never saw."[24]

My being denied tenure resulted not only from the university's failure to follow AAUP guidelines but also because there were no clear lines of authority within the history department and between the department and the dean's office. In just two years there were three actual, acting, or de facto heads of the department, not one of whom was fully cognizant of my activities during my probationary period. The acting chairman did not know about my being assigned a new course during my third year. Professor Doe evidently did not know about my option agreement with the Europa Verlag and probably didn't know that the acting chairman had supported my decision to write *The Habsburg Legacy* or that my research had been approved by a university committee.

This division of authority made it easy for all responsible parties to leave the ultimate decision to someone else. Dean Meyer could have overturned the decision, but that would have been a vote of no confidence in the very man he had just gone to a great deal of trouble and expense to hire as the new head of the department; so he deferred. Professor Doe, as the new chairman, had more influence than anyone else but said that he couldn't interfere in the department's decision, even though he had been crucial in shaping it through his negative evaluation of my manuscript. Even when it was certain that I was about to have two books published with prestigious presses, something that no history candidate for tenure had ever before accomplished at Wyoming, no one admitted making a mistake or took responsibility for correcting it.

So I was left to my fate, not even given a full year—the customary practice when tenure is denied—to look for a new job. I have often wondered whether I should have taken some legal action at the beginning of 1970. Such actions were rare at the time, although they became fairly common soon thereafter. Usually, however, such cases involved ethnic or gender discrimination. Protesting a tenure case was risky at best. If you lost you could be labeled a troublemaker, and your chances of getting a job elsewhere, even outside academe, could be seriously jeopardized. Winning could cause resentment, perhaps resulting in bad teaching schedules, lower pay raises, and delayed promotions. So I chose not to protest.

THE BLISS OF IGNORANCE

Sometimes ignorance is a good thing. If I had known at the start of 1971 the jeopardy my career as a historian was in I would have been terrified. However, for much of the spring semester of 1971, I was too busy revising my two books and teaching my three classes to be preoccupied with morbid thoughts. Only a month after the tenure decision was made, Professor Eubank responded enthusiastically to the third chapter of *The Habsburg Legacy*, which was on the Paris Peace Treaties. By the end of January the concluding chapter was finished, and by late March all the revisions had been completed and the manuscript had been sent to the copyeditor. On June 11 the senior project editor at Holt, Rinehart and Winston wrote that the manuscript would require only light editing. The title, oddly enough, was one of the last issues to be settled. On June 24, I wrote to Clifford Snyder and suggested *The Habsburg Legacy, 1867–1939*, saying that I thought it had a "certain intriguing quality which might invite a potential reader to open the book and find out more about its contents," a suggestion that he accepted by return mail.[25]

The Habsburg Legacy was adopted as required reading by such schools as UCLA, Colorado, British Columbia, Holy Cross, Washington State, Texas Tech, Maryland, Edinburgh, Salzburg, and, irony of ironies, the University of California at Santa Barbara, Professor Doe's former university. John Rath, founder and editor of the *Austrian History Yearbook*, used *The Habsburg Legacy* at the University of Texas. The same was true of Stephen Fischer-Galati, editor of the *East European Quarterly*, at the University of Colorado. Otto von Habsburg, the son of the last reigning Austro-Hungarian monarch, Karl I, thanked me for a copy of the book and said that he was "deeply impressed by the objective and clear way in which you re-establish historic truth. I do hope that the book will have the success it deserves."[26]

With work on *The Habsburg Legacy* essentially finished by late March I was able to start putting the finishing touches on *Hahnenschwanz und Hakenkreuz*—literally, "Rooster's tail and swastika." The Europa Verlag was prepared to publish my manuscript in German with no further changes, although the editor allowed me to make some revisions based on a few books and articles that had been published since my dissertation had been completed in 1966. Before the end of May all but a few minor changes were completed. By then I was able to argue that the Styrian Heimatschutz provided "an excellent example of the rise of a right-wing, para-military organization from the chaos of World War I, its growth, program, decline, and absorption by the Austrian National Socialists. And by discovering why and how the Nazis succeeded in taking over the *Heimatschutz* we can gain a new insight into the appeal of National Socialism, not only in Austria, but to some extent in Germany as well."[27]

Hahnenschwanz und Hakenkreuz attracted an astonishing amount of publicity in Austria when it was published early in 1972, something that is rarely true of scholarly books published in the United States. Around thirty newspapers and journals reviewed it. *Die Gemeinde* said that I showed a "remarkable ability to sympathetically understand an especially unhappy chapter of the pre-Nazi period . . . that shouldn't be forgotten." *Wissenschaft und Weltbild* called me "a good judge of Austrian contemporary history and the political camps of the interwar period." The Social Democratic magazine *Zukunft* was also effusive in its praise: "Only a few Austrians have dealt with this subject. . . . It isn't surprising that it is once again an American who couldn't resist undertaking an investigation of what we Austrians have called scum, an investigation whose thoroughness we won't dispute."[28] On the other hand, I was sharply criticized by the Communist newspaper *Die Volksstimme* for finding similarities between the Nazis and the Communists.

I have gotten ahead of my story. By the time *The Habsburg Legacy* and *Hahnenschwanz und Hakenkreuz* were published in early 1972, I was living in Orlando and teaching at Florida Technological University. Most of the five years I had spent in Laramie were among the happiest of my life, but I left feeling like a jilted lover. I was leaving a job, a home, and good friends for an unfamiliar part of the country, far from my parents in Lincoln and no closer to Marianne's family in Rochester. My disappointment, however, did not prevent me from returning to Laramie numerous times to enjoy its magnificent summer weather, write, hike in the mountains, and play golf. When we left Laramie in 1971, however, I was totally unaware that I was about to face a whole new set of challenges.

CHAPTER 12

From the Frying Pan into the Fire

"Fiscal facts are the worst kind of facts."

MY DESPERATE SEARCH FOR A NEW JOB

The loss of my job at the University of Wyoming came at the worst possible time. I naively imagined that with two forthcoming books I could easily land another job, and probably a better one at that. Two years earlier, perhaps even one, that would have been the likely scenario. Because of the large enrollments in PhD programs in history, I had seen as early as 1967 that a job shortage for historians would eventually develop, although I thought the shortfall would come on gradually and not get serious until about 1975. However, as the new decade began the job market for historians suddenly collapsed.

The period between 1945 and 1970, often known as the "Golden Age of Higher Education," was marked by the three P's: prosperity, prestige, and popularity.[1] It was no coincidence that this age also coincided with one of the biggest booms in the history of the American economy when the average annual growth rate was 3.5 percent.[2] Not surprisingly, the downturn in the economy during the 1970s was accompanied by devastating developments in higher education, which affected not only historians but also nearly all academic fields. Whereas only 6,420 PhDs in all fields had been awarded in 1949–50, that number had risen to 29,872 twenty years later.[3] Bachelor degrees granted in history nationally peaked in 1972 at 44,600. Thereafter, undergraduate degrees in history declined to around 16,400 in 1986, even though the number of degrees granted in all fields was increasing.[4] Meanwhile, higher education was experiencing a financial crisis brought on by operating costs, inflation, and decreased public and private income. Job openings disappeared virtually overnight. Many faculty were dismissed, including tenured professors at such universities as Wisconsin and Southern Illinois.[5]

Demography, which up to then had always been my friend, was now my enemy. I was competing for a job with the first cohort of baby boomers along with a massive wave of new PhDs.[6] Making matters worse was the death in June 1968 of Professor May, who might have been helpful in my finding a new job. Fortunately, Professor Salomone at the University of Rochester, the co-adviser for my dissertation, was sympathetic to my plight. He suggested a number of schools I could contact and wrote numerous letters of recommendation. Somewhat later, John Rath, the editor of the *Austrian History Yearbook* and a kindly gentleman if ever there was one, became a kind of substitute mentor.

Complicating the job search was the sheer time it took to write letters. In our age of word processing and e-mailing it is easy to forget that prior to the 1990s all letters had to be individually typed, even when they were identical except for the name and address of the recipient. A single serious mistake usually meant that the whole page had to be retyped. During my job hunt in 1970–71, I didn't even have an electric typewriter. I am still embarrassed to think of all the time my friends and former professors spent writing letters on my behalf.

Some of the job "openings" for the fall of 1971 evaporated because anticipated funding failed to materialize. I learned at the Boston convention of the American Historical Association in late December that there were only 250 available jobs in all fields of history for 1,700 applicants. Only eight positions were in my specialty, and at least three of these disappeared for budgetary reasons. Several department chairmen frankly told me that my credentials were "very impressive," something interviewers are not ordinarily inclined to do. Four others said they would definitely hire me if they had the funds. I even made inquiries at the U.S. Embassy in Vienna and at the Institute of European Studies, each time with no luck.

One of the job openings that disappeared was at Kansas State College of Pittsburg. In a letter to Dr. Larson, the chairman wrote that of all the recommendations he had received, the "most complete, illuminating, and helpful . . . on any candidate are those hymns of the praises of Bruce Pauley. Yours is one of five, and all argue his case fervently and forcefully. All five simply support my initial opinion of him and his outstanding record as a teacher and producing scholar. But fiscal facts are the worst kind of facts."[7]

FLORIDA TECHNOLOGICAL UNIVERSITY

Keith Eubank in many respects became another substitute mentor and soon saved my professional neck. In retrospect, it was almost miraculous that I had already written to him on November 3, 1970, about my tenure situation. My letter arrived just before he attended a meeting of the Southern Historical Association, where he learned that Florida Technological University (FTU) in Orlando was looking for someone in French or German history. Because the position was not advertised nationally, without his letter I never would have known about the opening, and my career as a historian would most likely have ended right then and there.

By April 1971, I was beginning to despair. I had written fifty or sixty letters to friends and former colleagues and had applied for every job that sounded like even a remote possibility. I had also heard nothing from the chairman of the history department at FTU, Leland Jackson, since he had responded to my application in January. I had pretty much given up on the school. On April 7, I wrote Jackson that I was "disappointed not to have heard from you as yet concerning your opening in German history. Do you have any idea when the decision might be made?" I learned later that he had forgotten all about the job vacancy until he received my letter. On the twenty-second he wrote back, inviting me to come to Orlando for an interview.

I was not terribly impressed by what I saw. The school, officially founded in 1963 but offering classes only since 1968, was nearly six miles from the nearest residential neighborhoods in Winter Park and Oviedo. Whereas the University of Wyoming campus had lush lawns, huge pine trees and cottonwoods, and beautiful flower beds, FTU's trees were barely visible, and much of its campus consisted of ugly parking lots. Wyoming had over 9,000 mostly residential students when I left, and a full range of cultural and Division 1 athletic events, whereas 90 percent of the 6,137 students at FTU (in the fall of 1971) were commuters and there were few social, cultural, or athletic activities on campus.[8] The name of the school was also completely misleading and had negative connotations for someone in the humanities and social sciences like myself. Although it had been founded with the idea of serving the technological needs of the nearby Space Center at Cape Canaveral, it was in practice a comprehensive state university, but many people, even in central Florida, did not know what FTU was or even where it was. The school was sometimes referred to as "the best-kept secret in central Florida."

I did have a friendly and productive interview with Dean Charles Micarelli, who was far more personable than my dean at Wyoming. However, I was shocked at the end of the day when Professor Jackson simply dropped me off at a motel on a busy street opposite a shopping center and told me to fend for myself for dinner. In contrast to the usual practice at Wyoming, there was no informal social gathering in which I could engage in casual conversations with the four members of the history department. Nor was I asked to give a presentation. However, the important thing was that on May 27, 1971, I received a phone call from Professor Jackson offering me the appointment at $12,000 a year—an increase of nearly $1,500 over my previous salary—and a promotion to the rank of associate professor. The threat of unemployment was finally over.

It turned out that 1971 was not just a bad time to be looking for an academic job. It was also a terrible time to find housing in the Orlando area. Disney World opened its Magic Kingdom in October, and nearly every apartment was filled. Most apartment complexes didn't even bother to answer our inquiries. We finally found a two-bedroom unit at the Summit Apartments in the suburb of Casselberry. Marianne was not too disappointed. She and the kids enjoyed the complex's swimming pool; five-year-old Mark soon amazed us by swimming the length of the pool *underwater*. Marianne and I also played a little tennis, and her health seemed to benefit from the mild climate. In general, she and the boys took an immediate liking to Florida because they enjoyed being outdoors on all but the hottest days. The beach, only an hour away, was also a welcome attraction.

For me, however, the move, if not catastrophic, was a major setback professionally. For starters, my five-minute, three-block walk to work had been replaced by a ten-mile drive on highways lined with billboards, strip malls, and fast-food restaurants. It also soon became apparent that we would need a second car if Marianne and the boys were not to be stranded at home all day.

Much more serious, however, was my teaching load. I'd had a nine-hour load at Wyoming and a teaching assistant to help grade papers in my Western Civ classes. A year or two after I left, their load was reduced to six hours a week. At FTU I had a twelve-hour load with no assistant. With rare exceptions my classes were huge; I sometimes had a total of two hundred students in four classes. Grading essay exams, which I regarded as indispensable for students of history, was enormously time consuming. The library, especially in my early years, was so small that it rarely had the books I needed for research. Fortunately, that was not as serious a problem as it might sound, because I was able to make use of the school's interlibrary loan service; in any event, I needed to go to Vienna if I wanted to do any serious original research.

With two books and also two articles accepted for publication just before leaving Wyoming, I expected our sojourn in central Florida to be brief. During my second year at FTU I applied for a job as director of the Institute of European Studies and had an interview at the headquarters of IES in Chicago. Later, the president of the institute, Robert Bosshart, flew down to Orlando for a second interview. Alas, a job offer never materialized, probably because I had no administrative experience. The following year I was one of ninety-nine applicants for the chairmanship at Clemson University.[9] I did at least have an on-campus interview but failed to get that job as well, probably for the same reason. I was also a finalist the same year for an opening in European diplomatic history at the University of Rhode Island from among well over 150 people who applied for the job.[10] In 1974, I also applied for a job at the University of Pennsylvania. That opening attracted more than 300 applicants and revealed just how grim the job market was for historians in the 1970s.[11]

I'm glad that Marianne and I did not absolutely count on an immediate move and instead started an early search for a house as close to the university as possible. We wanted to buy an existing home in Winter Park, a beautiful suburb of Orlando canopied by enormous live oak trees. However, we soon learned that the houses we liked were too expensive and the houses we could afford were too small and in neighborhoods inhabited mostly by senior citizens. Eventually we decided to build a house in Oviedo, a village of less than two thousand six miles north of the campus. The house was a "cookie-cutter," like all the houses in our Oviedo Oaks subdivision, and did not have nearly the charm or quality of construction as our house in Laramie.

TEACH OR PERISH

It didn't take me long to learn that the administration's attitude toward research at FTU was the exact opposite of what it had been at Wyoming. Now, suddenly, the emphasis was on teaching and having large classes; research was viewed with suspicion. This policy may simply have resulted from a belief that it was more important to attract students than to lure scholars who, in any case, were not likely to be impressed with FTU's research possibilities.[12] Consequently, if one's classes were smaller than average, administrators assumed that too much time was being devoted to research. I recall a meeting of the entire faculty with President Charles Millican in which a brave young member of the physics department stood up and said that he felt that doing research at FTU "was like cheating on your wife. If you absolutely had to do it, you should at least have the common decency to do it secretly."

Leland Jackson resigned as chair of the history department even before my arrival in September 1971. Dean Micarelli took over as de facto chair while we searched for a replacement. Unfortunately, the position was not advertised either nationally or locally as a department would be required to do today, so we had just two candidates. One had been the mentor of one of our department members. The other was my good friend and former colleague at Wyoming, Tom Kennedy, who was eager to leave his position there. When the department met to discuss the two candidates I pointed out Tom's diverse education at Antioch College, his Stanford PhD, and his ability to teach the history of India as well as American history. The other candidate had obtained all three of his degrees in state and was a specialist in Florida history. Much to my surprise, he gained the majority of the votes.

I was disappointed that Tom, with his even temper and courteous manners, did not get the chairmanship, but during his first year our new head seemed to be working out. In his annual evaluation of faculty in March he wrote that I took my "classes seriously, working long hours on preparation of lectures which he delivers with a thoroughness of which only the best prepared scholars are capable." Under "extent of creative effort" he wrote that I was "a rising scholar who is gaining a national reputation for his work in Austrian history." Under "overall value to the university" he concluded that I was "an asset to the department and the school." I was pleased that we had already developed such an excellent rapport.

However, at the end of the spring semester of 1973 an incident occurred that soured our relationship. Marianne and I and our sons left Florida in a hurry to be on time for Marianne's tenth college reunion in Rochester. I had given a student an incomplete grade because I had no record of his having taken the final exam, which he later insisted he took. (It is likely that he put his answers in the stack of questionnaires I threw out rather than in the answer pile as I had instructed.) At any rate, Dean Micarelli was angry at our chairman for letting me leave early, and our chairman in turn was angry at me for placing him in the middle of an awkward situation. The incident, in retrospect, although not trivial, was hardly monumental; the student was never in danger of not getting credit for the course. However, the episode marked the beginning of a tumultuous relationship between my chairman and me that continued for the next eighteen years until he finally resigned the chairmanship in 1991.

Putting me in a vulnerable position was my having had a canceled class in the spring and some other smaller-than-average classes during the year, although my classes had been at least average during my first year. Upon my return in September I had a meeting with my chairman in which he gave me a memorandum he had written in June stating that "the assigning of an 'Incomplete' in this case appeared to be a callous disregard of his responsibility to his students. It may even shed some light on why it is so difficult to get students to take his courses." The chairman told me that the college expected to lose positions in the coming year—the history department was overstaffed by one-half of one position—and it was inconceivable to him that he would release anyone who was maintaining satisfactory student enrollment while retaining someone who was not. He asserted this intention even though my combined enrollments for the coming fall semester were the largest in the department. However, it was in my upper-division courses, he maintained, that I was not attracting enough students. I "could not expect students to take my courses simply because [I] was a great Austrian scholar. That might work at other universities but not at FTU." The university's students were the "dumbest" he had encountered anywhere, and "to attract them one had to—[he] hated to use the word—'entertain' them."[13]

It was true that I had a class canceled in the spring of 1973 and another canceled that fall. The spring class had been the second half of my class on the history of German-speaking Europe, which covered the modern period since 1890. During the same quarter a "special topics" course on Nazi Germany had been offered by the political science department, and a course on tyranny—with Hitler being the primary tyrant—had been offered in the humanities department. My course that had been canceled in the fall had been scheduled to meet at 4:00 in the afternoon (one of three classes canceled out of four that had been scheduled at that hour), absolutely the worst time of the day for drawing students.

Making my situation all the more precarious was the lack of tenured members in the history department apart from the chair himself. Standing up to a chairman who was also a former sergeant in the air force was something no one was eager to do. Fortunately, three tenured full professors outside my department unexpectedly and without being asked came to my rescue: Richard Adicks, a friend and member of the English department; Stuart Omans, also from the English department; and David Mays from the theater department. One day they simply marched into Dean Micarelli's office and asked him indignantly why he was willing to allow the termination of an associate professor with nine years of teaching experience and numerous publications. Professor Adicks also took up the matter with the American Association of University Professors. On December 20 the executive committee of the AAUP at FTU sent a memorandum to the academic vice president, C. B. Gambrell, the academic deans, and the chair of the Faculty Senate stating that the AAUP's guidelines toward retrenchment were, first, that "no member of the faculty shall be dismissed solely for low productivity in his own classes, to the exclusion of other factors. The burden of productivity should be shared by a whole college, if not by the whole University"; and second, that "Any faculty member should have the right to appeal a notice of non-renewal to the Tenure and Academic Freedom Committee of his college or department (or its equivalent)."

The involvement by the AAUP induced my chairman to call a department meeting on January 10. He said that students "couldn't be forced to take courses from fact purveyors" (an oblique reference to me). His students "liked a story," since that way they "didn't have to take many notes." Finally, he turned more directly to the subject of retrenchment. His philosophy, he said, was that the person with the lowest number of students should be the one to go. He had been speaking with me about this matter during the fall, and I was his choice for the person to leave. He claimed I had acquired a reputation throughout the Western world from my publications and consequently would have the best chance of getting a new position. (I later told Dean Micarelli that if my reputation was really that good it should be a reason for retention, not dismissal.) He asked the faculty if anyone had any objections to my being dismissed. (I'm not making this up.) Not surprisingly, there was no comment; evidently, no one was eager to commit professional suicide. Near the end of the meeting he declared that he was opposed to the principle of tenure and thought it would soon disappear in Florida. Fortunately, he was wrong in that prediction (at least to date for university professors).

The actions of the AAUP turned out to be decisive. Soon thereafter, Dean Micarelli announced that the college would set up a committee to study the issue, consisting of one representative from each department except from the two departments where retrenchments were being contemplated. The dean's decision essentially removed my case from my chairman's jurisdiction. A short time later the dean said that he would not agree to my dismissal.

Thus ended my second brush with professional death, but not before I had lost fifteen pounds and a whole lot of sleep. Dean Micarelli and I were able to resume our cordial relationship, but my department head never fully got over his inability to fire me. On the other hand, after this affair he was more accommodating about my schedule and usually had nice things to say about my research in his annual faculty report. This episode, together with my experience at the University of Wyoming, demonstrated the importance of clear guidelines for tenure and dismissal. If Wyoming had followed the AAUP's standard of five full years of tenure probation, I would have had no trouble being tenured. The existence of established guidelines saved my job at FTU.

As it turned out, my teaching problem was easily corrected. I soon became aware that professors in other departments were giving their courses enticing titles. This was a game I too could play. The titles I had given my courses (or had already been on the books) at Wyoming were the standard "History of [a country] from [one date] to [some later date]." I eventually concluded that if I scrupulously avoided the word "history" and any mention of dates in the titles of my courses, students would sign up in droves. A new course on "The Second World War" I taught in the winter quarter of 1975 drew 50 students. A year later a total of 119 students in two sections signed up for the class. A course on "Hitler's Third Reich" attracted no fewer than 63 students during the spring quarter, whereas only 5 had signed up for the course two years earlier when it was the second half of "The History of German-Speaking Europe." Somewhat later I worked up new courses on "The Rise of Mass Culture and Democracy" and "Fascism and the Totalitarian Dictatorships." After that I introduced "War and Society from the Ancient Greeks to the First World War." Although these were not quite as popular as my World War II and Nazi Germany classes, enrollments were always substantial. While changing these titles I made no changes in my teaching philosophy, grading, or treatment of students. I was the same person students had presumably avoided because of my "callous attitude."

SUMMER DIVERSIONS

One good thing about living in hot and humid Florida was that we always had a tremendous incentive to leave in the summer and go where it would be cooler—which was virtually anywhere. Although the weather in central Florida was about the best in the country from November through April, and although May and October are usually tolerable, temperatures and humidity from June through September are invariably brutal. The summers in Laramie had been so delightful that we had little desire to leave.

Our whole family was able to spend the summer of 1972 in Vienna when I began researching the history of the Austrian Nazi Party, thanks in part to grants from the National Endowment for the Humanities (NEH) and the American Philosophical Society. One of the nice payoffs of publishing is that it makes attracting research grants much easier, which leads to more publications and still more grants. Soon after our arrival in Europe we rented a car in Innsbruck and spent two weeks exploring Italy as far south as Rome. Some of our friends thought we were crazy traveling with a three-year-old and a five-year-old. However, we did most of our sightseeing in the morning and early evening, and the kids would nap while we drove in the afternoon. We would then all go to bed early. The highlights of the trip for Marianne and me were Napoleon's first place of exile on the Island of Elba, Hadrian's Villa near Rome, the Roman Forum, and Byzantine churches in Ravenna. For the boys it was undoubtedly feeding pigeons in Venice's St. Mark's Square.

The Fulbright Commission in Vienna found us a spacious and conveniently located apartment on Sechsschimmelgasse, complete with a large living room and dining area, two bedrooms, a study, and a well-equipped kitchen. It was also near a streetcar line and next to a farmers market where Marianne was able to purchase amazingly delicious fresh fruits and vegetables daily. While I worked six or seven hours a day, Marianne and the boys visited nearly every museum in the city, including such esoteric ones as the Fire Fighters' Museum, the Clock Museum, and the boys' favorite, the Technological Museum with its old streetcars, bicycles, automobiles, and flying machines. The boys loved riding streetcars and exploring the city's imperial palaces and nearly every park in Vienna; however, they had a hard time understanding why they couldn't walk on the grass. (They would be sternly reprimanded by elderly Viennese ladies if they forgot.) For three weeks the boys attended a bilingual kindergarten, giving Marianne the welcome opportunity to see several art galleries and antique shops. In the evening the four of us frequently attended concerts performed by visiting symphony orchestras in a courtyard of the city's Rathaus. By the time we left Europe the boys were able to speak a few words of German and had been exposed to a very different way of life.

The summer of 1974 was especially exciting because I was invited to an international symposium on fascism held in Bergen, Norway. The conference was attended by forty scholars from both sides of the Iron Curtain as well as from North America. The discussions were stimulating, and ultimately the papers were published in a huge tome called *Who Were the Fascists? Social Roots of European Fascism*.[14] Our Norwegian hosts lavished the participants with hospitality. One particularly memorable evening was spent listening to music by Edvard Grieg played in his well-preserved summer home called Troldhaugen, overlooking Nordås Lake.

The following year witnessed a complete change of pace for the whole family. My old U of R friend, Gilbert McArthur, the same man who had identified Marianne several years earlier, did me a second big favor by inviting me to teach a five-week course on modern Russian history at the College of William and Mary in Williamsburg, Virginia, while he was doing research in the Soviet Union. He also offered us the use of his house, which was just two blocks from the restored area. Although I spent a great deal of time working up new lectures on the Russian Revolution, every school day I enjoyed riding a bicycle across the restored village to the campus on the opposite side. Meanwhile, Marianne and the boys, having free passes provided by the university, leisurely explored every nook and cranny of the colonial capital. The passes also gave us admission to films, concerts, and lectures about colonial America. On weekends we took several excursions to nearby historic sites such as Yorktown, Jamestown, and Mount Vernon.

Our family experienced still another complete change in the summer of 1976 when I was able to get a National Endowment for the Humanities (NEH) grant for college teachers to attend a seminar on comparative fascism at Vanderbilt University in Nashville. This was the first of three such grants I was to win, which went to professors who taught at schools not having a doctoral program and not having a major research-oriented library. So, ironically, I actually benefited in this instance from not teaching at a major research university. Charles F. Delzell, a specialist in Italian fascism, did an excellent job of leading the discussions, which took place three hours a day, three times a week and were invariably continued over lunch. The participants were twelve bright and personable professors from around the country, some of whom I have maintained contact with to this day. Our location in the center of Tennessee also enabled us to explore an unfamiliar part of the country, including numerous Civil War battlefields. My father, a Civil War buff, would have loved that aspect of our summer. At the end of the seminar we returned to Florida by way of the Great Smoky Mountains in western North Carolina.

HOME (AND ACADEMIC) IMPROVEMENTS

By 1977 I had become increasingly skeptical of being able to move to a more established, research-oriented university. Not only did the supply of new PhDs continue to far outstrip job openings in history, but history departments, under pressure from their higher administrations, placed an increasing emphasis on becoming more "diverse" by hiring more women and minorities. The few job openings were usually for untenured assistant professors who could be hired cheaply and fired easily if economic circumstances warranted. As history departments grew, fields they wanted to have filled became increasingly narrow. In the mid-1960s it had been sufficient to call oneself a modern Europeanist or perhaps a specialist in central European history. By the 1970s, if a department advertised for a historian in German history, the opening meant literally the history of Germany; Austrian history was not close enough. The few other jobs that were advertised nationally were for department chairmen, for which I lacked experience, and for endowed chairs, an elite status usually requiring the publication of four or five books, an accomplishment I would not attain until much later.

These realities convinced me that I might as well reconcile myself to remaining at FTU for a good long while, and quite possibly for the rest of my career. But did Marianne and I want to stay indefinitely in our small and poorly constructed house on Oak Drive? We had never been particularly thrilled about the house. When our neighbors, Tom and Karen Morgan, built a new house in 1975, a mile or so away from us, we lost one of the most attractive aspects of our location. We were also never happy with our house's floor plan. Particularly objectionable was the location of my study next to the family room, the site of our TV and a virtual playground when the boys couldn't go outside.

We were not eager to build a new house, because we knew it would be a long and complicated process. In addition, it was impossible to know how much we would like such a house once it was completed. However, the longer we looked at existing houses the less convinced we were that we could find one we liked. Nearly all of them had the very features we didn't like: a single story, a mammoth garage facing the street, a huge and often stained and cracked driveway, a dark family room, and no room that could become a quiet, isolated study. Florida houses were simply not constructed with scholars in mind. Reluctantly, we decided to build a custom home.

Fortunately, we found a perfect lot. Located at the end of a cul-de-sac, it was large—actually larger than we either wanted or needed—and pie shaped with fifty-foot-high trees. Being traditionalists in our taste as far as music and art were concerned, Marianne and I wanted a house that would reflect our artistic and personal values while being functional. We decided to build a two-story, modified colonial with a covered loggia and a big bay window in the dining room facing the street. Using the equity from our old house, we were able to make a 20 percent down payment on the $62,000 cost of the new house and lot. The 8.25 percent loan didn't seem like much of a bargain at the time. However, when the lending rate rose to 14.5 percent in 1979 and to 21.5 percent in 1981 we realized how fortunate we had been.[15] The purchase of our house was still another example of the importance of timing and dumb luck.

It took over nine months of dreaming, planning, lot clearing, and almost daily inspections of the construction, but we finally moved in January 1978. The house was well worth the wait. It was always a relief to arrive home after a hard day at work. Within a few years, the citrus trees I planted in our backyard were producing more fruit than we knew what to do with. On the other hand, we soon learned that there was a downside to having a big yard, even though we managed to reduce the area needing maintenance by planting hundreds of ferns. Unlike Laramie, plants, including weeds, bushes, grass and vines, grew all too easily and had to be cut frequently or uprooted. As the years passed I felt that I was trying to beat back a jungle.

In addition to becoming resigned to not finding another job, I was seeing positive changes at the university. By the mid-1970s FTU was beginning to evolve with the times. The emphasis on research that had reached the University of Nebraska around 1950 and the University of Wyoming in the mid-1960s was finally starting to affect FTU. It was now no longer possible to be tenured and promoted without publishing. I easily attained tenure in 1976, but the next year the higher administration, which had promoted some people to full professor with few if any publications, suddenly and drastically changed its criteria.

Fortunately, I was one of a fairly small number who benefited from this policy change. By 1977, in addition to my two books in print, a third was well under way. I had published three articles, had given seven scholarly papers at conferences, and had published nine book reviews. Consequently, I was just one of six professors in the college applying for a full professorship to be promoted, and one in only seven for the university as a whole to achieve that status.

This new emphasis on research became even more pronounced when H. Trevor Colbourn became our new president in 1978. A scholar on colonial American history in general and on Thomas Jefferson in particular, President Colbourn radically transformed the university during his eleven-year tenure. First and most traumatically for many alumni as well as engineering majors, he pushed for changing the name of the school to the University of Central Florida (UCF). Also controversial was his policy of establishing a football program. Colbourn made it clear that both good teaching and publications would be required for tenure and that very significant publications would be essential for promotion to full professor. What had been near heresy during the first decade of the school's operation was the new orthodoxy. At long last, my credentials matched the philosophy of the university where I was teaching.

Needless to say, many faculty members were unenthusiastic about the changes. For them the name change was probably the least controversial of the new policies; at last the community now knew what we were and where we were. Most of the opponents of the name change were in the engineering college. The reception to the new football program was mixed, and UCF was far slower to make the "big time" than schools like the University of South Florida, which had started its football programs several years later.

For many faculty the new stress on research and publishing was wrenching. They had been hired as teachers, and in many cases it had been years since they had written their dissertations. Resuming research after several years is not easy. It can take a year or more simply to become acquainted with the latest research results, techniques, and controversies. Many faculty members at UCF never managed to make the transition and felt increasingly isolated and disparaged. The concerns of the older faculty were not without some merit. UCF, like other regional and newer universities, lacked the financial resources to support research to the same extent as older and better endowed universities.[16] It also lacked doctoral programs with grad students who could help correct exams in large classes.

Colbourn's arrival coincided with my unexpectedly becoming chairman of the fifty-eight-member Faculty Senate. I was "drafted" by Marilyn Whisler, a well-connected member of the political science department. The position of chairman also automatically made me the chairman of the Senate's Steering Committee and a member of the Faculty Advisory Forum, a committee consisting of the faculty chairs of all ten of the state universities of Florida. My four specific objectives were to establish a distinguished professorship award, help revise the university's core curriculum, set terms for department chairs, and create a faculty exchange program with other universities. All but the last of these objectives were approved by the Senate. In a more general way, I hoped to improve relations between the faculty and higher administration, which were somewhat strained by all the recent changes. Ironically, I found it far easier to deal with administrators than with the faculty, which probably accounts for my narrow defeat when I ran for reelection a year later.

CHAIRMANSHIP PROBLEMS—AGAIN

A lasting benefit of my relationship with President Colbourn, which continued in an informal way for the remainder of his presidency and beyond, was that I had a court of last appeal should I ever have another serious confrontation with my chairman. After several years of relative calm, relations with my chairman soured again at the end of the decade. In 1979, I had a book nearing completion, two articles published and a third accepted for publication, and was elected to the University Tenure Committee as well as to a search committee for a new college dean. For these activities I received an "above average" overall evaluation, which, thanks to "grade inflation," in reality was no better than average. When we met to discuss my evaluation he said that "a serious scholar should not waste his time with an organization like the Faculty Senate." I replied that "President Colbourn did not consider it beneath his dignity to devote himself nearly full-time to administrative work. If scholars are not willing to do this kind of service, who should?"

I didn't take my evaluation lying down and appealed it all the way to President Colbourn. The outcome of meetings with my dean and the provost of the university, Leslie Ellis, as well as with President Colbourn himself, resulted in a very welcome 10.4 percent raise. However, although I had won a major battle, I did not win the war. My chairman was still in command, and I was still his subordinate. I doubt very much whether he was pleased that I had appealed my annual evaluation all the way up to President Colbourn and that he had been overruled.

Two years later, in 1981, I found myself in another battle over my annual evaluation. I had just completed the most productive year since my arrival in Orlando in 1971. My third book, *Hitler and the Forgotten Nazis* (described in the next chapter), had been published in March. I had written four book reviews, two of them for the prestigious *American Historical Review*. I also wrote an eight-page article titled "A Russian Diary" for UCF's magazine, *Emphasis*, describing my trip to the Soviet Union the previous summer (described in chapter 15). I had taught seven different courses during the school's three trimesters and a total of nine courses including two graduate courses. I had served on the time-consuming and critically important College Personnel Committee (for tenure and promotion) as well as on the University Personnel Committee. Finally, in the spring I was given the prestigious University Award for Excellence in Research, which was accompanied by a $2,000 prize. President Colbourn wrote me a congratulatory letter saying: "Thank you again for your outstanding contributions as a faculty member at our University. . . . I hope that you are aware of how much your extra efforts are appreciated."[17]

Nevertheless, I realized by this time that the better my performance, the worse would be my chairman's evaluation. In a letter to my parents dated April 5, 1981, I wrote: "Just as an experiment I decided that I would not say a word to my chairman about any of these accomplishments [beyond what I had submitted in my annual report] in order to see whether or not he would congratulate me on anything. So far he has not said a word to me. . . . I'm just wondering now [if] he won't try to find some way to [give] me a low annual evaluation the way he did after my year as Faculty Senate Chairman."

I didn't have long to wait. Six weeks later I received a copy of his "Chairman's Evaluation Summary." His *overall* evaluation assessment: "average." He rated me "low" in teaching because I allegedly "viewed history as a set array of facts to be divulged by one who knows to those who do not." (I plead guilty to believing that I knew more about the subjects I taught than my students.) I was "not sought out by students as are most of his colleagues." He recommended that I "spend some time in the following months reflecting on the apparently permanent decline in student preparation for college . . . and the professional health of an individual who derives satisfaction from failing students." I received an "outstanding" in research but ignored everything I had listed in my annual report except my book on the Austrian Nazi Party. Under "Service and Professional Development" he failed to mention my three months of research and travel in Europe and again rated me "average."

By now I had long since abandoned the passivity I displayed at the University of Wyoming. I was not going to allow my chairman to deny me the financial rewards of the grueling work that had gone into *Hitler and the Forgotten Nazis*. I pointed out in my three-page written response that "such an outcome, if upheld, would contradict the administration's emphasis on the importance of research and writing." When I asked him about the University Award for Excellence in Research he merely responded that he "did not regard the award as important."

As for his comment that I was "not sought out by students," I merely pointed out that in his evaluation of 1975–76 he had written that my "classes are constantly filled." In 1977–78 his comment was: "His classes are much in demand and well attended." As to the pleasure I allegedly took in failing students, I pointed out that I had given only ten failing grades to the 235 students I had had so far that year, actually an unusually low number for me. If I was deliberately trying to fail students, I had a strange way of going about it. I regularly handed out a list of review essay questions prior to every examination. I also offered optional examinations and optional book reviews and gave students detailed instructions on how to write reviews. I also dropped their lowest examination grade when calculating their final course average. Borderline cases I resolved in favor of the student.

Of course, a much larger issue was involved in my chairman's evaluation: academic freedom. Few aspects of that doctrine were (and are) more sacrosanct for professors than their right to assign grades they deem appropriate. Students at UCF had the right to appeal grades to a student-faculty committee. In my thirty-five years at the school, none of my students ever exercised this right, and only a handful complained to me about their course grade. As to failing grades, any professor whose grades are wildly out of line with his colleagues will soon find himself facing nearly empty classrooms. In any event, a grade of F or D can serve as a healthy wake-up call for students who don't take their courses seriously.

Ultimately, appeals to my dean and to the provost were successful and I received a handsome raise of over 21 percent. However, I was tired of having to go through the appeal process and thought there were more productive ways I could use my time. Amazingly, though, the administration approved my chairman for another term. However, once again overruled and apparently chastised, he gave me reasonable evaluations for the next few years.

So the 1980s began for me a whole lot better than had the 1970s. I had somehow survived two threats to my professional life. I had a secure if not always agreeable job and a new house built to the exact needs of my family. Marianne, like many other American women of her generation, was becoming restless with her role as full-time mother and housewife.[18] Consequently, she, like her cohorts, resumed her career in 1976 by landing a part-time job with the Seminole County Home/Hospital Program teaching children with injuries or non-contagious diseases. The boys were doing well in school. The remainder of the decade would witness a decided improvement in my life. Years of almost constant work were beginning to pay off.

CHAPTER 13

Hitler and the Forgotten Nazis

"A 'conspiracy of silence'"

PROBING THE POLITICALLY INCORRECT

Almost as soon as *Hahnenschwanz und Hakenkreuz* and *The Habsburg Legacy* were in print, back in 1972, I had begun work on a new project. Having written about Nazism and paramilitary extremism in one Austrian province, Styria, I was eager to expand my knowledge to include Austria as a whole. Scholars in Austria and the United States had done a good deal of research on various specialized topics related to the Austrian Nazis, but no one had published a comprehensive history of the movement. The same "conspiracy of silence" regarding the Austrian Nazis was just as alive in the 1970s as it had been in 1963–64, and indeed since the establishment of the Second Austrian Republic in 1945.

I made a good start researching my new topic during the two months we spent in Vienna in 1972 and the month following the symposium on international fascism that I had attended in Norway two years later. By the early 1970s my research in Austria benefited enormously from the introduction of microfilming and photocopying in Vienna's libraries and archives. It was no longer necessary to take notes for every document painstakingly by hand. Instead, I could determine its usefulness and have it copied after reading just a paragraph or two. What had taken me months could now be accomplished in days or weeks.

The highlight of my research in the summer of 1974 was my three-hour interview with two former leading Austrian Nazis: Leopold Tavs, who had been the Nazi *Gauleiter* (regional leader) in Vienna at the time of the Anschluss in 1938), and Eduard Frauenfeld, who had been the director of Nazi propaganda in the Austrian capital. Both men appeared eager to be interviewed and to advance their points of view. Frauenfeld kept urging me not to ridicule or insult the Nazis. In an attempt to prove my objectivity I read to him a passage from the preface of *Hahnenschwanz* in which I wrote that "the historian's task in dealing with extremist groups is not to condemn them . . . but to understand how such movements could originate at all." Frauenfeld was looking over my shoulder as I read directly from my book. Fortunately, he didn't notice that I had skipped the passage after the word "groups" where I wrote that "the naked facts can do that eloquently enough."[1]

Although I was sincere then and since in wanting to be nonpartisan and objective, I no longer believe that facts are always "naked." Historians are often confronted with contradictory accounts, making it difficult if not impossible to determine what actually happened. More problematic is how to decide which facts, among thousands that one has accumulated, are worth including in a publication. Most difficult of all is drawing appropriate conclusions from the facts that one has decided to publish. The question of objectivity becomes especially complex when dealing with a movement as reprehensible as National Socialism. Nevertheless, I still believe the goal of a historian is to understand and not to condemn. The word *understand*, however, has two definitions. The historian's role, in my opinion, involves the first: "to comprehend and to be thoroughly familiar with; to grasp the significance of." This does *not* mean that he or she adopts the second definition: "accepts as true; believe" or "accepts tolerantly or sympathetically."[2]

The need to "understand" the Austrian Nazis was accompanied by the necessity of deciding just what regions and time frames to include in my study. Should the Nazis of Bohemia be included? The Nazi Party had its start there in 1903, but the province had broken away from Austria when

Czechoslovakia became an independent state in 1918. Should Austrian Nazis be included after the country was annexed by Germany in 1938? These two areas lay well beyond what I had previously researched. However, they were familiar territory for two friends of mine: Ronald Smelser of the University of Utah, and Robert Schwarz, a Jewish refugee who had fled from Austria in 1939 and was, in the 1970s, a professor of philosophy at Florida Atlantic University in Boca Raton. Another scholar, Max Kele, at that time a professor at the University of Florida in Gainesville, was especially strong on the 1918–23 period as well as on the party's pre–World War I antecedents in Vienna. In December 1975 the four of us decided to pool our expertise, with me being the editor and coordinator. With this agreement made and my notes organized, I began writing the following month.

However, collaboration proved difficult and in the end impossible. My colleagues were too tied up with other obligations to devote much time to our project. During 1976 we managed to agree only on the title: "Hitler and the Forgotten Nazis: National Socialism in Austria and Czechoslovakia." We had not even completed a joint outline. Keith Eubank, my editor for *The Habsburg Legacy*, warned me in the spring of 1977 that publishers were leery of collaborative projects unless they were already in final form. On May 4, I wrote my colleagues that I had written ten chapters myself and was not willing to continue setting and then resetting deadlines indefinitely.

Two days later I received a terrible shock. An advertisement in a scholarly journal described a new book, *Fascist Movements in Austria*, by the well-known Austro-British historian Francis L. Carsten. I wrote my colleagues that I had "repeatedly warned [that] we have had plenty of competition in writing a book on the Austrian Nazis. It appears now as though we may have lost the race." I was so depressed with the thought that years of research and writing had been wasted that I stopped writing altogether until I had read Carsten's book.

Once I did so I discovered that Carsten had provided no general background information about the impact of World War I and the Bolshevik Revolution in neighboring Hungary on Austrian politics, Austria's humiliating treatment at the Paris Peace Treaties, and the consequences of the postwar inflation. The absence of Nazi newspapers was a shocking omission in his bibliography. Worst of all was the almost complete lack of new ideas and critical analysis. David C. Large, reviewing the book in the *Journal of Modern History*, put it succinctly: "In Carsten's hands history becomes simply 'one damn thing after another.'"[3]

By the summer of 1977 I had come to two conclusions. First, a collaborative book project proceeds, if at all, at the rate of the slowest collaborators. In the case of our book, it didn't proceed at all, at least not as a joint effort. By the fall of 1978 both Bob Schwarz and Ron Smelser had withdrawn from the project, although they were helpful in critiquing my manuscript. Second, I should not be deterred by other books whose titles seemed to overlap with my own work. These were valuable lessons for the future. Armed with this knowledge, I proceeded full-speed ahead on my own. In December Marianne wrote our parents that the family saw me "only at meal times and after 10:00 p.m. It has really been that way during most school years. . . . Luckily this point in the project is a very exciting time for him." At the end of the month I saw Malcolm Call, the editor in chief of the University of North Carolina Press, at the annual convention of the American Historical Association in New Orleans and gave him a copy of my book's table of contents and preface. Six weeks later he wrote me that "the book appears extraordinarily promising to me and to my colleagues and we are eager to consider it for our list as soon as it becomes available."[4]

Energized by this letter, I redoubled my writing efforts and was able to send the press all but the concluding chapter by mid-July 1978. In my cover letter to the editor I emphasized that "I have endeavored to make the book analytical, descriptive, and topical rather than a mere narrative of events. . . . I expect . . . the book's appeal to extend beyond scholars and university libraries to at least some of the educated public because it explores a little-known aspect of two highly popular subjects: Hitler and Nazism. . . . Precisely because of the book's potentially broad appeal I have deliberately avoided taking too much prior knowledge for granted from the reader. . . . Background information has been provided for all the important figures so that they become, hopefully, real people, not just faceless names."[5]

My elation at having been able to send the press what I hoped was a completed manuscript turned out to be short lived. On September 15, Malcolm Call informed me that he had "received a review of [my] manuscript.... You will note that our advisor finds much of merit in the manuscript but does not in the end recommend publication of it in its present form." This news was disappointing but not devastating. It is common for a university press to require authors to make revisions in their manuscripts before they are formally accepted for publication.

By early January 1979, I was able to send the revised manuscript back to the press. I can only sigh when I think of how much easier it would have been to revise the manuscript if I had had access to a computer in those days. Instead of simply deleting sentences and words that I no longer needed and typing only brand-new material, I had to completely retype well over one hundred pages of text and all seventy-six pages of endnotes. I can't say that the computer has made me a better writer, but it certainly has made revising vastly easier, faster, and a lot less tedious.

Having submitted my manuscript a second time, I again had to endure a long wait for the reader's report, which did not come until May. This time the news was almost purely positive. The editor reported that "our advisor has read the manuscript and ... told me that the work was, in his opinion, 'excellent' and that his recommendation would be unequivocally in favor of publication. The criticisms to be offered are, he says, of a copyediting nature. It seems to me, therefore, on the basis of this news that I will be able to present the project to our Board of Governors at its July meeting with a recommendation in favor of publication."[6] I was ecstatic; although several months of reviewing galleys and page proofs remained, five years of grueling work had finally paid off. My book was going to be published by one of the country's most prestigious presses.

The reader, Andrew G. Whiteside of Queens College, had made some excellent suggestions in his second report, ideas that I incorporated not only into the final draft but in subsequent publications as well. He thought that some of my paragraphs needed stronger topic sentences and that I should cut down on the use of the passive voice.[7] Whiteside also suggested that I provide each chapter with a brief summary and conclusion.

One of Whiteside's suggestions, however, I rejected outright. He preferred the book be called "Hitler and the Austrian Nazis," a title that I found bone dry. Shortly before the book was printed, Gwen Duffey, the managing editor of the press, suggested that it be called "something like *Forgotten Nazis: Austrian National Socialism* or *Swastika over the Alps*."[8] I responded that I thought the first title was too bland and the second title was inaccurate because not all of Austria was Alpine.[9] I might have added that not all the Alps are located in Austria. Fortunately, the editorial staff of the press endorsed my title, *Hitler and the Forgotten Nazis*, and merely suggested that I add the subtitle *A History of Austrian National Socialism*. I mention these details because it is probably not common knowledge that an author can only suggest a title. The publisher has the final word. A book's title is a form of advertisement and often has a great deal to do with whether or not it becomes a commercial success.

I took Professor Whiteside's description of my book as a "popular-scholarly work" more as a compliment than as a criticism. Most history books tend to be either scholarly or popular. I had consciously tried to bridge the gap, something rarely attempted by academic historians. Whereas research is emphasized in PhD programs in history in the United States, writing is not.[10] I pointed out in my response to Malcolm that "the only concession I make to the wider audience is to assume no prior knowledge.... However, I am quite sure that even many scholars will not be familiar with much of my background information. I have been at pains to avoid the vulgar aspects of popular history. There are no invented conversations in my book, no reading of minds, and no telling of stories merely for the sake of entertaining."[11]

My last chore in writing *Hitler and the Forgotten Nazis* was compiling an index. This turned out to be a tedious business lasting several weeks. I had to create a list of every event, proper name, geographic name, and even idea or concept on separate pieces of paper and then keep track of every page on which those items appeared in the text. Subcategories had to be created for the more important entries. Fortunately, there are professional indexers who are usually highly skilled and efficient in this type of work. In future publications I was more than happy to resort to their expertise even though it was expensive to do so.

Hitler and the Forgotten Nazis was published in March 1981, a little less than nine years after I had started my research in Vienna in the summer of 1972. What had I discovered in the roughly three hundred books, articles, and dissertations I had read, the thirty-three newspapers and numerous documentary collections I had examined, and the eight interviews I had conducted? For one thing, I was somewhat surprised to learn that many members of the Austrian Nazi Party "were inspired by a very real, if in our view perverted, idealism whose end they were willing to realize through violence."[12] Like most people, I had come to think of idealism as something purely positive. In studying the Austrian Nazis, however, I came to realize that many of them were sincere in their beliefs—although there were also, of course, plenty of opportunists—and willing to make great personal sacrifices to see the party's aims realized. There is no other way to explain the long hours they devoted to the cause, away from family and friends. Ultimately, of course, perverted idealism also led to great disillusionment for many party members after Austria was annexed by Germany in March 1938.

One of their ideals was the *Führerprinzip*, or leadership principle. Presumably, a talented, all-wise leader (*Führer* can also mean "guide") would be the answer to Austria's (and Germany's) economic and political problems and would restore greatness to the German-speaking people of central Europe. Unfortunately, the Austrian Nazis could never produce an effective leader of their own, thus causing almost constant quarrels between provincial leaders. Ironically, it was only when Hitler appointed a Reich German, Theo Habicht, as the leader of *all* the Austrian Nazis that the party had some effective leadership. Habicht, however, grossly overestimated the party's popular support and organized an ill-fated attempt to overthrow the Austrian government in July 1934. The resulting assassination of Chancellor Engelbert Dollfuss produced a worldwide revulsion and fears of a new world war. The false assumption that Hitler himself had organized the putsch led to his only serious diplomatic setback before the outbreak of World War II.

Until this July Putsch, I wrote, "Hitler showed surprisingly little interest in the Austrian Nazis for many years. His first ambition was to seize power in Germany. When that was accomplished he would rebuild the German armed forces. Only then would he turn his attention to the German-speaking people of Austria."[13] After July 1934 Hitler cut off all political and most financial ties between the German and Austrian Nazi parties and counseled Austrian Nazi leaders to exercise restraint until Germany was militarily strong. That moment came in 1938. Meanwhile, Hitler shrewdly counseled the same restraint for Nazis in neighboring countries such as Czechoslovakia and Denmark, not wanting to alarm foreign powers when Germany was still militarily weak.

Hitler and the Forgotten Nazis drew generally favorable reviews from around twenty scholarly journals and newspapers in the United States, Austria, Britain, and Canada. Austrian publications were impressed by my nonpartisan approach to the subject. *Die Presse*, one of the leading newspapers in Austria, said that the book was free of ideological and class considerations or a proclivity to lay blame. "Perhaps it is for this reason that Bruce Pauley writes with so much understanding about the interwar period in Austria. That is especially true of his analysis of conditions in this land in 1918 when it entered a changed Europe." I was pleased that the *Salzburger Nachrichten* thought the book could be "easily read by anyone who had not completely forgotten his middle school [high school in the United States] English."[14]

Reviews in American publications were also favorable. The *American Political Science Review* said: "The author skillfully traces the development of Austrian Nationalism from its beginnings in the 1880s until the famous Anschluss of 1938" and concluded that "this book is well worth reading both for its historical perspective and theoretical implications." *Choice* said that the book "blends solid research with a good general knowledge of Austrian and German affairs and offers some thoughtful reinterpretation of the 1938 annexation of Austria by Germany. . . . There is no questioning of his fairness in presenting these difficult and sometimes unsavory characters." *Social Science Journal* said that "Bruce Pauley's study is a fine piece of research on a rather important topic. . . . It is a knothole through which one can watch the whole drama of the First Austrian Republic. . . . Pauley captures the story with impeccable scholarship and delightful prose." *Magill's Literary Annual* of 1982 described it as "rigorously and thoroughly researched." The *Orlando Sentinel* wrote that "[Pauley] skillfully provides the minimum essential background to follow the intricate socio-politico evolution of Austria following World War I, with the maximum economy of words and trivia."[15]

Needless to say, I was pleased by the response. Both the hardback edition, published simultaneously by University of Carolina Press in the United States and by Macmillan in Britain, sold out, as did the paperback edition published in 1987. It should be noted, however, that scholarly books are not printed in huge numbers and rarely make their authors much money. A successful book, however, often leads to more grants and serves as an incentive to write still more books. Such was certainly true in my case.

POSTSCRIPT: SEARCHING FOR AN AUSTRIAN PUBLISHER

From the very beginning of my research on the Austrian Nazi Party I envisaged having the book translated into German and published in Austria. *Hitler and the Forgotten Nazis* was useful for American specialists in central European history and for a small portion of the general public in filling in a blank spot about Hitler and Nazism. For Austrians, however, the subject was essential in understanding one of their country's greatest catastrophes. Nevertheless, getting the book published in Austria was no easy task.

It turned out that for years the book was simply too "hot" for any Austrian press to publish. To be sure, in addition to the political incorrectness of the book at a time when most Austrians were still clinging to the half-truth that Austria was "the first victim of Nazi aggression," there were the usual difficulties standing in the way of such a publication. Austria's population in the 1980s was around 7.5 million, including several hundred thousand guest workers who had little or no interest in Austrian history. Furthermore, translating a book is very expensive for a publisher and in Austria often requires a subsidy from the government.

The official and to a considerable extent unofficial Austrian attitude toward its recent past changed suddenly and dramatically with the international uproar beginning in 1985 that soon came to be known as the Waldheim affair. Kurt Waldheim was a longtime Austrian diplomat who served two terms as secretary-general of the United Nations from 1971 to 1981. In 1985 he was cruising toward victory in the Austrian presidential election when the popular Austrian magazine *profil* revealed that his service in the German Wehrmacht included the Balkans, where many Nazi atrocities against Jews and Yugoslavs were committed, a fact that Waldheim had omitted in his just-published memoirs. The World Jewish Congress in New York caught wind of the article and began calling Waldheim a war criminal. The publication of a picture of Waldheim in a Wehrmacht uniform sealed his fate as far as many Americans were concerned. The Reagan administration put Waldheim on its watch list of people prohibited from entering the United States because they had "assisted or otherwise participated in the persecution of persons because of race, religion, national origin or political."[16] The prohibition remained even after an international committee of historians, called for by Waldheim himself, reported that there was no evidence that he had been personally involved in any crimes, although he must have known about them.[17]

The foreign attacks on Waldheim caused a "circling-of-the-wagons" mentality in Austria, although his ultimate election to a mostly ceremonial position was almost as much a result of the rejection of the scandal-ridden Socialist Party as it was an unequivocal endorsement of Waldheim. Eighty-five percent of Austrians, especially at first, resented the attacks on Waldheim. Former chancellor Bruno Kreisky, himself of Jewish origins, came to Waldheim's defense and, in a more limited way, so did the famous Austrian-Jewish Nazi hunter, Simon Wiesenthal.[18] After a time, however, the Socialist Party joined the attack on Waldheim, though it couldn't prevent his election in 1986.

The controversy raged for several years. Broader issues were involved. For example, what exactly was a war crime? Was mere knowledge of war crimes enough to make one a war criminal? Was service in the Wehrmacht, even as a draftee, a criminal offense? When I was in Vienna in 1988 to deliver a paper at a symposium related to the fiftieth anniversary of the Anschluss, Chancellor Franz Vranitsky told me and several other participants that "the Waldheim Affair had divided Austrian opinion like nothing else in the country's history." A scab had been removed from the country's history, and Austrians were forced to confront their country's controversial past.

Many members of Austria's intelligentsia had not fully subscribed to the victimhood interpretation of recent Austrian history. But for the majority of the population the Waldheim affair turned what had been taboo and politically incorrect into something that was openly debated. A dispassionate book by an American, with no ax to grind, might now have an audience in Austria. Thus a path had been cleared for an Austrian edition of *Hitler and the Forgotten Nazis*. Once again, I was able to take advantage of favorable timing.

Crucial in publishing the translation was Professor Gerhard Botz, one of Austria's leading historians of the interwar period and at the time a professor at the University of Salzburg. I had met him at the Bergen symposium on international fascism in 1974. He had already been enormously helpful in 1980 by allowing my whole family to use an apartment he owned in Vienna. With his assistance, two Viennese publishing houses, the Molden-Verlag and Verlag Kremayr und Scheriau, showed an interest in 1983 in publishing a German-language edition of my book. Ultimately, however, Kremayr und Scheriau rejected the book, because "this truly interesting book is too scientific [by which was probably meant "too scholarly"] and too specialized" for their readers.[19] I had trouble understanding how a book covering more than fifty years of Austrian history and the most disastrous political party in the country's history could be considered too specialized, but, of course, there was nothing I could do about the decision except look for another publisher.

Three years later the political atmosphere and the interests of Austrian readers and publishers had drastically changed. Again with the assistance of Professor Botz and also Dr. Irene Freudenschuss-Reichl of the Austrian Press and Information Service, the Österreichischer Bundesverlag (ÖVB, or Austrian Federal Publishing Company, which, despite its name, was not a government publishing house) showed a definite interest in a translation. In December 1986 the ÖVB asked Professor Isabella Ackerl, a highly respected Austrian historian and archivist, to critique the book. Three months later she recommended publication and suggested only a few changes which I could easily make.

The translation of a book is not as simple a matter as might be imagined. For many words and phrases the translation is merely an approximation of the original meaning. Translators must have a thorough knowledge of each language, and even then they cannot know exactly what was in the author's mind. There were many instances when my translators found a word in a German-English dictionary that appeared to fit the meaning of the English word but which, in fact, had quite a different connotation. Fortunately, I was able to assist in the translation, and most if not all such errors were avoided.

The Austrian edition of *Forgotten Nazis* was far more than just a translation of the American edition. I was able to add around fifty new sources to the bibliography and forty pages to the text; some minor mistakes in the English-language edition were corrected. The changes, however, did not substantially alter my conclusions. One new and interesting fact had emerged since the publication of *Forgotten Nazis*. I had learned that Hitler had indeed known in advance about the putsch plans that were carried out in July 1934, although he had not initiated them. He had accepted Theo Habicht's assurance that a putsch would enjoy the support of the Austrian army and the majority of the population. The führer had incorrectly assumed that if the putsch failed, he could deny any personal responsibility.

The Austrian edition also included a good many new details about Nazi propaganda, for example, instructions from party officials on how rank-and-file members could carry out person-to-person proselytizing. Likewise, I added information about the social composition of the Austrian Nazi Party and the role the party played in the last days leading up to the Anschluss. Perhaps the best addition to the German translation, which certainly added to the book's popular appeal, was a thirty-two-page section containing fifty-seven illustrations, most of them previously unpublished, which Professor Ackerl herself uncovered, only six of which had appeared in the American edition. They included a variety of periods, geographic areas, and topics related to the Austrian Nazi Party and favored action photos over portraits.

In the foreword to the Austrian edition I mentioned the advantage I thought I had in having no connection to any of the three political camps of the interwar period or to any contemporary political parties. In addition, I stressed that I did not approach the subject with any sense of moral superiority by virtue of simply being an American, mentioning our own history of slavery, racial segregation, the treatment of indigenous Americans, and our expansionist wars against Mexico in 1848 and Spain a half century later. Whereas Austrian Jewish professors had had difficulty being promoted during the interwar period, American Jews were not even hired at some of the country's most prestigious universities; Jewish students in the United States likewise were subjected to quotas when they applied for admission. I concluded the foreword by saying that the book was devoted less to casting blame than it was to uncovering mistakes that should be avoided in the future. At a time when Austria-"bashing" was popular in the United States, my approach was appreciated by Austrian reviewers, even though the book revealed a highly unflattering side of their country's history.

Der Weg in den Nationalsozialismus (The path to National Socialism), which I dedicated to three distinguished Austrian friends, Gerhard Botz, Walter Siegl, and Helmut Sohmen, was given broad publicity in the Austrian press. At least fifty reviews appeared in newspapers, magazines, and scholarly journals, about half of which were detailed and analytical and emphasized the book's readability, thorough research, and objectivity. Several mentioned that I had proven that National Socialism was no mere import from Germany. *Die Presse* called it "important and necessary."[20] Several reviewers praised the book's illustrations.

The book received still more publicity by virtue of my publisher's organizing a discussion in Vienna featuring three of its authors, including myself. All three gave brief speeches to an audience of about sixty journalists, publishers, and historians. I also had two radio interviews. During the same week in February 1988, I was one of twenty-six scholars—eight of them from Austria and the rest from other European countries, North America, and Israel—at the symposium in Vienna dealing with the Anschluss on the occasion of its fiftieth anniversary. We were dinner guests of the Viennese mayor and later chancellor Vranitsky. During the week I attended a huge anti-Waldheim rally. The highlight of the week, however, was a tour of the Nazi concentration camp at Mauthausen guided by one its former inmates. After my return to Florida I wrote Helmut Sohmen and his wife, Anna, that "altogether it was an exciting but hectic week and I'm not too sorry to have it over with."

After a two-week respite in Florida I was off to Europe again, this time with Marianne, to present a paper on "Anti-Semitism and the Austrian Nazi Party" at a symposium at Oxford University on "Politics and Culture in Austria: The 1930s." Following the conference we spent three delightful days sightseeing in London. It was a stimulating and gratifying period in my life. I was tempted to write President Waldheim a letter of thanks for making it all possible.

CHAPTER 14

Assessing Anti-Semitism

"It creates a special climate and atmosphere I can identify with."

A DAUNTING NEW PROJECT

The symposia in Oxford and Vienna in 1988, coinciding with German translation of *Forgotten Nazis,* highlighted the recognition I had been receiving since beginning of the decade both nationally and internationally in the form of requests to review books, both before and after their publication, and to present papers or commentaries at national and regional conventions. In 1983, I returned to Grinnell at the invitation of Joe Wall to give two lectures on Austrian anti-Semitism and Nazi propaganda. An especially exciting invitation came in 1984 from the Center for European Studies at Harvard University and the Austrian Institute in New York to participate in an international symposium on "Austrian Social Democracy, 1918–1934: The Socialist Experiment and Its Collapse." The Harvard paper was just one of sixteen scholarly presentations I made during the 1980s along with twenty-one reviews published in scholarly journals. In 1986 I began a three-year term on the executive committee of the German Studies Association, during which time I twice organized panels for papers related to twentieth-century history.

In the meantime I had begun work on an entirely new research topic. Already in the late spring of 1979, just after *Hitler and the Forgotten Nazis* had been all but formally approved by the University of North Carolina Press, I began thinking about a new project. I toyed with the idea of doing a social and political history of Vienna from 1914 to 1938. My primary mentor, Arthur J. May, had been working on this topic at the time of his death ten years earlier, and his widow had passed along his many notes to me. The subject, however, although neatly limited in time, seemed unwieldy in scope and would have a limited appeal in the United States to anyone who was not a specialist in the field.

I favored instead a book on the history of Austrian anti-Semitism, which I naively thought would be a little more manageable. I was more realistic in my belief that my study of the Austrian Nazis had already given me some useful information and insights about Austrian anti-Semitism. My interest had also been stimulated by my service as a consultant during the 1980s for the Holocaust Memorial Research and Education Center of Central Florida in nearby Maitland. I thought my publications would also make securing grants easier than if I had launched research into less familiar territory.

Anti-Semitism in Austria was both intriguing and daunting. The country's 220,000 self-identified Jews were three and a half times more numerous per capita than the 500,000 Jews of Germany, and the 200,000 Jews who made up 10.8 percent of Vienna's total population at the start of the interwar period were more numerous than the 173,000 Jews of Berlin, who made up only 3.8 percent of the German capital's population. Vienna, which had the sixth-largest Jewish population in the world, was especially interesting, because its Jewish population was divided between those people who were highly assimilated into Austrian culture and those who had recently emigrated from eastern Europe and followed Orthodox practices that set them apart from everyone else—both Gentiles and other Jews. By contrast, nearly all German Jews were highly assimilated; Polish, Romanian, and other eastern European Jews were much less assimilated into their local populations. Austrian anti-Semitism also reflected, in a far more pronounced way than anti-Semitism in Germany, traditional religious prejudices against the Jews. Thus a close study of Austrian anti-Semitism would throw much light on the whole prejudice. So I set out to learn as much as I could about anti-Semitism in general and not merely its Austrian version.

My first order of business was to make sure that my topic had not already been thoroughly explored by other scholars. Peter G. J. Pulzer's *The Rise of Political Anti-Semitism in Germany and Austria* was an excellent account of the phenomenon between 1867 and 1914. However, a careful check of all back issues of the *Austrian History Yearbook* revealed that, as was the case for Austrian Nazism, there were many articles and books that dealt with limited aspects of the topic but none that was comprehensive. Thus reassured, I decided to forge ahead. Sometimes it is best if we can't peer too far into the future. Had I known in 1979 that it would take me thirteen years to finish my new project, I'm not sure I would have undertaken it.[1]

Even more than in my study of the Austrian Nazi Party, I realized that I was entering a minefield. If I was too shrill in my denunciation of Austrian anti-Semitism, Austrians would view me as just another American bent on bashing Austria while ignoring his own country's historical sins. If I soft-pedaled the history of anti-Semitism in Austria, Jews in America and elsewhere would accuse me of whitewashing the phenomenon.

I was also concerned that American Jews might see me as an interloper in what I assumed they regarded as a Jewish preserve. I couldn't have been more wrong. Many Jews I met believed that Gentiles suspected Jewish historians of lacking objectivity in their study of anti-Semitism and the Holocaust. Tess Wise, the executive director of the Holocaust Memorial and Research Center of Central Florida, was instrumental in putting me in touch with local Austrian Jewish refugees. Professor Bill Wright, the director of the Center for Austrian Studies at the University of Minnesota, also helped me contact local Austrian Jewish refugees who were eager to help.

I began my research in the summers of 1980 and 1982 in Vienna. Thereafter, however, I made little progress until 1985, when I participated in a National Endowment for the Humanities summer seminar at Yale University on "Generic Fascism." Looking back, I can see a number of reasons for this hiatus. As mentioned earlier, the publication of a major work by a university press almost inevitably leads to invitations of various kinds. This was especially true of the years 1983–85. However, truth be told, these activities, along with numerous critiques of scholarly manuscripts and grant proposals, were probably not the only reasons why I had not devoted more time to the study of Austrian anti-Semitism. Photocopying and microfilming had enabled me to collect roughly twenty-five hundred documents in Vienna. The majority of these photocopies were of newspapers reduced to half their original size, often requiring a magnifying glass and sometimes a German-English dictionary. Consciously, or probably more likely unconsciously, I had allowed this multitude of documents to intimidate me. The prospect of reading and evaluating so much material in a foreign language was daunting, making smaller and more manageable projects all the more tempting.

The Yale seminar, directed by the distinguished historian Henry Ashby Turner, gave me access to the Yale University Library as well as the library of the Leo Baeck Institute in New York City. I used the seminar to write a paper on Jewish reactions to anti-Semitism in Austria. Even more important, however, was a semester-long sabbatical in the spring of 1986, only my second sabbatical in my twenty-two years in the profession and the first that was a full semester. The sixteen weeks free of teaching and committee duties enabled me to read and translate the majority of my documents.

COMBINING BUSINESS WITH PLEASURE: ISRAEL AND EGYPT IN 1986

From the beginning of my research I realized that a trip to Israel would probably be necessary. The archives of the Viennese Jewish Community (Kultusgemeinde) had been moved to Jerusalem sometime after World War II and were part of the Central Archives for the History of the Jewish People. The Central Zionist Archives, the archives of Yad Vashem—the Holocaust memorial in Jerusalem—and the Israeli National Library would also likely hold vital documents. The Holocaust Center of Central Florida provided me with a generous scholarship, facilitating what otherwise would have been an impossibly expensive trip.

The six weeks that Marianne and I spent in Israel in the summer of 1986 were the most enjoyable and interesting part of my years of research on Austrian anti-Semitism. The summer also marked a major change in our role as parents. Our sons, then nineteen and seventeen, were on their own, working as counselors at YMCA camps in New England. The documents I found in Jerusalem, although significant, did not consume a great deal of time. I also devoted three weeks to attending a seminar on the Holocaust at Yad Vashem. Because I had already read a good many books on the Holocaust, I was somewhat skeptical about whether I would learn much in such a short time. I also had some concerns that the seminar might have a Zionist agenda. Both of these apprehensions soon disappeared. Our group of thirty-three participants, consisting of teachers and directors of Holocaust centers, did make one brief trip to a Zionist headquarters where we received a rather one-sided view of the Israeli-Palestinian conflict. However, the seminar itself was excellent, particularly the lectures of Yehuda Bauer and Ezra Mendelssohn. Each day was filled with three or four lectures in addition to movies and discussions.

We were fortunate in having as one of the seminar members a professional tourist guide. Because the seminar met only from Monday through Thursday, there was plenty of time for our Israeli colleague to show us every corner of Israeli-controlled areas from the Golan Heights in the north to Eilat, Israel's only port on the Gulf of Aqaba, in the extreme south. Marianne and I were impressed not just by the beauty of the country but also by its biblical, Crusader, Turkish, and modern monuments and by its incredibly diverse topography.

Sightseeing was made all the more pleasant by the near absence of tourists in Israel in the summer of 1986. Only a few weeks before our arrival, President Reagan had ordered the bombing of Tripoli, Libya, in retaliation for alleged Libyan terrorism, thus scaring off tourists who didn't seem to realize that Tripoli was a thousand miles away from Israel. When we visited Masada, the mountaintop fortress where Jews made their last stand against Roman soldiers in the early second century, and probably the most frequently visited site in the country, we were almost alone. As it turned out, the only terrorism we encountered in Israel and later in Egypt was when we attempted to cross the streets of Jerusalem, Tel Aviv, and Cairo. Drivers maneuvered with one hand on their steering wheel and the other on their horn. Cars, not pedestrians, had the right of way.

Marianne and I lived for five weeks in a basement apartment in Jerusalem. It was not exactly luxurious. The landlady said it included a television set—which was true—but somehow she failed to mention that it didn't work. However, the apartment was in a beautiful and convenient neighborhood not far from the Mount Scopus campus of Hebrew University. We especially enjoyed evening walks along streets lined with flowers and bushes in small but well-cared-for yards. The yards were closely guarded by watchdogs, so whenever we went for a stroll we set off a chain reaction of howls. Walking, of course, was not the only way to get around Jerusalem. We soon discovered that the city had an excellent bus system—except on Saturdays when only Arab buses operated.

Marianne attended some of the lectures at Yad Vashem and audited a course on Middle Eastern politics at Hebrew University taught by a Canadian immigrant. I joined her class on a field trip to a West Bank settlement, where we discovered that most of its militant inhabitants had emigrated from the United States. On the other hand, we discovered that there were plenty of moderates in Israel who longed for peace with the Palestinians and surrounding Arab states. Most Israelis seemed to realize that the status quo was unsustainable in the long run, but there was widespread disagreement on how to resolve disputes. The more things change, the more they stay the same.

Toward the end of the Yad Vashem seminar we decided that as long as we had come this far, we might as well see Egypt. We thought that we were probably out of our minds to visit Egypt in August, where afternoon high temperatures averaged 105 degrees in the south. Once there, however, we quickly discovered that humidity levels around 5 percent made even the southern Egypt more comfortable than Florida. As long as one wore a broad-brimmed straw hat and constantly drank cold bottled water—readily available at every tourist site—sightseeing could be quite comfortable in the morning and evening. Our main meal was at noon, after which we took a long siesta, like the natives.

We spent three of our eight days in Egypt in Cairo and its environs. Cairo itself was incredibly crowded and polluted; our eyes began to burn five minutes after we stepped out of our hotel. We found the poverty and overcrowded streets and housing to be both depressing and nerve-racking. A standing joke in the Egyptian capital was: "Should we walk or do we have time enough to drive?" On the other hand, in southern Egypt, which we reached by an overnight, German-built train, we were greeted by bright blue skies. We especially enjoyed sailing in a felucca on the Nile while viewing the beauty of the golden and sometimes pink sand along with the green valley which was dotted by villages. We saw so many ancient ruins that by the time we left Egypt we had come to think of temples that had been built in 200 BC as relatively new.

GETTING ORGANIZED: THE WRITING OF *FROM PREJUDICE TO PERSECUTION*

In the summer of 1987, Marianne and I returned to Vienna for six and a half weeks so I could have one last look at the city's archives and libraries, above all the National Library. As my research progressed in Vienna I noticed that I was beginning to run across essentially the same information—a sure sign that my research was reaching the point of diminishing returns and could soon be ended. Once again we were able to use Gerhard Botz's apartment on Gumpendorferstrasse, which had recently been furnished not only with a refrigerator but also with a new shower and even a television set. We used the latter for an hour or so in the evening to improve our German. Sightseeing was limited to a bus trip to a special exhibition on the Age of Joseph II, such exhibitions being a favorite Austrian means of attracting summer tourists. We also went hiking in the Vienna Woods and sipped new wine in Grinzing.

After devoting much of 1987 and early 1988 to putting the finishing touches on the German translation of *Hitler and the Forgotten Nazis* and participating in the international symposia in Vienna and Oxford, I was able to resume my study of Austrian anti-Semitism in the summer of 1988. That summer saw the first of three straight years in which we returned to Laramie, where most of the book was written.

It was an ideal situation. The friends we had made at the University of Wyoming were still there. Our son Glenn, by that time a student at the

University of Wyoming, was able to find us rental housing each summer. I borrowed his word processor, so I needed only to bring relevant documents with me from Florida. An annual membership at the golf course in Laramie could be had for just $200 (or $350 today), enabling me to play three times a week. It was a marvelous break from my writing, which usually consumed six to eight hours a day. We also picnicked in the mountains, attended concerts, and went to excellent plays put on by grad students. Once a week there was an open-air band concert in Washington Park. Low temperatures and even lower humidity kept me feeling energized. It was an excellent way to combine writing with recreation.

Before I could write, I needed an outline. All historical writing involves compromises between chronological and topical approaches. Even diplomatic and military history, which lend themselves most easily to a chronological organization, must be treated to some extent topically, because many noteworthy events occur simultaneously. Any study of political anti-Semitism in Austria was bound to be particularly difficult to organize. It was influenced by great historical events such as the economic depression of the 1880s and 1890s, World War I, postwar inflation, and especially the Great Depression. Nevertheless, the character of Austrian anti-Semitism varied enormously from one political party to another and from one social class to another, and it depended on whether or not one was religious or secular. These differences could only be discussed topically.

After two trial outlines I hit on the idea of dividing the book into five major parts, each with its own introduction and three to five closely related chapters. The idea of using parts and preambles was inspired by the German journalist-historian Joachim Fest, who had written a best-selling biography of Hitler. Once I had an outline and had organized my notes accordingly, the writing itself went quickly. The whole project seemed like a giant jigsaw puzzle that gradually became a clear picture as I wrote. Bits of information that seemed irrelevant when I found them often made sense when placed side by side.[2] Without the distractions of lectures to give and committee meetings to attend, I could avoid multitasking, which, according to the latest research, slows the completion of a project by 50 percent.[3] I set a goal of writing a chapter a week and kept to it.

My writing was also enormously facilitated by my ability to use a Smith Carona word processor. It was not a full-fledged computer able to "cut and paste," automatically number and renumber footnotes, or check spelling; however, it did allow me to write with a certain abandon without worrying about whether I would later have to retype entire pages. I had always handwritten first drafts, including important business letters, on yellow legal pads. I would double-space, allowing plenty of room to make changes between lines. After crossing things out and rewriting passages numerous times, I would finally type out the manuscript. Then the process of editing and typing would begin all over again. It all seems practically medieval today and was indeed enormously time consuming and frustrating, but there was no realistic alternative. Fortunately, I could type fairly quickly and in time my writing became more and more fluent, so fewer drafts were necessary. Young people today have no idea how lucky they are to have computers, not just to write but also to look up facts.

By the end of 1988 my work had progressed to the point where I thought I could at least sound out publishers. I decided to begin my search with the University of North Carolina Press. With the exception of the long time it had taken to get responses from outside reviewers, I was more than satisfied with its production of *Hitler and the Forgotten Nazis*. If they adopted my new work they could publicize both books simultaneously. Consequently, on December 5 I sent an outline and the book's preface to Lewis Bateman, the executive editor at the press, advising him that "in 1979, shortly before completing *Hitler and the Forgotten Nazis*, I decided to give 'equal time' to the Nazis' victims, the Jews. . . . [My book] will be the first comprehensive work in any language on the history of Austrian anti-Semitism and the Jewish response to it."

Barely a week later I received a phone call from Bateman, followed the next day by a letter offering a contract, contingent on my sending the completed manuscript of 450 pages by September of the next year. I was stunned. I had not imagined so quick and positive a response. My only reservation was that I doubted that I could limit the manuscript to 450 pages. I also made it clear that I wanted a completely separate contract with the Österreichischer Bundesverlag in Vienna, which had already shown a strong interest in my proposed book. As it turned out, I missed the deadline by only two days. I also exceeded the 450-page maximum length by a good 150 pages, although the press wasn't upset by that issue either.

Nearly every major research enterprise, whether it is in history or in some completely different area, requires the collaboration of other scholars in closely related areas of expertise. Some of my colleagues at the University of Central Florida, such as Elmar Fetscher and Moshe Pelli, gave me valuable advice, as did Bob Schwarz of Florida Atlantic University. The most useful and thorough recommendations, however, came from Donald Niewyk of Southern Methodist University and John Haag at the University of Georgia. Professor Niewyk had published *The Jews in Weimar Germany*, and Haag had written several articles on political anti-Semitism at the University of Vienna. Both gave me indispensable advice. Especially helpful was Niewyk's suggestion that I "tighten up [my] anti-Semitic typologies [and] distinguish more dramatically between the Nazis' vicious, racial anti-Semitism and varieties of Judeophobia that were qualitatively different as measured by, among other things, the ways in which they hoped to solve the 'Jewish problem.'"[4]

Evidently my choice of critics was good, because Bateman later asked the same two men to submit confidential evaluations of my manuscript directly to him. Niewyk wrote in his commentary that he was "happy to report that [my manuscript] was a fine piece of work. Pauley has written a pioneering study of anti-Semitism, and Jewish reactions to it, during the short life of the First Austrian Republic. . . . No one before has examined interwar Austrian anti-Semitism with such breadth, depth and sensitivity."[5] Haag wrote that "[Pauley's] knowledge of Austrian conditions for this period is strong, his judgments well-reasoned and usually persuasive, and his research impressive. . . . He is far ahead of Austrian historians who have only come into their own in the last decade or so in terms of substantially digging into this difficult and controversial segment of their own national history."[6] It took me another six months to carry out the revisions they suggested and resubmit my manuscript. Both men approved of these changes in July 1990. In early October, Bateman confirmed that the press would publish my book.[7]

There still remained the usual problem of a title. For several years I intended to call it "In the Shadow of Death: Jews and Anti-Semitism in Austria from Emancipation to Destruction." I thought the main title, which of course was from Psalms ("Yea, though I walk through the valley of the shadow of death . . ."), accurately and dramatically depicted the situation of the Jews of Austria in the interwar period. Unfortunately, however, someone had used the quotation for a book title before I could get my work into print. Don Niewyk suggested the title *From Prejudice to Persecution*. I was not enthusiastic about it, probably because I had not thought of it myself, but I agreed to it for lack of a better alternative. I don't recall who came up with the subtitle: *A History of Austrian Anti-Semitism*.

By the time my book was accepted for publication I had made four research trips to Vienna (1980, 1982, 1987, 1989) and one to Israel (1986). I had read 58 different newspapers and around 450 books, dissertations, and articles in addition to thousands of documents in thirteen archives in Austria, Israel, Germany, and the United States. What had I learned about Austrian anti-Semitism? I began my concluding chapter by saying that "it would probably not be an exaggeration to suggest that 'Jewish predominance' was the single most pervasive and persistent issue in Austrian politics in the six decades preceding the Anschluss in 1938. No other idea was denounced more frequently and by so many political parties and private organizations over so long a period of time. No political party of any significance entirely ignored the issue for long."[8]

Anti-Semitism was also the perfect vehicle of anti-democrats wishing to embarrass the federal government. There was always some "Jewish problem" that the government could not possibly solve by democratic means or whose solution would be rejected by the international community at a time when impoverished and isolated Austria needed all the outside help it could get. On the other hand, no political party in Austria was dependent on anti-Semitism for its very existence, not even the Nazis, whose "anti-Marxism" (anti-Socialism and anti-Communism) was more important and more popular than its anti-Semitism.

An odd discovery was that all but the most extreme anti-Semites had no problem with reading Jewish-edited newspapers, attending plays by Jewish playwrights, shopping in Jewish-owned department stores, and patronizing Jewish physicians and lawyers. The conclusion I finally reached was that for the most part Austrian anti-Semites disliked Jews in the abstract, but not necessarily Jews they knew personally.

Another interesting discovery I made resulted in part from interviews and correspondence with twelve Jewish refugees living in Florida and Minnesota. It gradually became apparent to me how differently they had been affected by anti-Semitism. Some Jews, especially middle- or upper-middle-class Jews living in overwhelmingly Gentile areas, were hardly even aware that the prejudice existed. Others, especially those living in heavily Jewish areas in Vienna such as the Leopoldstadt and students at Austrian universities, witnessed it almost on a daily basis. Some Jews encountered physical violence, whereas others happily socialized with Gentiles and often married them. Indeed, intermarriage and a low birthrate threatened the very survival of the Jewish community in Austria over the long run, something never acknowledged by anti-Semites.

Jews also responded in very different ways to anti-Semitism, which both reflected and aggravated divisions within the Jewish community. The more-assimilated Jews thought it was a temporary phenomenon that would eventually disappear. In the meantime it could either be ignored or fought within the legal system. Zionists, who became stronger after Hitler's rise to power in 1933, thought that the prejudice was permanent and could be avoided only if Jews withdrew from Gentile society and eventually emigrated to what was then called Palestine. Orthodox Jews thought anti-Semitism was God's punishment for Jews abandoning their traditional faith. These radically differing ideas prevented Austrian Jews from forming a common front, although even such a front almost certainly would not have saved them because of their small numbers and the scarcity of Christian sympathizers.

A pleasant discovery in my research was that the U.S. government succeeded in protecting American students—many of them Jewish—who had been assaulted at the University of Vienna. On the other hand, it was dismaying to discover how frequently Austrian anti-Semites referred to American racial laws and discrimination toward Jews to justify their own anti-Semitic policies.

Finding an Austrian publisher for *From Prejudice to Persecution* was easy compared to the long struggle I had had getting *Forgotten Nazis* published in a German translation, reflecting a clear change in how Austrians viewed their own past after the Waldheim affair. As soon as it became apparent that the University of North Carolina Press would publish the book, I contacted Dr. Karin Wolf, my editor for the Austrian edition of *Forgotten Nazis* at the Österreichischer Bundesverlag in Vienna. She replied that "there are many books on Jews and anti-Semitism, but not one that even comes close to being as comprehensive as yours."[9]

Just when it appeared that the ÖBV would publish my book, something happened that all authors dread: a change in the management staff at the ÖVB. Eventually the new management decided that it would no longer publish history books. Fortunately, all was not lost, as Dr. Wolf, supported by my friend Gerhard Botz, took the initiative in contacting another major Viennese publisher, Kremayr and Scheriau, the same publisher that had rejected *Hitler and the Forgotten Nazis* because it was "too scholarly." Its editor in chief, Gerhard Kellinger, wrote me that it was "important, in this time of great revolutions . . . and when nationalism and fascism threaten to appear, that a book such as yours be published."[10] The translation went smoothly and was aided by my having included all of the original German text in the quotations I had made in the American edition. Several reviewers later commented on the quality of the translation.

The American edition of *From Prejudice to Persecution* was published in 1992, the Austrian edition a year later. As with *Forgotten Nazis*, my Austrian publisher wanted me to come to Vienna to help "present" the book to the public. This involved a public discussion at the Jewish Community Center of Vienna and interviews on two radio stations. The interviews went well because they were recorded and all my long, awkward pauses were deleted. I was leery, however, of a discussion where I couldn't speak from prepared notes. I was afraid that my imperfect German would make me look like a dimwit. As it turned out, I was saved by a long exchange between the famous Nazi hunter, Simon Wiesenthal, an Austrian historian (Dr. Gerhard Jagschitz), and the leader of the Jewish Community Center, all of whom had nice things to say about the book. It seemed odd at the end of the evening when Wiesenthal asked me to autograph his copy of my book; I thought it should be the other way around.

REVIEWS AND AWARDS

The hardback and paperback English editions of the book as well as the Austrian edition all sold out. The latter reached fourth on the best-seller list. As with the Austrian edition of *Forgotten Nazis*, however, this status was less impressive than it sounds because of Austria's relatively small population. Historians almost always have to think of royalties as modest bonuses, not as a substantial part of their income.

Far more rewarding for me than the sales were the reviews I received in the United States, Austria, Britain, and Israel. The *Jerusalem Post* wrote that "Professor Pauley's brilliantly presented account of over a century of anti-Semitism in Austria . . . deserves to be read not only by every Jew, but by every Austrian. In its scope (it actually begins in the Middle Ages), it is one of the best books on anti-Semitism ever written." The *American Historical Review* said the book "provides the most comprehensive analysis of Austrian anti-Semitism to date. . . . Pauley attempts to present a balanced account of both the perpetrators of anti-Semitism and their victims." Other scholarly journals described the book as a "magisterial study of Austrian anti-Semitism" and a "success in analyzing the forms of anti-Semitism [and] . . . the variety of responses among Jews. *Modern Austrian History* described it as "evenhanded" and "readable," and *Patterns of Prejudice* called it "authoritative [and] readable."[11]

Reviewers in Austria were also complimentary. The book was described as "fair, ambitious, and expansive" and as "required reading for Austrians interested in history and politics. . . . No school library should be without it." Herbert Steiner, at the time the director of the Resistance Movement Archive in Vienna and someone who had helped me a great deal in my research, wrote that "[Pauley] is a friend of Austria, but nevertheless is an objective foreigner who was predestined to grapple with this difficult problem in Austrian history."[12]

Every book author's dream is to win an award. I was fortunate enough to receive two such awards for *From Prejudice to Persecution*. The prize committee for the Austrian Cultural Institute described the book on its plaque as "a pioneering study of anti-Semitism and Jewish reactions to it. . . . It is not only exhaustively researched, but [also] presented with admirable clarity and vivid detail. It is indeed a masterful piece of work." The award was accompanied by a $2,000 research grant from the institute. The other recognition was the Charles Smith Award of the European History Section of the Southern Historical Association. The award committee wrote that it was "unanimous in agreeing that Professor Pauley's book . . . [displays] authoritative scholarship and literary style which combine to make [it] an outstanding historical study of a tragic period in the history of Austria and Europe. Of the twenty-six books from American presses nominated for the Charles Smith Award, Bruce F. Pauley's book [is] clearly the superior work in the committee's judgment."

As gratifying as the reviews and awards were, I derived almost as much satisfaction from letters I received from Jewish readers of the book. Harold Stern of Willow Grove, Pennsylvania, wrote that he "had never understood the deep set anti-Semitism that pervaded the atmosphere until I read your book. . . . Your wonderfully researched reports from various angles were an eye opener to many things that I have never understood about the Austrian phenomenon." Thomas O. Schlesinger, a professor of political science at Plymouth State College in New Hampshire, wrote that he had "rarely felt so enriched. Your book is enormously informative on anti-Semitism in general, not only on the place and time on which it is focused. A great contribution. And it is just plain well written." Lillian Axel, an Austrian Jewish émigré, wrote me that the book "makes fascinating and easy reading and I have a problem to put it down. For me, it will fill many gaps in my knowledge of the evolution of anti-Semitism in Austria. [It] creates a special climate and atmosphere which I can identify with." A young Austrian historian, Dr. Brigitte Lichtenberger-Fenz, who herself had worked on Austrian anti-Semitism, wrote that she believed that "this book, will be a standard work. It has fostered many new insights and points of view."[13]

It wasn't just refugees and scholars who read the book either. My friend Walter Siegl ordered several copies for the Austrian Foreign Ministry. His initiative evidently produced results. When I met the Austrian ambassador to the United States at a meeting of the German Studies Association in Washington, he told me that he was reading the book at that very time. The ultimate reward (in part) for writing *From Prejudice to Persecution* came many years later, in April 2010. At that time another Austrian ambassador to the United States, Christian Prosl, personally presented me with the highest Austrian award for scholarship and art, the Ehrenkreuz erste Klasse für Wissenschaft und Kunst (Cross of Honor First Class for Scholarship and Art) at a ceremony in Orlando.

Researching and writing of a book—especially a big book—is an act of faith. Even an advance contract does not guarantee its publication. Nor is there any way of knowing its real impact on its readers. Sales and reviews are obvious indicators, but the number of people reading a used academic book or a copy borrowed from a library might be several times larger than the number of new copies sold. Nevertheless, based on the amount of research involved, its sheer length, and the number and quality of the reviews it engendered, *From Prejudice to Persecution* was undoubtedly my most important book. Excluding the time I had been distracted by other projects, I had devoted roughly eleven years to the project by the time the Austrian edition was published in 1993. It had become an integral part of my life. Henry Turner at Yale, who had labored many years on his mammoth work *German Big Business and the Rise of Hitler*, said it well in a letter he wrote me shortly after the publication of *From Prejudice to Persecution*: "I know it's a relief to have it done, but I also know from experience that publishing a long-term work of that sort is a bit like having a limb amputated. You'll miss it, I predict."[14] The great English historian Edward Gibbon, author of the monumental *Decline and Fall of the Roman Empire*, remarked upon its completion that "a sober melancholy was spread over my mind by the idea that I had taken my everlasting leave of an old and agreeable companion."[15]

CHAPTER 15

Hot on the Trail of the Cold War

"We didn't find a single 'true believer.'"

"TOTALLY" NEW INTERESTS

Professor Turner was right: the study of Austrian anti-Semitism had been part of my life for such a long time that I could hardly imagine being involved in another subfield of history. By the time the Austrian edition of *From Prejudice to Persecution* was published in 1993, I had been studying some aspect of Austrian history since 1957. Although I had always tried to place Nazism and anti-Semitism in their broadest possible context, Austria had remained my geographic focal point. Fortunately for me, the Waldheim affair continued to arouse popular and scholarly interest in Austria between 1986 and 1988, the fiftieth anniversary of the country's annexation.

In November 1989, however, international attention had shifted to the collapse of the Communist regime in East Germany, followed soon thereafter by the overthrow of Communist governments in Russia's other satellite states and the secession of the Baltic States from the Soviet Union. Two years later the Soviet Union itself collapsed into its component parts. The disintegration of the Soviet Union and its empire made it possible for the first time to compare all three dictatorships—the Nazi, Communist, and fascist regimes—from their origins to their demise. Moreover, the term "totalitarianism," which had been in disrepute during times of improved relations between the United States and the Soviet Union, was again in vogue, especially among people who had been living behind the Iron Curtain. The 1990s, therefore, were an ideal time to study Hitler's Germany, Stalin's Russia, and Mussolini's Italy.

In 1989 Keith Eubank had asked if I was interested in writing a book for the European History series, which he was editing for the Harlan Davidson Publishing Company.[1] According to its guidelines, the series was "[not] intended to supplant textbooks but rather to provide more in-depth, analytical interpretations. . . . The subject of each volume [was to be] an issue, event, or era that has posed a problem of interpretation for historians and which is a major point of interest in European history. . . . Each volume [was to] be an interpretive essay combining analysis and narration with a synthesis of the best scholarship."[2] I was flattered by Professor Eubank's proposal, but in 1989 I was too involved in my anti-Semitism book to consider anything else. Fortunately, Eubank renewed his offer three years later, suggesting I write a sequel to *The Habsburg Legacy*. The proposition was tempting, because I was convinced that the ethnic and political quarrels of east-central Europe during the interwar period were bound to reappear now that the heavy hand of the Communist dictatorships had been lifted.

However, I felt better prepared to write a book on the totalitarian dictatorships and believed that such a book would have an even broader appeal. I had been teaching an honors course called "The Rise and Fall of Totalitarianism" for several years in addition to my courses on Nazi Germany and World War II. I also had 150 annotated books related to the totalitarian dictatorships in my personal library. Moreover, I had traveled extensively in European countries that once had totalitarian regimes. Especially valuable were trips to Czechoslovakia in 1957 and 1969, to Bulgaria, Romania, and Hungary in 1964 Most important of all were trips to East Germany in 1969 and 1987 and to Russia in 1980 and (later) 1996. Documents, books, and articles are the bread and butter of historical research. However, there is also no substitute for actually witnessing the everyday life of societies whose regimes purported to be totalitarian.

EAST GERMANY, 1969 AND 1987

Two trips to Czechoslovakia and East Germany (known then as the Deutsche Demokratische Republik, or DDR) were fascinating. The first, taken with my grad school friend Jim Bachman, was in 1969, just one year after Czechoslovakia's "Prague Spring," an attempt to liberalize the country's still largely Stalinist regime. The movement was brutally suppressed by troops from the Communist Warsaw Pact countries. We could see the results of the crackdown on the streets of Prague, where the people were slovenly dressed and looked utterly dispirited and the buildings were even more decrepit than in 1957.

The eight days we spent in East Germany following our departure from Prague were, if anything, even more spellbinding. Traveling by car rather than in an organized group enabled us to engage in numerous private conversations with locals. Nineteen sixty-nine was the twentieth anniversary of the founding of the DDR, a fact driven home by numerous posters around the country. Other posters asserted that the DDR "is our state," demanded that it be admitted to the United Nations, and claimed that its Communist government, under Walter Ulbricht, was responsible for the "longest period of peace in modern German history."

At the Czech–East German border it took us ninety minutes to obtain visas, special East German license plates, car insurance, hotel reservations, and gas coupons; the latter enabled Western visitors to buy high-grade gasoline unavailable to East Germans. All meals and hotel reservations had to be paid for in advance in hard Western currency, though we were free to eat wherever we pleased. We soon discovered that we were nearly the only tourists traveling independently. At the former Nazi concentration camp at Buchenwald a cheerful East German guide asked to which group we belonged and seemed shocked when we said "none." Our hotel accommodations were usually adequate, but not remotely the luxury class they claimed to be. On the other hand, the DDR actually looked relatively prosperous and tidy compared to Czechoslovakia. The East Germans were better dressed and more carefully groomed than the pedestrians we had seen in the Czech capital.

However, Dresden, our first stop, was depressing. British and American planes had done a thorough job of obliterating the historic and beautiful city center but had left the ugly, nineteenth-century industrial outskirts untouched. Empty fields remained where beautiful baroque buildings once stood. The city's famous cathedral, the Frauenkirche (now completely rebuilt), was a pile of rubble. The new streets were wide but nearly devoid of traffic, whereas a prewar postcard showed streets crowded with automobiles. The new buildings lining the streets were sterile and utterly lacked the charm for which the city had been famous.

We spent much of one day in Dresden trying to repair a damaged tire. A garage was almost impossible to find; the new tire proved costly and lasted only about forty or fifty miles before falling apart. Traveling was not made easier by the autobahns, which had obviously not been properly maintained since the fall of the Third Reich. The pavement was so bumpy that we were rarely able to drive faster than forty miles an hour. Also poorly maintained were the royal palaces in Potsdam.

After viewing the destruction that had been wrought on Dresden, I was surprised to discover how much of prewar Berlin's city center had survived the war more or less intact. To be sure, there was plenty of evidence of fighting during the war's last days, as witnessed by the many holes in buildings caused by bullets and shrapnel. But many prewar buildings that were missing in 1969, such as Kaiser Wilhelm II's palace, had been deliberately torn down by the Communist government—despite worldwide protests—to make way for a "People's Palace." After reunification in 1990 the latter was itself torn down as a health hazard. East Berlin, by the way, was never referred to in the DDR as East Berlin, but simply as "Berlin, the capital of the DDR." City maps showed only blank spots for the western sectors of the city.

A highlight of East Berlin was the Museum of German History. Located in the former Prussian royal armory, the museum had exhibits covering the period from just before the French Revolution to the establishment of the DDR in 1949. In reality the museum didn't cover the history of Germany but instead the history of the working-class movement. No mention was made of the Protestant Reformation, the classical German authors and great composers, or even the fact that German universities were the world's best in the nineteenth century. Instead, the museum's theme was that nothing really good happened in Germany before the founding of the DDR. German history simply consisted of militarism and capitalist exploitation salvaged only by the growth of class consciousness among the lower classes.

Some of the omissions were downright hilarious. One exhibit said that the democratic Weimar Republic, which had preceded the establishment of the Hitler's Third Reich in 1933, had been secretly rearming "abroad." Somehow it failed to mention that it had been rearming in the Soviet Union. Elsewhere a chart showed all the countries with which the Soviet Union had established non-aggression pacts during the 1930s without including the Nazi-Soviet Non-Aggression Pact of August 1939. The museums displays were excellent illustrations of how history could be distorted as much by omissions as by blatant lies.

Before leaving the DDR we were privileged to meet the brother and nephew of the University of Wyoming's chief landscape architect, Otto Dahl, in Rostock, on the Baltic Sea. Both men were physicians and acknowledged that they enjoyed a decent standard of living, especially since so many East German physicians had escaped to the West before the wall divided East and West Berlin in 1961. However, like other East Germans they were able to watch West German television and so were well aware how much poorer they were than their peers in the West. By far their biggest complaint, as well as that of other East Germans we met, was their inability to travel in the West or even to Czechoslovakia or Yugoslavia. Bulgaria was the only country heavily promoted. Excursions to capitalist countries, of course, were completely out of the question except for retirees who could leave permanently, thus sparing the regime the cost of their pensions.

As the two physicians spoke about their inability to travel I recalled a moment that had occurred a few days earlier in East Berlin. Standing on the eastern side of the Brandenburg Gate gazing into West Berlin, I realized that if I had been an East German it would have been easier to travel six thousand eastward to Vladivostok on the Pacific Ocean than to walk a hundred yards to the west. Being able to walk those hundred yards anytime I pleased left me with a certain sense of guilt. I could do so merely because of the accident of my birth.

It was remarkable that among all the people with whom we spoke we didn't find a single "true believer," not even among the younger generation that had been thoroughly schooled in Marxist ideology. The general attitude toward the regime ranged from skepticism to sullen but resigned hostility. On the other hand, we didn't get the impression that East Germans were living in a constant state of terror. People spoke about their grievances quite openly, even though in most cases we were total strangers, something that would have been unthinkable in the Third Reich. This relaxed attitude almost certainly resulted from the solidarity of the opposition to the regime. As in other totalitarian states, the East Germans were well aware that they couldn't trust their newspapers.

The most politically sensitive issue was relations with Soviet Union. When East Germans mentioned it they always lowered their voices. We found it revealing that every advertisement for a concert included a piece by a Russian composer. The only American composition performed that summer in the DDR was Leonard Bernstein's *West Side Story*, which "confirmed" Communist assertions about the violence and ethnic divisions of American society. Of course, the East German government was not alone in using culture for political purposes after World War II. All of the Allies tried to promote their culture in their zones of occupation, although Americans were less active in doing so than Russians.[3]

When leaving East Germany, Jim and I had to have our documents checked twelve miles before even reaching the border. At the border our luggage was thoroughly scrutinized; the examination of our car included not only the trunk but also the engine. The backseat was even removed by a machine-gun-toting guard to see if we were trying to smuggle out any human contraband. Once these inspections were completed, a guard opened a heavy iron gate. To proceed we had to drive through a ditch and then slowly zigzag through an obstacle course of huge concrete pillars on either side of the narrow road. Thus, even the most intrepid East German would think twice about trying to blast his way across the border in some sort of heavily armored homemade vehicle. Beyond the road, on both sides, was an area a quarter of a mile wide filled with rows of barbed-wire fences and mine fields. Once we reached the West German side of the border we felt like we had just left a concentration camp. Indeed, the "wall" encompassing East Germany was far more imposing than the one surrounding the Nazi concentration camp at Dachau, which we had seen two weeks earlier.

Just after reaching West Germany, I wrote Marianne a postcard stating, "We're out! What a relief. E. Germany was very interesting, but a nerve-racking experience. An unbelievable amount of red tape. . . . Now it seems as though we're almost back in the States."[4] A day later I wrote that the "people of the DDR [are] friendly & talkative, but I felt terrible sympathy for them. [There are] Russian and propaganda signs everywhere."

Eighteen years later, in 1987, I returned to the DDR, this time with Marianne. We were participants in a Bradley Berlin Seminar sponsored by the East and West German governments and organized by Bradley University in Illinois. Our ten days included visits to virtually all the country's important cities: Wittenberg, Erfurt, Eisenach, Weimar, Dresden, Potsdam, Torgau, and East Berlin, most of which were associated with Germany's cultural and historical icons such as Martin Luther, Johann Sebastian Bach, Johann Goethe, Friedrich Schiller, and Frederick the Great. Designed for historians, political scientists, and teachers of German language and literature, the group met professors, a mayor, officials in the Foreign Ministry, the director of a machine tool factory, the manager of a collective farm, and a former inmate of Bergen-Belsen who gave us a guided tour of the former Nazi concentration camp. The East Germans, of course, were trying to make a favorable impression on our group, but their propaganda was mostly "soft sell." I'm sure that our hosts knew that the hard-sell type would be counterproductive.

By 1987 East Germany had recovered from the war far more thoroughly than the Soviet Union and easily enjoyed the highest standard of living of any Eastern Bloc country. If it was truly prosperous, however, the wealth was well hidden. East Berlin remained like Havana: an antique car lover's paradise with numerous cars dating back to the prewar period. Scars from the war were still obvious. The autobahns were no better than in 1969; the top realistic speed was still around forty miles an hour. Russians, however, were evidently still convinced that the DDR was indeed prosperous. In 1969 I had noticed Russian officers gazing through shop window with childlike wonderment. Eighteen years later, when we were in Dresden, I asked our East German guide what kinds of questions Russian tourists asked when they visited the country. He said they always wanted to know if the day's itinerary could be scrapped so that they could go shopping. We wondered what they could possibly want to buy. Considering the low quality of products sold in Russia, East Germany apparently looked like a shopper's paradise. Russians also wanted to know how it was possible that the DDR, a defeated country, could enjoy a higher standard of living than the victorious Soviet Union.

One big change I noticed in 1987 was the regime's attitude toward German history. Evidently it had decided that its constant denigration of Germany's prewar past was counterproductive in creating support for the state. The Museum of German History was closed for "renovation." The most obvious indication of a new policy was the return of an equestrian statue of Frederick the Great to its original location on the city's grand boulevard, Unter den Linden.

Few could have predicted in 1987 that the Communist regime would cease to exist and that Germany would be reunited in little more than two years, even though President Reagan issued his famous plea to the Soviet leader, Mikhail Gorbachev, to "tear down this wall" at the very moment Marianne and I were leaving East Berlin.

THE SOVIET UNION AND POLAND, 1980

My most important insights about totalitarianism most likely came from a trip to the Soviet Union in 1980. Marianne, the boys, and I began the summer with a weeklong exploration of London while visiting our friends Helmut and Anna Sohmen. Thereafter, we enjoyed fifteen days in the Low Countries and Scandinavia, saving money by using Eurail passes and sleeping on overnight trains or in youth hostels. The only exception to this routine was three days we spent visiting West Berliners whom we had befriended in Wooster. Besides being thrilled to sleep in real beds again, we enjoyed seeing the prosperous residential districts of West Berlin that had been left relatively unscathed by Allied bombing.

What interested us most about Berlin, however, was the difference between Communist and non-Communist TV. Stations in East Berlin were still broadcasting in black and white; those in West Berlin were in color. News reports from the East were almost invariably about a ceremony in which the manager of some factory was being given an award for surpassing his quota. Any American who hates negative news would have loved the news coming out of East Germany, or any other totalitarian state for that matter. The only bad news reported by East German television and newspapers was confined to events in the West.

Soon after our visit to West Berlin we settled down in Vienna, where I began researching Austrian anti-Semitism. Sometime in late August, shortly after Marianne and the boys returned to Florida to start the school year, I received an unexpected phone call from Walter Siegl, now the chargé d'affaires at the Austrian embassy in Moscow, a rank just a notch below that of ambassador. He insisted that I visit him. I had some qualms about suspending my research in Vienna, but the opportunity to see the capital of the Soviet Union, which appeared (misleadingly) to be at the height of its power and influence, seemed too good to pass up.

Thanks to an official invitation from the Austrian embassy in Moscow, I could get a Russian visa at their Viennese embassy in fifteen minutes. It was far more expensive and time consuming, however, merely to obtain *transit* visas for Czechoslovakia and Poland. The Russian consul told me that I could acquire a Czech visa in fifteen minutes; in reality it took two hours. A Polish visa necessitated two trips to their embassy. Crossing the borders of Czechoslovakia, Poland, and the Soviet Union was even more time consuming. My train, the *Chopin*, stopped for two hours at the Austro-Czech border, two more at the Czech-Polish border, and another three hours at the Polish-Russian border for a total of seven hours of wasted time during a thirty-seven-hour trip. Even in those days, before the formation of the European Union, trains rarely stopped in Western Europe at an international border for more than ten minutes if they stopped at all, and examination of passports was cursory. The Communist countries, by contrast, were just as suspicious of each other as they were of the non-Communist West, a fact Marianne and I had noticed already during our travels in the Balkans in 1964.

The Iron Curtain separating Czechoslovakia and Austria was the most carefully guarded of all the borders I crossed in 1980. A high wire fence paralleled both sides of the track for a distance of at least half a mile, and the whole area was brightly illuminated in order to foil any escape attempts. I was reminded of the feeling I had when entering and especially when leaving East Germany in 1969: a sense of being in a gigantic concentration camp.

After a restless night I awoke in Poland. Everything looked run-down and neglected, far more so than what I had seen in East Germany, Hungary, and Czechoslovakia. Weeds were growing along the tracks, and I noticed a number of high-rise prefabricated apartment buildings in the larger towns. The quality of construction was so poor that it was hard to tell whether a building was going up or coming down.

Another powerful image was Polish technology, or rather its backwardness. At times I almost rubbed my eyes in disbelief; it was like turning the clock back several decades. Steam locomotives, which in the States had spewed their last puff of steam by the mid-1950s, were the rule, not the exception.[5] Even more amazing was the sight of horse-drawn wagons at every train crossing and farmers walking behind horse-drawn plows, something that had become a rarity in the United States by the 1940s.[6] Bicycles were plentiful, and rural roads were mostly unpaved. At least the Poles were not consuming much oil.

Everything in Moscow was on a grand scale. The avenues, about a hundred yards wide, had doubled or tripled in width since the revolutions of 1917. Compensating for the near absence of cars was the excellent 180-mile subway system built by Stalin in the 1930s under the supervision of Nikita Khrushchev, the later Soviet leader. Nevertheless the city's subway trains and buses were horribly overcrowded. On the other hand, the government-subsidized fares were low: a subway ride was the equivalent of only about eight cents; tram and bus fares were even cheaper.

The official Russian guidebook called Moscow "one of the most beautiful cities in the world." In reality its architecture was a mishmash of styles reflecting the city's largely non-Western history and its transformation under Stalin and his successors. Nonetheless, Moscow, a city of 8 million and the fourth largest in the world at that time, looked considerably more "picked up" than Poland. I was also somewhat surprised by the near absence of political billboards, until Walter told me that many "hard-sell" propaganda posters had been removed and the city had been sanitized because of the Olympics, much like what the Nazis did with anti-Semitic posters during the Berlin Olympics in 1936.

Among Moscow's most interesting sights were those churches that had not been included in the hundreds that Lenin and Stalin had ordered destroyed in the 1920s and 1930s. The demolition had included the huge cathedral Christ the Savior, which was torn down before geologists determined that the soil on which it stood would not support what was supposed to be the world's tallest building. Instead, the church was replaced by a swimming pool. Only forty Russian Orthodox churches were still functioning in Moscow in 1980, whereas there had been eight hundred active churches in 1914 for a population of 1.2 million. In Leningrad (today's St. Petersburg), just fourteen churches were left to serve a population of 4.5 million.

One evening Walter and his wife, Gundi, took me to the Bolshoi Theater, built in the mid-nineteenth century and internationally renowned since 1900 for its ballet productions. We saw a ballet performed by an Estonian troupe whose dancing was excellent; but the clothing worn by the audience was tacky. The atmosphere was totally different from Vienna's elegant Staatsoper. During the intermission, sandwiches were weighed and sold by the gram as in a market.

Walter and I spent one day visiting the nearby religious center of Zagorsk, ironically named for a hero of the Bolshevik Revolution. Much of the drive through a landscape resembling Wisconsin or Minnesota was on a new, albeit bumpy, four-lane highway. At a checkpoint we had to slow down so a soldier could record our foreign license plate and pass it on to another checkpoint, where we again had to drive momentarily at a snail's pace. Failure to reach the second checkpoint within a reasonable time could arouse suspicion.

Zagorsk featured the most important remaining Russian Orthodox seminary as well as several churches built between the fourteenth and eighteenth centuries. All the religious buildings were closed soon after the Bolshevik Revolution, but they were reopened during World War II as a means of improving the regime's popularity and support for the war.

The worshippers included people of all ages and both sexes, although older women predominated. Openly practiced religion was not dead in Russia, but it was on life support.

Aside from Moscow's churches and various public monuments, I was especially interested in Moscow's stores. Shop display windows were unimaginative, probably because store managers were well aware that demand already far outstripped supply. Stores were so packed with shoppers that I could hardly move. Gundi, who took me shopping to give me an idea of everyday life in the Russian capital, told me that on any given weekday there were a million non-Muscovites in the city who were there simply to shop. There were often long lines outside stores. Muscovites were so eager to buy scarce products that only after they joined a line did they bother to inquire what was for sale. I saw a crowd of people on a side street waiting to buy tomatoes. In a meat market I saw chicken heads and feet being sold to help satisfy the demand for meat. Separate lines existed inside each store as well. Customers stood in one line to make an order, in another to pay for the purchase, and in still another to pick up their merchandise. Having three clerks doing the job that one did in the United States assured both full employment and long lines. The Siegls told me that the average Russian spent the equivalent of one day a week simply standing in line.

What I found both amusing and pathetic was the existence of special stores for diplomats and high-ranking officials in the Communist Party. These stores offered products—mostly chocolates, liquor, and American cigarettes—that were unavailable to ordinary citizens in the workers' paradise. Venetian blinds made sure that curious Muscovites would be unable to catch a glimpse of the forbidden capitalist goodies. The nicer restaurants were also limited to the foreign and domestic elite. Even souvenir shops for Western tourists were hidden from curious Russian eyes, not that there was much worth buying beyond the famous Matryoshka nesting dolls. If a Western diplomat wanted to do any serious shopping, the best option was a weekend excursion to Helsinki on Finnair for $260 ($680 in today's currency). An American diplomat I met for lunch surprised me only slightly by saying that his wife had told him that if they were Soviet citizens she would want him to join the Communist Party.

Shopping was just one issue that the Siegls had to confront in Moscow. Every summer they had to do without hot water for three weeks while the system in their apartment house was cleaned. Heat was not available until October 1, even though the average temperature then was forty-six degrees. Diplomats assumed that their apartments were bugged. I noticed at a dinner party that when discussing current politics no one spoke above a whisper. Diplomats also had to cope with a number of restrictions and insecurities. Without special permission they could not travel outside a certain radius from Moscow.

After considerable finagling Walter managed to make train reservations enabling me to go first to Leningrad and then to Warsaw. Given the crowded conditions of the overnight train to Leningrad, he suspected that some poor Russian had been kicked off in order to make a room for a "distinguished" foreign visitor. Most impressive about Leningrad was the loving care and expense that had gone into restoring the one-third of the city that had been destroyed during World War II. Hardly a trace of war damage remained. Although the city and its inhabitants looked drab, it was still a showpiece of baroque and neoclassical architecture. The Hermitage art gallery, in the former Winter Palace of the Romanovs, with more than 3 million works of art, was probably second only to the Louvre in its collection of paintings and statues.

An English-speaking guide and university student in Leningrad told a tour group I joined that each Russian was guaranteed fifteen square meters of living space—about 170 square feet. Rent consumed only about 3 percent of the average Russian's income, but Muscovites often waited two years for an apartment. When our bus passed a shoe factory our guide said that it manufactured 500,000 shoes a month; but in a revealing statement he added that an effort was being made to improve quality. Shoes were just one example of the poor quality of consumer goods in the Soviet Union. The whole system was designed to satisfy the desires of the supervisory bureaucracy, not the consumer. For consumers the problem was not availability; there were warehouses full of clothes that no one wanted to buy. Nothing else, not even the absence of civil liberties, caused so much dissatisfaction in the Soviet Union and its satellites as the lack of quality consumer goods.

As in other Communist countries I had visited, the people I saw on the streets of Moscow and Leningrad were not dressed in rags. No one looked abjectly poor, but neither did I see anyone fashionably dressed. The Soviets could be credited with eliminating the desperate poverty that was so prevalent in Russia before the revolution. But there was a drab sameness not only in the appearance of the people but also to the whole way of life. Every city dweller who was not among the 13 percent of the population belonging to the Communist Party lived in a tiny apartment in a huge apartment building. Only rural people continued to live in quaint pre-revolutionary log cabins with ornate window frames.

Shortly after my Warsaw-bound train left Leningrad, a lecture was broadcast through the intercom system. Not knowing Russian, I didn't know exactly what was being said. However, the tone resembled a sermon with the Russian equivalent of "socialism" (sotsializm) and "communism" (kommunizm) being frequently repeated. I concluded that the broadcast was a panegyric on the Soviet system. There was no way that passengers could turn it off. The whole thing reminded me of George Orwell's *1984*. If Big Brother wasn't watching me, he was at least talking to a captive audience.

When the train reached the Polish border, three hours were spent jacking up the cars and replacing the wide, Russian-gauge wheels with the narrower wheels that are standard in the rest of the world (except for Finland and the Baltic States). While this was going on, the usual army of Soviet soldiers and customs officials searched the train for contraband and potential escapees. The officials looked under every seat and even under the flooring in the aisles. The soldiers must have spent at least thirty seconds scrutinizing every passport photo. A customs official even flipped through every page of a souvenir book I had purchased in Moscow until she accidently ran across the official invitation given me by the Austrian embassy in Moscow, which bore a Russian stamp of approval. Walter had told me that Soviet citizens were impressed by official stamps. He was right. Seeing this symbol of authority the agent immediately stopped her inquisition.

Warsaw was the last stop on my ten-day trip into Communist eastern Europe. Unfortunately, most of my time in the Polish capital was devoted to finding a way back to Vienna. I ruefully recalled the Russian consul telling me to buy a round-trip ticket before leaving Vienna. The next morning I decided that my first priority was to purchase a ticket back to Austria. After waiting an hour for the ticket window to open, I was informed by a surly agent that second-class tickets to Austria were sold out for the next two months; even first-class tickets were unavailable for two weeks. By this time I began to break out in a cold sweat wondering whether I would be spending the fall semester in Poland. I considered throwing myself on the mercy of the American embassy, since our embassies are known to help stranded Americans. Fortunately, however, I accidently discovered that credit cards could sometimes be used in Warsaw. A call to Austrian Airlines revealed that it had space on a flight to Vienna that very day. After a thorough search of my luggage at the airport, my last remaining obstacle was a gun-toting soldier standing next to the plane's entrance to prevent any Pole from making a dash for freedom. Once on the plane I was greeted by Viennese waltzes and Western newspapers. I was already "home."

The sense of freedom and a strange combination of relaxation and exhilaration that I felt upon returning to the West after a visit to the Communist bloc is difficult to describe to someone who hasn't experienced it. Being able to understand people and read signs and newspapers again was obviously a factor—but far from the only one. My German was good enough that language was not an issue in East Germany. Yet I still had the same anxiety there in 1969 that I had in Russia and Poland. Far more important to my sense of relief was knowing that I was no longer in a police state where every facet of life was subject to an almost infinite number of regulations that could be unwittingly violated no matter how careful I was.

WAR AND REVOLUTION IN THE BALKANS, 1991

Although totalitarian regimes disappeared in East Germany in 1989 and in other satellite states shortly thereafter, it can hardly be said that the old order disappeared without a trace. Plenty of remnants were still in evidence when Marianne and I visited Albania in 1991 and Russia in 1996.

In 1991, I was invited to teach at the University of New Orleans International Summer School program in Innsbruck. On earlier trips to Austria we had visited several countries besides Austria itself. Even though Yugoslavia was a neighboring state, neither of us had explored it thoroughly. I had seen a bit of Zagreb, Belgrade, Niš, and Skopje in 1958, but Marianne and I had sped through the country in our little Volkswagen Beetle in 1964, eager to get to the warmth and sunshine of Greece as quickly as possible. We had never seen the most beautiful part of the country, the Adriatic (or Dalmatian) Coast. It was our good fortune that Walter Siegl had just become the Austrian ambassador to Yugoslavia—the last person to hold that title, as it turned out. As soon as he learned that we were in Austria, he urged us to come to Belgrade for a visit. Our timing was interesting, to put it mildly.

Walter and Gundi Siegl were their usual hospitable selves. (Walter later told us that if we had arrived just a few days later he "would not have had even five minutes to spare for us" because of the crisis caused by Yugoslavia's disintegration.) We spent the first few days exploring the Yugoslav capital, which we found rather ugly, not surprising perhaps in view of its having been destroyed numerous times throughout its history. What few historic and architecturally interesting buildings it may have had before World War II were mostly obliterated by Nazi bombers in April 1941. Postwar buildings were usually high-rises without any character and, like those in other Communist countries, often in a bad state of repair.

Soon after we arrived in Belgrade, Walter asked where we were headed next. I told him that I had tried to obtain Albanian visas while we were still in the United States but had not been successful. No problem, he said: he would call the Albanian embassy and see that we obtained the necessary documents. Fifteen or twenty minutes after we arrived at the embassy the next morning we had our visas.

We had some qualms about entering Albania because of our fear that we would be unable to find unleaded gasoline for our rental car, or spare parts if the car should break down. Crossing the border itself, however, was easy, and the border officials were friendly. However, once into Albania we felt as if we were in a time warp. The few people we saw in the barren eastern part of the country were tending goats, sheep, or donkeys. We hesitated to stop the car, because every time we did so we were immediately surrounded by children begging for chewing "gummy" or pencils. We saw women washing their laundry in a river and scrubbing the clothes on rocks, just like in the Middle Ages. It took us four hours to traverse the eighty miles from the border to Tirana, the country's capital.

Albania had been a hermit state ever since the Communist takeover at the end of World War II. Its only ally was faraway China. By 1991, few if any tourists had visited the country in half a century, and I'm sure that very few foreigners had seen the country before then. When we occasionally stopped our car, people quickly crowded around to look at it, much like what I had experienced on the way to Prague in 1957.

As we drove deeper into the country, the roads were filled with goats, cattle, horse-drawn wagons, and occasionally bicycles. Only rarely would we even see a truck. The three cars we encountered all had foreign license plates. Albanians wanting to go to a neighboring town did so by foot. The highways were even worse than East Germany's. Thirty-five miles an hour was as fast as we could drive without causing damage either to our car or to ourselves. The country's only two stoplights were in Tirana, and no one paid the least attention to them.

We spent our one night in Tirana in one of only two hotels deemed suitable for foreigners. (We were told to leave our car in a well-lit and closely guarded parking lot.) As was true of the capitals of other Communist countries, Tirana was supposed to be a showpiece, and indeed there were a few attractive buildings along the main avenue, which contrasted sharply with dilapidated buildings elsewhere. A student we met in our hotel dining room admitted that the city's best buildings had been built by the Italians after fascist Italy occupied the country in 1939. In 1991, Italian television was the Albanians' only source of information about the outside world. On the other hand, foreign influences could be seen in the American-style jeans worn by young boys. Many women in rural areas, however, wore white pantaloons and red overskirts revealing a strong Turkish influence.

One reason why there were so many Albanians wandering around aimlessly in the streets was because the country's economy, never exactly robust, had collapsed even before the overthrow of the Communist regime a few months earlier. About half the shops and factories were completely shut down and had broken windows. Store shelves were almost empty, and the unemployment rate was 50 percent. Two Americans we met in Tirana, who were there to teach two-week courses in English, told us that the people were depressed in every way: intellectually, emotionally, and financially. To cope with the hardships, the Albanians appeared to have strong emotional attachments to each other. We frequently saw people of both genders and all ages walking arm in arm. Men and women kissed both cheeks and embraced on the streets.

After two days in Albania we headed north, stopping briefly in the former Montenegrin capital of Cetinje and the onetime Austro-Hungarian naval base of Kotor. We detoured inland to visit Mostar in Bosnia-Herzegovina, with its well-preserved Turkish quarter and sixteenth-century bridge (shortly thereafter destroyed by shelling and still later rebuilt). It was in Mostar that we first noticed the absence of tourists. Not a single patron was in an outdoor restaurant, which had a beautiful view of the turquoise-colored Nereiva River. The same was true of romantic rooftop restaurants in the famous walled city of Dubrovnik. We felt sorry for the waiters, who had nothing to do except stand around. The coastal highway, which ordinarily was crowded with foreign cars, was almost deserted. In each major town we stopped at a tourist agency to see if it was safe to travel further north. In Split, the largest town on the Dalmatian Coast, we saw hand-drawn maps of Croatia, which had just proclaimed its independence from Yugoslavia. In every Croatian home and store we noticed the colors of the newborn republic. The only place where we saw Yugoslav flags was in military installations.

We were witnessing, as I later wrote in an article published in the *Orlando Sentinel*, the partial unraveling of the Paris Peace Settlement of 1919, which had theoretically been founded on the principle of self-determination. However, the Croatians and Slovenes had had no representation in Paris. Almost the only thing attracting them to Serbia had been their common fear of Italy, which was largely nonexistent by 1991. The fact that most of the people of Yugoslavia spoke Slavic languages turned out to be much less important than their historical differences. Oddly enough, the U.S. government, which had encouraged the disintegration of the four-hundred-year-old multinational Habsburg Monarchy in 1918, opposed (unsuccessfully) the breakup of the equally polyglot Yugoslav Republic in 1991.

Our last coastal stop was in Pula, where we learned that fighting had broken out in Slovenia and its borders were closed; a tourist office advised us to leave the country with a specially chartered ferryboat headed for Trieste. We got in line at the dock at 2:00 p.m., only to wait until 10:00 for our departure. We arrived in Trieste at 1:30 a.m. and finally disembarked an hour later. By then all the hotels and motels in the area were either booked solid or closed for the night. We had no choice but to keep driving until we found a rest stop next to our *autostrado*, where we managed to sleep in our car for a couple of hours. We were never in much danger, but we did have some notion of what it was like to be war refugees.

After summer school ended in Innsbruck, Marianne and I went to Poland to see Cracow (Kraków) and the nearby Nazi concentration camp of Auschwitz-Birkenau. Auschwitz had changed little since it had been liberated by the Russians in January 1945. Unlike other death camps such as Treblinka and Sobibor, the Nazis had been unable to destroy the evidence of their brutality. The Holocaust is often described by statistics. But for us the most enduring images were the pictures of victims and the names and cities that appeared on suitcases they had brought with them, not to mention the huge piles of human hair and prostheses of all kinds. The importance of this visit for my book on totalitarianism cannot be exaggerated.

RUSSIA, THE BALTIC STATES, AND POLAND, 1996

Greatly aiding my understanding of totalitarianism and its aftermath was my return to Russia in the summer of 1996. Once again, Walter Siegl was a catalyst. He was back in Moscow, this time as the Austrian ambassador to Russia and eight other former Soviet states. Marianne and I were eager to see more than just Moscow and St. Petersburg. After a little investigating we discovered that it was possible to see both cities, plus numerous points in between, by riverboat. Our eight-hundred-mile route followed the Neva Riva upstream to Lake Ladoga, the largest lake in Europe. From there we went to Lake Onega and then by canals to the Upper Volga River. Still more canals, constituting a bigger project than either the Suez or Panama canals, finally brought us to Moscow. Knowing very little at that time about my

Volga German ancestors, I was completely unaware that we were following in part the same route they had traversed in 1766–67. Thanks to canals that Stalin had built with conscript labor during the 1930s, including quite possibly some of my distant relatives, we were able to cruise from St. Petersburg to Moscow in just a week. By 1996, of course, the Soviet Union and its Communist regime had been gone for almost five years. Nevertheless, much of what we saw during our two-week trip told us a great deal about totalitarianism and its legacy.

It took twenty-four hours to fly from Florida to St. Petersburg via Vienna. We were pleasantly surprised, however, that getting through Russian passport and customs controls was a breeze compared to what I had experienced in 1980. We spent our first night in a huge, dreary Soviet-era hotel. The first thing we noticed in our room was horrible brown water that gurgled from our faucets. Although we were in need of baths, we decided that could wait until we boarded our riverboat the next day. Our room and beds were small, but we could get CNN on our TV, something that would have been unthinkable in Soviet times. Newer, far more elegant hotels were located near St. Petersburg's famous St. Isaac's Cathedral in the center of town. Patronized mostly by foreigners, they even provided their guests with free English-language newspapers, the *St. Petersburg Times* and the *Moscow Times*.

By chance, my old Rochester friend Gilbert McArthur, still a Russian history professor at the College of William and Mary, along with his seventeen-year-old daughter, Grace, happened to be in St. Petersburg doing research at the very time we were there. He was able to show us how to use the fast and clean subway system, which cost the equivalent of just twenty-five American cents—a bargain for Americans, but far from cheap for Russians, whose average monthly income at that time was just $100 ($137 today). The subways had been deep enough to use as bomb shelters during the war. Even though subway trains came along every three minutes, they were always crowded, especially near the city center. The passengers, both in St. Petersburg and later in Moscow, were quiet, polite, and neatly although not fashionably dressed. The stations were also remarkably free of graffiti, as were the subway trains themselves.

On the second day of our trip we were able to board our riverboat, the *Krasin*, and join our shipmates on a city tour. We passed many tall, dilapidated apartment houses that were obviously prefabricated. They were built during and after Khrushchev's time (1955–64) as part of his push to alleviate housing shortages. Apartment houses built under Stalin had been more substantial in construction but had not kept up with demand as Soviet cities experienced a population boom caused by the Soviet dictator's push for rapid industrialization. World War II then took a heavy toll on what was already an enormous housing shortage. Khrushchev tried to catch up by favoring quantity over quality; five-story buildings didn't even have elevators. The result was that by 1996 many apartment houses ringing St. Petersburg looked almost uninhabitable. Each Russian was still, as in 1980, supposedly guaranteed around 170 square feet of living space, but that was well below that of other former Communist states and only about one-sixth to one-seventh the space found in apartments in Western Europe.

There were only 136 (mostly very well-traveled) passengers on the *Krasin*, which was operated by the Uniworld travel company. Built by East Germans in 1989 for top-level Communist Party members in the Soviet Union, it was upgraded in 1995 and provided with an elegant dining room and three tastefully furnished lounges. This refurbishing made it all the more ironic that our boat and Stalin's canals were now used for the benefit not of Communist bigwigs but of Western capitalists. At least half the boats we saw along the way were carrying tourists, rather than the heavy freight for which the canals had been built.

Our cabin was reasonably comfortable. The onboard entertainment by eight Russian music students dressed in colorful native costumes was excellent; they all came from small provincial towns where folk music was still popular. The boat's food, however, was mediocre at best, in part because 50 percent of the country's grain and 60 percent of its fruit rotted in fields, because of poor infrastructure, and never reached markets, even though 24 percent of the Russian population was engaged in agriculture (compared to less than 2 percent in the United States). Gundi Siegl later told us that as the wife of the Austrian ambassador even she had trouble obtaining quality foodstuffs for entertaining at the embassy.

Every time we took a city tour or our boat was docked we were greeted with peddlers hawking books, dolls, jewelry, watches, lacquered bowls, T-shirts, postcards, war memorabilia, shawls, and a number of other mostly homemade items. Fortunately, they were not aggressive and took no for an answer, unlike vendors we were to encounter on trips to China and India. Sometimes we would be met by small bands playing Dixieland jazz or marches. At other times middle-aged ladies offered fresh flowers from their gardens. We admired them for not begging, and many passengers on our boat gave them tips or bought their products. Our guides told us that the Russians were discovering entrepreneurial talents that they didn't even know they had. This was all the more remarkable when one remembers that the Communist regime had equated "business" with "crime." Likewise, there was no tradition of respect for private property. Even the czars had confiscated much property, especially that belonging to ethnic Germans.

The small towns we visited during our river cruise were mostly impoverished. Side streets were either unpaved or littered with huge potholes. Many people still depended on public wells for their water. Little pre-Bolshevik Revolution log houses, however, often had charming, highly decorated window frames. Everyone seemed to have a garden, and many people owned a goat. In one town we were able to get into three dachas, little garden houses in the countryside used by people who lived in apartments in nearby cities. On their tiny plots they could grow badly needed vegetables. What they wanted in exchange for their hospitality of tea and cookies were vegetable seeds.

We were impressed with a kindergarten in the middle of a big complex of nine-story apartment buildings in Kostrama, not far from Moscow. Parents had to pay 15 percent of their income to enroll their children, and it probably had well-above-average amenities: beautifully equipped scaled-down furniture, dolls, a tropical garden, exercise room, ballet room, and a swimming pool. Its children seemed happy. However, Russia's birthrate was far below the replacement level, and what few children we saw were usually well dressed and obviously pampered. Girls were often decked out in frilly white dresses and had big bows in their hair, much like the ones my mother had worn nearly a century earlier.

Our guides, who were all women, were often teachers of English during the school year. They were highly trained, charming, and usually beautiful. To maintain their licenses they had to take rigorous annual tests. We were also fortunate to have on our boat a fifty-seven-year-old economist from the Moscow Institute of International Relations, Eduard Vertumian, who was "moonlighting" on our cruise in order to earn some much-needed hard currency. Most of the problems he described in four lectures were holdovers from the Soviet era, although some had worsened since the fall of the Soviet regime in 1991.

The basic reason for the collapse of the Soviet Union, Professor Vertumian maintained, was the failure of the regime to provide a decent standard of living for its citizens, a standard that actually declined starting in the late 1970s. By the 1980s Russians could no longer accept the shopworn excuses that the czars or World War II was to blame for their country's economic backwardness. Mikhail Gorbachev, the Soviet Union's last leader (1985–91), recognized the fundamental problems but could not solve them. We learned that following the collapse of the Communist regime and the Soviet Union itself, industrial productivity fell 60 percent between 1992 and 1996 and by 40 percent in agriculture. Seventy-five percent of St. Petersburg's factories and 50 percent of Moscow's had been devoted to military purposes, compared to 12 percent that had produced consumer goods. With the disintegration of the Soviet Union, military spending had been cut by two-thirds, leaving 75 to 80 percent of the population living barely above subsistence. Salaries of state employees had fallen by 70 to 75 percent. Professors' salaries were so low that Dr. Vertumian was too embarrassed to reveal his own. People on fixed income and people over forty, especially retirees, were among the 50 percent of the population who were worse off than under the Soviet regime, compared to the 10 percent who had prospered since its downfall. For them, every problem, medical or mechanical, was a potential disaster.

Professor Vertumian's lectures on economics, public health care, education, and crime and other social problems were fascinating. State spending on health care, he said, had dropped by half to 3 percent of the country's GNP, compared to 12 percent at that time in the United States (and 17 percent in 2014). Twenty-five percent of Russian hospitals lacked central heating, connections to sewers, and baths. Cats were used to catch mice. Consequently, infant mortality was three to four times higher than in Western Europe. Twenty times as many mothers died in childbirth as in developed countries. In the mid-1990s there were more than twice as many abortions—5 million annually—as live births. Forty-five percent of drug needs went unfilled.

Alcoholism, a problem in Russia for centuries, was getting worse. Gorbachev's efforts to reduce it had simply led to an increase in homemade brews. Forty to 60 percent of the Russian population lived in environmentally dangerous places. Twenty-five percent of Russian children were born with environmentally caused health problems. Air pollution, Dr. Vertumian claimed, was 20 times greater than in Western Europe. Adding to the pollution were American cigarettes, which we noticed had no health warnings. One of first things we saw as we came into Moscow was an eighteen-story apartment house with an enormous Marlboro man painted on the side of the building. Not surprisingly, lung cancer was becoming an increasing problem in Russia.

Professor Vertumian also told us that the Russian population had been "traumatized" to learn from Russian historians, using previously top-secret documents, that socialism was a fraud and that Lenin was an unscrupulous demagogue, terrorist, and mass murderer. It was therefore all the more surprising that we saw statues of Lenin in nearly every town we visited, usually pointing to a glorious future. And, of course, Lenin's body was (and is) still on display in Red Square in Moscow. On the other hand, we saw no statues or pictures of Stalin.

We found Moscow to be a good deal more prosperous than St. Petersburg and the towns we had seen en route. Thirty percent of Moscow's population was classified as "New Russians," most of whom were relatively young, fairly well off, and not affiliated with the old regime. Many of them were employed by twelve hundred U.S. joint venture companies. Such companies, which were particularly numerous in Moscow, paid their employees $3,000 to $4,000 a month. Many other New Russians bought consumer goods in Finland, Poland, or Germany and then resold them for big profits in Russia. We saw many of them selling their wares from the backs of trucks, in small booths near subway stations, or even along busy sidewalks. Around 70 percent of these people, however, had much of their profits skimmed off by the Russian mafia, which did not hesitate to threaten their children if they did not pay protection money. Nevertheless, the New Russians were able to buy cars and build new homes or at least live in renovated apartment houses in nice neighborhoods. Unfortunately, their success only aroused the envy of those Russians who were less successful, which led to increased theft.

For Russia as a whole, only 10 percent of the population fell into the New Russian category. These relatively prosperous people were most obvious in what we were told was the biggest McDonald's restaurant in the world. I counted no fewer than fifty lines of people ordering food with eight to ten people in each line. McDonald's restaurants were not the only sign of American influence. Pepsi-Cola, which had been the only American company I had seen in 1980, had now been joined by Pizza Huts, T-shirts, jeans, and baseball caps.

Since pensioners earned only about sixty dollars a month, it is easy to see why most of the patrons at McDonald's were in the late teens to thirties and fell well within the New Russian category. Evidence of prosperity could also be seen at the famous pre-revolutionary shopping mall called GUM, whose stores had been almost empty when I saw them in 1980. Meanwhile, they had been renovated. There, with sufficient money, a major qualification, one could buy most anything from nearly anywhere in the world. More evidence of growing wealth could be seen on the streets of Moscow. Whereas there had been only 300,000 cars on the capital city's streets as recently as 1986, there were 3 million ten years later.

We were impressed in Moscow and other Russian cities by the apparent revival of religion. A church on Red Square, which Stalin had ordered torn down because he could see it from his office in the Kremlin, was restored to its exact condition and location. Another of Stalin's victims and Moscow's largest church, Christ the Redeemer, was also being rebuilt on the same site and in every detail, including its golden dome. We noticed the same effort to rebuild crumbling churches in some of the towns we visited during our cruise.

We encountered a number of other small and sometimes not-so-small ways that illustrated how Russia was abandoning its totalitarian past. For example, our city guide in Moscow told us that her daughter found it impossible to believe that her mother had not been able to travel anywhere she pleased. An exhibition at the Tretyakov Art Gallery featured early-twentieth-century impressionist and abstract art, paintings that Stalin and his successors denounced as decadent and contrary to "socialist realism." When I had seen the gallery in 1980 it was an old wreck of a building; now it was in a beautiful new structure on a street closed to vehicular traffic. The Pushkin Museum had a special exhibit called "Moscow-Berlin, 1900–1950," which juxtaposed fascinating examples of Nazi and Communist art. One of the paintings depicted Stalin surrounded by happy children. Another, titled *In the Beginning Was the Word*, featured a young Hitler addressing a small group of Nazis. Especially interesting were old films showing plans to rebuild both Berlin and Moscow on a giant scale. Still another sign of the new era was election posters showing a right-wing politician comforting an impoverished old woman with a church in the background, two subjects that would have been unimaginable in Soviet times. On the other hand, a clear legacy of the Communist past that had not changed, although perhaps for good reasons, was the unwillingness of the Russians to believe anything they were told by the government.

The new era was also illustrated by something as mundane as a picnic the Siegls organized to celebrate their daughter's eleventh birthday. A group of Russian children picnicking nearby challenged our group of Austrian and German children to a soccer match. The Russian adults invited us to join their picnic. Walter told me that such "fraternization" with foreigners had been unthinkable in Soviet times. Even our departure from Russia was a far cry from what I had experienced in 1980. The inspection of our luggage this time was perfunctory; in fact, the officials examined only one of three suitcases before declaring that we were "good people." It was illustrative of the poor quality and cost of Russian goods, however, that a Finnish customs official told us that 99 percent of the Russians who came to Finland by car, train, or bus—some ten thousand on any given day in Helsinki—did so to go shopping.

We therefore left Russia with mixed feelings about its future, impressions that I incorporated into the concluding chapter of my book on totalitarianism.

On the one hand, there was far more freedom in the new Russia than there had been during the Soviet period. Some people had clearly profited, and businesses were learning how to become more efficient. The Soviet educational system had produced a fairly well trained labor force, although most Russians still lacked business and computer skills and very few knew English, even though by 1996 it was clearly the number one international language. On the other hand, crime (mostly nonviolent), corruption, and health care had all worsened. Most problematic of all, many Russians still lacked a strong work ethic; centuries of dependency on either an autocratic or a paternalistic government (or both) had become ingrained. There was considerable nostalgia for the "good old days," especially among older people and state employees, who longed for the stability of the old regime when almost everyone was provided with the basics of housing, food, jobs, education, and medical care, even if the quality of all these things had been poor. Unlike Italy, and especially Germany, the jury was (and is) still out on whether Russian democracy and capitalism would succeed in the long run.

After leaving Russia we spent twelve days in Finland and the Baltic States—Estonia, Latvia, and Lithuania. They offered interesting contrasts to our eighteen days in Russia. Suddenly, fresh fruits and vegetable were available in Finland even though its climate was less suitable for agriculture than Russia's. In the Baltic States, all of which had belonged to the Soviet Union between 1945 and 1989, we saw the numerous examples of the same type of Soviet-era prefabricated apartment houses we had seen in Russia, but they were far better maintained. Apparently, a pre-Communist work ethic had somehow survived the Soviet occupation.

Our tour also revealed the mixture of disdain and fear the Baltic nationalities had toward the Russians. When we asked a student-age taxi driver in the Finnish capital what Finns thought of the Russians, he replied that it was "hard to find a sober and honest one." Our guide in Vilnius, the capital of Lithuania, perhaps captured the general attitude best when she said: "We are fed up with the Russians." The anti-Russian attitude of the Baltic States was also seen in the complete lack of bilingual signs—with the partial exception of Tallinn—despite the Russians making up 34 percent of the population of Latvia, 30 percent in Estonia, and 9 percent in Lithuania.

COMPARING DICTATORSHIPS

By the summer of 1996, my book on totalitarianism was nearing completion. I was determined from the outset to avoid writing separate histories of the Soviet Union, Nazi Germany, and fascist Italy. Such a book would have been impossibly long. Rather than summarizing well-known events, I wanted to make systematic comparisons. After describing the ideological foundations of the regimes, I used a chronological approach only when explaining the regimes' rise to power and later in analyzing their collapse. In between I had chapters on "Personalities and Policies of the Dictators," "Totalitarian Economics," "Propaganda, Culture and Education," "Family Values and Health," and "Totalitarian Terror."

The three totalitarian regimes, I concluded, are best known for their dogmatism and fanaticism. However, I also discovered that the dictators could at times be pragmatic, thus making their regimes look almost "normal," especially when it came to health care, entertainment, and to some extent (in Germany and Italy) economic policies. Pragmatism, however, was merely a ploy. As soon as the regimes felt economically and militarily secure, they returned to their long-term goals: territorial expansion and ethnic purity in the case of Germany and Italy, and a one-party state, a command economy, and labor camps for anyone who objected in the case of the Soviet Union. The dogmatism of the three dictatorships was self-destructive. Mussolini suppressed intellectuals, causing their emigration. Hitler forced out two-thirds of Germany's Jewish population and killed the remainder, thus losing some of the country's most creative and productive people. Stalin killed or forced into labor camps the hardest-working and most prosperous peasants (the so-called kulaks) and anyone with unorthodox ideas. Each dictator ultimately achieved the exact opposite of what he had wanted. Germany lost a quarter of its territory and left racism utterly discredited; Italy lost its colonial empire; Stalin left in his wake increased corruption and scars on the Russian environment that will last for centuries.

For once, there was no argument about a title. By mutual agreement, my rather pedantic suggestion, *The Totalitarian Dictatorships: Their Rise and Fall in Twentieth-Century Europe*, was replaced by *Hitler, Stalin, and Mussolini: Totalitarianism in the Twentieth Century*, which seemed both attractive and descriptive. I regretted that the book was not published first as a hardback and in a larger format, which might have appealed to the general public and not just to undergraduates, to whom it was primarily marketed. However, as supplementary reading for a variety of undergraduate courses it has been a great success.

The downside to publishing a book based almost entirely on secondary sources is that such works are rarely reviewed in scholarly journals and seldom result in invitations to speak at professional meetings. However, I was pleased to receive a number of comments from friends and scholars. The Austrian political scientist Anton Pelinka, at the time a visiting professor at Stanford, wrote that I had "mastered the complexity of comparative analysis." He thought the book would be helpful for the teaching of both history and political science. Michael Geyer of the University of Chicago wrote that "just the very ability to put these three very difficult histories on paper with such economy is a feat—and among the writers of history writing economically is something of a trade secret. I further thought that your treatment of the three regimes is very even-handed." Lionel B. Steiman of the University of Manitoba wrote: "Your study . . . has a wonderful freshness (given the topic), a remarkable range, and a richness of detail rare in so compact but so broad a work." John Rath of the University of Minnesota "marvel[ed] at how quickly [I] manage[d] to publish first-rate books." Radomir Luza, professor emeritus of history at Tulane, said the book addressed "a sensitive topic of central importance. Much of what you say rings true. Your narrative, well structured, provides fresh insight into the calendar of epic-historical times in contemporary Europe." My old friend and fellow Austrian history specialist Evan Bukey of the University of Arkansas "applauded [my] objectivity and detachment in dealing with a highly emotional and still controversial topic." Keith Eubank admitted in a letter he wrote to a UCF research prize committee that he had been "concerned about how well Pauley could handle three such diverse topics within the space limitations of this series of books. There was no need for my worry."[7]

POSTSCRIPT: CUBA, 2013

The publication of *Hitler, Stalin, and Mussolini* in 1997 did not end my study of totalitarianism. A revised and expanded second edition was published in 2003, and a third edition appeared in 2009. By 2013, I needed to prepare a fourth edition for a new publisher, and it seemed like a good time to study totalitarianism in an entirely different part of the world: Cuba.

An eleven-day visit that year revealed some similarities between the island nation and the Communist countries of eastern Europe: Buildings in Cuba were in an equally poor state of repair, because no one owned them or had a vested interest in repairing them. Traffic was light, because few people could afford to buy cars or even motorcycles. Clotheslines were even more common than in eastern Europe, because few people had enough money to buy driers or even the electricity to run them. Newspapers reported only positive news and especially avoided topics like crime. Private enterprise resembled Lenin's New Economic Policy of the 1920s, being very modest in scale: barbershops, restaurants, fruit and vegetable stands, and handmade souvenir stands. Political posters touting the glories of socialism and Communist heroes again reminded me of what I had seen in eastern Europe. As with Russia after the collapse of the Soviet Union, the future of Cuba, especially after the death of the Castro brothers, is very much in doubt.

Although I encountered numerous similarities between Cuba and the totalitarian countries I had seen in Europe, I also noticed some significant differences. "Socialist realism" depicting heroic workers and muscular peasants in massive paintings and statues was entirely absent, not only in contemporary Cuban art but also in any artistic form dating back to the beginning of Communist rule in 1959. Health care in Cuba is evidently far superior to anything that the Soviet Union and its satellites ever experienced, because life expectancy is higher, and even higher than in the United States and Canada, not to mention today's Russia. Cuba's skies and surrounding seas have remained unpolluted. Most different of all, of course, is the climate, which allows Cubans to escape their tiny apartments and spend much of their time socializing in public squares, something that for most of the year was impossible in cold and dreary Russia and its satellites. Indeed,

Cubans appear to be happy, no doubt in part because of their love of music, dancing, and art. The fact that Cuba's government is "homegrown" rather than imposed by a foreign power certainly differentiates it from Russia's satellites. Finally, Cuba's tropical climate and geographic location near the population centers of North America give it far greater potential as a tourist destination than most of the former Communist countries of eastern Europe.

CHAPTER 16

Phasing Out

"They were such vital people, with lust for life, humor, and intellectually curious."

"Travel is fatal to prejudice, bigotry, and narrow-mindedness."

NEW OPPORTUNITIES

Hitler, Stalin, and Mussolini was published in early 1997. It was my fifth book (counting revised, translated edtions) in sixteen years. Since 1960, when I started to work on my master's thesis, my life had nearly always revolved around some big research project. Now approaching my sixtieth birthday, I was ready for a major change.

Fortunately, a number of tempting offers for less-ambitious undertakings did materialize in the middle and late 1990s. In 1995, I was asked to give a paper on "Austria's Press, 1933–1938" at a symposium on "Journalism and the Holocaust, 1933–1945" at Yeshiva University in New York. The paper was later published in a book titled *Journalism and the Holocaust*.[1] In 1996, I accepted an invitation to join the editorial board of the *Austrian History Yearbook*. One opportunity I did turn down was an invitation in 1997 to apply for the chairmanship position at the University of South Carolina, although I certainly would have been receptive to the offer if it had come a few years earlier.

An entirely different opportunity came in 1998 when the War Crimes Division of the Department of Justice of the Canadian federal government asked me to be an expert witness in a deportation hearing. The case involved a former member of the Austrian gendarmerie from northern Styria, a hotbed of Nazi sympathizers in the early 1930s. The accused had secretly joined the Austrian Nazi Party in 1933 when it was illegal. In so doing he was in a position to pass on vital information to higher Nazi authorities in Austria and Germany about the Austrian Army's weapons depots and its anti-Nazi activities. After the war he was part of a general amnesty given by the Austrian government and managed to immigrate to Canada in the early 1950s by not disclosing his Nazi past. The whole affair was a case study of someone who always knew which way the political winds were blowing.

The hearing dragged on for two years and involved at least five trips to Ontario. My testimony ended with a cross-examination by the defense in October 1999. The nice thing about being an expert witness was that I knew far more about the subject than the defense attorney, much like when I defended my dissertation. However, the hearing also taught me that it is much harder to prove someone's legal guilt than it is for a historian to make sweeping generalizations about a whole country. The hearing ended suddenly in 2000 when the accused died before a verdict was reached. I regretted that the case had not come up years earlier, rather than when the accused was ninety and near death. It is also a shame that the hearing was ignored in the Canadian press, thus eliminating its potential educational value. The edifying value of the hearing was at least not lost on me, however, and I also enjoyed the opportunity to do some sightseeing in Ottawa.

THE MATURATION OF A UNIVERSITY

Meanwhile, the 1990s had brought encouraging changes at the University of Central Florida. In 1989 the university's president, Trevor Colbourn, resigned after eleven years at the helm—a stint that was well above average for a university president. The school's location and mission were no longer well-kept secrets. Academic standards for faculty and students had risen significantly. Colbourn had supported tenure and promotion committees at both the college and university level and had encouraged open forums where the faculty could question all members of the administration. That policy was risky, because professors often posed sharp, sometimes even hostile questions. President Colbourn was always able to respond with good humor and objectivity.

After a brief interregnum, President John C. Hitt helped raise the university's profile still more, while enrollment more than doubled by 2013, to 59,000, making UCF the second-largest university in the country and nearly four times the 15,000 students the school was projected to have "someday" when it was founded in 1963.[2] Its rapid growth reflected a growing trend at urban universities. Entrance requirements for students had risen dramatically since my early years at the school. Reflecting national trends, the teaching load for faculty had declined from twelve hours a week to nine or fewer. The controversy over publishing had diminished with the retirement of older faculty. However, another national trend—decreasing support from the state government—had resulted in growing class sizes, especially after the turn of the new century. This trend, in turn, led to ever more machine-graded examinations, fewer written assignments, and less time for faculty to advise students, also part of a nationwide trend.[3]

Happily, UCF's campus was becoming more attractive. Trees, which had been minuscule when I arrived in 1971, provided a good deal of much-needed shade thirty years later. Several ugly surface parking lots had been replaced by parking garages. New sidewalks were built where students actually walked, and a good deal of beautiful landscaping was added. The library more than doubled in size, and its collection of books and documents multiplied several times. The honors program acquired a handsome new building of its own, one of many new buildings on the campus, including a huge student union and a football stadium that seated forty-five thousand. Unfortunately, the history department and my office remained in one of the oldest and least desirable buildings, but at least I enjoyed a window with a nice view. What UCF didn't have, like other relatively new universities, was a big endowment and a performing arts center.

Making life much more pleasant for me was a new department chairman,

Richard (Dick) Crepeau, whose tenure between 1991 and 2001 coincided with the most satisfying years of the thirty-five I spent at UCF. At last we had regular meetings, committees, a growing number of students, and several fine additions to the faculty in whose selection all members of the department participated. On numerous occasions Dick stopped by my office just for a friendly chat, something that his predecessor hadn't done once in nineteen years. No longer did I have to protest annual evaluations.

PREPARING FOR RETIREMENT

In other respects, during the last few years of the 1990s I began to turn my attention to the mundane business of planning for my retirement. Given the volatility of the U.S. economy and stock market, it is fortunate that Florida's State Retirement System still offered defined-benefit pensions. However, my first seven years of teaching at Wooster, Nebraska, and Wyoming didn't contribute to my pension. Therefore, I needed to teach as much summer school as possible, a practice I had avoided through most of my career in order to devote as much time as possible to research and writing. Consequently, starting in 1995 I taught summer school for five of my last six years of full-time employment at UCF.

I was also fortunate that I was not entirely dependent on summer income to boost my eventual pension. Starting in 1993, the ten state universities in Florida began granting generous salary increases for the Teaching Incentive Program (TIP) award and later for the Professorial Excellence Program (PEP), in which research was critical. Putting together huge application folders was time consuming, as was the selection process of ad hoc college committees. Proving that one is an outstanding teacher is especially difficult. The first time I applied for the TIP award I emphasized the importance of my research in classroom teaching. I found out later that the committee had been badly split on the merits of my application. Members who had weak publication records argued that the award was strictly for teaching, not for research. Those who had strong research records thought I had an excellent folder. The controversy over the relevance of research to teaching was obviously still not entirely dead at UCF.

The following year I applied again, but this time I said next to nothing about my three books that had been based on original research. Instead, I cited *The Habsburg Legacy* and *Hitler, Stalin, and Mussolini* as books intended for undergraduate courses. I stressed the importance of my interviews with historically important people, the seventeen trips I had taken to historical sites in over fifty foreign countries, and the numerous lectures I had given at various American, British, and Austrian universities. I also included copies of instructions I always handed out to students on how to take classroom notes, how to prepare for exams, strategies to use while taking exams, and how to write book reviews. At the back of my inch-and-a-half-thick folder I included several eight-by-ten-inch prints made from slides I had taken at historical sites in Egypt, Turkey, Italy, Austria, and Poland. This time I won the $5,000 award, which was added to my base salary. I won the award again in 1999.

Much more difficult to obtain were PEP awards, which first became available in 1997. Applicants had to have been a full professor for at least ten years and were judged on their entire record during those years. Research and other creative activities were the most important components, but teaching and service were also appraised. The criteria amounted to requirements for a promotion. Approximately one hundred professors applied for the awards the first year they were offered; I was one of the ten recipients and received a 9 percent raise in salary.

In the same year, President Hitt decided to establish a Presidential Award for Special Merit for professors who had recently won a national award of some kind. Winning the Best Book Prize from the Austrian Cultural Institute in 1994 enabled me to win a Presidential Award as well. Altogether, between 1994 and 1999 I had increased my salary substantially, and together with my summer school teaching I had helped boost my future pension to a comfortable level, enabling me to consider some expenditures I otherwise would not have deemed possible.

THE RETURN OF A NATIVE

During the middle and late 1990s, I was gaining recognition not just from UCF but also from the University of Nebraska–Lincoln (UNL). In 1996 its history department nominated me for a College of Arts and Sciences Alumni Achievement Award. The following year I was asked to deliver an address on "Remembering the Holocaust," for the Jewish Days of Remembrance commemoration at the state capitol. I was grateful for these honors, which reminded me of how much I owed both the University of Nebraska and my father, who had helped inspire my love of history and made possible my higher education. These events induced me to think of ways I might credit my father for his unflagging support of my career and at the same time do something to advance the historical profession in general and UNL's history department in particular.

My father had emerged from the Great Depression as a fiscal conservative. If he couldn't afford to pay cash for something, he couldn't afford to buy it, period. He had scrupulously saved money in what he thought were ultra-safe investments—since 2008 we have learned that there is sadly no such thing—for the next great depression he was sure would eventually come. Once my mother died and my parents' inheritance was divided between my sister and me, I invested my share in the stock market just as it was beginning to boom, another example of pure luck. By 1997 my portfolio had grown to the point where it exceeded our personal needs. What could we do with my inheritance that would simultaneously honor my father and benefit my profession? One day it occurred to me that establishing an endowment in my father's name for a distinguished speakers' series administered by UNL's history department would be the perfect answer. My father had always loved history, had taken courses in the Nebraska history department, was a loyal Nebraskan, and had prospered because of his Nebraska customers. I feel certain that he would have approved of the endowment, although had he established it himself he would have been far too modest to attach his name to it. Some years later I made a similar donation to UCF.

As it turned out, the awards and the Pauley Endowment were only the beginning of a reconnection with my home state. A third opportunity came in 2002 when I was asked to teach Czech history at UNL as a guest professor. In the 1980s, an Omaha businessman of Czech ancestry had given the history department a substantial endowment "to advance the study of the

Czech heritage in Nebraska and the Great Plains."[4] Even though I was not a Czech history specialist, a good deal of Czech history was included in *The Habsburg Legacy*. Furthermore, I had traveled extensively throughout the Czech lands on five different occasions, most recently in 2000.

The last trip was especially important. I had spent ten days in the Czech Republic at the beginning of the Prague-Berlin Seminar sponsored by Bradley University, the same traveling seminar that I had joined in 1987 when the itinerary was limited to East and West Germany. The Czech Republic in 2000 was a sharp contrast to Russia in 1996, not to mention the Czechoslovakia I had seen in the 1950s and 1960s. Although its standard of living was about the same as it had been when the country regained its freedom during the "Velvet Revolution" of 1989, Czech living standards were beginning to improve, in part due to a flourishing tourist industry. And whereas most Russian towns in 1996 looked shabby, Prague was "golden" once more. Most of the Gothic, baroque, and art nouveau buildings of the old city had been restored. Teaching a new course in Czech history kept me busy, even though I had prepared several lectures on their history early in my career. About half of the students in my class were of Czech heritage, which made the course all the more interesting.

My semester in Lincoln in the fall of 2002 proved to be one of the most enjoyable in my teaching career. I immediately felt at home. The one big personal change that had taken place in my long absence was the demise of the Pauley Lumber Company in 1999 after eighty-four years of business at Twenty-Seventh and E Streets. It had been hard enough for me to imagine my father not working at the lumberyard. Even harder to visualize was its disappearance. My cousin David Pauley, the lumberyard's last manager, felt that a small, family-owned business could not compete with conglomerates like Home Depot and Ace Hardware. I had no cause for complaint. I had made it clear many years earlier that I had no interest in the family business. It is actually commonplace for family businesses not to survive the third generation.

While we were in Lincoln, Marianne and I rented a small house on Pawnee Street, just two blocks from where I had grown up. Built in the late 1920s, the house was small but had a modern kitchen and an attractive, enclosed backyard. To give Marianne full use of our one car, I walked three blocks to catch the same "Arapahoe" bus that I had taken as a youngster. It was a five-minute walk to the bus stop, a ten-minute ride to the campus, and another five-minute stroll to my office. The bus ride was free because of an agreement between the university and the city government. Obviously, I also had no need to worry about finding a parking place. The experience of riding a bus made me wonder why our society had become so dependent on cars. Unfortunately, our car culture has created urban sprawl, and urban sprawl has made buses, with their frequent stops and transfers, far more time consuming than when Lincoln and other cities were much smaller and more compact. Urban sprawl in Lincoln also caused department stores to move to shopping malls, leaving the downtown area looking almost like a ghost town.

Compensating for the decline of the downtown area were dramatic physical improvements in the university's campus since I had taught there in 1965–66. Gone were the ugly parking lots south of Burnett Hall and north of the Student Union. Three streets—Tenth, Twelfth, and Fourteenth, all of which had cut into or through the campus—had been replaced with walkways and lush landscaping, vastly improving the overall appearance of the campus. Adding to our cultural enjoyment was the existence of the new Lied Center of the Performing Arts and the Great Plains Art Museum, both on the southern edge of the campus and both built since I last taught at Nebraska. UNL by this time was no longer a jumping-off place for greener pastures but a school where top scholars were willing to spend their entire careers and live in a city that was ideal for raising a family.[5]

My renewed relationship with the University of Nebraska remained close even after the fall of 2002. In 2005 the university's alumni association, with the support of the history department, selected me to receive a senior Alumni Achievement Award for my "outstanding dedication and commitment to academics." The letter informing me of the award went on to say that the association applauded my "many accomplishments as a scholar and teacher."[6] My parents, my father in particular, would have been thrilled by the award. The following year I was again invited to teach Czech history and also a graduate seminar on totalitarianism.

The winding down of my teaching career roughly coincided with the end of Marianne's career, too. After four years teaching remedial reading and math and another four years teaching gifted middle school students, she returned to teaching in Seminole County's homebound and hospitalized program in 1985. It was a job she loved until her retirement in 2000. The most common "illness" of her students was postpartum recovery. She soon learned a lot about teenage motherhood. She especially liked being able to work with students individually, although during the latter part of her career she also did some telephone conferencing with up to eight students at a time. Either way she was able to see real progress in her charges and know that she was making a significant impact on their lives.

Mark and Glenn were undergoing far more drastic and difficult changes, earning their undergraduate degrees and moving on to graduate school. Mark obtained a bachelor's degree in chemistry at the University of Florida in 1989 before earning a master's in chemistry at the University of North Carolina. He spent an extra year at UNC and North Carolina State University studying computer science before earning a PhD in chemistry at UNL. However, the years of research in windowless laboratories for the benefit of his major professor killed most of his enthusiasm for the subject, so he ultimately turned his attention to computer science.

Mark managed to survive his long graduate school ordeal in large part because of his marriage, in December 1990, to Maria Hart. They had met at the University of Florida; Mark was a resident assistant at the time, and Maria, who was majoring in business administration and accounting, was an undergraduate in the same dorm. She soon proved herself to be a highly competent and hardworking businesswoman as well as a thoughtful and caring wife and mother. The more we got to know Maria, the more impressed we were with Mark's choice.

Glenn's experience with graduate school was no picnic either. He graduated Phi Beta Kappa from the University of Wyoming in December 1991, majoring in wildlife management, before earning his master's degree at the University of Calgary in Alberta. His thesis on conservation easements enabled him to land a job as the founding executive director of the Southern Alberta Land Trust Society (SALTS). His position gave Marianne and me the excuse to explore western Canada every time we visited him.

Whereas things were looking up at UCF and eventually for Mark and Glenn, the same could not be said for my parents. In several phone calls in the last few months of my father's life, he mentioned how forgetful *they* were becoming. In retrospect, I think he was talking mostly about my mother. His sudden death in 1987 of an aneurysm revealed the true extent of her memory loss caused by arteriosclerosis. During their last few years together my father's relatively good memory had compensated for my mother's memory loss while her physical stamina made up for his frailty. Chances are, however, that they would not have been able to live unassisted for more than another year or two.

My mother had many friends and belonged to numerous clubs—common for middle-class women of her generation—but she was lonely living by herself. Finally, she decided to move to Gateway Manor, a retirement home in Lincoln where she knew many people. Had she been in good mental health she might have spent many relatively happy years there. However, after just three months it became obvious that her mental condition was deteriorating, resulting in serious damage to her apartment and even to the building when she left her stove on and her bath water running. Consequently, she had to leave because of the danger she posed to herself and to the building.

Fortunately, an assisted living facility called Orchard Park had just opened up at this time (1989), and my uncle Gordon helped her move. My mother had no choice and accepted the change without complaint. In fact, she entertained the residents with daily piano concerts so much that Orchard Park used her in a TV advertisement. It was remarkable how well she could play up to a year before her death. By early 1991 her needs grew so numerous that she had to be moved to Homestead, a full-fledged nursing home. Her "concerts," which drew quite a crowd, continued even there for a time.

People suffering from Alzheimer's or some other memory-robbing condition either become ornery and difficult to manage or even sweeter and more cooperative than they had previously been. My mother fell firmly into the latter category, never complaining, always treating others politely, lovingly, and gratefully. Within the space of just a few years she lost her sister, my father, her home, her car, and two apartments. Through it all she remained stoic and cheerful. She died on July 15, 1992, four days before her eighty-fourth birthday. A few days later, my old friend Jim Bachman wrote that "it is hard to realize that both your parents are gone. I believe that I last saw them nine years ago, in Florida. They were such vital people, with lust for life, humor, and intellectually curious. For people with so many endowments, it seems a bit unfair that their life spans must ever run out, *nicht wahr*?"[7]

My two guest professorships at the University of Nebraska also provided Marianne and me with more opportunities to see Mark and Maria and their growing family. In February 1996, Alena Marie became the first member of the seventh generation of Nebraska Pauleys. Marianne and I wrote in our Christmas letter of 1996 that "Alena immediately had us all falling madly in love with her. She has acted like a gigantic magnet drawing us to Lincoln. . . . She lights up an entire room with her nearly constant smile and never cries without a very legitimate reason. A test administered to her by her pediatrician around her third birthday showed that she had memorized the alphabet, could count to ten, and recognized the spelling of her own name. Her doctor wanted to know 'in how many languages she could do these things.'"[8]

In 1997, Mark landed a half-time job at the University of Nebraska–Omaha helping to develop a computer laboratory at the College of Information Science and Technology. The following year he became a full-time laboratory manager, and in 2004 he began teaching bioinformatics. Life became a little easier for both Mark and Maria when Maria got a banking job in Omaha, thus eliminating their long commute from Lincoln.

In 2001 Mark and Maria presented us with our first grandson, Benjamin Isaac Pauley. As soon as Ben was old enough to walk and talk he became almost obsessed with anything related to dinosaurs: books, clothes, videos, toys—you name it. His delightful sense of humor kept us constantly entertained. Meanwhile, once in school, Alena excelled in just about everything academic, but especially in science, math, reading, and spelling.

The start of the new century brought major changes for Glenn as well. He liked his job with SALTS, which was featured in several magazine and newspaper articles, as well as in radio and television programs for its land conservation activities. In 1998 the Canadian government gave his organization a major grant to help make it a prototype for similar organizations around the country. Nevertheless, after eight years studying and working in Canada he welcomed the opportunity to return to the States and accepted an offer to become the executive director of the Wyoming Stock Growers Agricultural Land Trust, a land conservation organization in Cheyenne.

Glenn's new work facilitated another kind of hunting: hunting for a wife. At a professional conference in 2003 he met Lucy Hansen, who was a "mediator" for the Wyoming Department of Agriculture. Lucy was cheerful and outgoing, and Marianne and I liked her immediately. Two years later they were married, and two years after that we gained a third grandchild, William Frederick Pauley; his second name coincided with his maternal grandfather's first name and my middle name. Within a few years "Will" developed an interest in hunting and firefighting. In 2008 Glenn was able to get out of the precarious nonprofit business—in the nick of time, given the changed economic circumstances—and secured a job with the Wyoming Game and Fish Department, a position for which he had seemingly been preparing his whole life. Just seven months after the start of his new job, he and Lucy had Reina Victoria Pauley, a beautiful little girl with blonde hair, blue eyes, and a playful personality. Thus we had a nice even number of grandchildren: two granddaughters and two grandsons, all of them happy and healthy, and at the risk of bragging, also smart.

SURVIVING HURRICANE CHARLIE AND OTHER ADVENTURES

May 2001 marked the end of my full-time employment at the University of Central Florida. Although Marianne and I, with one exception, had managed to escape from Florida at least part of each summer during the thirty years we had lived in the Sunshine State, we had never become accustomed to the heat and humidity that persist from May to October. Each time we returned to Florida in August after spending the summer in Vienna, Laramie, Williamsburg, Nashville, or New England, it seemed as if we were being punished for some crime we hadn't committed. The start of the new academic year painfully reminded us of how gorgeous and invigorating the summers and early falls were in the Rocky Mountains. On the other hand, we were also well aware that winters and springs were beautiful in Florida, although we had usually been too busy during the school year to enjoy them.

The phased retirement program for Florida's state universities enabled us to combine the best of both worlds. I had to be in Florida only from early January until the end of April when teaching during UCF's spring semester. The remainder of the year we were free to live and travel wherever we pleased. The question was, where would we spend our summers and falls? I thought Laramie was a possibility. The weather there from June to September was almost unbeatable, but May and October could often be downright cold. The number of good restaurants was limited, and the nearest international airport, in Denver, was two and a half hours away. Most decisive of all, Laramie lacked maintenance-free condominiums, something we regarded as indispensable if we were to have two homes.

Fort Collins, Colorado, on the other hand, sixty-five miles south of Laramie, seemed more attractive. Its growing season was almost two months longer than Laramie's, making temperatures in May and October as well as during the summer months almost ideal. There were a dozen golf courses in the vicinity, a huge choice of restaurants, and plenty of inexpensive local entertainment provided by Colorado State University in Fort Collins and the University of Northern Colorado in Greeley. Denver was just an hour to the south, and Rocky Mountain National Park was only an hour to the west. Northern Colorado also had excellent medical facilities, something we were likely to appreciate as we got older.

We began our house hunting in Fort Collins in 1999 and continued it the following summer. The irony was that after focusing on Fort Collins, and to a lesser extent its neighbor, Loveland, we ended up in a planned neighborhood in Windsor, a much smaller town a few miles to the east. Although we were farther from the mountains than we would have been in either Fort Collins or Loveland, our view of the snowcapped Continental Divide was not obstructed by foothills. Just two months after we moved to

Windsor in 2001, Glenn moved to Cheyenne, an hour to the north. Mark and his family were just nine hours to the east.

Our Colorado home had numerous attractive features, the most important of which was that we were didn't have to worry about yard maintenance or snow removal. The unit was just a hundred feet from a sandy beach and a small lake that reflected gorgeous sunsets. Across the lake we could see a hiker/biker trail, the Poudre River, a golf course, and snowcapped mountains. By an amazing coincidence we discovered that Volga Germans had played a critical role in the settlement and economic development of Windsor in the first half of the twentieth century.[9]

When we purchased our Colorado summer/fall home we had no intention of selling our Oviedo house on Whippoorwill Lane. We had designed it exactly to our needs and preferences. The house was filled with wonderful memories of our children growing up and annual visits from our parents. We were close to old friends and to UCF. By 2001 Oviedo was no longer so isolated from everyday conveniences like grocery stores and shopping malls the way it was when we moved there in 1972. Yard maintenance was a concern, but as long as I could find someone to take care of it, the problem was not too serious.

All these happy considerations were upset when we received a phone call at 7:15 on the morning of August 14, 2004. A neighbor in Oviedo informed us that Hurricane Charlie had made a direct hit on our house. The winds had brought a huge water oak tree—which, unbeknownst to us, had a rotten core—crashing into the second story of our house. Our neighbor urged us to return to Florida as soon as possible.

What greeted us in Oviedo was surreal; the devastation looked like something straight out of a disaster movie. Once we were within about a mile of our house we began seeing broken limbs piled up along the streets to a height of at least eight feet, allowing room for only one lane of traffic. When we reached our house we could see a tree firmly embedded in my study. Altogether we were without power for seven days and with it our air-conditioning; we now had to bear the full brunt of Florida's heat and humidity. Our one stroke of luck was that unlike most people, we still had an old-fashioned dial-up phone that was not dependent on electricity. The phone, however, was of only limited value. When trying to reach a tree surgeon or a contractor it was rare for someone to actually answer the phone, and recorders were usually filled. In practice, we often had to track down repairmen whenever we could actually see them in the neighborhood. Sometimes this involved stalking them by car for a mile or two.

Superstorm Sandy in 2012 as well as Hurricane Katrina in 2005 put Charlie in a whole new perspective. Many houses in Oviedo had damaged roofs and missing windows, but the town did not look as if it had been hit by an atomic bomb. UCF and my job were both still intact. We were lucky that our house had two stories. Although the upper story was largely uninhabitable, our main floor, which included our master bedroom, had survived relatively unscathed except for water stains on the ceilings, walls, and carpets. We never lacked for running water, and once power was restored a modicum of normalcy returned to our lives. Many of our neighbors were not so fortunate, having to live in trailers or motels for up to a year while their houses were repaired. We were able to engage a tree-removal service and a house contractor relatively quickly.

Temporary repairs enabled us to survive Hurricanes Frances and Jeanne—which struck Florida a few days after Charlie—without further damage, although we did find out what it was like to sleep on the floor under a sturdy table for extra security. We had suffered at most a minor inconvenience. We had not been injured; we lost very little personal property; most of the more than $100,000 of damage was covered by insurance; and we had a second home where we could wait out the reconstruction of our Oviedo home. After five hectic weeks we were able to return to Colorado, where we remained until our house was at least habitable in December.

Hurricane Charlie also forced us to reconsider where we wanted to live in Florida. Towering trees overhanging our house, which seemed like such a wonderful asset when we built our house in 1977, now seemed more like Damocles' sword, ready to strike us again at any moment. Yard maintenance remained an issue. I had services to mow, fertilize, and spray our yard for weeds; however, dead branches, potato vines, and out-of-control volunteer trees were a constant headache. Did I really want to spend my "golden years" worrying about a big lawn and big trees? By 2006, I was ready to concede that I had lost my twenty-eight-year battle against the jungle and was ready to declare unconditional surrender. By then our boys had long since left the nest and all of our parents were dead. It was time to move into something smaller and easier to maintain.

About the time I began phased retirement in 2001 we had seen an advertisement for an "over 55 active adult community" named Victoria Gardens in DeLand, a college town of about twenty-seven thousand a half hour north of Oviedo and an equal distance from the Atlantic. DeLand was the home of Stetson University and had a charming "historic" downtown area and many stately, turn-of-the-century mansions. Victoria Gardens was representative of a new concept in retirement living. Until the 1960s, physicians generally told their elderly patients to avoid strenuous exercise, and only the wealthy could afford an active retirement. In the 1990s isolated golf course communities, surrounded by "McMansions," were very much in vogue throughout the United States. But by the 2000s many Americans, especially seniors, were far more interested in having a real sense of community.

Victoria Gardens had that sense of community we sought: a big clubhouse with a fitness center and café, a hiking trail, tennis courts, a jacuzzi, and a huge heated swimming pool surrounded by tropical vegetation. We would still be reasonably close to our old friends and just an hour from Orlando International Airport, where we could catch a nonstop four-hour flight to Colorado. After we moved I was even able to continue teaching by offering abbreviated courses to appreciative Victoria Gardens residents.

By the spring of 2005 we were ready to take the plunge and made a down payment on a future house. A year later, only a few months before the completion of our new house and just after I finished my fifth and final year of phased retirement at UCF, we sold our home on Whippoorwill Lane to the second couple to see it. Our timing for both transactions was perfect: the cost of housing construction continued to rise between the time we made our down payment on our new home and the time we moved in fourteen months later. We sold our old house in May 2006 when house prices were at their peak. Once again the date of my birth had been critical. Had I retired a year later, the price of a new house would have been substantially higher and the difficulty of selling our old house would have been enormous.

DISTANT DESTINATIONS

With the completion of the first edition of *Hitler, Stalin, and Mussolini*, I felt that our summer travels no longer had to be confined to areas related to my research and teaching. I had been to Europe seventeen times, ten with Marianne. That did not preclude visits to previously unexplored parts of Europe, but the time seemed ripe to see other parts of the world.

Our first such foray into an exotic area was to China in 1997. We followed the usual tourist route starting with Shanghai and then going to nearby Suzhow to see the eighth-century Grand Canal. After Wuhan we spent five days on a boat going eight hundred miles up the Yangtze River to view its spectacular gorges. We disembarked in Chongjing and flew to Xian to see the eight thousand terra-cotta soldiers that had been buried in 200 BC. Our tour ended in Beijing, its Forbidden City, and the nearby Great Wall of China.

A number of things impressed us about China. On the negative side, we were horrified by the terrible air pollution, which prevented us from having a single day of truly blue skies in two weeks. We were also surprised that there were so few old buildings compared to Europe and disappointed that we saw no one, aside from fashion models on our river cruise, wearing traditional Chinese clothing. American jeans, we were to discover on this and other trips to remote countries, with the exception of India, Peru, and Egypt, seem to have conquered most of the world. On the other hand, we were amazed by the amount of new construction in China, particularly in Shanghai. We also noticed how few overweight people we saw—three men altogether—compared with the United States. That condition is already changing as the Chinese abandon their bicycles in favor of motorcycles and cars. One can only shudder at the prospect of still more pollution, noise, and congestion which that change will create.

Turkey, where we spent two weeks in 1998, was in many ways less exotic than China but every bit as interesting and enjoyable. It turned out to be a paradise for anyone who has the least interest in history, beautiful scenery, and good food. We saw everything from the ruins of Troy to monuments for the Gallipoli campaign of World War I, as well as the impressive mausoleum of the founder of the Turkish Republic, Kemal Pasha Atatürk, in Ankara.

In between we visited the best-preserved Greek stadium in the world, the most-intact Roman theater, the inspiring and partially reconstructed ruins of Ephesus, and numerous Byzantine churches and beautiful mosques. Traditionally dressed rural Turks (especially women), folk music, and Turkish baths were all part of the local color which we enjoyed.

Much less foreign but equally enjoyable was the "Country Roads of France" tour that we took in 1999. Although we spent five days in Paris at the end of our nineteen days in France and Monaco, most of the trip featured charming medieval towns in the eastern and southern parts of the country. The tour included everything from vineyards to glaciers. We didn't encounter any of the unfriendliness that we had been led to expect, not even in Paris.

Of our next five international trips—Costa Rica in 2001; Spain and Portugal in 2003; Rome, southern Italy, and Sicily in 2004; a river cruise from Amsterdam to Vienna in 2005; and Greece in 2007—the last was the most enjoyable, probably because of the weather and the beauty of the Greek islands and coastlines. We were impressed by the friendliness of the Greeks, their close family ties, traditional music, and the low crime rate. Spain and Portugal were much more prosperous than when I had last seen them in 1958. The river cruise, though easy and relaxing, involved too much eating and too little time to explore on our own.

In 2008 our yearning to see faraway places led us to Southeast Asia in January and parts of South America in December. We were especially impressed with the gentleness and politeness of the people of Southeast Asia. The ornate Buddhist temples of Bangkok were amazing, but not as amazing as the enormous twelfth-century temple of Angkor Wat or the floating village at Tonle Sap (the "Great Lake") in northern Cambodia. However, probably the longest-lasting impression we took away from Cambodia was the near absence of middle-aged and elderly people, the two generations that had been nearly exterminated by the Communist Khmer Rouge. Vietnam was an interesting mixture of ancient Chinese and indigenous Vietnamese culture, traces of French colonialism, and modern Western influence. We were surprised at the friendliness of the people, given the destructiveness of our intervention in the Vietnam War. We were also taken aback by how much trash there was in the streets except in the central parts of Saigon and

Hanoi, the location of upscale hotels and shops. By contrast, Hong Kong, where we were hosted by my longtime Austrian friend Helmut Sohmen, was almost spotless, and its public transportation system was superb. In Guilin, northwest of Hong Kong, where the fantastic mountains depicted by traditional Chinese artists are located, we were such oddities that several people wanted to have their picture taken next to us.

Those parts of Chile, Argentina, and Brazil that we saw in December 2008 seemed quite European, not terribly surprising for the first two countries, since 97 percent of their population had come from Europe and the indigenous people had been nearly wiped out by the newcomers. Buenos Aires, with its broad avenues and heroic equestrian statues, was faintly reminiscent of Paris. Santiago's climate and vegetation were much like those of the Mediterranean and southern California. The area around Puerto Varas further south, as well as Bariloche on the Argentinean side of the Andes, revealed strong German and Austrian influences. Peru, with the exception of Lima, was a strong contrast to the ABC countries of South America. Traditional costumes were the rule, not the exception, although small children could often be seen in jeans and baseball caps. Machu Picchu's mountaintop location was jaw-dropping.

Southeast Asia and South America turned out to be mere preludes to an even more exotic destination at the end of 2009: India. The subcontinent is not for the faint of heart. Aside from the thirty-two hours it took to reach New Delhi from Orlando and the thirty-six hours required for our return, we had to endure air pollution far worse than China's, death-defying drives on unbelievably congested streets, gauntlets of aggressive vendors at every tourist site, and trash almost everywhere we looked.

Nevertheless, India was by far the most fascinating and exciting country we had ever seen. It had been Grandmother Pauley's favorite destination in the 1950s and was the "overwhelmingly interesting highlight" of my parents' trip around the world in 1976. My mother described it as having "grandeur, color, drabness," and above all "many people." Mark Twain wrote in 1897 that it was "the land of dreams and romance, of fabulous wealth and fabulous poverty, of splendor and rags, of palaces and hovels, of famine and pestilence."[10]

India, of course, has one of the world's four oldest civilizations, and one that is still comparatively untouched by westernization and modernization, at least in rural areas. Certainly the Portuguese, French, and especially the British have all left their marks on the country, marks that are readily visible in New Delhi, Mumbai (Bombay), and Cochin. We were surprised, however, to find that English is spoken by only 3 percent of the population. Much of rural India, in many ways, is still living in the Neolithic period. Farm animals and monkeys coexist with humans, and not just on farms. In some areas, water for irrigation and drinking is brought to the surface by waterwheels driven by water buffalo. The latter, along with cows, being regarded as holy by Hindus, provide not meat but milk, ice cream, fertilizer, and even fuel.

The temples, palaces, and forts we saw in Delhi, Agra, and Jaipur, not to mention the religious ceremonies we witnessed in the holy city of Varanasi, were all especially exotic. Architecture and religion were only two obvious differences between India and the West. Another was the dress of men and especially women in both villages and cities. Traditional costumes were still favored in India, in part a product of Indian nationalism and a conscious rejection of the Western norms.[11] If you put a group of typically American women next to a group of Indian women of any class, you would have a tough time telling which group lived in an impoverished country.

On the other hand, the opening of India to international investors after 1990 had brought tremendous changes. On the outskirts of larger cities we saw evidence of a new middle class—estimated to be around 250 to 300 million—in new high-rise apartment complexes and streets crowded with new automobiles. However, the rural population, which still makes up 70 percent of the country's 1.15 billion people, survives on $1.75 a day. Despite this, the Indians we met seemed happy and optimistic about their country's future.

On the negative side, we were appalled not only by India's air pollution but even more by the trash we saw everywhere, even in national parks, where presumably only wealthier Indians visit. As in Southeast Asia, much of the trash was plastic. Whereas in the past much of the uncollected garbage was eaten by cows, goats, and pigs that still wander the streets of even big cities, plastic cannot be eaten, or at least not digested, and will last virtually forever. Rarely did we see evidence of regular garbage collection.

Our trip to Australia and New Zealand and the Fiji Islands in 2011 resembled India only in the distances covered. All of them, even the Fiji Islands (which is still very much a developing country), were free of trash. Sydney impressed us not only with its iconic opera house but also with its excellent public transportation system, museums, and parks. Australia and New Zealand are clearly also benefiting from the favorable balance between natural resources and population density along with their mild climates.

A cruise to the western Caribbean with our two older grandchildren, Alena and Ben, in the spring of 2012 hardly qualifies as a "distant destination." Nevertheless, it was interesting to see how much travel by ship has changed over the last century. Until World War I, oceangoing ships carried immigrants, cargo, mail, and a handful of the super-rich from one continent to another. For most passengers, the voyage was an ordeal. From the 1920s to the 1960s ships were used primarily to transport tourists in relative comfort to exotic destinations. Nowadays, oceangoing ships and even some riverboats have become almost purely ends in themselves with recreation and pleasure being the primary purpose. Learning about other cultures is at best secondary; contact with local residents other than tour guides is next to impossible.

A cruise on the Danube from the Black Sea to Budapest in the summer of 2012 gave us an opportunity to compare that region to what we had seen in 1964. The entire area was more prosperous than it had been thirty-eight years earlier, and no one with whom we spoke longed to return to a Communist dictatorship. On the other hand, many people regretted their loss of job security and were overwhelmed by the choices they now have to make. It was especially interesting to compare the orderliness, tidiness, and relative prosperity of Croatia and Hungary, former parts of the Austro-Hungarian Monarchy, with Bulgaria and Serbia, which had never been part of the monarchy and its efficient and honest civil service. Our need to have different currencies in each of the five countries through which we traveled was also a sobering contrast to the monarchy, which had a single currency for its eleven nationalities.

A nostalgic return to Austria in the summer of 2013—my nineteenth since 1954—as well as to Germany and Switzerland enabled my wife and me to make still more comparisons between central Europe today and the areas we had visited nearly a half century earlier. The most obvious and dramatic difference was the increase in the number of cars. In 1964 Marianne and I had driven through every country between Turkey and France without incident or anxiety. That feeling of freedom and relaxation remained in trips through East Germany in 1969, Italy in 1972, and Yugoslavia in 1991. By contrast, driving in central Europe was a harrowing experience in 2013. Finding a parking place in a town of any size required a costly permit from an automated machine. Driving on an autobahn meant competing with cars going between forty and over a hundred miles an hour. Motoring in small towns was no picnic either, filled as they were with blind corners and impatient drivers. I returned to the United States with a greater appreciation for American driving habits and a vow that I would never again drive a car in Europe. Terrifying as the German autobahns were, they did at least give us a glimpse of how the Germans have turned to wind and solar power as new sources of energy. This transition is all the more surprising considering the relative scarcity of sunshine and wind in central Europe.

Fortunately, driving is not a necessity in Europe, and especially not in Vienna. The Austrian capital's public transportation system, already very good in the early twentieth century, is better than ever. In contrast to my student days, the Austrian capital now has a complete network of subways as well as a new set of streetcars. Subway stations even have huge screens broadcasting the latest news headlines as well as the arrival of the next train. Walking is also more pleasurable than it was a half century ago. Streets in the central sections of Vienna, Graz, Munich, and Salzburg, as well as many other European cities, once filled with noisy and smelly cars, are now reserved for pedestrians and outdoor restaurants. And streets that were lined with pre–World War I buildings in desperate need of paint or plaster in the 1950s and 1960s have now been restored to their former splendor. Also noteworthy are supermarkets—nonexistent in the early 1960s—some with underground parking lots and escalating ramps for carts, thus conserving land and enabling shoppers to park without being exposed to the elements.

Marianne and I also discovered in 2013 that many problems now confronting the United States also exist in Europe, often in a more serious form. Austria and Germany are confronted with an aging population and a birthrate so low that population stability can be retained only through immigration, much of it illegal. According to our friends, people coming from areas once belonging to the Austro-Hungarian Monarchy, with the exception of the Muslims of Bosnia-Herzegovina, have relatively little difficulty assimilating into their new surroundings. It is another story, however, for immigrants from the Middle East or Africa, whose inability or unwillingness to learn the local language makes it nearly impossible for them to enter the middle class in Austria, Germany, and other European countries.

International travel has raised the question of why some countries are filled with trash while others are immaculately clean. Peru was strewn with garbage until quite recently, when the government decided that if it was serious about international tourism the country needed to clean up its act. China, including Hong Kong, was not noted for its public cleanliness a half century ago, yet today at least the cities seem to be very clean (although we saw a great deal of refuse in the Grand Canal and in some villages in 1997 and 2008). China's long history of strong central government appears to have made public cleanliness easier to enforce there. The lack of a strong central government in India is apparent in that country's trash and chaotic traffic. Our guide told us that Indians consider traffic lights and lanes to be mere suggestions. We saw vehicles driving on the wrong side of divided multi-lane highways because it was "more convenient" than making a U-turn at the next exit. The Indian government has also been ineffective in enforcing compulsory education and child labor laws, a phenomenon reminiscent of the United States at the beginning of the twentieth century.

My travels since the 1950s have left me with three lasting impressions. The first is the impact of globalization, and not just economically. Especially during my first two trips to Europe in 1954 and 1957–58, Americans could easily be spotted a hundred yards away. Now jeans, baseball hats, and T-shirts can be found from San Francisco to Paris to Shanghai. With the exception of India, of the seventy-plus countries I have visited, only the rural areas of states commonly called third-world countries still cling to more traditional clothing. Glass-and-steel skyscrapers are also no longer the monopoly of big American cities. The omnipresence of American fast-food restaurants in Russia, China, and even India (where they serve chicken burgers) is creating a boring and depressing sameness around the world.

The second big impression, especially pronounced in the countries Marianne and I have visited since the late 1990s, is how much many have invested in infrastructure. In 1998 we were impressed by France's TGV (train à grande vitesse, or very fast train), which we rode between Bordeaux and Paris at speeds of up to 180 miles an hour. Not a single fatality has been recorded on them, and they use one-sixth as much energy as airplanes. China is spending $300 billion building a nationwide network of high-speed rail lines. On our trips to China, Southeast Asia, Australia, and New Zealand we encountered new airports in Beijing, Bangkok, Siem Riep (Cambodia), Hong Kong, Tokyo, Sydney, and Auckland. In 2003 we traveled in Spain by bus on brand-new superhighways. In Santiago we landed at a new airport and were whisked into the center of the city on an equally new multi-lane highway.

The third impression has to do with how much the American transportation system has deteriorated, especially since about 1970. When Marianne and I lived in Laramie my parents could drive to Omaha, relish a nice dinner, and board a Union Pacific Pullman (sleeping) car on a side track anytime after 9:00 p.m. Their car would be hooked up to a passing train around midnight; they woke up in Cheyenne the next morning about 7:00, just in time for them to breakfast while crossing the Laramie Range. They loved not having to drive. Today, no passenger train comes through Laramie, or any other town in Wyoming for that matter. The only public means of crossing Nebraska today, from the Iowa border to Wyoming, is by a Greyhound bus. A trip from Omaha to Cheyenne takes between fifteen and nineteen hours, depending on departure times. A Chinese bullet train could cover the same five hundred miles in less than three hours.

During the last half century we have made dramatic improvements in transferring and retrieving information through direct-distance dialing, cell phones, e-mails, smartphones, and the Internet. However, air travel is far slower today than it was in the 1960s. In 1970 one could arrive at most

American airports just thirty minutes before departure and expect to catch a flight. There were no security lines or even metal detectors. Today, passengers are supposed to get to large airports at least two hours in advance. In the meantime, service has nosedived, especially on domestic flights. The one aspect of air travel that has improved is cost, although the price of aviation fuel has recently caused increased fares and will likely continue to do so in the future. We have gone from having the best public inter-urban and intra-urban transit system in the world at the beginning of the twentieth century to one of the worst among developed countries a century later.

The sad fact is that Americans have invested in costly wars, huge houses, big cars, and gargantuan meals rather than in the country's infrastructure, especially its transportation network. Even our bridges and water and sewage systems have deteriorated to a dangerous degree, causing our infrastructure to rank twenty-fifth in the world. The result is enormous federal deficits, dependence on cars and therefore foreign oil, and bulging waistlines that will inevitably increase chronic health issues such as diabetes, cancer, and heart disease. These diseases, in turn, will enormously increase health-care costs, especially now that the baby boomers are reaching retirement age.

Despite the increased expense and inconveniences of traveling, Marianne and I have never tired of it, and we hope to continue our travels well into old age. We return to the States having learned as much about our own country, through comparisons, as we have about the countries we visited. In general, I wholeheartedly agree with Mark Twain—the best-traveled American of the nineteenth century—who said that "travel is fatal to prejudice, bigotry, and narrow-mindedness. . . . Broad, wholesome, charitable views of men and things can not be acquired by vegetating in one little corner of the earth all one's lifetime."[12] My only regret is that I can no longer pass on what I have learned to a classroom of students.

CHAPTER 17

Reflections

THREE FAMILY TRAITS

In October 2009, Marianne and I were able to track down the house that my great-great-grandfather Heinrich built around 1880. A mile east of Harvard, Nebraska, it had obviously not been lived in for decades. All the windows were broken. A kitchen stove and bathtub, both no doubt installed long after the house was built, had been tossed out. Numerous outbuildings were falling apart. However, the buildings were still surrounded by trees that my great-great-grandfather and his sons had planted. The house had three modest-size rooms downstairs, each roughly twelve by fourteen feet. There were two even smaller rooms upstairs and no closets to be seen anywhere, as was the norm in the late nineteenth century. There was no evidence that the house ever had electric lights or an indoor toilet. Heinrich died in this house, and my grandfather Pauley was born there in 1886. Undoubtedly, my father, born in 1908, visited the house before Heinrich's death in 1914.

Later that same day, Marianne and I drove five miles south to the Clay County courthouse to see if we could find Heinrich's last will and testament. After some searching, a clerk brought us a thick packet of documents dating back to 1906. The will listed Heinrich's assets and how they were to be distributed after his death. But what interested us most was his "signature." In beautiful handwriting was his anglicized name, Henry Pauley. But between his first and last names was a + sign. Above the + was the word "his"; below was the word "mark." Here was proof that my great-great-grandfather could not even write his name!

With this evidence I confirmed that I had not descended from a long line of scholars. However, what Heinrich had lacked in education he more than made up for in his pioneering and adventuresome spirit, good luck, and hard work. If he had lacked those characteristics he never would have brought his family to Nebraska, and the history of my family would have been unrecognizably different. One also has to wonder, where else at that time, other than the High Plains frontier, could a semi-literate man have been so successful?

A pioneering spirit, good luck, help from the Russian government, and hard work were certainly needed for Philip Jacob Paulÿ and his wife, Maria Elizabeth, to make their epic journey from Germany to the Volga in 1766–77. It took nearly as much courage for Heinrich to bring his family to Nebraska 111 years later. It was pure luck that Wilhelm Staerkel exhorted his congregation in Norka to seek economic, political, and religious freedom on the American frontier. It was either luck or happenstance that Heinrich had three sons at or near draft age, which helped persuade him to immigrate to America, thereby avoiding the horrors that would have befallen the family had it remained in Russia. Heinrich was the least educated of my Pauley ancestors of whom I have detailed knowledge. However, his decision to come to America was the most important contribution to the destiny of the Pauley family and its pioneering traditions.

The pioneering and adventuresome characteristics of my ancestors can again be seen in my great-grandfather Conrad. He was the first fully literate Pauley, the first to enter the business world, and the first to show a real interest in education by joining the Harvard, Nebraska, school board. Almost certainly this interest encouraged his children to complete high school. My grandfather Ludwig Pauley, entered the lumber business in 1902 at the age of sixteen and began managing a lumberyard the next year, a time when construction was booming. He was lucky to have a generous and trusting father, but it was his own intelligence and ambition that enabled him to establish numerous enterprises. It was also he who began a family tradition of academic achievement, encouraged a love of music and traveling, and provided the financial means to pursue those passions. In the same year, 1902, that my grandfather Pauley started his business career, my grandfather Hulsebus entered the hardware and telephone business. Eight years later he got into the automobile business, just when cars were beginning to be mass produced and were replacing horse-drawn vehicles.

The good fortune that both of my grandfathers enjoyed from the beginning of their careers evaporated in the Great Depression. They were lucky not to lose their businesses altogether. If anything, however, the Depression made an even bigger impact on my father, whose business career was just beginning as the Depression was deepening. For eleven years he was barely able to make a living. The Depression was a traumatic experience from which he never entirely recovered. He worried about its recurrence to the end of his business career in 1975; it made him ultraconservative about his business ventures as well as his investments.

If his business career was not blessed with a good deal of luck, my father did inherit much of his parents' adventuresome spirit. By the time he was twenty-one he had seen nearly every important city in the United States. He and his parents traveled to California in 1925 at a time when paved roads west of Lincoln were virtually unknown. My parents' trip to Europe in 1930, the time when they met, was the inspiration for our memorable family adventure of 1954, when all four of us went to Europe for nearly three months. That trip, in turn, made me want to spend my junior year in Vienna in 1957–58, and I have been an ardent traveler ever since.

Although my father was extremely cautious when it came to business and investing, he was downright daring regarding World War II. He was not satisfied to sit safely at home and witness the war vicariously through radio and newspaper accounts. He wanted to be where history was being made, hence his decision to volunteer for the navy in 1942 and his involvement in a ferocious naval battle in the Mediterranean in 1944. His three years of active duty were filled with so many adventures that he devoted a third of his memoirs to his war years.

Certainly luck (mostly good but sometimes bad), hard work, and the help of my parents and mentors have been the dominant themes in my own life. Most of the good fortune I experienced throughout my life was related to my birth year. It was truly the gift that kept on giving. From kindergarten through high school I belonged to an age cohort that did not have to endure overcrowded schools. When I was ready for college they were eagerly seeking applicants. Scholarships were plentiful for graduate students. By the time I began looking for a permanent teaching job in 1963 the market for historians was at an all-time high.

My birth year even aided me in the timing of my retirement. People born in 1937 belonged to the last cohort that could collect full Social Security benefits upon reaching their sixty-fifth birthday. I was also lucky to end full-time employment at the University of Central Florida just before it and most other American universities entered a period of ever tighter budgets and increasing class sizes. Good luck was even involved in the sale of our house in Oviedo in the spring of 2006, just before the housing bubble burst. Marianne and I have retirement pensions at a time when they are being reduced or eliminated elsewhere.

I was amazingly lucky to meet a beautiful, charming, and intelligent young woman named Marianne Utz who was taking the same history course that I was at the University of Rochester. It was also my good fortune, though not mere luck, that I chose to specialize in Austrian history, thus turning trips to Austria into both vacations for me and my family as well as opportunities for serious original research.

By the same token, I was almost unbelievably unlucky in the circumstances surrounding the loss of my job at the University of Wyoming in 1970. In this instance timing worked against me. It was simply bad luck that I came up for tenure when the history department had three de facto chairmen in two years, none of whom was fully aware of my scholarly activities. It was also unfortunate that the university did not yet have the tenure guidelines that were well established at other American universities. On the other hand, it was pure luck that the editor of *The Habsburg Legacy* happened to see a notice at a historical convention announcing an opening in German history at Florida Technological University, thus saving my career.

My half century as a student of history was marked by a great deal of work. Delivering twelve lectures a week to large classes during much of my career, correcting enormous piles of bluebooks, and attending numerous committee meetings was not easy. Even more demanding was the writing of numerous books, articles, and reviews, which consumed most of my weekends and vacations. A long attention span and an enthusiasm for one's project are essential prerequisites for writing, especially for writing a book. Fortunately, I seemed to have those characteristics, though no doubt this sometimes came at the expense of the time I would have otherwise devoted to my wife and sons. Perhaps most of all, I have been extremely lucky in the friendships I have made and maintained over more than half a century.

THE EVOLUTION OF AN AMERICAN FAMILY

In many ways the Pauley family typifies generational changes that were taking place all over America between the late nineteenth and the early twenty-first centuries. Like most other immigrants to this country, my ancestors on both sides of my family arrived on our shores with little more than the clothes on their backs and a burning desire to work hard and make a better life for themselves. A big part of that desire to "get ahead" was education. My great-great-grandfather Heinrich could read but not write. My great-grandfather Conrad could read and write but had no more than an elementary education. My grandfather Pauley was quite likely the first German from Russia in Nebraska to graduate from high school. My father graduated from college, and I went on to obtain a PhD. The progression from generation to generation is obvious. The length of time required for males in the Pauley family to reach full adulthood, if adulthood is defined in part as an ability to be financially self-supporting, is also obvious and typifies the evolution of the American family during the last hundred years. My grandfather Pauley entered the business world at the age of sixteen, my father when he was twenty-one. I acquired my first full-time job when I was twenty-six; Glenn was twenty-eight when he began working full-time, and Mark was thirty-one.

The lives of my female ancestors have also mirrored trends in this country over the last century. My great-great-grandmothers and their predecessors spent most of their prime adult years being pregnant, giving birth, and raising large families, all without the benefit of trained physicians and labor-saving devices. My great-great-grandmother Elizabeth had twelve children, only seven of whom survived into adulthood. My great-grandmother Alice had eight children, all born in Nebraska, and all of whom survived into adulthood, a stark contrast to the many Pauleys and Hulsebuses who were born in Russia or Germany and died in infancy or childhood. On the other hand, my grandmothers reflected the early-twentieth-century trend among non-farm families of having only two children, a family size that has characterized the Pauleys to the present day.

It was during the lifetimes of my grandmothers that the lives of American women began to change radically. My grandmother Pauley graduated from high school and even had one year of college, both exceptional achievements in early-twentieth-century America. Like nearly all married women of her generation and earlier, she did not work outside the home, although she did do some bookkeeping for my grandfather. She and my grandmother Hulsebus belonged to the first generation of women to enjoy such luxuries as electric stoves and vacuum cleaners, telephones, washing machines, and radios. However, ironically, all the new labor-saving devices, rather than reducing the domestic workload, led to higher expectations regarding cleanliness. However, my grandmother Pauley was able to become a world traveler not just while her husband was alive but even more so after his death.

My mother in many respects reflected the "New Woman" of the 1920s. Typically, her skirts were short and her hair was "bobbed" in the latest fashion. She was also athletic and was the first of my female ancestors to graduate from college. Likewise, she was the first to earn a living outside the home. By the 1920s and 1930s working outside the home was not all that unusual for American women. However, my mother did so in an extremely adventuresome fashion by teaching in France for a year and on Cape Cod for two years. Yet, she was old-fashioned in never smoking and favoring Prohibition—until her year in Europe. Once married and with children, however, she was again typical of her generation by never again working full-time outside the home. Like most women of her generation she believed that her role in marriage was to be a homemaker and that my father's job was to be a provider.

My sister, Patricia, was part of a generation that was torn between the post–World War II cohort of women who were anxious to be housewives and mothers and the generation of the 1960s that demanded equal rights, especially the right to work outside the home without any stigma being attached. My wife, Marianne, born seven years after my sister, belonged to a generation for whom working outside the home had become commonplace even for mothers, although the practice is still not universally applauded. For Marianne and other American women in the 1960s and 1970s, the ideal was to work before having children and again after they were in school full-time. For our daughters-in-law, Maria and Lucy, perceived economic needs dictated continuous work, except for a few months after the birth of their children—again a common phenomenon for women at the turn of the twenty-first century.

The Pauley family has reflected a major aspect of the American family in the demise of the family business, the Pauley Lumber Company, in 1999. After eighty-four years at the same location, it could not compete with huge chain stores. We have also been far too typical in living far from our parents, children, and grandchildren.

The Pauley family was characteristically American in experiencing huge changes in lifestyle after 1900. My grandparents belonged to the first generation to own cars, telephones, and radios and to live in houses equipped with electric lights and many appliances. The electric refrigerator my father purchased in the mid-1930s was a big improvement over the earlier icebox, which had caused my father so much aggravation. Significant improvements in comfort came when he bought a window air-conditioner in the early 1950s. At the end of that decade he built a house that was fully air-conditioned, thus making Nebraska summers reasonably tolerable. Air-conditioning was even more important when Marianne and I moved to Florida. It was air-conditioning that was largely responsible for making Florida's summers bearable and enabling its population to grow from 1.5 million in 1940 to 19 million by 2013. The computer, which I began to use in the mid-1990s, has also had a substantial impact on American society. It has certainly aided my research and speeded up my writing.

In some ways, however, American lifestyles have changed for the worse since about 1960. Houses and yards are now much larger, but paying for them often necessitates two incomes rather than one. The clarity of television pictures has improved remarkably since the snowy black-and-white pictures of the 1950s, but the quality of much of the programming has declined substantially. My social studies teacher at Lincoln High School solemnly predicted in 1955 that one of the biggest problems facing Americans by the end of the century would be a surplus of leisure time. Now that we are well into the twenty-first century I doubt very much whether fully employed people even have as much free time as we did more than a half century ago. The size of our homes and yards, the length of our commutes to work, and the need for two incomes to pay for it all have greatly reduced free time and even opportunities for exercise for most Americans. We have added years to the end of our lives, but many of those years are spent in nursing homes. It is doubtful that our level of happiness has increased, if at all, nearly as much as our waistlines.

Our interstate highways are a big improvement over the two-lane roads of my youth, but their existence effectively put passenger trains out of business. Nowadays, highways such as I-80 across Nebraska are overcrowded with huge semis. Jets are much faster than the propeller-driven planes of the 1950s, not to mention steamships, but the speed of air travel has if anything actually declined since the late 1960s, and the comfort level of flying has fallen precipitously. Nobody still claims that "getting there is half the fun." As a percentage of one's income, it is far cheaper to fly to Europe now than it was in the 1950s and 1960s, but the cost of sightseeing for an American tourist is much higher, owing to the steep decline in the value of the dollar.

PIONEERING HISTORY

How much have I lived up to my own family heritage? I have never been so daring as to pull up roots so drastically as Philip Jacob Paulÿ did in 1766 when he moved his family to the Russian frontier. Nor have I been as bold as my great-great-grandfather Heinrich, who made the audacious decision to bring the family to another frontier in Nebraska. I never had to endure the heavy farm work of Heinrich or Conrad Pauley or the incredibly long hours my grandfather and father put into the Pauley Lumber Company. I don't know if I would have had the courage to volunteer to fight in World

War II, as my father did. And I was certainly grateful (and lucky) to have been too young for the Korean War and too old for Vietnam.

In terms of physical comfort, the avoidance of hard manual labor, economic security, and opportunities for foreign travel, my life is one that my ancestors could not have imagined. And yet, I can take some credit for having been a different kind of pioneer, one who has entered previously unexplored or at least inadequately explored areas of history. Evaluating the dissolution of the Habsburg Monarchy and its successor states, seeking the causes for Nazi successes and failures, examining the roots and consequences of anti-Semitism, and pointing out the common denominators of totalitarianism have involved both hard work and a sense of adventure, albeit of an intellectual kind. To have played a role in the Austrians' coming to terms with their problematic recent history has been enormously gratifying. I hope these achievements will be as much a source of pride for my descendants as the accomplishments of my ancestors have been for me.

My family, work, friends, and educational travel have been the biggest sources of my happiness. I have been fortunate in all these areas. I had loving parents who provided me with marvelous educational opportunities and supported me in every phase of my career. I have been privileged to have an incredible wife who has shared all my joys and hardships for half a century. I have two sons, two daughters-in-law, and four grandchildren who have been an enormous source of pride and satisfaction. I have loved my profession so much that it has often been hard for me to distinguish between work and entertainment. Whereas my Volga German ancestors rarely traveled outside their village, I have been able to make over thirty international trips to exotic and beautiful destinations on six continents. I hope my children, grandchildren, and their descendants will be as fortunate in their lives and choices as I have been throughout my life.

Notes

PREFACE

1. Gibbon, *Memoirs of My Life*, 154–55.
2. For an excellent description of historians' autobiographies see Popkin, *History, Historians, and Autobiography*.
3. On the importance of birth dates see Gladwell, *Outliers*.

1. PIONEERS ON THE RUSSIAN FRONTIER

1. The best general surveys of the Volga Germans are Koch, *Volga Germans*; Long, *From Privileged to Dispossessed*; and Walters, *Wir Wollen Deutsche Bleiben*.
2. The spelling of my family name has undergone numerous changes. The current spelling, "Pauley," is rarely used today in German-speaking countries, although "Pauly" and "Pauli" are fairly common. Even though the pronunciation has evidently never changed, or has changed only slightly, the earliest spelling was apparently "Pauly̆," the y̆ now being archaic in the German language. When the family arrived in New York in 1878, the ship's manifest listed the family as "Pauli." Such spelling changes, of course, were quite common for immigrants whose names and their spellings were unfamiliar to immigration officials. The name continued to evolve after the family came to Nebraska. An article that listed all the names of the first Volga Germans to come to Nebraska in 1876 and 1878 spelled the name "Pauly." When my great-grandfather Conrad applied for American citizenship in 1878 his name was spelled "Paule" (Hölzer, "Die ersten Wolgadeutschen in Sutton, Nebr.," 44–45). Just two years later, however, the census of 1880 had the name spelled "Paulie." In what year the name acquired its current spelling is unknown to me. I know only that when my father's father, Ludwig, graduated from high school in 1902 the family name was Pauley. Furthermore, the tombstone of my great-great-grandfather Heinrich, who died in Harvard, Nebraska, in 1914, also uses that spelling. Fortunately, the lack of an obvious German identity for the name meant that there was no need for additional spelling changes when anti-German hysteria erupted in the United States during World War I.
3. See Khodarkovsky, *Russia's Steppe Frontier*, 1–2, 196, 213.

4. Erickson, *Great Catherine*, 270.
5. Giesinger, *From Catherine to Khrushchev*, 9.
6. Williams, *The Czar's Germans*, 51–88.
7. Walters, *Wir Wollen Deutsche Bleiben*, 52.
8. Scheuerman, *The Volga Germans*, 46.
9. Mai, *Transport of the Volga Germans*, i.
10. Beratz, *German Colonies on the Lower Volga*, 52–53.
11. Mai and Reeves-Marquardt, *German Migration to the Russian Volga*, xxx. Today, Saratov is a major city that boasts a large number of very German-style buildings dating back to the first three decades of the twentieth century.
12. Toepfer and Dreiling, *Conquering the Wind*, 26.
13. Mai, *Transport of the Volga Germans*, vi.
14. Long, *From Privileged to Dispossessed*, 2–3.
15. "The Early Years—1767 to 1775," *Norka: A German Colony in Russia*, http://www.volgagermans.net/norka/early_years.html.
16. "The Early Years—1767 to 1775."
17. Olson and Reisbik, *Norka*, 48; "Origins," *Norka: A German Colony in Russia*, http://www.volgagermans.net/norka/origins.html.
18. "Williams, *The Czar's Germans*, 156.
19. Dixon, *Catherine the Great*, 188.
20. Vaccinations were by no means accepted by all Russians. A century later none other than Josef Stalin contracted the disease, which left his face pockmarked for life.
21. In 1865 there were 214 teachers in all the Volga German villages attempting to instruct 43,269 students. See Koch, *Volga Germans*, 147.
22. Spring, *The American School*, 151–52.
23. Bonwetsch, *Geschichte der deutschen Kolonien*, 79.
24. While searching for information about my great-grandfather and great-great-grandfather I was astonished to see in the Harvard, Nebraska, newspaper a list of all the visitations that had occurred in the town during the previous week.
25. Schwabenland-Haynes, "German Russians," 64.
26. Rife, *German and German-Russians in Nebraska*, 116.
27. Lincoln, *The Great Reforms*, 156; Williams, *The Czar's Germans*, 178.
28. Toepfer and Dreiling, *Conquering the Wind*, 92. The Volga Germans reminded Czar Alexander II that Catherine had promised them the freedom to leave Russia if they so desired.
29. Koch, *Volga Germans*, 198.
30. Long, *From Privileged to Dispossessed*, 37.
31. Williams, "History of the German-Russian Colony in Lincoln," 56–57; Hill, "Volga German Occupance," 59.
32. Bonwetsch, *Geschichte der deutsche Kolonien*, 110.

33. Woodard, *American Nations*, 290. The value of the dollar over time can be found at http://www.usinflationcalculator.com.

34. Egan, *The Worst Hard Time*, 65.

35. Griess, *The German Russians*, 221. See also Kinbacher and Thomas, "Shaping Nebraska," 191–92.

36. Kinbacher and Thomas, "Shaping Nebraska," 192. However, railroad agents and agricultural publication as well as local newspapers endorsed the widely held fantasy that "rain follows the plow," that is, the very act of plowing would increase rainfall. See Wishart, *Last Days of the Rainbelt*, especially p. 36.

37. Johannes (1805–69) and Catharina (1807–67) were the only Pauly̆ couple to spend their entire lives in Russia. Johannes's father, also named Johannes (1758–1821), was born in Germany, although his wife, Catharina Weitzel (b. 1768), was born in Norka.

38. Harvard History Book Committee, *Harvard, Nebraska*, 301. Such letter writing was encouraged by the Burlington Railroad. James Griess, interview by the author, Lincoln, Nebraska, October 29, 2010.

39. Williams, *The Czar's Germans*, 199.

40. Hölzer, "Die ersten Wolgadeutschen in Sutton, Nebr.," 44–45. Hölzer spells the name "Pauley," but he was writing in 1926 and probably had no idea about how the family spelled its name fifty years earlier.

41. H. Paul Brehm, "The Yost Family" (unpublished manuscript, 1951), n.p.

42. Williams, "A Social Study of the Russian Germans," 142, 144. Sixty-five percent of Volga Germans who came to Lincoln did so on tickets purchased for them by relatives and friends already in Nebraska. See Schwabenland-Haynes, "German Russians," 112.

43. Wolmar, *Blood, Iron and Gold*, 222.

44. The same was true of my wife's parents. Having left Germany in 1930, my mother-in-law never saw her parents again, and my father-in-law saw his parents only once, in 1938.

45. Giesinger, *From Catherine to Khrushchev*, 251.

46. Koch, *Volga Germans*, 265.

47. Spach, "Sad Pages of History," 23.

48. Morris, *American History Revised*, 246.

49. Morris, *American History Revised*, 246. Some immigrants returned to their homelands in triumph or out of nostalgia, others because they felt defeated economically or because they could not adjust to such a divorce society. The exact number of returnees can only be estimated, because no government records were kept until 1908. See Donna Przecha, "Immigrants Who Returned Home," http://www.genealogy.com/96_donna.html.

50. Sklar, *The Plastic Age*, 2.

51. Rippley, *The German-Americans*, 126.

2. A NEW LIFE ON THE GREAT PLAINS

1. Harvard History Book Committee, *Harvard, Nebraska*, 388.
2. Manifest of the SS *Wieland*, photocopy at the American Historical Society of Germans from Russia. For pictures of the interior and exterior of the Wieland see "Norway-Heritage, Hand Across the Sea, S/S. Wieland, Hamburg America Line," http://www.norwayheritage.com/p_ship.asp?sh=wiela.
3. "Volga Germans, First Ships," http://www.webbitt.com/volga/firs2t-ships.html.
4. "Steerage Passengers—Emigrants between Decks," http://www.norwayheritage.com/steerage.htm.
5. Daniels, *Coming to America*, 273.
6. Hill, "Volga German Occupance," 65; Scheuerman, *The Volga Germans*, 100, 116.
7. Harvard History Book Committee, *Harvard, Nebraska*, 301. The possibility of such a freight-train ride was confirmed to me by James Griess in an interview in Lincoln on September 29, 2010.
8. Shrock, *The Gilded Age*, 228; Urbach, "Our Parents Were Russian German," 21.
9. Wolmar, *The Great Railroad Revolution*, 170.
10. Hölzer, "Die ersten Wolgadeutschen in Sutton, Nebr.," 45; Schwabenland-Haynes, "German Russians," 110.
11. Lears, *Rebirth of a Nation*, 54.
12. Baltensperger, *Nebraska*, 63.
13. Fink, *Agrarian Women*, 35.
14. Luebke, *Nebraska*, 102–3. See also Dick, *Sod-House Frontier*, 206.
15. Fink, *Agrarian Women*, 44; Wishart, *Last Days of the Rainbelt*, xvi, 112.
16. *The World Almanac and Book of Facts, 2008*, 592; Dick, *Sod-House Frontier*, 224.
17. Wishart discusses this ordeal in *Last Days of the Rainbelt*.
18. Egan, *The Worst Hard Time*, 56.
19. Luebke, *Immigrants and Politics*, 19.
20. Hickey, *Nebraska Moments*, 109. See also George Gale, "*History of Old Clay County*," County Scrapbook, Nebraska State Historical Society Library, Lincoln.
21. Rippley, *The German-Americans*, 94.
22. Harvard History Book Committee, *Harvard, Nebraska*, 388–89.
23. Overton, *Burlington West*, 531.
24. Schwabenland-Haynes, "German Russians," 104.
25. June 1, 1880, U.S. Census, Lynn Precinct, Clay County, Nebraska, Series T9 Roll: 745, 68, Household no. 111.
26. Wishart, *Rainbelt*, 88.
27. Harvard History Book Committee, *Harvard, Nebraska*, 301, 388–89.
28. Harvard History Book Committee, *Harvard, Nebraska*, 388.
29. Fink, *Agrarian Women*, 31.
30. Hill, "Volga German Occupance," 106–7.

31. Handlin and Handlin, *Wealth of the American People*, 124; Dick, *Sod-House Frontier*, 299.
32. Luebke, *Nebraska*, 88; Dick, *Sod-House Frontier*, 354.
33. E-mail from Frederick Luebke to the author, August 20, 2009; Griess, *The German Russians*, 180.
34. Luebke, *Nebraska*, 95.
35. Larsen et al., *Upstream Metropolis*, 45, 162.
36. Crichton, *America 1900*, 10.
37. Hayes and Cox, *History of the City of Lincoln, Nebraska*, 10.
38. Griess, *The German Russians*, 183. See also H. Johnson, *Johnson's History of Nebraska*, 169, which lists Clay County's population as seven thousand in 1878.
39. *World Almanac and Books of Facts for 1950*, 462; "Clay County, Nebraska," *Wikipedia*, http://wnwikipedia.org/wiki/Clay_County,_Nebaska.
40. June 1, 1900, U.S. Census, Harvard Precinct, Clay County, Nebraska, Series: T623 Roll: 920, p. 67 Family: 307.
41. June 1, 1900, U.S. Census, Harvard Precinct, Clay County, Nebraska; Historical Plat Book of Clay County, Nebraska, Drawn from Personal Observations and the County Records under the direction of Geo. W. Davy and J. S. Dunlap, C. E. (Davy & Dunlap Publishers, 1886).
42. April 15, 1910, U.S. Census, Ward 1, Harvard City Precinct, Clay County, Nebraska.
43. Last Will and Testament of Henry [Heinrich] Pauley, June 28, 1906, Court Records, Clay County Courthouse, Clay Center, Nebraska.
44. Harvard History Book Committee, *Harvard, Nebraska*, 187.
45. Historical Committee of Clay County, *History of Clay County*, 17–18; H. Johnson, *Johnson's History of Nebraska*, 270.
46. Harvard History Book Committee, *Harvard, Nebraska*, 275; Kazin, *A Godly Hero*, 134.
47. Crichton, *America 1900*, 162.
48. Harvard History Book Committee, *Harvard, Nebraska*, 159.
49. Harvard History Book Committee, *Harvard, Nebraska*, 25–30, 59, 111, 117.
50. H. Johnson, *Johnson's History of Nebraska*, 139.
51. Knoll, *Prairie University*, 8.
52. Luebke, *Nebraska*, 165. Nebraska was the twenty-second state to make education compulsory. Massachusetts was first, in 1852, and Mississippi was last, in 1918. See Good, *History of American Education*, 376.
53. Dudley, "Nebraska Public School Education," 68.
54. Dick, *Sod-House Frontier*, 320.
55. Last Will and Testament of Heinrich Pauley. Of Heinrich's $12,000 estate only $300 went to Margaret. However, it is likely that she had an adequate inheritance from her first husband.
56. June 1, 1900, U.S. Census, Lynn Precinct, Clay County, Nebraska.

57. "Memoirs of Selma Pauley Brehm, 1973," 2, in H. Paul Brehm, ed., "The Pauley Family" (unpublished genealogy, 1988).
58. Harvard History Book Committee, *Harvard, Nebraska*, 245–46.
59. Carroll R. Pauley, "An Autobiography" (1976) (unpublished manuscript, Love Library, University of Nebraska–Lincoln), 1.
60. Dick, *Sod-House Frontier*, 303, 304.
61. Mintz and Kellogg, *Domestic Revolutions*, 90, 99, 120.
62. Stratton, *Pioneer Women*, 72.
63. McBride and Nief, *The Mindset Lists of American History*, 46; Shrock, *The Gilded Age*, 79–80.
64. Coontz, *Social Origins of Private Life*, 253.
65. C. R. Pauley, "Autobiography," 2.
66. Griess, *The German Russians*, 256.
67. Bruntz, *Children of the Volga*, 93.
68. Harvard History Book Committee, *Harvard, Nebraska*, 193.
69. Urban and Wagoner, *American Education*, 187.
70. Franciosi, *Rise and Fall of American Public Schools*, 114.
71. "Harvard, Clay County, Nebraska Early Days," http://www.nebraskagenealogy.com/clay/Photo_%20Album/harvard.htm. Nationally, 70 percent of American teachers were women in 1900, whereas in 1830 nearly all U.S. teachers had been men. See Hofstadter, *Anti-Intellectualism in American Life*, 317.
72. Dudley, "Nebraska Public School Education," 69. In 1900, 78 percent of all Nebraska teachers were women; ten years later the percentage rose to 88 percent. See Dudley, "Nebraska Public School Education," 82.
73. Barzun, *From Dawn to Decadence*, 745.
74. Good, *History of American Education*, 253. See also Hofstadter, "The Development of Higher Education in America," 31.
75. In North Dakota only one Volga German was elected to a school board between 1913 and 1940, compared to twenty-five Norwegians. See Janssen, *Von Zarenreich in den amerikanischen Westen*, 238.
76. Dudley, "Nebraska Public School Education," 82.
77. Harvard History Book Committee, *Harvard, Nebraska*, 193–94.
78. Harvard History Book Committee, *Harvard, Nebraska*, 193–94.
79. See Kazin, *A Godly Hero*, especially p. 10.
80. *Harvard (NE) Courier*, May 24, 1902, 5.
81. Salins, *Assimilation American Style*, 7.
82. E-mail from Frederick Luebke to the author, November 21, 2009.
83. Janssen, *Von Zarenreich in den amerikanischen Westen*, 240.
84. Janssen, *Von Zarenreich in den amerikanischen Westen*, 232–36.
85. Schwabenland-Haynes, "German Russians," 142.

86. Dudley, "Nebraska Public School Education," 69.
87. *Harvard Courier*, March 7, 1908.
88. Dudley, "Nebraska Public School Education," 84.
89. *The World Almanac and Book of Facts, 1929*, 293.
90. *The World Almanac and Book of Facts for 1950*, 444.
91. The fire, which was apparently caused by a spark from a passing Rock Island train, caused $75,000 worth of damage (close to $1million in today's currency) and destroyed two nearby houses. See the *Lincoln Star* and *Nebraska State Journal*, July 2, 1925.
92. Watkins, *The Hungry Years*, 48; P. Johnson, "Calvin Coolidge and the Last Arcadia," 8.
93. Luebke, *Immigrants and Politics*, 192–93.
94. Rippley, *The German-Americans*, 176.
95. Rippley, *The German-Americans*, 35.
96. Schwabenland-Haynes, "German Russians," 156, 158.
97. "Medium Age at First Marriage, 1810–2010," http://www.infoplease.com/ipa/A0005061.html.
98. Rippley, *The German-Americans*, 178.
99. E-mail from David Holmes to the author, December 30, 2005.
100. Hill, "Volga German Occupance," 113.
101. *Harvard Courier*, March 7, 1908, 5; Apple, "Constructing Mother," 198. According to Apple "domestic science" was both a new term and a new academic discipline at the beginning of the twentieth century.
102. Coontz, *The Way We Never Were*, 156.
103. Leuchtenburg, *The Perils of Prosperity*, 202.
104. Kelley, *Shaping of the American Past*, 500.
105. Fuester, *The Hülsebus Families.*
106. Hupmobiles were another luxury car that went out of business during the Depression.
107. McElvaine, *Great Depression*, 18.
108. Allen, *The Big Change*, 7, 121, 124; Derks, *The Value of a Dollar*, 182.
109. Allitt, *I'm the Teacher*, 128.
110. Larsen et al., *Upstream Metropolis*, 193.
111. By 1925 more than two-thirds of new cars were bought on credit. Installment buying was commonplace at that time for other consumer items as well, such as phonographs, washing machine, and vacuum cleaners. See Shannon, *Between the Wars*, 98.
112. Leinwand, *1927*, 39.
113. Rasenberger, *America, 1908*, 21, 148.
114. Kyvig, *Daily Life in the United States*, 38.
115. Rasenberger, *America, 1908*, 80.
116. Leuchtenburg, *The Perils of Prosperity*, 184–85.
117. Watkins, *The Hungry Years*, 345.
118. *Harlan (IA) Republican*, March 19, 1931.

119. Roth, *The Great Depression*, 20.

120. Folsom, *New Deal or Raw Deal*, 32.

3. EDUCATION, TRAVEL, AND THE GREAT DEPRESSION

1. Weinwald, *1927*, 10, 36.
2. Watkins, *The Hungry Years*, 8.
3. Woodring, *Higher Learning in America*, 11.
4. Wall, *Grinnell College*, 110.
5. Wall, *Grinnell College*, xv.
6. Kelley, *Shaping of the American Past*, 500; Lucas, *American Higher Education*, 204, 206.
7. *The Cyclone 1931* (Grinnell College yearbook).
8. Coons and Varias, *Tourist Third Cabin*, 25, 32.
9. C. R. Pauley, "Autobiography," 23–24.
10. *Harlan (IA) Tribune*, February 25, 1931, 6.
11. C. R. Pauley, "Autobiography," 22.
12. *Harlan (IA) Republican*, September 18, 1930.
13. *Harlan Tribune*, January 14., 1931, 3.
14. Blanche Hulsebus to her family, November 26, 1930.
15. *Harlan Republican*, December 4, 1930.
16. Blanche Hulsebus to her family, September 14, 1930.
17. *Harlan Republican*, March 5, 1931.
18. *Harlan Tribune*, February 25, 1931, 6.
19. *Harlan Tribune*, April 29, 1931, 8.
20. *Harlan Tribune*, April 29, 1931, 8.
21. Blanche Hulsebus to her family, February 25, 1931.
22. C. R. Pauley, "Autobiography," 14.
23. C. R. Pauley, "Autobiography," 18.
24. Coontz, *Social Origins of Private Life*, 275.
25. Luebke, *Germans in the New World*, 31.
26. Good, *History of American Education*, 462–63.
27. In 1921 the University of North Dakota registered only one German from Russia out of 1,215 students, and the situation had changed little by 1940. See Janssen, *Von Zarenreich in den amerikanischen Westen*, 239.
28. Schwabenland-Haynes "German Russians," 142.
29. Schmalz, "*Volk auf dem Weg*," 3.
30. Hicks, *My Life with History*, 131.
31. Axtell, *The Pleasures of Academe*, 216–17.
32. Leuchtenburg, *The Perils of Prosperity*, 202.
33. Thelin, *History of American Higher Education*, 155.
34. Woodring, *Higher Learning in America*, 261.

35. Knoll, *Prairie University*, vii.
36. Brooks, *The Social Animal*, 10.
37. Kennedy, *Freedom from Fear*, 165.
38. Scott and Wishy, *America's Families*, 441.
39. Handlin and Handlin, *Wealth of the American People*, 199.
40. Handlin and Handlin, *Wealth of the American People*, 162–63.
41. Raynard, *It Started in Nebraska*, 39, 59.
42. Luebke, *Nebraska*, 279–80.
43. Harvard History Book Committee, *Harvard, Nebraska*, 362.
44. Harvard History Book Committee, *Harvard, Nebraska*, 87.
45. Coontz, *The Way We Never Were*, 158.
46. Braeman, "The American Polity," 37.
47. A Gallup poll taken in 1935 revealed the three-fourths of all women disapproved of married women holding a job. See Kelley, *Shaping of the American Past*, 819.
48. McElvaine, *Great Depression*, 74.
49. Kennedy, *Freedom from Fear*, 40.
50. Quoted in McElvaine, *Great Depression*, 75.
51. Morris, *American History Revised*, 202.
52. C. R. Pauley, "Autobiography," 20.
53. Kennedy, *Freedom from Fear*, 59.
54. McElvaine, *Great Depression*, 320–29.
55. Kelley, *Shaping of the American Past*, 604.
56. My father's annual salary of $1,200 in 1933 was roughly comparable to the national average for public school teachers between 1932 and 1934 ($1,227) and about half that of a college professor ($3,111). See Bowen, *This Fabulous Century*, 24.
57. C. R. Pauley, "Autobiography," 25.
58. U.S. Census of April 1, 1940, Lincoln, Nebraska.
59. Mintz and Kellogg, *Domestic Revolutions*, 56.
60. See Mintz and Kellogg, *Domestic Revolutions*, 203–37.
61. April 1, 1940, U.S. Census for Harlan, Iowa.
62. Lord, *The Good Years*, ix.

4. WAR, PEACE, AND PROSPERITY

1. Kyvig, *Daily Life in the United States*, 192; *The World Almanac and Book of Facts, 2012*, 609.
2. Estimates of unemployment for 1937 vary widely. Folsom, *New Deal or Raw Deal*, cites a figure of 13.2 percent (243). Hiltzik, *The New Deal*, says it was 9 percent (431).
3. Tuttle, "America's Home Front Children," 234.
4. Shlaes, *Forgotten Man*, xiii, 318.
5. Watkins, *The Great Depression*, 309–10.

6. *Evening State Journal*, January 1, 1937, 6. See also Roth, *The Great Depression*, 196.
7. *Evening State Journal*, January 8, 1937, 1.
8. *Evening State Journal*, January 8, 1937, 3.
9. Hiltzik, *The New Deal*, 377–78.
10. Watkins, *The Hungry Years*, 506.
11. Kennedy, *Freedom from Fear*, 298.
12. Shlaes, *Forgotten Man*, 3, 352. For a daily chart of the Dow Jones Industrial Average between 1920 and 1940 see http://stockcharts.com/charts/historical/djia19201940.html.
13. Mintz and Kellogg, *Domestic Revolutions*, 51.
14. Mintz and Kellogg, *Domestic Revolutions*, 120.
15. Kyvig, *Daily Life in the United States*, 121.
16. Quoted in Leuchtenburg, *The Perils of Prosperity*, 162–63.
17. See Sandler, "American Nightmare," 76.
18. Christopher Solomon, "The Swelling McMansion Backlash," *MSN Real Estate*, December 1, 2011, 1.
19. Wright, *Building the Dream*, 156.
20. Tuttle, "America's Home Front Children," 232.
21. C. R. Pauley, "Autobiography," 46.
22. C. R. Pauley, "Autobiography," 47.
23. My father also told me that he feared he would be drafted if he didn't volunteer. He evidently was influenced by the navy's recruitment slogan to "choose while you can" rather than risk being conscripted as a sailor or a foot soldier. I think that was unlikely considering that only one in five fathers was ever drafted. Of course, my father had no way of knowing that in 1942. Many years later he and I toured a destroyer escort in Boston harbor that was identical to the one on which he served during the war. He showed me what an officer's cabin looked like. Although small, compared to the cramped sleeping quarters of the sailors it looked downright luxurious. See Kennedy, *American People in World War II*, 210.
24. C. R. Pauley, "Autobiography," 74.
25. Patricia Pauley, "The Island of Curacao" (unpublished MS), September 24, 1945, 4 pp.
26. Woodard, *American Nations*, 290. See also H. F. May, *Coming to Terms*, 283.
27. Brokaw, *The Greatest Generation*, 15.
28. Popkin, *History, Historians, and Autobiography*, 133. See also Hans A. Schmitt, *Lucky Victim: An Ordinary Life in Extraordinary Times, 1933–1946* (Baton Rouge: Louisiana State University Press, 1989), 32.
29. Good, *History of American Education*, 441; Urban and Wagoner, *American Education*, 201, 236–37, 239.
30. I encountered my favorite social science teacher at Irving one evening at a movie theater. The ticket puncher, in a fancy uniform, said "Hello, Bruce." I was shocked

to see it was my teacher. He had taken the second job to make ends meet. This may have been my first clue that public school teaching was not for me.

31. Kazin, *A Godly Hero*, 172.
32. Wolmar, *Blood, Iron and Gold*, 286–87.
33. Knoll, *Prairie University*, 60.
34. Hawes and Nybakken, *American Families*, 160.
35. Kyvig, *Daily Life in the United States*, 102.
36. McBride and Nief, *The Mindset Lists of American History*, 113.
37. McBride and Nief, *The Mindset Lists of American History*, 56.
38. Kennedy, *Freedom from Fear*, 91.
39. Paradoxically, soft drinks with their high caffeine were seen as being perfectly healthy in the United States, whereas two decades earlier, Nazi Germany regarded Coca-Cola as unhealthy for German children. See Proctor, *The Nazi War on Cancer*, 149.
40. Knoll, *Prairie University*, 101.

5. THE AUDACITY OF YOUTH

1. McBride and Nief, *The Mindset Lists of American History*, 121.
2. McKee, *Lincoln, the Prairie Capital*, 102.
3. Okrent, *Last Call*, 37, 55–56.
4. Established as a volunteer ambulance corps in France at the start of e World War I, AFS set up an exchange program shortly after World War II for European and American high school students.
5. Mark Twain spent several weeks in Switzerland for much the same reason in 1878. In *A Tramp Abroad* he wrote: "Others came nearer formulating what they felt: they said they could find perfect rest and peace nowhere else when they were troubled: all frets and worries and chafings sank to sleep in the presence of the benignant serenity of the Alps" (184). See also an explanatory footnote by Kerry Driscoll on page 347.
6. C. R. Pauley, "Autobiography," 84.
7. C. R. Pauley, "Autobiography," 85.
8. Twain, *A Tramp Abroad*, 160–62.
9. See Dolmetsch, *"Our Famous Guest,"* especially p. 21.
10. I later wrote about the issue of the South Tyrol in *The Habsburg Legacy*.
11. For a discussion of the family backgrounds of future historians see Popkin, *History, Historians, and Autobiography*, 120–50.

6. FROM GRINNELL TO VIENNA AND BACK

1. Lucas, *American Higher Education*, 228.
2. *The World Almanac and Book of Facts, 1929*, 393.
3. Grinnell College *Cyclone* yearbooks for 1931, 1956, and 1959.
4. Grinnell College *Cyclone* yearbooks for 1931, 1956, and 1959.

5. Thelin, *History of American Higher Education*, 292, 322.
6. Arum and Roksa, *Academically Adrift*, 96.
7. *The Economist*, December 1, 2012, 30.
8. Folsom, *New Deal or Raw Deal*, 238.
9. Palmer, *Gentleman's Club*, x.
10. Leinwand, *1927*, 232–33.
11. See, for example, Billington, *Dr. B*, 110.
12. Brubacher and Rudy, *Higher Education in Transition*, 381, 390. See also Woodring, *Higher Learning in America*, 123.
13. E-mail from John R. Price to the author, March 19, 2010.
14. In the 1980s, IES expanded and was renamed the Institute of European and Asian Studies. In the 1990s it was enlarged again to include South America and South Africa and changed its name once more to the Institute for International Education of Students in order to maintain its IES acronym, and finally to IES Abroad. It is now one of the largest (if not the largest) provider of international education with twenty-three centers on six continents, over five thousands annual participants, and an annual budget of some $80 million. For a history and description of the program today see McMillan, *60 Years of Study Abroad*.
15. The issue of American students abroad living in a bubble is still a problem, although it is being addressed by colleges and international programs. See *Denver Post*, September 27, 2011, 8D.
16. McBride and Nief, *The Mindset Lists of American History*, 164.
17. Evan Burr Bukey has written a very good book on this subject: *Hitler's Hometown: Linz, Austria, 1908–1945* (Bloomington: Indiana University Press, 1986).
18. For a description of the youth hostel system in Germany see http://www.jugendherberge.de/en; http://www.hiusa.org/aboutus.
19. The Amerika Haus in Vienna was just one of 137 Amerika Häuser and reading rooms established in the American zones of occupation in Germany and Austria during the period of occupation, 1945–55. See MacDonogh, *After the Reich*, 248.
20. MacDonogh, *After the Reich*, 288.
21. Letter from the author to his parents, October 14, 1957.
22. E-mail from Ambassador Walter Siegl to the author, April 28, 2009.
23. *Harlan (IA) Tribune*, March 18, 1931, 4.
24. Letter from the author to his parents, March 17, 1958.
25. Popkin, *History, Historians, and Autobiography*, 130–31.
26. Letter from the author to his parents, August 19, 1958.
27. David Brooks, "Testing the Teachers," *New York Times*, April 20, 2012. See also Arum and Rosipa, *Academically Adrift*, 3.
28. See, for example, Hughes, *Gentleman Rebel*, 237.
29. Sheehy, *New Passages*, 25, 32.

30. Ashby, *With Amusement for All*, 263, 282.
31. Coontz, *The Way We Never Were*, 24.
32. Coontz, *The Way We Never Were*, xv, 29; *New York Times*, September 13, 2011, 1.

7. THE ORDEAL OF GRADUATE SCHOOL

1. Banner and Gillis, *Becoming Historians*, xiii. See also Popkin, *History, Historians, and Autobiography*, 140; Billington, *Doctor B*, 104–5; Hughes, *Gentleman Rebel*, 109, 311; and H. F. May, *Coming to Terms*, in which the author describes his time in graduate school as a period of "loneliness and depression" (224–25).
2. See Axtell, *The Pleasures of Academe*, 29.
3. Post, *Memoirs of a Cold War Son*, 58.
4. This problem was confirmed by the report of the Truman Commission on Higher Education in 1962, which said that at "some universities graduate students had to wait several months to arrange for appointments with their advisors." Westmeyer, *Analytical History of American Higher Education*, 115.
5. James T. King to the author, November 28, 1961.
6. Knoll, *Prairie University*, 69.
7. *The World Almanac and Book of Facts, 1929*, 394.
8. Knoll, *Prairie University*, vii–viii.
9. Robert Koehl, *RKFDV: German Resettlement and Population Policy, 1939–1945: A History of the Reich Commission for the Strengthening of Germandom* (Boston: Harvard University Press, 1957); Robert Koehl, *The Black Corps: The Structure and Power Struggles of the Nazi SS* (Madison: University of Wisconsin Press, 1983).
10. Derks, *The Value of a Dollar*, 204.
11. Palmer, *Gentleman's Club*, 87–88, 116.
12. In 1974, Gilbert C. Fite, a former president of the Southern Historical Association, sent a questionnaire to seventy-six history departments concerning teaching. Sixty-one of the respondents said that they did not bother much about teaching students to teach at the college level. Fite noted that Dexter Perkins was exceptional in pointing out such a need in his presidential address to the American Historical Association in 1956. See Adelson, *Speaking of History*, 96. The distinguished diplomatic historian Norman A. Graebner wrote in his memoirs that he had "never attended a meeting in which teaching was the primary subject of discussion." See Graebner, *A Twentieth-Century Odyssey*, 153.
13. Woodring, *Higher Learning in America*, 129.
14. Keller, *My Times and Life*, 68. This lack of teacher training for future professors may finally be changing. At the State University of New York at Albany they have had a special course for would-be professors since about 1990, as has Harvard University. Professor Donald Birn, interview by the author, Fiji Islands, December 24, 2011. Since the early 1990s the University of Pennsylvania has had a program to prepare graduate students to enter the academic job market. Professor Rosalind Beiler, interview

by the author, Orlando, January 23, 2012. In 2011 roughly 50 percent of doctoral students had an opportunity to take a course in teacher training. See Arum and Roksa, *Academically Adrift*, 133.

15. Quoted in Arum and Roksa, *Academically Adrift*, 6.
16. Perkins, *Yield of the Years*, 171–72.
17. For a brief discussion of IWA and Professor Gay's experiences in Nazi Germany see Gay, *My German Question*, 182.
18. Graebner, *Twentieth-Century Odyssey*, 118.
19. Letter to the author from his father, December 16, 1962.

8. ROMANCE AND MARRIAGE

1. Adelson, *Speaking of History*, 133.
2. "Median Age at First Marriage, 1870–2010," http://www.infoplease.com/ipa/A0005061.html; *Orlando Sentinel*, March 17, 2013, A14. See also Mintz and Kellogg, *Domestic Revolutions*, 179, 181.
3. Brooks, *The Social Animal*, 11.
4. Letter forwarded to me by Anton Porhanzl (Vienna), August 12, 1963.
5. Sohmen to the author, November 28, 1963. Laura Gellott, professor emerita of history at the University of Wisconsin–Parkside, had a similar experience with Austrian professors at the University of Vienna in 1979. E-mail to the author, June 20, 2012.

9. SEVEN MONTHS OF BLISS

1. CARE (an acronym for Cooperative for American Remittances to Europe) packages were first allowed into the American zone of occupation in Germany in June 1946.
2. Arthur J. May to the author, April 4, 1963.
3. Woodward, *Thinking Back*, 30.
4. Adelson, *Speaking of History*, 175.
5. Anton Porhanzl to the author, October 29, 1963.
6. Robert Koehl to the author, October 17, 1962.
7. Andrew Whiteside to the author, March 25, 1963. Whiteside had just published a book titled *Austrian National Socialism before 1918* (The Hague: Martinus Nujhoff, 1962).
8. Arthur J. May to the author, July 29, 1963.
9. Pauley, *Hitler and the Forgotten Nazis*, xv.
10. See my book *From Prejudice to Persecution*, especially pp. 221–30.
11. Mark Twain remarked in *The Innocents Abroad* that "when the work of the day is done, they forget it. Some of them go, with wife and children, to a beer hall, and sit quietly and genteelly drinking a mug or two of ale and listening to music; others walk the streets, others drive in the avenues; others assemble in the great ornamental squares in the early evening to enjoy the sights and fragrance of flowers and to hear military bands play" (130).

10. THREE JOBS IN THREE YEARS

1. McDonald, *Recovering the Past*, 141.
2. Brubacher and Rudy, *Higher Education in Transition*, 378.
3. Langer, *In and Out of the Ivory Tower*, 123.
4. Banner and Gillis, *Becoming Historians*, xiv.
5. See, for example, Hughes, *Gentleman Rebel*, 125.
6. See, for example, John R. Gillis, "Detours," in Banner and Gillis, *Becoming Historians*, 160; and James M. Banner Jr., "Historian, Improvised," in Banner and Gillis, *Becoming Historians*, 279.
7. Palmer, *Gentleman's Club*, 51.
8. Allen D. Patterson, Assistant to the President, to the author, February 25, 1964.
9. May to the author, May 4, 1964.
10. Professor Olson was the author of a biography of J. Sterling Morton and a history of Nebraska. During the year I was in Lincoln he became the graduate dean. Later he became the president of the University of Missouri at Kansas City and still later the president of the main campus of the University of Missouri in Columbia.
11. Olson to the author, May 6, 1964.
12. Knoll, *Prairie University*, 135.
13. Knoll, *Prairie University*, 140, 143–44.
14. Palmer, *Gentleman's Club*, 99.
15. Clough, *University of Wyoming, 1887–1964*, 19; Clough, *University of Wyoming, 1887–1937*, 113.
16. A. J. May, *History of the University of Rochester*, 140; Clough, *University of Wyoming, 1867–1964*, 19.
17. Clough, *University of Wyoming, 1867–1964*, 255.
18. Hardy, *Wyoming University*, 257, 51, 182.
19. Chafe, *The Paradox of Change*, 99. World War I doubtless affected the percentage of women attending graduate school in 1918.

11. PUBLISHING AND PERISHING

1. Woodring, *Higher Learning in America*, 118; Spring, *The American School*, 155–56.
2. Palmer, *Gentleman's Club*, 14.
3. Axtell, *The Pleasures of Academe*, 29.
4. Axtell, *The Pleasures of Academe*, 56.
5. Lucas, *American Higher Education*, 180, 278 (quote).
6. Carlson quoted in Hardy, *Wyoming University*, 233.
7. About the time Meyer was insisting that the University of Wyoming history department have a PhD program, the history faculty at New Mexico State University, which was about the same size as Wyoming, was promoting the same idea. The departmental chairman at New Mexico State, however, wisely vetoed the proposal on the grounds

that the department lacked the faculty, the library had insufficient resources, and the market was too saturated with PhD candidates. See Billington, *Doctor B*, 180–81.

8. Hardy, *Wyoming University*, 248.
9. My mentor, Arthur J. May, wrote me: "It seems to me unusual . . . that a man of your years should already be asked to direct a graduate seminar, but I think you have planned the work intelligently and selected a theme [on American opinion of Nazi Germany] well-worth exploring." May to the author, October 2, 1967.
10. Jedlicka to the author, March 11, 1968.
11. Göbhart to the author, n.d.
12. Mosse, *Confronting History*, 173.
13. Pauley, *The Habsburg Legacy*, 162.
14. The author to Eubank, March 24, 1969.
15. Eubank to the author, March 29, 1969.
16. The author to Eubank, February 21, 1970. At the top of the copy of the letter I showed to the acting chairman he wrote: "Bruce—I think this is well put. Roger."
17. The author to Eubank, September 22, 1970.
18. Eubank to the acting chairman, October 14, 1971.
19. The author to the incoming chairman, November 3, 1970. Dean Meyer's skepticism was understandable. History professors were notorious for abandoning research once their dissertation was published and they had been granted tenure. See Palmer, *Gentleman's Club*, 201.
20. Letter from the incoming chairman to the author, November 6, 1970.
21. Westmeyer, *Analytical History of American Higher Education*, 146, 148.
22. E-mail from Professor Ronald Surdam to the author, June 13, 2011.
23. "John Doe" to the author, June 26, 1984.
24. "John Doe" to the author, December 6, 1984.
25. Clifford Snydor to the author, June 24, 1970.
26. Otto von Habsburg to the author, October 24, 1972.
27. Pauley, *Hahnenschwanz und Hakenkireuz*, 197.
28. *Die Gemeinde*, June 14, 1972; *Wissenschaft und Weltbild*, March 1973; *Zukunft*, March 1973.

12. FROM THE FRYING PAN INTO THE FIRE

1. McDonald, *Recovering the Past*, 141; Thelin, *History of American Higher Education*, 260.
2. Palmer, *Gentleman's Club*, xvi.
3. Palmer, *Gentleman's Club*, 317–18.
4. Adelson, *Speaking of History*, 259.
5. Brubacher and Rudy, *Higher Education in Transition*, 384. At Wisconsin the history department shrank from seventy in 1970 to forty-seven in 1982. See Palmer, *Gentleman's Club*, 175–83.

6. Contrary to conventional wisdom, the birthrate in the United States began increasing rapidly as early as 1940. See Kennedy, *American People in World War II*, 356.
7. Dudley T. Cornish to T. A. Larson, March 3, 1971.
8. Sheinkopf, *Accent on the Individual*, 102.
9. Hewitt D. Adams to the author, April 2, 1974.
10. James Findlay to the author, March 15, 1974.
11. Werner L. Gundersheimer to the author, January 31, 1974.
12. Westmeyer, *Analytical History of American Higher Education*, 173.
13. Memorandum of a conference with my department chairman, September 10, 1973, p. 2.
14. *Who Were the Fascists? Social Roots of European Fascism*, ed. Stein Ugelvik Larsen et al. (New York: Columbia University Press, 1980).
15. Derks, *The Value of a Dollar*, 384, 405.
16. Thelin, *History of American Higher Education*, 357.
17. Colbourn to the author, April 3, 1980.
18. Coontz, *The Way We Never Were*, xx.

13. HITLER AND THE FORGOTTEN NAZIS

1. Pauley, *Hahnenschwanz und Hakenkreuz*, 11.
2. *Random House College Dictionary* (New York: Random House, 1988), 1432.
3. David C. Large, review of *Fascist Movements in Austria*, by Francis L. Carsten, *Journal of Modern History* 50, no. 4 (December 1978): 791.
4. Call to the author, February 20, 1978.
5. The author to Call, July 16, 1978.
6. Call to the author, May 16, 1979.
7. This practice was recommended by William Strunk and E. B. White in their classic handbook *The Elements of Style* (New York: Macmillan, 1935), which also greatly influenced my writing.
8. Duffey to the author, April 3, 1980.
9. The author to Duffey, April 10, 1980.
10. Russo, *Clio Confused*, 119–20, 123.
11. The author to Call, August 21, 1979.
12. Pauley, *Hitler and the Forgotten Nazis*, xiii.
13. Pauley, *Hitler and the Forgotten Nazis*, xv.
14. *Die Presse* (Vienna), July 23–24, 1983; *Salzburger Nachrichten*, January 8, 1983.
15. Review by William D. Pederson, *American Political Science Review* 76 (1982): 437–38; *Choice*, November 1981, 514; *Social Science Journal* 21, no. 1 (January 1984): 122–23; *Orlando Sentinel*, June 7, 1981.
16. Quoted in Bassett, *Waldheim and Austria*, 178.
17. For a detailed discussion of Waldheim's controversial wartime career see Herzstein, *Waldheim*.

18. Herzstein, *Waldheim*, 4; Bassett, *Waldheim and Austria*, 122.
19. Werner Ortner (Vienna) to Anne L. Tice (Chapel Hill NC), November 14, 1983.
20. *Die Presse*, July 9–10, 1988.

14. ASSESSING ANTI-SEMITISM

1. Other historians have made the same observation with even more justification. For example, Will Durant, the author of *The Story of Civilization*, remarked that "If I had been told that the enterprise would take eleven volumes and forty-six years (1929–75) . . . I might have turned and fled. Innocence and Ariel drew me on." Durant and Durant, *A Dual Autobiography*, 140.
2. C. Vann Woodward and doubtless most other historians have had similar experiences when writing. See his *Thinking Back*, 49–52.
3. Brooks, *The Social Animal*, 92.
4. Niewyk to the author, September 25, 1989.
5. Commentary submitted by Niewyk to Bateman on November 2, 1989.
6. Commentary submitted by Haag to Bateman, n.d.
7. Bateman to the author, October 3, 1990.
8. Pauley, *From Prejudice to Persecution*, 318.
9. Wolf to the author, January 24, 1989.
10. Kellinger to the author, June 14, 1991.
11. *Jerusalem Post*, October 4, 1993; review by Harriet Pass Freidenreich, *American Historical Review* 98 (February 1993): 200; review article by Laura Gellott, *Austrian History Yearbook* 26 (1995): 216; review by Michael J. Zeps, *Catholic Historical Review* 79, no. 1 (January 1993): 125; *Modern Austrian Literature* 26, no. 2 (1993): 174; review by Richard Mitten, *Patterns of Prejudice* 26, nos. 1–2 (1993): 124, 126.
12. *Austrian History Yearbook* 24 (1993): 230; review by Thomas Winkelbauer in *Das Waldviertel*, Heft 1 (1994), 87; *Der neue Mahnruf*, June/July 1993.
13. Stern to the author, January 11, 1993; Schlesinger to the author, October 15, 1993; Axel to the author, December 27, 1991; Lichtenberger-Fenz to the author, September 27, 1993.
14. Turner to the author, January 17, 1992.
15. Gibbon, *Memoirs of My Life*, 180.

15. HOT ON THE TRAIL OF THE COLD WAR

1. Eubank to the author, May 8, 1989.
2. Revised guidelines of Harlan Davidson, Inc., May 1, 1990.
3. MacDonogh, *After the Reich*, 244–49.
4. Postcard dated July 24, 1969.
5. Wolmar, *Blood, Iron and Gold*, 313.
6. Raynard, *It Started in Nebraska*, 13.

7. Pelinka to the author, March 14, 1977; Geyer to the author, 1997; Steiman to the author, June 26, 1997; Rath to the author, February 2, 1997; Luza to the author, February 26, 1997; Bukey to the author, April 20, 1997; Eubank to Richard Crepeau, January 11, 1999.

16. PHASING OUT

1. *Journalism and the Holocaust*, ed. Robert Moses Shapiro (New York: Yeshiva University Press, 2003), 269–95.
2. *Orlando Sentinel*, November 6, 2010, A2; Kenneth G. Sheinkopf, *Accent on the Individual: The First Twelve Years of Florida Technological University* (Orlando: Florida Technological University Foundation, Inc., 1976), 27.
3. Axtell, *The Pleasures of Academe*, xi.
4. Quoted in a letter from Kenneth J. Winkle to the author, November 16, 2001.
5. Knoll, "A Change in the Weather," 51.
6. Marti Paquette to the author, April 7, 2005.
7. Bachman to the author, July 21, 1992.
8. E-mail from Maria Hart Pauley to the author, February 17, 1999.
9. See Hill, "Volga German Occupance."
10. Twain, *Following the Equator*, 26.
11. Ferguson, *Civilization*, 224.
12. Twain, *The Innocents Abroad*, 491–92.

Bibliography

UNPUBLISHED SOURCES

Bailey, Lillian. Pauley Family Tree. American Historical Society of the Germans from Russia, Lincoln, Nebraska.

Brehm, H. Paul, ed. "The Pauley Family." Unpublished family genealogy, 1988.

———. "The Yost Family." Unpublished manuscript, 1951.

Brehm, Selma Pauley. "Memoirs of Selma Pauley Brehm" (1973). In "The Pauley Family," ed. H. Paul Brehm. Unpublished family genealogy, 1988.

Gale, George. "History of Old Clay County." County Scrapbook, Nebraska State Historical Society Library, Lincoln.

Hulsebus, Blanche. Diaries, 1930–31 (France, Italy, and Germany), 1976 (around-the-world cruise).

———. Letters to her family from France, 1930–1931.

———. [Pauley]. Taped interview with Bruce F. Pauley, Orlando FL, December 30, 1989.

Pauley, Bruce F. Diaries: 1954 (Europe), 1957–58 (Europe), 1963–64 (Europe), 1996 (Russia and the Baltic States).

Pauley, Carroll R. "An Autobiography." 1976. Unpublished manuscript in Love Library, University of Nebraska–Lincoln.

———. Diary, 1930 (Europe).

Pauley, Henry [Heinrich]. Last Will and Testament, June 28, 1906, Clay County Courthouse, Clay Center, Nebraska.

Pauley, Marianne B. Diaries: 1964 (Europe), 1980 (London, Scandinavia, and Austria), 1991 (Austria), 1996 (Russia and the Baltic States).

Pauley [Guy], Patricia. "The Island of Curacao." Unpublished MS, September 24, 1945.

PUBLISHED SOURCES

Adelson, Roger, ed. *Speaking of History: Conversations with Historians*. East Lansing: Michigan State University Press, 1997.

Allen, Frederick Lewis. *The Big Change: America Transforms Itself, 1900–1950*. New York: Harper and Brothers, 1952.

Allitt, Patrick. *I'm the Teacher, You're the Student: A Semester in the University Classroom.* Philadelphia: University of Pennsylvania Press, 2005.

Apple, Rima D. "Constructing Mother: Scientific Motherhood in the Nineteenth and Twentieth Centuries." In *American Families Past and Present: Social Perspectives on Transformations*, ed. Susan M. Ross, 191–207. New Brunswick NJ: Rutgers University Press, 2006.

Arum, Richard, and Josipa Roksa. *Academically Adrift: Limited Learning on College Campuses.* Chicago: University of Chicago Press, 2011.

Ashby, LeRoy. *With Amusement for All: A History of American Popular Culture since 1830.* Lexington: University Press of Kentucky, 2006.

Axtell, James. *The Pleasures of Academe: A Celebration and Defense of Higher Education.* Lincoln: University of Nebraska Press, 1998.

Baltensperger, Bradley H. *Nebraska: A Geography.* Boulder: Westview Press, 1985.

Banner, James M., Jr., and John R. Gillis, eds. *Becoming Historians.* Chicago: University of Chicago Press, 2009.

Barzun, Jacques. *From Dawn to Decadence: 500 Years of Western Cultural Life, 1500 to the Present.* New York: Harper Collins, 2000.

Bassett, Richard. *Waldheim and Austria.* New York: Viking, 1989.

Beratz, Gottlieb. *The German Colonies on the Lower Volga: Their Origin and Early Development.* Trans. Leona W. Pfeifer, LaVern J. Rippley, and Dona Reeves-Marquardt. Ed. Adam Giesinger. Lincoln NE: American Historical Society of Germans from Russia, n.d.

Billington, Monroe Lee. *Doctor B: The Making of a History Professor.* Ruidoso: New Mexico Historical Consultants, 2000.

Bonwetsch, Gerhard. *Geschichte der deutschen Kolonien an der Wolga.* Stuttgart: Verlag von J. Engelhorns Nachf., 1919.

Bowen, Ezra., ed. *This Fabulous Century, 1930–1940: The Thirties.* New York: Time-Life Books, 1969.

Braeman, John. "The American Polity in the Age of Normalcy: A Reappraisal." In *Calvin Coolidge and the Coolidge Era*, ed. John Earl Haynes, 14–62. Washington DC: Library of Congress, 1998.

Brokaw, Tom. *The Greatest Generation.* New York: Random House Trade Publications, 1998, 2005.

Brooks, David. *The Social Animal: The Hidden Sources of Love, Character, and Achievement.* New York: Random House, 2011.

Brubacher, John S., and Willis Rudy. *Higher Education in Transition: A History of American Colleges and Universities, 1636–1976.* New York: Harper and Row, 1976.

Bruntz, George G. *Children of the Volga.* Ardone PA: Dorrance and Company, 1981.

Chafe, William H. *The Paradox of Change: American Women in the 20th Century.* New York: Oxford University Press, 1991.

Clough, Wilson O. *A History of the University of Wyoming, 1867–1937*. Laramie: University of Wyoming, 1937.

———. *A History of the University of Wyoming, 1867–1962*. Laramie: Laramie Printing, 1965.

Coons, Lorraine, and Alexander Varias. *Tourist Third Cabin: Steamship Travel in the Interwar Years*. New York: Palgrave Macmillan, 2003.

Coontz, Stephanie. *The Social Origins of Private Life: A History of American Families, 1600–1900*. New York: Verso, 1988.

———. *The Way We Never Were: American Families and the Nostalgia Trap*. New York: Basic Books, 1992, 2000.

Crichton, Judy. *America 1900: The Turning Point*. New York: Henry Holt, 1988.

Daniels, Roger. *Coming to America: A History of Immigration and Ethnicity in American Life*. New York: Harper Collins, 1990.

Derks, Scott, ed. *The Value of a Dollar, 1860–1999, Millennium Edition*. Millerton NY: Grey House, 1999.

Dick, Everett. *The Sod-House Frontier, 1854–1890: A Social History of the Northern Plains from the Creation of Kansas and Nebraska to the Admission of the Dakotas*. Lincoln: University of Nebraska Press, 1995.

Dixon, Simon. *Catherine the Great*. New York: Harper Collins, 2009.

Dolmetsch, Carl. *"Our Famous Guest": Mark Twain in Vienna*. Athens: University of Georgia Press, 1992.

Dudley, Richard E. "Nebraska Public School Education, 1890–1910." *Nebraska History* 26 (Spring 1973): 65–90.

Durant, Will, and Ariel Durant. *A Dual Autobiography*. New York: Simon and Schuster, 1977.

Egan, Timothy. *The Worst Hard Time: The Untold Story of Those Who Survived the Great American Dust Bowl*. Boston: Houghton Mifflin, 2006.

Erickson, Carolly. *Great Catherine*. New York: Crown, 1994.

Ferguson, Niall. *Civilization: The West and the Rest*. New York: Penguin, 2011.

Fink, Deborah. *Agrarian Women: Wives and Mothers in Rural Nebraska, 1880–1940*. Chapel Hill: University of North Carolina Press, 1992.

Folsom, Burton, Jr. *New Deal or Raw Deal? How FDR's Economic Legacy Has Damaged America*. New York: Threshold Editions, 2008.

Franciosi, Robert J. *The Rise and Fall of American Public Schools: The Political Economy of Public Education in the Twentieth Century*. Westport CT: Praeger, 2004.

Fuester, John R. *The Hülsebus Families: Their Roots in Ostfriesland*. Privately published, 1999.

Gay, Peter. *My German Question: Growing Up in Nazi Berlin*. New Haven: Yale University Press, 1998.

Gibbon, Edward. *Memoirs of My Life*. New York: Funk and Wagnalls, 1966.

Giesinger, Adam. *From Catherine to Khrushchev: The Story of Russia's Germans*. Winnipeg, Manitoba: Marian Press, 1974.

Gillis, John R. "Detours." In *Becoming Historians*, ed. James M. Banner Jr. and John R. Gillis, 152–73. Chicago: University of Chicago Press, 2009.

Gladwell, Malcolm. *Outliers: The Story of Success*. New York: Little, Brown, 2008.

Good, H. G. *A History of American Education*. New York: Macmillan, 1962.

Graebner, Norman A. *A Twentieth-Century Odyssey: Memoir of a Life in Academe*. Claremont CA: Regina Books, 2002.

Griess, James R. *The German Russians: Those Who Came to Sutton*. 2nd ed. Henderson NE: Service Press, 2008.

Handlin, Oscar, and Mary F. Handlin. *The Wealth of the American People: A History of American Affluence*. New York: McGraw-Hill, 1975.

Hardy, Deborah. *Wyoming University: The First 100 Years, 1886–1986*. Laramie: University of Wyoming Press, 1986.

Harvard History Book Committee. *Harvard, Nebraska: 100 Years + 2*. Harvard NE: Centennial Committee, 1973.

Hawes, Joseph, and Elizabeth I. Nybakken, eds. *American Families: A Research Guide and Historical Handbook*. New York: Greenwood Press, 1991.

Hayes, A. B., and Sam. D. Cox. *History of the City of Lincoln, Nebraska; with brief historical sketches of the state and Lancaster County*. Lincoln: State Journal Co., 1889.

Herzstein, Robert F. *Waldheim: The Missing Years*. New York: Arbor House, 1988.

Hickey, Donald R. *Nebraska Moments: Glimpses of Nebraska's Past*. Lincoln: University of Nebraska Press, 1992.

Hicks, John D. *My Life with History: An Autobiography*. Lincoln: University of Nebraska Press, 1968.

Hill, Alton David, Jr. "Volga German Occupance in the Windsor Area, Colorado." Master's thesis, Department of Geography, University of Colorado, Boulder, 1959.

Hiltzik, Michael. *The New Deal: A Modern History*. New York: Free Press, 2011.

Historical Committee of Clay County. *A History of Clay County, Nebraska*. Sutton NE: E. H. White, 1876.

Hofstadter, Richard. *Anti-Intellectualism in American Life*. New York, Vintage Books, 1963.

———. "The Development of Higher Education in America." In *The Development and Scope of Higher Education in the United States*, by Richard Hofstadter and C. DeWitt Hardy, 3–134. New York: Columbia University Press, 1952.

Hölzer, Pastor John. "Die ersten Wolgadeutschen in Sutton, Nebr., und ein Teil ihrer Geschichte." In *Illustrierter Kirchenbote Kalender 1927*, 43–49. Redfield SD: Redfield College Press, 1927.

Hughes, H. Stuart. *Gentleman Rebel: The Memoirs of H. Stuart Hughes*. New York: Ticknor and Fields, 1990.

Janssen, Susanne. *Von Zarenreich in den amerikanishcen Westen: Deutschen in Russland und Russlanddeutsche in den USA (1871–1928): Die kulturelle Adaption einer ethnischen Gruppe in Kontakt zweier Staaten*. Münster: LIT, 1997.

Johnson, Harrison. *Johnson's History of Nebraska*. Omaha: Henry Gibson, 1880.

Johnson, Paul. "Calvin Coolidge and the Last Arcadia." In *Calvin Coolidge and the Coolidge Era*, ed. John Earl Haynes, 1–13. Washington DC: Library of Congress, 1998.

Khodarkovsky, Michael. *Russia's Steppe Frontier: The Making of a Colonial Empire, 1500–1800*. Bloomington: Indiana University Press, 2002.

Kazin, Michael. *A Godly Hero: The Life of William Jennings Bryan*. New York: Knopf, 2006.

Keller, Morton. *My Times and Life: A Historian's Progress through a Contentious Age*. Stanford CA: Hoover Institution Press, 2010.

Kelley, Robert. *The Shaping of the American Past*. 3rd ed. Englewood Cliffs NJ: Prentice Hall, 1982.

Kennedy, David M. *The American People in World War II: Freedom from Fear, Part Two*. New York: Oxford University Press, 1999.

———. *Freedom from Fear: The American People in Depression and War, 1929–1945*. New York: Oxford University Press, 1999.

Kinbacher, Kurt E. "Immigration, the American West, and the Twentieth Century: Germans from Russia, Omaha Indians, and Vietnamese-Urban Villagers in Lincoln, Nebraska." PhD diss., University of Nebraska–Lincoln, 2006.

Kinbacher, Kurt E., and William G. Thomas III. "Shaping Nebraska: An Analysis of Railroad and Land Sales, 1870–1880." In *Faculty Publications, Department of History*, 190–207. Lincoln: University of Nebraska, 2008.

Knoll, Robert E. "A Change in the Weather: Storm Clouds of the Seventies Give Way to Clear Skies, Bright Future for UNL." *Nebraska: Special 125th Anniversary Issue* 90, no. 1 (Spring 1994): 48–51.

———. *Prairie University: A History of the University of Nebraska*. Lincoln: University of Nebraska Press, 1995.

Koch, Fred C. *The Volga Germans in Russia and the Americas from 1763 to the Present*. University Park: Pennsylvania State University Press, 1977.

Kyvig, David E. *Daily Life in the United States, 1920–1930: Decades of Promise and Pain*. Westport CT: Greenwood Press, 2002.

Langer, William L. *In and Out of the Ivory Tower: The Autobiography of William L. Langer*. New York: Neale Watson Academic Publications, 1977.

Larsen, Lawrence H., Harl A. Dalstrom, Kay Calamé Dalstrom, and Barbara J. Cotrell. *Upstream Metropolis: An Urban Biography of Omaha and Council Bluffs*. Lincoln: University of Nebraska Press, 2010.

Lears, Jackson. *Rebirth of a Nation: The Making of Modern America, 1877–1920*. New York: Harper Perennial, 2009.

Leinwand, Gerald. *1927: High Tide of the Twenties*. New York: Four Walls Eight Windows, 2001.

Leuchtenburg, William E. *The Perils of Prosperity, 1914–1932*. Chicago: University of Chicago Press, 1958.

Lincoln, W. Bruce. *The Great Reforms: Autocracy, Bureaucracy, and the Politics of Change in Imperial Russia*. DeKalb: Northern Illinois University Press, 1990.

Long, James W. *From Privileged to Dispossessed: The Volga Germans, 1860–1917*. Lincoln: University of Nebraska Press, 1988.

———. "The Volga Germans and the Zemstvos, 1865–1917." *Jahrbücher für Geschichte Osteuropas* 30 (1982): 344–61.

Lord, Walter. *The Good Years: From 1900 to the First World War*. New York: Harper, 1960.

Lucas, Christopher J. *American Higher Education: A History*. New York: St. Martin's Press, 1994.

Luebke, Frederick C. *Germans in the New World: Essays in the History of Immigration*. Urbana: University of Illinois Press, 1990.

———. *Immigrants and Politics: The Germans of Nebraska, 1880–1900*. Lincoln: University of Nebraska Press, 1969.

———. *Nebraska: An Illustrated History*. Lincoln: University of Nebraska Press, 1995.

MacDonogh, Giles. *After the Reich: The Brutal History of the Allied Occupation*. New York: Basic Books, 2007.

Mai, Brent Alan, trans. and ed. *Transport of the Volga Germans from Oranienbaum to the Colonies on the Volga*. Lincoln NE: American Historical Society of Germans from Russia, 1998.

Mai, Brent Alan, and Dona Reeves-Marquardt. *German Migration to the Russian Volga (1764–1767): Origins and Destinations*. Lincoln NE: American Historical Society of Germans from Russia, 2003.

May, Arthur J. *A History of the University of Rochester*. Ed. and abridged by Lawrence Eliot Klein. Rochester NY: University of Rochester, 1977.

May, Henry F. *Coming to Terms: A Study in Memory and History*. Berkeley: University of California Press, 1987.

McBride, Tom, and Ron Nief. *The Mindset Lists of American History: From Typewriters to Text Messages, What Ten Generations of Americans Think Is Normal*. Hoboken NJ: Wiley, 2011.

McDonald, Forrest. *Recovering the Past: A Historian's Memoir*. Lawrence: University Press of Kansas, 2004.

McElvaine, Robert S. *The Great Depression: America, 1929–1941*. New York: Times Books, 1984.

McKee, James L. *Lincoln, the Prairie Capital: An Illustrated History*. Lincoln NE: J & J Lee Co., 1984.

McMillan, Amy Ruhter, ed. *60 Years of Study Abroad*. Chicago: IES Abroad, 2010.

Mintz, Steven, and Susan Kellogg. *Domestic Revolutions: A History of American Family Life*. New York: Free Press, 1988.

Morris, Seymour, Jr. *American History Revised: 200 Startling Facts That Never Made It into the Textbooks*. New York: Broadway Books, 2010.

Mosse, George L. *Confronting History—A Memoir*. Madison: University of Wisconsin Press, 2000.

Okrent, Daniel. *Last Call: The Rise and Fall of Prohibition*. New York: Scribner, 2010.

Olson, Marie Miller, and Anna Miller Reisbik, eds. *Norka: A German Village in Russia*. Lincoln NE: American Historical Society of Germans from Russia, 1986..

Overton, Richard D. *Burlington West: A Colonization History of the Burlington Railroad*. Cambridge: Harvard University Press, 1941.

Palmer, William. *From Gentleman's Club to Professional Body: The Evolution of the History Department in the United States, 1940–1980*. New York: Booksurge, 2008.

Pauley, Bruce F. *From Prejudice to Persecution: A History of Austrian National Socialism*. Chapel Hill: University of North Carolina Press, 1992.

———. *Eine Geschichte des österreichischen Antisemitismus: Von der Ausgrenzung zur Auslöschung*. Vienna: Kremayr and Scheriau, 1993.

———. *The Habsburg Legacy, 1867–1939*. New York: Holt, Rinehart and Winston, 1972.

———. *Hahnenschwanz und Hakenkreuz: Steirischer Heimatschutz und österreichischer Nationalsozialismus, 1918–1934*. Vienna: Europa Verlag, 1972.

———. *Hitler and the Forgotten Nazis: A History of Austrian National Socialism*. Chapel Hill: University of North Carolina Press, 1981.

———. *Hitler, Stalin, and Mussolini: Totalitarianism in the Twentieth Century*. 3rd ed. Wheeling IL: Harlan Davidson, 2009.

———. *Der Weg in den Nationalsozialismus: Ursprünge und Entwicklung in Österreich*. Vienna: Österreichischer Bundesverlag, 1988.

Perkins, Dexter. *Yield of the Years: An Autobiography*. Boston: Little, Brown, 1969.

Popkin, Jeremy D. *History, Historians, and Autobiography*. Chicago: University of Chicago Press, 2005.

Post, Gaines, Jr. *Memoirs of a Cold War Son*. Iowa City: University of Iowa Press, 2000.

Proctor, Robert N. *The Nazi War on Cancer*. Princeton: Princeton University Press, 1999.

Rasenberger, Jim. *America, 1908: The Dawn of Flight, the Race to the Pole, the Invention of the Model T, and the Making of a Modern Nation*. New York: Scribner, 2007.

Raynard, Phil. *It Started in Nebraska: My Life in Bio Bits*. Morgan Hill CA: Bookstand Publishing, 2010.

Rife, Janet Warkentin. *Germans and German-Russians in Nebraska: A Research Guide to Nebraska Ethnic Studies*. Lincoln NE: Center for Great Plains Studies, 1980.

Rippley, La Vern J. *The German-Americans*. Boston: Twayne, 1976.

Roland, Charles P. *My Odyssey through History: Memoirs of War and Academe*. Baton Rouge: Louisiana State University Press, 2004.

Roth, Benjamin. *The Great Depression: A Diary*. Ed. James Ledbeter and Daniel B. Roth. New York: Public Affairs, 2009.

Russo, David J. *Clio Confused: Troubling Aspects of Historical Study from the Perspective of U.S. History*. Westport CT: Greenwood Press, 1995.

Salins, Peter D. *Assimilation American Style*. New York: Basic Books, 1997.

Sandler, Lauren. "The American Nightmare: We Have Everything the American Dream Prescribed. So Why Aren't We Happy?" *Psychology Today*, March/April 2011, 70–77.

Scheuerman, Richard D. *The Volga Germans: Pioneers of the Northwest*. Moscow: University of Idaho Press, 1980.

Schmalz, Eric J. "*Volk auf dem Weg*: The Germans from Russia in the Americas." Germans from Russia Heritage Collection. Fargo: North Dakota State University Libraries, October 2011. 7 pp.

Schwabenland-Haynes, Emma." German Russians on the Volga and in the United States." Master's thesis, University of Colorado, 1929.

Scott, Donald M., and Bernard Wishy, eds. *America's Families: A Documentary History*. New York: Harper and Row, 1982.

Shannon, David A. *Between the Wars: America, 1919–1941*. 2nd ed. Boston: Houghton Mifflin, 1979.

Sheehy, Gail. *New Passages: Mapping Your Life across Time*. New York: Random House, 1995.

Sheinkopf, Kenneth G. *Accent on the Individual: The First Twelve Years of Florida Technological University*. Orlando: Florida Technological University Foundation, 1976.

Shlaes, Amity. *The Forgotten Man: A New History of the Great Depression*. New York: Harper Perennial, 2007.

Shrock, Joel. *The Gilded Age*. Westport CT: Greenwood Press, 2004.

Sklar, Robert. *The Plastic Age (1917–1930)*. New York: George Braziller, 1970.

Spach, Alexander. "Sad Pages of History." *Journal of the American Historical Society of Germans from Russia* 35, no. 1 (Spring 2012): 22–27.

Spring, Joel. *The American School: 1642–2000*. Boston: McGraw-Hill, 2001.

Stratton, Joanna L. *Pioneer Women: Voices from the Kansas Frontier*. New York: Simon and Schuster, 1981.

Thelin, John R. *A History of American Higher Education*. Baltimore: Johns Hopkins University Press, 2004.

Toepfer, Amy Brungardt, and Agnes Dreiling. *Conquering the Wind: An Epic Migration from the Rhine to the Volga to the Plains of Kansas*. Ed. Victor C Leiker. Garwood NJ: Victor C. Leiker, 1966.

Tuttle, William M., Jr. "America's Home Front Children in World War II." In *American Families Past and Present: Social Perspectives on Transformations*, ed. Susan M. Ross, 227–43. New Brunswick NJ: Rutgers University Press, 2006, pp. 227–43.

Twain, Mark. *Following the Equator: A Journey around the World*. Vol. 2. New York: Harper and Brothers, 1897.

———. *The Innocents Abroad or, The New Pilgrims' Progress*. 1869. New York: Modern Library, 2003.
———. *A Tramp Abroad*. Intro. Kerry Driscoll. 1880. New York: Modern Library, 2003.
Urbach, William. "Our Parents Were Russian German." *Nebraska History* 48, no. 1 (Spring 1967): 1–26.
Urban, Wayne J., and Jennings L. Wagoner Jr. *American Education: A History*. Boston: McGraw Hill, 2000.
U.S. Department of Commerce, Weather Bureau, *Climates of the States, Nebraska*. Washington DC: Government Printing Office, 1959.
Wall, Joseph Frazier. *Grinnell College in the Nineteenth Century: From Salvation to Service*. Ames: Iowa State University Press, 1997.
Walters, George J. *Wir Wollen Deutsche Bleiben: The Story of the Volga Germans*. Kansas City MO: Halcyon House, 1982.
Watkins, T. H. *The Great Depression: America in the 1930s*. New York: Little, Brown, 1993.
———. *The Hungry Years: A Narrative History of the Great Depression in America*. New York: Henry Holt, 1999.
Weinwald, Gerald. *1927: The High Tide of the Twenties*. New York: Four Walls Eight Windows, 2001.
Westmeyer, Paul. *An Analytical History of American Higher Education*. 2nd ed. Springfield IL: Charles C. Thomas, 1997.
Williams, Hattie Plum. *The Czar's Germans: With Particular Reference to the Volga Germans*. Ed. Emma S. Haynes, Phillip B. Legler, and Gerda S. Walker. Lincoln NE: American Historical Society of Germans from Russia, 1975.
———. "The History of the German-Russian Colony in Lincoln." Master's thesis, University of Nebraska, 1909.
———. "A Social Study of the Russian German." PhD thesis, University of Nebraska, Lincoln, 1916.
Wishart, David J. *The Last Days of the Rainbelt*. Lincoln: University of Nebraska Press, 2013.
Wolmar, Christian. *Blood, Iron and Gold: How the Railroads Transformed the World*. New York: Public Affairs, 2010.
———. *The Great Railroad Revolution: The History of Trains in America*. New York: Public Affairs, 2012.
Woodard, Colin. *American Nations: A History of the Eleven Rival Regional Cultures of North America*. New York: Viking, 2011.
Woodring, Paul. *The Higher Learning in America: A Reassessment*. New York: McGraw-Hill, 1968.
Woodward, C. Vann. *Thinking Back: The Perils of Writing History*. Baton Rouge: Louisiana State University Press, 1986.
The World Almanac and Book of Facts for 1950. New York: New York World Telegram, 1950.

The World Almanac and Book of Facts, 1929. Facsimile Edition. New York, American Heritage Press, 1971.
The World Almanac and Book of Facts, 2008. New York: World Almanac Books, 2007.
The World Almanac and Book of Facts, 2012. New York: World Almanac Books, 2011.
Wright, Gwendolyn. *Building the Dream: A Social History of Housing in America*. New York: Pantheon Books, 1981.

Index

OTHER WORKS BY BRUCE F. PAULEY

The Habsburg Legacy, 1867–1939

Hahnenschwanz und Hakenkreuz: Steirischer Heimatschutz und österreicher Nationalsozialismus, 1918–1934

Hitler and the Forgotten Nazis: A History of Austrian National Socialism

Der Weg in den Nationalsozialismus: Ursprünge und Entwicklung in Österreich

From Prejudice to Persecution: A History of Austrian Anti-Semitism

Eine Geschichte des österreichischen Antisemitismus: Von der Ausgrenzung zur Auslöschung

Hitler, Stalin, and Mussolini: Totalitarianism in the Twentieth Century